Our Minds on Freedom

OUR MINDS ON
FREEDOM

Women and the Struggle for Black Equality
in Louisiana, 1924–1967

SHANNON FRYSTAK

LOUISIANA STATE UNIVERSITY PRESS

BATON ROUGE

Published by Louisiana State University Press
Copyright © 2009 by Louisiana State University Press
All rights reserved
Manufactured in the United States of America
Louisiana Paperback Edition, 2020

Designer: Michelle A. Neustrom
Typeface: Chaparral Pro, AT Sakers Gothic
Typesetter: J. Jarrett Engineering, Inc.

LIBRARY OF CONGRESS CATALOGING-IN-PUBLICATION DATA
Names: Frystak, Shannon L. (Shannon Lee), 1968– author.
Title: Our minds on freedom : women and the struggle for black equality in Louisiana, 1924–
  1967 / Shannon Frystak.
Description: Louisiana paperback edition. | Baton Rouge : Louisiana State University Press,
  2020. | Includes bibliographical references and index.
Identifiers: LCCN 2019041653 (print) | LCCN 2019041654 (ebook) | ISBN 978-0-8071-7236-0
  (paperback) | ISBN 978-0-8071-3662-1 (pdf) | ISBN 978-0-8071-4675-0 (epub)
Subjects: LCSH: Women civil rights workers—Louisiana—History—20th century. | Civil rights
  movements—Louisiana—History—20th century. | African American women civil rights
  workers—Louisiana—History—20th century. | African Americans—Civil rights—Louisiana
  —History—20th century. | Louisiana—Race relations—History—20th century.
Classification: LCC E185.93.L6 F79 2020 (print) | LCC E185.93.L6 (ebook) | DDC 323.092—dc23
LC record available at https://lccn.loc.gov/2019041653
LC ebook record available at https://lccn.loc.gov/2019041654

Cover photographs used by permission of Connie Bradford Harse

For
Elizabeth "Miss Bettie" Dorsey Purcell,
the quintessential southern woman

CONTENTS

ACKNOWLEDGMENTS

When I was thirteen, I read the Pulitzer prize–winning (and sometimes controversial) novel *To Kill a Mockingbird*, by Harper Lee. I had already cultivated a love of literature reading voraciously every night, but I quickly discovered that this book was different; I read it in one sitting. The story of Tom Robinson affected me as much as it did Lee's erstwhile characters, Jem, Dill, and Scout. I questioned how a country so rooted in democracy, professing "all men are created equal," could let such an obviously innocent man lose his life, even in a fictional setting. I had been raised in a fairly conservative household, but due to state-mandated busing adopted in the 1970s in an attempt to achieve racial parity in the public schools, I attended an integrated Chicago elementary school. Because of this experience, I firmly believed the words an innocent Scout spoke to her brother in her attempt to come to grips with racial and class differences in the South: "Naw Jem, I think there's just one kind of folks. Folks." The story stuck with me and, ultimately, led me to investigate, advocate for, and now write and teach about the social, economic, and racial disparities that exist in America. Thanking Harper Lee for writing *To Kill a Mockingbird* may seem trite, but her work has shaped who I am ideologically; I couldn't have written my book without her words in my head.

I began my investigation into the story of Louisiana's female civil rights activists while working on my master's degree at the University of New Orleans. I took my very first graduate class from Professor Raphael Cassimere and was inspired by his own story of leadership in the New Orleans civil rights movement. Madelon Powers and Arnold Hirsch supported my work on the integration of the League of Women Voters of New Orleans and encouraged me to meet and interview the surviving women who fought for a biracial organization in the South at a time when many considered it improper to do so. My dissertation committee at the University of New Hampshire, including my mentor and friend, Harvard Sitkoff; J. William Harris, the best editor one could ask for and one of my biggest cheerleaders, professionally and personally; and Janet Polasky, Ellen Fitzpatrick, and Cliff Brown all deserve my sincere thanks. As this work took shape, friends have read it in part or as a whole. I wish to thank the late Bettie Purcell, Elizabeth Palumbo, and Sarah Gerkensmeyer not only for their sincere interest, but also for their numerous suggestions that only made me think more clearly about how I was framing my arguments. Kate Clifford Larsen, my friend and fellow graduate student from UNH, is an amazing writer and historian who didn't hesitate, even amid her own busy writing and teaching schedule, to read the full manuscript. This book is all the better for her efforts.

Staff members of the numerous archives and libraries I have visited over the years have been indispensible to my work. I wish to thank the staff at the Special Collections at Tulane University; the Earl K. Long Special Collections at the University of New Orleans; the New Orleans Public Library; the Louisiana State University Special Collections; the Moorland-Spingarn Center and the Ralph Bunche Civil Rights Documentation Project at Howard University; the State Historical Society of Wisconsin at the University of Wisconsin, Madison; the Amistad Research Center in New Orleans, especially Brenda Square and Shannon Burrell; and the staff at the Library of Congress in Washington, D.C.

None of these trips would have been possible without the financial assistance that I received from a variety of sources. I received numerous research grants from the Department of History at the University of New Hampshire, including a Gunst-Wilcox Research Grant. The University of New Hampshire's Graduate School also provided me with several summer research fellowships and travel grants as well as a dissertation fellowship, which allowed me to finish my research and writing. Newcomb College Center for Research on Women granted me a Visiting Scholar position at Tulane University, which allowed me the use of their extensive library system and Special Collections. Even more, the center provided me a place to discuss my research and writing in an academically challenging, yet comforting and convivial environment. I am grateful for the Thursday morning reading groups, for the Friday afternoon Louisiana Women's History group, and, especially, for the support of the center's director, Beth Willinger. Through the Newcomb Center, I was awarded an Emily Schoenbaum Foundation grant, which allowed me to travel to Washington, D.C., to complete my research at the Library of Congress. Finally, the Faculty Research and Development Fund at East Stroudsburg University of Pennsylvania provided me with funds to help defray the costs of a few last-minute trips to New Orleans.

I don't even know where to begin to thank the enormous group of family and the family of friends who have been in my corner since the very beginning of my academic career, but I will try: the Emerald Isle, North Carolina, gang; Tim and Jeff Jurkovac; Alice and Mike Kelleher; Barbara and the late Mike Palumbo; the Cables—Bill, Chris, Jen, and Shelly; Owen and Jane Phelps; Kristin and Nic, Gina G, Joey, Maria, and Elizabeth Guehlstorf; Eric and Robin Phelps, and Shannon Phelps; my mother, Charlotte, and her husband, Jim Russell; my brothers, Jerry, Brandon, and Dean Strow; and my sisters, Ashley Frystak and Megan Schwitz. This work would not have been possible without the love, support, and encouragement of my father, who never finished college himself but who understands what this accomplishment means to me. Skeet Hanks allowed me to live with him rent-free while I researched in New Orleans for six months. Although he has relocated to Nashville permanently since Hurricane Katrina, he'll always be my New Orleans family. Tim Tyson, my academic "cousin," inspires me through his work and his life. In D.C., thanks to the gang at Tonic, especially Patrice Hammond, Silvano "Bano" Vigil, Jeremy Pollok, Eric "Bernie" Bernstrom, Kevin Twine, Tricia Cominsky, Terence Samuel, and Shola Mapaderun. In West Virginia, I thank my dear friends Elizabeth and Ken Fones-Wolf and Martha McCauley. Here at East Stroudsburg University, I have the support of my department and, particularly, my dear friend Michael Gray.

I am fortunate to say that I have a group of women who surround me and sustain me, and for that, they are irreplaceable. I cannot begin to express my gratitude to them. Marilyn Frystak, Diana Kerr- Brown, Julia Fafard, Tracy Wallace, Shirley O'Hare, Rose Donna, Marla McGuire, Sarah Gerkensmeyer, Susan Hershey, Denise Maruna, Kathleen Lavelle, Katherine Mellen Charron, and Michelle Wallace and her daughter, Elena, bless my life in countless ways. Colleen Purcell, along with her husband, Ben, and my nephew Christian, have not only supported me emotionally, but also opened their home to me whenever I needed. I thank my longtime friend, editor, and confidante Elizabeth Palumbo and her partner, Sean O'Donnell.

I cannot end this without thanking the innumerable women who participated in the Louisiana civil rights movement. Although they are too numerous to mention, I would like to thank in particular those women who allowed me to interview them, many for hours on end: Miriam "Mimi" Feingold, Betty Wisdom, Felicia Kahn, Millie Charles, Katrina Jackson NaDang,

Connie Bradford Harse, Margaret Leonard, Jill Finsten, Dorothy "Dottie" Zellner, Kathy Barrett, Julia Aaron, Inez Hale Cassimere, Madelon Cochrane, Lorraine Poindexter Ambeau, Elizabeth Rack, Jean Boebel, and Sybil Haydel Morial. I was fortunate enough to interview Rosa Freeman Keller before she died in 1997. It was her story that inspired me to continue research on other women who played pivotal roles in the Louisiana movement. Special thanks also go to Kim Lacy Rogers, who had the foresight to interview a number of women whose stories may have been lost; and to Mary Hebert of LSU-Baton Rouge, and Greta de Jong for their recent interviews with women in rural Louisiana.

My partner of the past four-plus years, Brandon McAuliffe, has put up with a two-year, sometimes frustrating long-distance relationship, two moves, writer's block, my obsessive cleaning bouts due to writer's block (which he calls "the sickness"), wine nights, numerous academic trips that take me away from home and leave him to play single-parent to our dog, Magnolia, and my constant pursuit of perfection in all areas of my life. Brandon is my best friend, and I can't imagine how I could have ever completed this project without his effortless love, encouragement, and support. Thanks, babe!

Three years ago, we tragically and quite suddenly lost one of the most vibrant, funny, intelligent, progressive, crazy, lovely women that I have ever had the sheer luck and pleasure to know. Miss Bettie Purcell was my dear friend, editor, mentor, fellow wine lover, and one of the best southern "ladies" around. I miss her every day. This book is dedicated to her spirit that lives on in me and, in those whose lives she touched.

CIVIL RIGHTS TIMELINE

1896   Supreme Court decides in *Plessy v. Ferguson* that "separate, but equal" will become law

1909   Founding of the National Association for the Advancement of Colored People (NAACP)

1917   Supreme Court rules in *Buchanan v. Warley* that racial segregation housing ordinances are illegal

1933–1935   President Franklin Delano Roosevelt institutes the New Deal, establishes a "Black Cabinet"

1942   Roosevelt adopts Executive Order 8802, eliminating discrimination in government and defense industry; Congress of Racial Equality (CORE) founded

1944   Supreme Court rules in *Smith v. Allwright* that the all-white Texas primary violates the Fifteenth Amendment

1950   NAACP begins to build case leading to *Brown v. Board of Education;* sees significant wins with *Sweatt v. Painter,* requiring immediate admission for blacks to the all-white University of Texas law school, and *McLaurin v. Oklahoma State Regents,* which required the state to admit black students on a desegregated basis

1953   Baton Rouge Bus Boycott

1954   Supreme Court rules in *Brown v. Board of Education of Topeka, Kansas* that "separate is inherently unequal"

1955   Emmett Till murdered; Montgomery Bus Boycott

1956   Tallahassee Bus Boycott

1957   Southern Christian Leadership Conference (SCLC) founded; Little Rock, Arkansas, desegregation crisis

1958   Youth March for Integrated Schools—Washington, D.C.

1960   Sit-ins begin in Greensboro, North Carolina; Nashville Student Movement organized; New Orleans sit-ins and boycotts; Student Non-Violent Coordinating Committee (SNCC) founded; Civil Rights Act of 1960; New Orleans Public Schools desegregation crisis begins

1961   Freedom Rides organized by the Congress of Racial Equality; voter registration begins in Mississippi; Baton Rouge student protests

1962   Council of Federated Organizations (COFO) founded

1963   March on Washington—Martin Luther King Jr. gives "I have a dream" speech; Medgar Evers murdered

1964   Freedom Summer—voter registration/education projects in Mississippi and Louisiana; murders of James Chaney, Michael Schwerner, and Andrew Goodman; Deacons for Defense and Justice founded in Louisiana; comprehensive Civil Rights Act passed upholding the Fourteenth Amendment; Free Southern Theater founded; Lowndes County Freedom Organization founded in Alabama

1965   Malcolm X murdered; Voting Rights Act passed; Watts Riot; Poor Peoples Campaign begins; Selma to Montgomery March

1966   Call for Black Power; James Meredith begins March Against Fear and is shot in Mississippi

1967   Martin Luther King Jr. publicly opposes the Vietnam War; Supreme Court rules in *Loving v. Virginia* that miscegenation laws are unconstitutional

1968   Memphis Garbage Workers strike; Martin Luther King Jr. assassinated

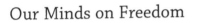

Our Minds on Freedom

INTRODUCTION

Don't mourn, organize.

JOE HILL, labor organizer

Oone afternoon in 2003, I came across an article in *Mother Jones* about a woman who escaped the Rwandan massacres. In the spring of 1994, seventeen-year-old Joseline Mujawamariya, along with her sister and brother, hid for three days while rival Hutus raped and murdered her Tutsi family, friends, and neighbors. For two months, Mujawamariya, her siblings, and other Tutsi refugees survived on food they found in "corpse-littered gardens" and rainwater they "collected in cupped hands." Mujawamariya survived the infamous genocide, and today, armed with only a primary school education, she leads the redevelopment of her region. She supervises the reconstruction not only of her village's "shattered infrastructure," but also of its health-service system, educational system, and economy. Forging ahead amid such devastation, Mujawamariya is "rebuilding her neighbors' lives while struggling to rebuild her own." She is not mourning; she is organizing *and* leading.[1]

Mujawamariya's story is not unique, but one most often left at the margins of history. Like Mujawamariya's story, this study reveals that in the struggle for human rights, women are often at the forefront. In the nineteenth century, black and white women worked together in the successful

1. Kimberlee Acquaro and Peter Landesman, "Out of Madness, A Matriarchy," *Mother Jones*, January/February 2003. Most recently, the *Washington Post* published an article detailing the significance of women to the revitalization of Rwanda's economy. As the author notes, the large presence of Rwandan women "speaks to a seismic shift in gender economics in Rwanda's post-genocide society, one that is altering the way younger generations of males view their mothers and sisters while offering a powerful lesson for other developing nations struggling to rebuild from the ashes of conflict. . . . Rwanda's economy has risen up from the genocide and prospered greatly on the backs of our women" (see Anthony Faiola, "Women Rise in Rwanda's Economic Revival," *Washington Post*, 16 May 2008).

abolitionist movement and organized powerful antislavery societies. The first women's rights convention, held in Seneca Falls, New York, in 1848, sparked a biracial movement of women who quite vocally demanded the right to vote. Women formed the backbone of the moral and social reform movement during the Progressive Era and organized women's "clubs" around issues of temperance, crime, drug use, public housing, public health, and child welfare. They ultimately succeeded in prohibiting alcohol and gaining the right to vote. In the 1930s, women joined unions for better pay and working conditions, sued to equalize teacher salaries, and fought for equal access to public accommodations. And although the term "civil rights" did not come into widespread usage until the 1940s, women's organizations protested discrimination in education, voting, housing, employment, and public transportation. Perhaps the Louisiana civil rights activist Isaac Reynolds put it best in 1970: "One of the things that anybody that's really been involved in the civil rights movement knows is that the women have always been at the forefront. If you called a meeting and went to a civil rights meeting, nine out of twelve people sitting in the audience . . . would be women. To really, sort of, get some action started, seventy to eighty percent of the participants would be females."[2]

Our Minds on Freedom focuses on the significant roles women took on in the struggle for racial justice in Louisiana from the early 1920s through the late 1960s. Following the latest research, which challenges the dominant narrative that dates the modern civil rights movement "proper" from the *Brown* decision in 1954 to Martin Luther King Jr.'s assassination in 1968, this study begins in 1924, when Louisiana women openly fought the unequal and discriminatory racial status quo in their communities and across the state.[3] Most notably, this book highlights some of Louisiana's prominent local protest communities. It was impossible to include the stories of all of the thousands of Louisiana women who joined unions and civil rights organization, marched, attended church meetings, registered to vote, canvassed, or supported the movement in myriad other ways, often at risk to their lives and livelihoods. The following pages, however, contain the stories

2. Isaac Reynolds, interview by James Mosby, 27 May 1970, Box 298, Ralph Bunche Civil Rights Documentation Project, Moorland-Spingarn Research Center, Howard University, Washington, D.C. (hereafter cited as RBCRDP).

3. Specifically, see Jacquelyn Dowd Hall, "The Long Civil Rights Movement and the Political Uses of the Past," *Journal of American History* 91, no. 4 (March 2005); and, most recently, Glenda Elizabeth Gilmore, *Defying Dixie: The Radical Roots of Civil Rights, 1919–1950* (New York: Norton, 2008).

of a diverse group of courageous women who fought alongside their brothers and fathers, uncles and cousins, to achieve a more racially just Louisiana. The study concludes in 1967, when the Congress of Racial Equality, arguably Louisiana's most important civil rights organization in the 1960s, ended its formal tenure in the state movement, and Black Power arose as the new mantra.

Our Minds on Freedom draws on and contributes to the historiography of the civil rights movement in three ways: it highlights the integral role of women in the Louisiana movement; it adds to our understanding of the impact of gender in a social movement structure; and it expands the literature on leadership in the movement where the diversity of women's experiences—race and class—contributed to their ability to attain leadership positions in a social movement structure largely dominated by men.

Traditional movement literature highlights the role of men in the civil rights movement, most notably the male ministerial leadership and young black revolutionaries; men like Martin Luther King Jr. and Stokely Carmichael are at the forefront of many movement narratives. To be sure, this trend is changing. With the onset of the second wave of feminism in the 1970s and 1980s, feminist scholars paid increasing attention to the role of women in the struggle for black equality. In 1977, the editors of *Southern Exposure*, the magazine of the Southern Conference Educational Fund, devoted an entire issue to women in the movement in which scholars and activists alike contributed essays on subjects such as the differing roles and experiences of white and black women and women's consciousness in a southern black movement.[4] In October 1988, activists and scholars convened in Atlanta to consider the role of women in the civil rights movement. Out of this conference, one of the first scholarly studies of female civil rights activists emerged: *Women in the Civil Rights Movement: Trailblazers and Torchbearers, 1941–1965*.[5] Since then a number of works have focused on the impact of women on the successes in the civil rights movement. Through personal recollection and scholarly research, these studies have shown that women were much more than followers in a male-led movement; they were leaders *and* organizers, as well as supporters in both local and national civil rights organizations.[6]

4. See *Southern Exposure* 4, no. 4 (Winter 1977).
5. Vicki L. Crawford, Jacqueline Anne Rouse, and Barbara Woods, eds., *Women in the Civil Rights Movement: Trailblazers and Torchbearers, 1941–1965* (Bloomington: Indiana University Press, 1990).
6. See Anne Braden, *The Wall Between* (New York: Monthly Review Press, 1958); Virginia

Sociologists have contributed much of the pioneering scholarship on female civil rights activists. Rhoda Lois Blumberg and Bernice McNair Barnett have written on issues such as white mothers as activists; the "careers" of female civil rights activists; women leaders; and activist women as revolutionaries. The sociologists Doug McAdam, Belinda Robnett, and Mary Aikin Rothschild have all contributed important works on gender as a mediating experience in social movement structures.[7] In a recent study, and most important to this work, M. Bahati Kuumba treats social movements as "gendered terrain." Kuumba suggests that there is much to be learned by viewing the civil rights movement through a gendered lens; that "gender is a basic organizing principle in human society and that gender roles, relations, and inequalities impact social processes in complex ways." Kuumba views the movement as a societal mirror that reflects a "gendered division of labor, [where] women and men are not only assigned different roles and responsibilities, [but] these positionings are valued differently and placed in rank

Durr, *Outside the Magic Circle: The Autobiography of Virginia Foster Durr* (Tuscaloosa: University of Alabama Press, 1985); Ellen Cantarow, ed., *Moving the Mountain: Women Working for Social Change* (New York: Feminist Press, 1980); Mary King, *Freedom Song: A Personal Story of the 1960s Civil Rights Movement* (New York: Morrow, 1987); Jo Ann Robinson, *The Montgomery Bus Boycott and the Women Who Started It* (Knoxville: University of Tennessee Press, 1987); Cheryl Lynn Greenburg, ed., *A Circle of Trust: Remembering SNCC* (New Brunswick, N.J.: Rutgers University Press, 1998); Chana Kai Lee, *For Freedom's Sake: The Life of Fannie Lou Hamer* (Urbana: University of Illinois Press, 1999); Constance Curry et al., *Deep in Our Hearts: Nine White Women in the Freedom Movement* (Athens: University of Georgia Press, 2000); Sarah Mitchell Parsons, *From Southern Wrongs to Civil Rights: The Memoir of a White Civil Rights Activist* (Tuscaloosa: University of Alabama Press, 2000); Bettye Collier-Thomas and V. P. Franklin, eds., *Sisters in the Struggle: African-American Women in the Civil Rights-Black Power Movement* (New York: New York University Press, 2001); Elizabeth Higginbotham, *Too Much to Ask: Black Women in the Era of Integration* (Chapel Hill: University of North Carolina Press, 2001); Lynne Olson, *Freedom's Daughters: The Unsung Heroines of the Civil Rights Movement from 1830 to 1970* (New York: Scribner, 2001); Catherine Fosl, *Subversive Southerner: Anne Braden and the Struggle for Racial Justice in the Cold War South* (New York: Palgrave Macmillan, 2002); and Barbara Ransby, *Ella Baker and the Black Freedom Movement: A Radical Democratic Vision* (Chapel Hill: University of North Carolina Press, 2003); Dorothy Height, *Open Wide the Freedom Gates: A Memoir* (New York: Public Affairs, 2003); and Gail S. Murray, ed., *Throwing Off the Cloak of Privilege: White Southern Women Activists in the Civil Rights Era* (Gainesville: University Press of Florida, 2004).

7. See Mary Aikin Rothschild, "White Women Volunteers in the Freedom Summers: Their Life in a Movement for Social Change," *Feminist Studies* (Fall 1979); Rhoda Lois Blumberg, "White Mothers in the American Civil Rights Movement," in *Research in the Interweave of Social Roles: Women and Men*, ed. Helen Lopata, vol. 1 (New York: JAI Press, 1980); Rhoda Lois Blumberg, "Careers of Women Civil Rights Activists," *Journal of Sociology and Social Welfare* (1980); Rhoda Lois Blumberg, "Women in the Civil Rights Movement: Reform or Revolution?" *Dialectical Anthropology* 15 (1990); Rhoda Lois Blumberg, "Rediscovering Women Leaders of the Civil Rights

order." It is clear that, in Louisiana, gender affected recruitment, participation, experiences, organizing strategy, and outcomes.[8]

Outside of the cosmopolitan city of New Orleans, Louisiana was like much of the rest of the Jim Crow South, predominantly rural and poor. After Reconstruction, the state depended on its pre–Civil War plantation economy, with many farms relying on a cheap labor force of poor, illiterate, and dependent blacks. Tenant farming and sharecropping dominated the northern and southeastern parishes, with cotton and sugar the primary crops, perpetuating a permanent system of dept-peonage and economic dependency among many black families. In 1898, Louisiana adopted a new constitution that made voting conditional on passing literacy tests, paying poll taxes, and satisifying residency requirements, virtually disfranchising the state's African American population. Segregated public schools further separated the state's blacks from economic opportunity. As in the rest of the South, segregation, discrimination, and disfranchisement set the parameters for African American life in rural Louisiana well into the twentieth century. Louisiana's white elite enforced the subordination of its black citizenry by threat of violence, when necessary, making the state one of the most repressive in the South.[9]

Movement," in *Dream and Reality: The Modern Black Struggle for Freedom*, ed. Jeanne Swift (New York: Greenwood Press, 1991); Doug McAdam, "Gender as a Mediator of the Activist Experience: The Case of Freedom Summer," *American Journal of Sociology* 97 (March 1992); Sherry Cable, "Women's Social Movement Involvement: The Role of Structural Availability in Recruitment and Participation Processes," *Sociological Quarterly* 33 (1992); Bernice McNair Barnett, "Invisible Southern Black Women Leaders in the Civil Rights Movement: The Triple Constraints of Gender, Race, and Class," *Gender and Society* 7 (June 1993); Belinda Robnett, "African American Women in the Civil Rights Movement, 1954–1965: Gender, Leadership, and Micromobilization," *American Journal of Sociology* 101 (May 1996); Belinda Robnett, *How Long? How Long?: African-American Women in the Struggle for Civil Rights* (New York: Oxford University Press, 1997); and Jenny Irons, "The Shaping of Activist Recruitment and Participation: A Study of Women in the Mississippi Civil Rights Movement," *Gender and Society* 12 (December 1998).

8. M. Bahati Kuumba, *Gender and Social Movements* (New York: AltaMira Press, 2001), 2, 11–12.

9. Edward Ayers, *Promise of the New South: Life after Reconstruction* (New York: Oxford University Press, 1992); C. Vann Woodward, *The Strange Career of Jim Crow* (New York: Oxford University Press, 1974); C. Vann Woodward, *Origins of the New South* (Baton Rouge: Louisiana University Press, 1951); Adam Fairclough, *Race and Democracy: The Civil Rights Struggle in Louisiana, 1917–1995* (Athens: University of Georgia Press, 1995); Leon Litwack, *Trouble in Mind: Black Southerners in the Age of Jim Crow* (New York: Knopf, 1998); V. O. Key, *Southern Politics in State and Nation* (New York: Vintage Books, 1949); Greta de Jong, *A Different Day: The African-American Freedom Struggle and the Transformation of Rural Louisiana, 1900–1970* (Chapel Hill: University of North Carolina Press, 2002); Patricia Sullivan, *Days of Hope: Race and Democracy*

The distinct, if not peculiar, nature of Louisiana's political structure only contributed to the difficulties faced by African Americans. Between 1896, the year that saw the defeat and resultant demise of the Populist Party, and the 1930s, when Huey Long rose to power, a one-party system dominated the state. Long's Share Our Wealth program gave him support from both poor whites and blacks, though his regime operated under a system of patronage, nepotism, corruption, and, at times, outright violence. Even after Long's assassination in 1935 and his brother Earl's subsequent rise to political power as a two-term governor, state power remained concentrated in the hands of a few—the political machine of New Orleans. This group was comprised of New South entrepreneurs and industrialists in the oil, lumber, and shipping industries and a large, rural planter class concentrated in the Black Belt cotton and sugar parishes in the south of the state.[10] These factors added to the already enormous disparities between the rich and powerful and the poor and powerless.

It was under this system of government that Louisiana citizens found themselves living from the 1920s through the 1950s. On the eve of the Great Depression, almost half of African Americans lived in the rural South, and the rest had few options in the severely distressed urban areas of the nation.[11] Yet even within these limited economic and social conditions, a number of African Americans emerged to become important leaders in the black struggle for civil rights. According to historians of the New Deal era, the 1930s provided the foundation for the ensuing modern civil rights movement.[12] Louisiana women were among those actively pursuing the cause of racial justice. Through local and national civil rights organizations such as the National Association for the Advancement of Colored People (NAACP), local teachers' unions, and women's "club" organizations like the Young Wo-

---

in the New Deal Era (Chapel Hill: University of North Carolina Press, 1996); Harvard Sitkoff, A New Deal for Blacks: The Emergence of Civil Rights as a National Issue (New York: Oxford University Press, 1978); constitution of the State of Louisiana (1898), cited in Greta de Jong, A Different Day, 16.

10. Anthony J. Badger, "Huey Long and the New Deal," in Nothing Else To Fear: New Perspectives on America in the Thirties, ed. Stephen W. Baskerville and Ralph Willett (Manchester; and Dover, N.H.: Manchester University Press, 1985), 68, 69; Allen Sindler, Huey Long's Louisiana: State Politics, 1920–1952 (Baltimore: John Hopkins University Press, 1956); T. Harry Williams, Huey Long (New York: Bantam Books, 1970); A. J. Liebling, The Earl of Louisiana (Baton Rouge: Louisiana State University Press, 1961); Key, Southern Politics.

11. Sitkoff, A New Deal for Blacks, 35.

12. Sitkoff, A New Deal for Blacks; Sullivan, Days of Hope; Fairclough, Race and Democracy, xii.

men's Christian Association (YWCA), Louisiana's female activists advocated for voting rights, equal pay for black teachers, admission for blacks to the state's all-white universities, and amelioration of economic and social constraints that restricted the full participation of blacks in the American democratic ideal outlined in the Constitution.

Studies of the movement in Louisiana are few. In a state with such a diverse ethnic and religious base, concentrating on any aspect of politics, society, or culture can be a daunting task. Additionally, the unique nature of Louisiana politics, and the state's peculiar legal system, based on French civil law and the Napoleonic Code, only add to the complexity of any scholarly study of the state. Historian Adam Fairclough wrote the first and arguably most sweeping study of the civil rights movement in Louisiana, *Race and Democracy: The Civil Rights Struggle in Louisiana, 1915–1972*. But Fairclough's important study slights the contributions of the many women who participated.[13] Historians Kim Lacy Rogers and Pamela Tyler rectified this deficiency in their respective works on civil rights activists and women and politics in New Orleans. Through oral history and research in the manuscript collections of women's organizations, both Rogers and Tyler give voice, and credit, to the black and white female activists in the New Orleans movement.[14] Most recently, historian Greta de Jong has published an important study of the civil rights struggle in rural Louisiana. Like Rogers, de Jong conducted interviews with former civil rights activists; her work highlights the various local women who participated in the grassroots movement and the significance of their activism to Louisiana's rural communities.[15] Like the works of historians Rogers, Tyler, and de Jong, as well as a number of sociologists and political scientists, *Our Minds on Freedom* is a holistic study, utilizing both oral history—to uncover what research in archives alone cannot—and personal and organizational manuscript collections to explore how the women viewed themselves and their roles in the Louisiana movement.

I have diverged from the traditional historical narrative in the last chapter in a discussion of "women-centered organizing." While this concept could certainly be argued for in all of the activities black and white women engaged

13. Fairclough, *Race and Democracy*.

14. Kim Lacy Rogers, *Righteous Lives: Narratives of the New Orleans Civil Rights Movement* (New York: New York University Press, 1993); Pamela Tyler, *Silk Stockings and Ballot Boxes: Women and Politics in New Orleans, 1920–1963* (Athens: University of Georgia Press, 1996).

15. de Jong, *A Different Day*.

in, it was in rural Louisiana and the latter stages of the "classical" movement that "women-centered" organizing was most noticeable.[16] In rural Louisiana and certainly in many localities across the South, gender was central to the ways in which women organized, interacted with, and worked in their community structures. Susan Stall and Randy Stoecker's work "Community Organizing or Organizing Community? Gender and the Crafts of Empowerment" sheds light on the important relationships women cultivated that enabled them to sustain the movement, and themselves, "through the long and dangerous struggles" that defined the movement writ large. The focus of much of the literature on the civil rights movement, as Stall and Stoecker so keenly assert, is that "what people see is the flashy demonstration, not knowing the many hours of preparation entailed in building relationships and providing for participants' basic needs." This was the "grassroots" work that was most often performed by women and, in the more rural areas, by African American women who, according to the authors, were excluded from traditional notions of what constituted the "private sphere" of home and family for women. According to Stall and Stoecker, "women of color and low-income women expanded the boundaries of mothering and the private sphere beyond the private household as they raised and nurtured children in extended family networks and communities," which became the foundation for black women's activism.[17] While white women across the state of Louisiana used race and class to cultivate power relationships that afforded them some unique opportunities to incite change, indigenous female leaders were central to the success of the rural Louisiana movement and to sustaining momentum through the more than a decade that constituted the civil rights movement "proper."

In keeping with this "multidimensional" view of leadership, then, the varied stories of the numerous women who make up the Louisiana civil rights movement show that women were not simply followers, but also leaders with duties similar and equal to those of men. This study supports the work of a number of social scientists who have found that the civil rights movement provided women with an unusual opportunity to achieve positions of leadership, especially in their local communities.[18] To be sure, Louisiana women performed all of the "leadership roles" Bernice McNair Bar-

16. See Susan Stall and Randy Stoecker, "Community Organizing or Organizing Community? Gender and the Crafts of Empowerment," *Gender and Society*, 12, no. 6 (December 1998).

17. Stall and Stoecker, "Community Organizing," 731–32.

18. Barnett, "Invisible Southern Black Women Leaders"; Blumberg, "Rediscovering Women Leaders."

nett identifies—the ability to articulate the needs of followers; to define/ set goals; to provide an ideology justifying action; to formulate tactics and strategies; to initiate action; to mobilize/persuade followers; to raise money; to serve as an example to followers and leaders; to organize/coordinate action; to control group interactions; to teach/educate/train followers and leaders without alienating colleagues and followers; to lead or direct action; to generate publicity; and to obtain public sympathy and support.[19]

Charles Payne's 1995 work *I've Got the Light of Freedom: The Organizing Tradition and the Mississippi Freedom Struggle* in many ways pioneered the study of women in the movement. In it, he asserts that women were overrepresented in the Mississippi movement, estimating that women from thirty to fifty years of age were three to four times more likely to be active in the movement than men. Moreover, Payne argues that class affected women's participation in that "poor black women in rural areas have had to fulfill social roles not commonly played by more privileged women." Payne's well-known formulation that the "men led, women organized," however, is long overdue for reassessment, particularly for Louisiana.[20] This study does that by reevaluating women's qualifications, activities, and leadership roles in Louisiana's struggle for black equality.

As has been shown to be the case across the South, Louisiana has a long tradition of women fighting against racial injustice. Chapters 1 and 2 expand the traditional timeline of the civil rights movement by illuminating the female tradition of dissent in Louisiana prior to the 1954 *Brown* decision. From the Depression years through World War II, and into the postwar years, black women joined and led in local unions and civil rights organizations, agitating for equal treatment in the public arena, for voting rights, in employment, and for equal admission to Louisiana's institutions of higher learning. At the same time, black and white women began to find common ground in organizations such as the Young Women's Christian Association (YWCA), the National Association for the Advancement of Colored People (NAACP), and the National Urban League (NUL).

This protest tradition continued into the 1950s, as middle-class black

---

19. Barnett, "Invisible Southern Black Women Leaders," 167.

20. Charles Payne, *I've Got the Light of Freedom: The Organizing Tradition and the Mississippi Freedom Struggle* (Berkeley and Los Angeles: University of California Press, 1995); Charles Payne, "Men Led, but Women Organized: Movement Participation of Women in the Mississippi Delta," in *Women in the Civil Rights Movement: Trailblazers and Torchbearers, 1941–1965*, ed. Vicki L. Crawford, Jacqueline Anne Rouse, and Barbara Woods (Bloomington: Indiana University Press, 1990).

and white women created biracial organizations, integrated previously all-white organizations, and expanded their work for greater equality in the public and political arenas. Chapter 3 highlights the bravery and tenacity of black and white mothers prior to *Brown* who protested, organized, and sustained a bus boycott in Baton Rouge and, on behalf of their children and students, organized a successful boycott of the historic McDonogh Day Parade in New Orleans. Chapter 4 addresses how women acted as leaders in the day-to-day struggle to alter the system of unequal education throughout Louisiana, and especially in New Orleans. Louisiana women created organizations to address the issues that arose after the Supreme Court's ruling in *Brown v. Board of Education,* and they fought fiercely to see that the desegregation of Louisiana's public school system happened as smoothly as possible. In New Orleans, specifically, black and white women led the fight for integrated schools, escorting their own and, at times, other women's children to the newly integrated schools, educating the public, and appearing before the state legislature to address the importance of complying with the *Brown* decision.

In 1960, the sit-in movement ushered in a new phase of the struggle for black equality. Chapters 5 through 8 explore the work of a new generation of female activists who joined their older female counterparts to work with organizations such as the NAACP, the Congress of Racial Equality (CORE), and a number of local, grassroots civil rights organizations, campaigning for equal treatment in public accommodations in voting rights and in the political arena. Women dominated the membership in many national and local civil rights organizations, acting as chairpersons and serving on executive committees, among other positions. They joined the Freedom Rides, the sit-ins, and numerous demonstrations protesting the inequitable treatment of the nation's African American population. In Louisiana, despite very real dangers working in the state's rural areas, women acted as field directors in CORE's numerous voter education projects, and they canvassed and taught in voter registration clinics and Freedom Schools. At the same time, local women bravely welcomed civil rights workers into their homes, at great risk to themselves and their families. And when the civil rights movement began to wane and Black Power became the new slogan, women adapted and altered strategy, continuing to work toward a more democratic Louisiana.

Our Minds on Freedom expands the traditional civil rights movement narrative—what Jacqueline Dowd Hall deems the "long civil rights movement"—highlighting the activism of Louisiana women long before the civil rights movement of the 1950s and 1960s. The persistence, perseverance, and dedication of Louisiana women were crucial to the successful implementation of movement initiatives and attainment of movement goals. In many ways, women's activities were a logical extension of the role that society had bred into them, but the civil rights movement allowed women to step out of their socially prescribed roles as wives, mothers, and daughters and become significant actors and leaders in the history of the United States. The movement provided a unique opportunity for those widely considered "ordinary" individuals—in this case, women—to act in extraordinary ways. As Belinda Robnett so eloquently notes: "It was, in point of fact, women's extraordinary acts of courage that defined their leadership. It was precisely during these emotionally charged, courageous moments that women, despite threats to life and limb, propelled the movement forward, thereby sustaining its momentum."[21] Women became leaders in a historically limiting public sphere of political and social action. In the daily struggle for civil rights in Louisiana, women exemplified the movement spiritual, "I woke up this morning with my mind on freedom."[22]

21. Belinda Robnett, "African-American Women in the Civil Rights Movement: Spontaneity and Emotion in Social Movement Theory," in *No Middle Ground: Women and Radical Protest*, ed. Kathleen Blee (New York: New York University Press, 1998), 87–88.

22. Words and music by Reverend Osby and Bob Zellner, 1961–62, *Sing for Freedom: The Story of the Civil Rights Movement through Its Songs*, Smithsonian Folkways Collection, 1990.

I

MAY THE DAY HASTEN

Louisiana Women and Early Struggles for Racial Justice

> [W]e pray that . . . the day will come that all men and women regardless of color will have their rightful place in this nation and that we will no longer be the FOOT MATS of this American country and will not be Semi-slaves as we are but Americans. Living and moving with ease them the words of the Holy Bible. . . . "Of one Blood God have made all nations to dwell upon the face of the earth" will be practice [sic] in reality. And although I may be sleeping in my grave, "May the day hasten."
>
> GEORGIA M. JOHNSON, president of the Alexandria branch of the NAACP, April 30, 1945

In October 1924, police arrested a New Orleans schoolteacher, "Mrs. Beck," for moving into a house that she had purchased on a "white" block. The National Association for the Advancement of Colored People (NAACP) believed that it had found its test case to challenge a residential segregation ordinance passed by the city earlier that September. Hoping to avoid "tedious delays and possible adverse decisions of the State Courts," the New Orleans branch's legal team sought to move the case directly to the Fifth District Court and, eventually, to the United States Supreme Court. To accomplish this end, the NAACP attempted to secure a writ of habeas corpus, which stated that should she surrender bail, jailing Mrs. Beck was a violation of the U.S. Constitution.[1] Along with the NAACP's National Legal Committee, the women's auxiliary of the NAACP worked actively on the campaign and

---

1. Dr. Robert W. Bagnell, Director of Local Branches of the NAACP, to Dr. George W. Lucas, President of the New Orleans NAACP, October 15, 1924, II, D, Louisiana State Files, National Association for the Advancement of Colored People Papers, Library of Congress, Washington, D.C. (hereafter cited as NAACP Papers). Unfortunately, "Mrs. Beck's" first name does not appear on any of the legal transcripts.

"plann[ed] a large entertainment to raise funds."[2] According to the president of the New Orleans branch, interest in the case was "high and our people are stirred as never before. The Mrs. Beck case is a genuine case."[3]

The initial enthusiasm surrounding the Beck case, however, was short-lived. The president of the New Orleans branch, Dr. George W. Lucas, quickly informed the national association that if she surrendered bail, Mrs. Beck could run the risk of remaining in jail for several hours, or even several days. Lucas continued that "Mrs. Beck[,] [being a woman] and a teacher in the public schools," could not risk going to jail at all, much less remaining in jail for several days as the school board might "take advantage of the situation and possibly dismiss her entirely." Lucas regretted that "Mrs. Beck is not a *man* who had the time and interest in the affair to spend the required time in prison and prevent the delay in carrying our cases through the lower courts." He subsequently recommended they pursue another case, involving "Mr. Harmon," to challenge the residential segregation law.[4]

The NAACP achieved its desired ruling in *Harmon v. Tyler* when a local judge, Hugh C. Cage, ruled unconstitutional the residential segregation law that prevented "Negroes living in white neighborhoods and whites living in Negro neighborhoods without the consent of a majority of the residents of either color." The judge stated, however, that he believed the "ordinance a just and proper one, based on traditions and beliefs" of the South. Judge Cage further hoped that the matter would eventually make it to the U.S. Supreme Court, which could then decide whether the law was within the "police powers of this state."[5] Under appeal, *Harmon v. Tyler* made its way to the Louisiana State Supreme Court, where on March 2, 1925, the higher court overturned Judge Cage's ruling and upheld the segregation ordinance, arguing that the law protected blacks and whites equally.[6]

Two days later, apparently undeterred by the court's ruling, Miss Prudhoma Dejoie was arrested for "attempting to interfere with an officer" when she was ordered to stop construction on a house she had purchased in a pre-

2. "New Orleans Colored People Stirred by Fight Against Segregation," 10 October 1924, I, D, NAACP Papers.

3. George W. Lucas to Robert W. Bagnell, 7 October 1924, II, D, NAACP Papers.

4. Dr. George W. Lucas to Dr. Robert W. Bagnell, 21 October 1924, II, D, NAACP Papers (emphasis mine).

5. "Race Zoning Law Is Ruled Against in District Case" and "Segregation City Law Invalid," *New Orleans Times-Picayune*, n.d., II, D, NAACP Papers.

6. "Race Segregation Law Is Upheld," *New Orleans States-Item*, 2 March 1925, II, D NAACP Papers.

dominantly white neighborhood.[7] The NAACP took the Dejoie case all the way to the U.S. Supreme Court, where it argued that the New Orleans ordinance violated a 1917 ruling that "no state or municipality could enact residential segregation ordinances." In 1927, the United States Supreme Court reaffirmed its 1917 *Buchanan v. Warley* decision and threw out the New Orleans ordinance.[8]

The Beck case and the incident involving Mrs. Dejoie illustrate two important points about the history of women's early civil rights activism. First, although women pursued the fight for black rights, early histories marginalize and often omit the actions of women like Mrs. Beck and numerous others. The Harmon case was exceptional for its time, but might never have played out if not for the actions of Mrs. Beck. Second, women were significant actors in the tradition of dissent that existed well before what many historians term the beginning of the modern civil rights movement in the 1950s. Inspired by the reformist zeitgeist of the Progressive Era and the emergent women's "club movement" of the early twentieth century, black and white southern women recognized and keenly felt the unjust nature of southern race relations and worked to change it.

As recent historians have shown, there is good reason to expand the traditional timeline of the civil rights movement beyond the boundaries set by the *Brown* decision in 1954 and the assassination of Dr. Martin Luther King Jr. in 1968.[9] And the "foremothers" of the movement "proper" deserve mention in their own right. In Louisiana, black and white women protested against Jim Crow segregation and discrimination as early as the 1920s and well into the 1940s, a period when it was dangerous to do so in the Deep South. Though association records clearly indicate that women were widely represented within civil rights organizations, they were more than simply rank-and-file members; they participated in numerous legal "test" cases, joined and agitated through unions, registered to vote, and fought stridently, if not openly, for black rights in public space.[10] Louisiana women were, to be sure, an integral part of a well-established protest tradition before civil rights came to the forefront of national politics in the 1950s.

7. "Segregation Act Test to Be Made in Delachaise St.," *New Orleans Times-Picayune*, 5 March 1925.

8. Press release, 12 March 1926, II, D, NAACP Papers.

9. In particular, see Jacquelyn Dowd Hall, "The Long Civil Rights Movement and Political Uses of the Past," *Journal of American History* (March 2005); and, most recently, Glenda Gilmore, *Defying Dixie: The Radical Roots of Civil Rights, 1919–1950* (New York: Norton, 2008).

10. See Robin D. G. Kelley's discussion of the "hidden transcript" in *Race Rebels: Culture, Politics, and the Black Working Class* (New York: Free Press, 1994).

Still, prior to the 1950s, protest activities in Louisiana were sporadic and mainly local. Thousands of women throughout the state supported the movement not only by attending meetings, but also by agitating within their local communities, acting as spokeswomen, and creating both formal and informal community networks to address the severe poverty, racism, and discrimination experienced by many Louisiana blacks.[11] Although many historians have cited the outright "exclusion and limited participation of women in traditionally male-headed civil rights groups," particularly in early civil rights organizations like the NAACP, Louisiana women seem to have worked around, and within, these limitations.[12] The stories of black and white women opposing the racial status quo by working through the NAACP, unions, and progressive women's organizations illustrate the long tradition of activism that existed in many Louisiana communities prior to 1954.

"YOU DO NOT SEEM TO REALIZE THAT THE SOCIAL ORDER HAS CHANGED"

The NAACP was the first and arguably most significant organization to work for black rights in Louisiana. Founded in 1909, a group of like-minded men and women institutionalized and led the movement for racial equality at a time when most white progressives paid little attention to blacks. The founders and early membership of the NAACP were uniquely an integrated group of liberal-minded individuals dedicated to the ideals of racial justice and equality.[13] As one historian has noted, in Louisiana the NAACP "pro-

---

11. Vicki Crawford, "We Shall Not Be Moved: Black Female Activists in the Mississippi Civil Rights Movement, 1960–1965" (Ph.D. diss., Emory University, 1987), 67.

12. Crawford, "We Shall Not Be Moved," 63. There is much literature that addresses the subordination of women in the civil rights movement, but most noteworthy are Sara Evans, *Personal Politics: The Roots of Women's Liberation in the Civil Rights Movement and the New Left* (New York: Vintage Books, 1979); Angela Davis, *Women, Race, and Class* (New York: Random House, 1981); Paula Giddings, *When and Where I Enter* (New York: Bantam Books, 1984); Jacqueline Jones, *Labor of Love, Labor of Sorrow: Black Women and the Family from Slavery to Freedom* (New York: Basic Books, 1985); Vicki Crawford, Jacqueline Anne Rouse, and Barbara Woods, eds., *Women in the Civil Rights Movement: Trailblazers and Torchbearers, 1941–1965* (Bloomington: Indiana University Press, 1990); and, more recently, Constance Curry et al., *Deep in Our Hearts: Nine White Women in the Freedom Movement* (Athens: University of Georgia Press, 2000); and M. Bahati Kuumba, *Gender and Social Movements* (New York: Altamira Press, 2001).

13. Adam Fairclough, *Better Day Coming: Blacks and Equality, 1890–2000* (New York: Penguin, 2001), 69–70; Harvard Sitkoff, *A New Deal for Blacks: The Emergence of Civil Rights as a National Issue* (New York: Oxford University Press, 1978), 14.

vided the backbone of the freedom struggle."[14] In 1914, the year the United States Supreme Court reaffirmed its 1896 *Plessy v. Ferguson* decision giving final legal backing to the de facto "separate, but equal" doctrine that ensured the unequal status of the nation's African American population, the first NAACP chapter was organized in the Deep South, in Shreveport, in northwestern Louisiana. The branch lasted for just ten years, yet by 1930 eight more branches were organized throughout the state, including one in New Orleans established in 1915.

In the early years of the NAACP's existence, many rural branches in Louisiana, and throughout the Deep South, found it difficult to sustain a stable membership base. Extreme poverty, illiteracy, lack of a black professional class, absence of paved roads to travel to meetings, and, perhaps most problematic for Louisiana, a language barrier in the rural, southern area of the state where many spoke only French, all contributed to the NAACP's inability to establish a solid base, much less flourish in the smaller, more rural cities and towns. The New Orleans chapter, however, as well as other urban chapters, held steady and were integral to the success of the larger freedom struggle in the state.[15]

The NAACP's integrated membership consisted mostly of professionals and small businessmen, together with women who were most often housewives or teachers. As early as 1917, the New Orleans branch created a Women's Auxiliary, which, among other actions, organized a committee to protest the use of "colored women prisoners on the streets and in the public markets" and the segregation of women in the red-light district of the city.[16] In 1925, the New Orleans branch was awarded the Madam C. J. Walker Scholarship for the "biggest advance in membership in 1924."[17] Well into the 1940s, the NAACP continued its work on numerous test cases in an effort to break down the segregation laws enacted at the height of the Jim Crow era. The "Mrs. Beck" residential segregation case of 1924 proved to be only the tip of the iceberg.

Although the NAACP remained active during the Depression years, member participation in all civil rights organizations decreased during the 1930s

14. Adam Fairclough, *Race and Democracy: The Civil Rights Struggle in Louisiana, 1915–1972* (Athens: University of Georgia Press, 1999), xiv.

15. Fairclough, *Race and Democracy*, 20. The other NAACP chapters organized in Louisiana in the early years were Alexandria (1919), Ama (1920), Baton Rouge (1919), Clarence (1922), Lake Providence (1927), Madison Parish (1928), and Monroe (1927).

16. NAACP New Orleans to Roy Nash, 25 March 1917, I, G, NAACP Papers.

17. Telegram to the New Orleans Branch, 5 January 1925, I, G, Louisiana State Files, NAACP Papers.

due to a variety of factors. The unprecedented extension of federal power during the Depression benefited some Louisiana blacks: they participated in adult education and vocational programs, literacy training, and, minimally, in public works projects such as the Civilian Conservation Corps (CCC) and the Works Progress Administration (WPA). Though racism and discrimination existed throughout the nation, African Americans in the South were forced to contend with entrenched racist bureaucratic systems and discriminatory local officials put in charge of public assistance programs. In many ways, at both the local and national levels, the New Deal "reinforced existing power relationships." President Franklin Roosevelt, for instance, refused to support an antilynching bill, fearful of losing the support of southern politicians for his New Deal initiatives.[18] Discrimination and violence, including lynching, increased as poor whites and blacks vied for the already inadequate relief from local administrators. During the New Deal years, the NAACP often found little success when investigating lynchings and discrimination against blacks receiving aid through government programs.

Although membership in the Louisiana branches decreased during the Depression years, it rose again as the United States entered World War II. During the war years, the country embraced a new patriotism, and African Americans saw an opportunity to claim victory at home as well as abroad. During the 1940s, 1 million African Americans migrated from rural to urban areas, and more than 2 million southern blacks migrated north and west for opportunities in the wartime industries. Along with an enhanced awareness of their status as second-class citizens, African Americans embraced a new militancy, believing it their time to fight for their rights as Americans. The number of registered black voters in the North as well as the South climbed, and NAACP branches across the South benefited; membership grew from 50,000 in 355 branches in 1940 to almost 450,000 in 1,073 branches in 1946.[19]

Even as jobs related to the wartime buildup seemed to abound, racial discrimination still existed at every level. Blacks, and particularly black women, still performed the most menial and subordinate tasks. Due to a wartime

18. Fairclough, *Race and Democracy*, 42–44; Greta de Jong, *A Different Day: African American Struggles for Justice in Rural Louisiana, 1900–1970* (Chapel Hill: University of North Carolina Press, 2002), 86–99. See also William E. Leuchtenburg, *The White House Looks South: Franklin D. Roosevelt, Harry S. Truman, Lyndon B. Johnson* (Baton Rouge: Louisiana State University Press, 2005).

19. Robert Korstad and Nelson Lichtenstein, "Opportunities Found and Lost: Labor, Radicals, and the Early Civil Rights Movement," *Journal of American History* 75, no. 3 (December 1988): 786–87.

shortage of workers, many African American women were able to leave domestic service, but they usually found themselves relegated to the worst positions in the industrial plants. Much like their male counterparts, black women actively embraced the new racial awareness of the war era; between July 1943 and December 1944, nearly one-quarter of all complaints brought before the Federal Employment Practices Commission (FEPC) established by President Roosevelt were by black women.[20]

Gradually, women began to challenge racial discrimination in the public arena. In Alexandria, Louisiana, Georgia Johnson presided over the NAACP chapter, attacking the system of unequal voting rights. In Baton Rouge, Viola Johnson helped break down segregation in the state's professional schools, while throughout the state, other black women worked with the national NAACP to attack discrimination in teachers' pay. Others cooperated with white women to press for equal treatment in teachers' unions. At the same time, progressive white women worked for racial justice in their own organizations, including the YWCA, and joined predominantly black organizations such as the NAACP and the National Urban League.

During the war years, African American men and women protesting their place in southern society were met with extreme white resistance. Alexandria, Louisiana, located in the rural midsection of the state, exemplifies the militancy that erupted in many southern communities during the 1940s. A concentration of military bases in the area may have contributed to heightened racial tensions; a strong NAACP branch added to the volatility of the situation. On behalf of Alexandria's black citizens, the NAACP relentlessly pursued action against police brutality and voter registration abuses. The NAACP also sued to use city-owned buildings for black functions.[21]

Black troops stationed in Alexandria had already experienced violence at the hands of whites when, in 1942, a black soldier resisted arrest by a white military officer; twenty-nine black soldiers were injured in the resulting violence, three critically. During the melee, black female employees of a local diner also experienced severe repercussions. In the pursuit of justice, a female witness, Mary Scales, reported the incident to the NAACP. Scales, a twenty-two-year-old waitress, was shot during the conflict; having witnessed the imbroglio, she wrote the national organization requesting that President Roosevelt investigate "the race riot there." Another woman, Mary

20. Giddings, *When and Where I Enter*, 238.
21. Fairclough, *Race and Democracy*, 78.

Trotter, similarly reported that a white military policeman struck her, causing her to fall on her mouth and knock out some of her teeth. Before she could get up, he kicked her in the side. Trotter further reported a lot of "hollering and cursing." According to the black-owned *Louisiana Weekly*, women were beaten, kicked, and thrown out of other Alexandria establishments. Another waitress, who wished to remain anonymous, stated that she and another woman hid two black soldiers in the back of the diner and, when white soldiers attempted to enter, locked the door. Finally, after things quieted down, they let the "two soldiers slip out the back way." One witness called the incident a "Little Pearl Harbor."[22] Illustrative of this renewed commitment to achieving equality, and despite the dangers, the women persisted in their fight, not only by aiding their black soldier brothers, but also in pushing the NAACP to investigate.

At the center of the Alexandria movement was a controversial and fiercely determined newspaper editor and businesswoman, Georgia Johnson, chairperson of the Alexandria NAACP during the mid-1940s. Little is known about Johnson's background, and her status as chairperson of the branch throughout the years appears unclear. Yet, her involvement with the Alexandria NAACP illustrates a high level of commitment as well as strong leadership abilities in this predominantly male-led organization. Her voluminous correspondence with NAACP officials, particularly attorneys, illustrates Johnson's ability to provoke action and, at times, annoyance, from the national male leadership.

In the early 1940s, Johnson began petitioning the national NAACP, often to no avail, on behalf of a number of Alexandria's black citizens who had routinely been subject to police brutality. In one case, Johnson was commended for the "energy and ability, which you have shown as chairman of your legal committee which made it possible for us to prepare to take this case to the Supreme Court of the United States."[23] When the national NAACP looked into the practices of the Democratic white primary in the state, it was Georgia Johnson who provided association attorneys with numerous examples of complaints against the practices of the local registrar. In 1944, working with the Right to Vote Movement in Alexandria, Johnson requested that the National Legal Committee file suit on behalf of blacks who had been

22. War Department Memo, 23 January 1942, Walter White to Thurgood Marshall on behalf of Mary Scales, 20 January 1942, I, C, NAACP Papers; *Louisiana Weekly* article, 24 January 1942.

23. J. A. Williams to Georgia Johnson, 10 July 1944, I, C, Alexandria, Louisiana, Files, NAACP Papers.

refused the right to register.[24] And, in 1945, Johnson succeeded in getting local newsstands to sell black newspapers and even persuaded one "white man to carry 'The Crisis.' "[25]

In her correspondence with the well-known NAACP attorney Thurgood Marshall, Johnson often expressed indignation at the apparent slowness with which the national NAACP reacted to her appeals. Johnson's impatience with the NAACP's methodical approach caused her to be viewed as somewhat of a nuisance. In one instance in 1944, Johnson became angry with Thurgood Marshall for not pursuing a voter registration lawsuit. In another incident, Johnson pressed Marshall to act on behalf of a soldier's wife from Mississippi who, during her stay in Louisiana, was beaten by police and thrown in jail. In response, Marshall stated, "[W]e certainly will not be able to get along if everything I do is going to be looked upon with suspicion by you," though he offered to meet with her to discuss the case.[26]

Looking for a friendly ear, Johnson turned to Ella Baker, director of NAACP branches during the 1940s. Johnson expressed her dismay that New Orleans attorney A. P. Tureaud and regional director Daniel Byrd did not take her seriously enough. In Johnson's opinion, they were "seeking favor with local [white] reactionaries." Proclaiming her loss of respect for the NAACP, she claimed to regret "that I took an active part in the activities of the Alexandria Branch because it is dangerous to be militant in the reactionary south. . . . Some day I will be able to show some one how one has suffered by being militant alone."[27] Johnson appeared no less dismayed in another letter to Baker by what she deemed the actions of the "Uncle Tom's" [sic] within the larger NAACP. Citing her embarrassment at some of the actions of the organization and the lack of protection afforded her from the national organization, Johnson continued, "Although all over this country Negroes are fighting for the rights of the group, the NAACP with its militant principles will do more harm to an individual or set of individuals when Branches are existing for personal gain and managed by Negro stools for leading white people." Apparently finding herself in a "dangerous spot" for her ostensibly solo militant activities, Johnson refused to further "push her neck out . . . in these reactionary southern cities."[28]

24. Georgia Johnson to the National Legal Committee, 1 September and 30 September 1944, I, B, NAACP Papers.

25. Georgia Johnson to Roy Wilkins, 23 June 1945, I, C, NAACP Papers.

26. Thurgood Marshall to Georgia Johnson, 5 October 1944, I, B, NAACP Papers.

27. Georgia Johnson to Ella Baker, 29 December 1945, I, C, NAACP Papers.

28. Georgia Johnson to Ella Baker, 20 January 1946, I, C, NAACP Papers.

In 1947, still working within the Alexandria branch, Johnson became embroiled in yet another dispute with the national NAACP. During the war, the city of Alexandria allowed its black residents the use of an assigned USO building for community functions. However, when the war ended, the city reclaimed the building. Still under the leadership of Georgia Johnson, the Alexandria NAACP filed a petition with the mayor to allow it to use the building for its organizational functions, claiming that it was paid for, in part, by (black) taxpayer dollars. The Alexandria City Council rejected the proposal, with the mayor asking the group to "be reasonable." In a letter to the National Legal Committee of the NAACP, Johnson stated that she would not compromise, except under "a court order."[29] In a follow-up letter to Daniel Byrd, Johnson eloquently cited the 1944 opinion in *Smith v. Allwright,* in which the Supreme Court ruled the all-white Texas primary unconstitutional, and asked Byrd to "think of the suit . . . [as] it has opened the door to all citizens of Negro blood in the South." Believing that the Alexandria branch had a federal case that could be put before the Supreme Court, she continued, "SO THIS IS WHAT I THOUGHT THE NAACP STOOD FOR. If it does not, we as militant members and officers are in a bad fix because the reactionaries can close us up or do anything they want to do to us."[30]

Johnson relentlessly pursued her proposed lawsuit, corresponding with the national NAACP, Daniel Byrd, and Louis Berry, a Howard University law student. Urging immediate action, Johnson noted that the mayor of Alexandria deemed the local NAACP and its president—Georgia Johnson—"radicals" and refused to budge. Louis Berry eventually took the case, and on the first day of trial, he met in conference with the defense attorneys and reached a compromise. Dissatisfied, Johnson openly insulted the judge, stated that her branch did not accept such a compromise, and insisted that they would take the matter all the way to the Supreme Court if necessary; for this action she was thrown out of the courtroom.[31] Although Thurgood Marshall agreed to attend the state conference and meet with Johnson to discuss the matter, the national NAACP, apparently reluctant to get involved in yet another controversy begun by Johnson, continued to forestall action.

29. Letter to the Mayor of Alexandria, 11 April 1947, signed by Mrs. Fannie K. Fontenot, President of the PTA, Mrs. Dora Wallace, Mrs. Beatrice Redford, Doretha Anderson, President of the YWCA Alexandria; petition, 1 May 1947, signed by five individuals, among them Mrs. Georgia Johnson, Mrs. Elizabeth Williams, and Miss Mildred Morgan, Treasurer of Alexandria NAACP; Georgia M. Johnson to NAACP National Legal Committee, 23 May 1947, I, B, Alexandria, Louisiana, Files, NAACP Papers.
30. Georgia Johnson to Daniel Byrd, 23 July 1947, I, B, NAACP Papers.
31. Georgia Johnson to Daniel Byrd, 4 August 1947, I, B, NAACP Papers.

In the end, branch members accused Johnson of embezzling monies and rigging elections. A local male minister ultimately replaced her as branch president. With the matter of the building use by local blacks still under review, the national NAACP decided not to pursue the case to the Supreme Court as Johnson had wished. Although she produced affidavits accounting for all the money in question, her tenure as leader in the Alexandria NAACP officially ended.

It appears that Georgia Johnson was accused of embezzlement in essence to shut her up, but this was not the first time, nor the last, that the national NAACP leaders found themselves arguing with Johnson over what she believed to be their lack of action. There was no evidence to suggest that Johnson had misappropriated any funds. Furthermore, Georgia Johnson's discharge was not the only time a woman was accused of these allegations. In Iberville Parish, a black teacher who performed organizational work for the state NAACP office was accused of embezzling money from the Iberville Parish Teachers Club. In that case, too, the missing money was accounted for.

Regardless of the charges, in 1948 Johnson was still working as chairperson of the Alexandria Legal Committee, as well as acting state organizer for the NAACP and the Federated Clubs.[32] Although it is apparent that many thought Johnson a problem, her grasp of the constitutional rights of blacks, as well as her persistent pursuit of justice, is noteworthy; that year she argued that "registrars who refuse citizens the right to register stand liable to be imprisoned, fined or both upon conviction in court." She continued to ask all "colored women of Louisiana, wake up and do as women of other races are doing by playing our part in helping to make this our great Nation, a still greater force in the postwar world."[33] That same year, Johnson penned a letter to the Alexandria registrar of voters, stating indignantly: "You do not seem to realize that the social order [has] changed. Over ten thousand Negro men and women died in WWII for 'World Democracy,' when you are denying it at home." She enclosed numerous affidavits from black Alexandrians who had attempted to register and went on to note that not only were

32. Georgia Johnson to Daniel Byrd, 4 August 1947; Daniel Byrd to Frank H. Williams, August 15, 1947; Daniel Byrd to Thurgood Marshall, 12 September 1947; Daniel Byrd to Reverend J. M. Murphy, 5 November 1947, NAACP Papers, I, B; Edith Jones to National NAACP, 31 December 1946, I, B, NAACP Papers.

33. "Women of Louisiana Urged to Exercise Constitutional Rights," 26 January 1948, unidentified newspaper clipping, I, C, NAACP Papers.

they refused registration, but also that a number of registration cards legally obtained had been destroyed or misplaced. Georgia Johnson continued her pursuit of voting rights through the 1950s, though her leadership and constant efforts on behalf of black rights were overshadowed by the continuing controversies beleaguering her and the Alexandria branch.[34]

Johnson's exhaustive petitioning on behalf of the black citizens of Alexandria appears a nuisance on the surface. It is quite possible that the national NAACP office thought it unwise to use its limited resources, or perhaps it opted to focus on other priorities. However, considering what scholars of the movement have uncovered regarding traditional gendered attitudes in the NAACP and, specifically, Martin Luther King Jrs.'s sometimes easy dismissal of Ella Baker, it is fair to assume that had Johnson been a man, the NAACP might have been more willing to take her requests seriously. Instead, Johnson came across as pushy. Both Johnson and Baker stepped outside of what were considered "proper" gender roles, and they therefore found it difficult to effect change.

"WILLFUL NEGLECT OF DUTY"?

Through the 1940s, the militant and not-so-militant activities of women like Georgia Johnson continued to bring small, but significant changes to the social, political, and racial structure of Louisiana. A discernable reduction in the willingness of women to suffer their subordinate status in the state is most noticeable in the increase in the NAACP's legal efforts in education. As early as the 1920s, Louisiana women petitioned local school boards requesting equal pay. During the Depression years, union-affiliated teacher associations, both black and white, grew in number.[35] The NAACP's lawsuits on behalf of black teachers and students in the 1930s and 1940s laid the foundation for greater successes in the 1950s and 1960s. Even during the early Depression years, when the NAACP found itself somewhat impotent, interest in fighting for equal pay for black workers, specifically black teachers, increased. In 1936, the NAACP filed its first lawsuit challenging differentials in teacher salaries, part of attorney Charles Hamilton Houston's strategic campaign to overturn the *Plessy* decision. By 1939, the NAACP created a separate

34. Georgia Johnson to Nora Windon, Registrar of Voters—Alexandria, 18 August 1948, I, C, NAACP Papers.

35. See Edith Rosepha Ambrose, "Sarah Towles Reed: Teacher and Activist," *Louisiana History* (Winter 1996).

Legal Defense and Education Fund to raise monies for these "test cases," eventually culminating in the 1954 *Brown v. Board of Education* ruling.[36]

In 1940, Louisiana had approximately four thousand black school teachers, the majority of them female; they were paid anywhere from 30 percent to 75 percent of the salaries of white teachers of similar education, experience, and tenure.[37] In 1939, a reorganized NAACP Shreveport branch sought assistance from the national NAACP in gaining equal pay for its African American teachers. The secretary of the local branch, Ruth Burks, noted that the black teachers in her parish were paid approximately half of what the whites earned and that she already had one teacher willing to file a suit.[38] Thus, Louisiana teachers, most of them women—black and white—were among the first to actively challenge the status quo.

In the 1940s, inquiries were made to NAACP Special Counsel Thurgood Marshall regarding a group of teachers in New Orleans who were "greatly interested in equalizing the salaries paid to Negro and white teachers," and who were "prepared to initiate a test case in the courts." By 1941, Marshall had met with the group and initiated the case marking the "third state in addition to Maryland and Virginia whose campaigns to equalize teachers' salaries is being carried on through legal procedure." The NAACP filed suit in June 1941 "individually and on behalf of others similarly situated"; in early 1942, Judge Wayne Borah of the Eastern District Court of Louisiana overruled the Orleans Parish School Board's attempted to have the case dismissed.[39]

The salary equalization case, filed as *McKelpin v. Orleans Parish School Board*, was the first of its kind in Louisiana and continued in the court system until 1943. The NAACP had every reason to look forward to success, citing "a sweeping decision" in 1940 wherein the Supreme Court equalized black and white teacher salaries, to take effect within a two-year period. The NAACP chose to extend the *McKelpin* suit, however, when the Orleans Parish School Board declined to abide by the Supreme Court's ruling. Sarah Towles Reed, a white schoolteacher and a political agitator who taught in the

36. See Mark V. Tushnet, *The NAACP's Legal Strategy Against Segregated Education, 1925–1950* (Chapel Hill: University of North Carolina Press, 1987).

37. Fairclough, *Race and Democracy*, 62; "Orleans Parish School Board Salary Schedule" re: white and black teachers and principals, 1940, II, B, NAACP Papers.

38. Ruth Burks to Walter White, 2 November 1939, II, D, NAACP Papers.

39. Donald Jones to Thurgood Marshall, 14 March 1941; telegram to Thurgood Marshall from NAACP New Orleans, 17 March 1941; Mrs. Crump to Thurgood Marshall, memorandum, 14 June 1941; A. P. Tureaud to Thurgood Marshall, 28 July 1941; NAACP press release, 6 February 1942, II, B, Legal Files, Teachers Salaries—General, NAACP Papers.

state from 1910 to 1951, greatly influenced the outcome of the case. Reed's unwavering commitment to women's equality through her union affiliations makes her, in the words of her biographer, a woman "conspicuously ahead of her time." As a teacher for the Orleans Parish school system, Reed constantly worked for equal pay for women, founding first the New Orleans Public School Teachers Association (NOPSTA) in 1925 and, then, the union-affiliated New Orleans Classroom Teachers Federation (NOCTF) in 1935. Reed believed that a trade union would possess more clout during the New Deal years than simple professional associations. Although NOPSTA and NOCTF were successful in gaining raises for white teachers, Reed continued to fight on behalf of African American teachers.

In 1937, Reed and Veronica Hill, a prominent African American teacher and civil rights activist, supported by an interracial delegation of women, petitioned the New Orleans school board for equal pay for black teachers. When an elevator operator stopped them from entering the meeting, Reed and Hill climbed a fire escape and slid the petition under a locked door. Black teachers not only got a raise, but, with Reed's assistance, they successfully formed the League of Classroom Teachers (LCT), American Federation of Teachers, Local 527, affiliated with the all-white NOCTF, Local 353.[40] For years, Reed served as the link between the white NOCTF and the black LCT, attending both unions' meetings and working persistently on helping the groups achieve both their respective and their common goals.

Thought by conservative leaders to be "a radical, a threat to such time-honored Southern traditions as white supremacy and complacent woman-hood," Reed often found herself mired in controversy.[41] In 1938, Reed attended the organizational meeting of the Southern Conference for Human Welfare (SCHW)—thought by many to be a communist front group. Such activities, combined with her unique teaching style, which included field trips to the police stations, jails, and courtrooms as lessons in democracy, and student debates over differing political philosophies such as communism, capitalism, fascism, and socialism, led to great personal and legal troubles for Reed.[42] The House Un-American Activities Committee (HUAC) and the conservative New Orleans Young Men's Business Club (YMBC) investigated her for many years.

40. Ambrose, "Sarah Towles Reed," 43–45; Leslie Parr, "Sarah Towles Reed, Class of 1904," in *Lives of Learning in a Southern Setting: The Education of Women at Newcomb College*, ed. Beth Willinger and Susan Tucker (Baton Rouge: Louisiana State University Press, forthcoming).

41. Ambrose, "Sarah Towles Reed," 47–48.

42. Fairclough, *Race and Democracy*, 52; Ambrose, "Sarah Towles Reed," 55.

In June 1943, Reed informed A. P. Tureaud, council for the NAACP of New Orleans, of her intent to attend a meeting in Baton Rouge on behalf of black teachers, called by the nonunion and all-white Louisiana Teachers Association (LTA). The meeting was seemingly an attempt on the part of white teachers to thwart the establishment of equal salary scales based on qualifications and experience. The LTA made it clear that "the whites would quit teaching if Negro teachers received the same pay."[43] Due to the efforts of Sarah Reed and the NAACP, in October, the Louisiana Supreme Court ruled for "complete equalization of salaries of Negro teachers with that of the white teachers in the schools of New Orleans . . . the first payment of salaries [i]n the 1943–44 term."[44] In 1958, the white union, Local 353, voted against integration, and the national American Federation of Teachers (AFT) revoked their charter. Subsequently the integrated black union, Local 527, remained the only teachers' union in New Orleans.[45] Because of Reed's diligence, Louisiana's black and white teachers eventually did find common ground at a time when white southerners overwhelmingly avoided interracial affiliations.

In Jefferson Parish, Louisiana, located only a few miles southeast of Orleans Parish, another significant battle was being waged on behalf of African American teachers. In December 1942, Miss Eula Mae Lee, a graduate of Southern University who had taught in the public school system for nine years, filed a petition to equalize salaries for teachers and principals in the Jefferson Parish public school system. The Jefferson Parish School Board countered with a petition of its own, citing twenty-one separate incidents, between February 9 and May 5, 1943, where Lee was "tardy." The principal of her school testified to her lateness; however, noting the lateness of buses and of other teachers, he deemed her competency as a teacher "relative."[46] In an obvious attempt to punish Lee for filing a lawsuit, the school board dismissed her under the Teacher Tenure Act, citing "tardiness" and "willful neglect of duty."[47]

Believing her dismissal "unlawful, illegal, and void," in October, Lee filed

43. A. P. Tureaud to Thurgood Marshall, 13 June 1943, II, B, Teacher Salaries—General NAACP Papers.

44. A. P. Tureaud to Thurgood Marshall, 2 October 1943, II, B, Teacher Salaries—General NAACP Papers.

45. Ambrose, "Sarah Towles Reed," 53–54, 59.

46. NAACP Petition, 31 December 1942; A. P. Tureaud to Thurgood Marshall, 6 October 1943, II, B, NAACP Papers.

47. Jefferson Parish School Board to Eula Mae Lee, 15 October 1943, II, B, NAACP Papers.

her case with the Judicial District Court of Jefferson Parish. In her petition, Lee cited the provisions of the state legislature that provided that "no teacher in the Public schools of [Louisiana] shall suffer any loss or deduction of pay for tardiness, unless such tardiness has caused loss of time from her official class duties, on more than two occasions and for a period of one hour or more, during any one school year." Lee further noted that the Jefferson Parish School Board used a truck to transport children to the African American school in Kenner where she taught, and that she and another teacher were given permission by the principal to take the truck to the school as she lived in New Orleans and needed transportation to get to the Kenner "Colored School." Lee argued that the truck was often late arriving to the school, thus she often opted to take a bus in order to arrive on time. Lee, who lived with her seriously ill mother, noted that "on many occasions she should have remained at home with her mother but knowing the difficulty of securing the services of a substitute teacher in her place, she nevertheless reported for duty." Lee requested that she be rehired and have her salary restored with back pay.[48] The judge ruled in her favor, but the Jefferson Parish School Board appealed.

Eula Mae Lee v. Jefferson Parish School Board continued at the local and state court levels for five more years, eventually ending up at the Louisiana State Supreme Court. While the NAACP fought on her behalf, Lee moved to Washington, D.C., for work. The NAACP combined Lee's case with a case against the Jefferson Parish public school system, requesting that Lee be restored to her position for the 1948–49 school term, that she receive a salary based on the previous school year, *and* that the board further agree to pay "colored teachers the same salary as white teachers with similar degrees."[49] Although the school board again sought dismissal by the state Supreme Court, it was eventually settled by consent decree, and Lee returned to her teaching career in Louisiana.[50]

Both the *Lee* and *McKelpin* cases were significant in establishing precedents in the state with regard to equalization of salaries. Suing for equal pay on behalf of teachers who, for the most part, were female, was a significant aspect of the NAACP's legal strategy against segregation in the southern public schools. As the *Lee* case illustrates, the women involved in the early

48. *State of Louisiana, ex rel, Eula Mae Lee, Realtor v. Jefferson Parish School Board,* and Lem Uel W. Higgins, Respondent, November 1943, II, B, NAACP Papers.

49. A. P. Tureaud to John E. Fleury, District Attorney for Jefferson Parish, 12 April 1948, II, B, NAACP Papers.

50. A. P. Tureaud to Thurgood Marshall, 30 July 1948, II, B, NAACP Papers.

civil rights battles took initiative and proceeded in these lawsuits often at great risk to their livelihoods.

Although the 1950s and 1960s would bring many more achievements in the struggle for black equality in the South, the protest activities by black and white women in the years prior to the modern civil rights movement are significant. As early as the 1920s, black and white women in Louisiana worked to better the status of the African American community, not only by creating interracial alliances within integrated organizations like the NAACP, but also by directly challenging the racial status quo through the courts. And, although integrated organizations such as the NAACP and the National Urban League were progressive for their time, when it came to gender issues, women still retained a place subordinate to that of men. Thus, women had to contend not only with the usual racial intimidation, harassment, and violence for their efforts, but also with direct challenges from men with whom they found themselves in constant competition. It is understandable that many women chose to work exclusively within women's organizations.

Certainly within the black community, women were acutely aware of their subordinate status due to race and gender and acted in both subtle and overt ways to challenge this racial caste system. In Louisiana, African American women were a distinct part of the protest tradition working within organizations such as the NAACP or teachers unions, filing lawsuits, attempting to register to vote, and advocating for equal pay and better working conditions. By the 1940s, economic considerations had become a priority in the fight for equal rights. To be sure, in many areas of the country the fight for economic equality superseded requests for equality in the public arena, and women, in particular, fought to be included in the newly emerging "consumer republic."[51] Class considerations became part and parcel of women's quotidian resistance to racism and discrimination in much the same way it had been a defining aspect of their community structures.

Women such as Georgia Johnson, who acted as president of an NAACP branch in a particularly violent area of the state, and Sarah Towles Reed, who risked her life and livelihood protesting the inequitable treatment of the state's black teachers, were important leaders in these early struggles for racial justice. Both women subverted strictly defined racial and gender categories to advance the cause of civil rights. Sarah Reed's actions must

51. For more information on African American economic struggles in the 1940s, see Lizabeth Cohen, *A Consumers' Republic: The Politics of Mass Consumption in Postwar America* (New York: Knopf, 2003).

certainly have been perceived as an assault on the entire foundation of the South, which, in the main, rested on a specific set of assumptions about the role of white women. Their actions illustrate a strong tradition of dissent, a tradition that formed the bedrock for the civil rights movement "proper" of the 1950s and the 1960s.

2

SUBVERSIVE WOMEN
Interracial Alliances

> It's so obvious when somebody thinks somebody else is second-class. It sticks out all over them. It's not what they say . . . , it's just there. It's a presence. I don't know how to describe it, but you can feel it . . . when somebody thinks you're second-class and you know that. *We're all women,* and you certainly must have felt it.
>
> ROSA FREEMAN KELLER, civil rights activist

During the nineteenth century, interracial cooperation was the hallmark of the abolition and women's rights movements. After the Civil War and the failure of Reconstruction, interracial activism floundered with the rise of Jim Crow and legal and de facto segregation of African Americans, particularly in the South. The Progressive Era of the early twentieth century, however, ushered in a new biracial activism that became the bedrock of twentieth-century civil rights struggles. Perhaps the most historically significant interracial alliance emerged in 1909, when black and white progressives met in Harpers Ferry, West Virginia, and organized the National Association for the Advancement of Colored People (NAACP) to work on behalf of social, political, and economic equality for African Americans. A year later, in 1910, another integrated organization, the National Urban League (NUL), was founded to aid African Americans migrating to the North in search of better economic and social opportunities. In 1919, a group of southerners founded the Commission for Interracial Cooperation (CIC) to address the problems blacks faced in the postwar world, most notably, lynching. Like the NAACP and the NUL, the CIC included established white and black members of the southern community, including Dr. R. R. Moton, president of Tuskegee Institute in Alabama; George Foster Peabody, a highly successful New York investment banker who at one time served as a trustee of Hampton University, a historically black university; and Harry F. Byrd, the governor of Virginia from 1926 to 1930.[1] All of these organizations were part and parcel of the reformist zeitgeist of the Progressive Era. Although these organizations persevered during the Great Depression, all achieved nominal success for African American civil rights.

As the Depression decade came to a close, white liberals' concern about equal opportunity in America increased; so too did their participation in civil rights activities and organizations. In 1938, the integrated National Urban League founded a chapter in New Orleans, one of the first to be organized in the South. Although it was predominantly supported and led by a group of "conservative, segregation-minded whites," it also included a number of Jewish liberals, many of them new migrants to the state, and women, who would continue to address issues of racial inequality well into the 1960s. In its early years, the New Orleans Urban League focused on issues of employment and wage inequalities and, later, police brutality and discrimination in public housing. Similarly, in 1939, the pro-labor Catholic Committee of the South (CCS) was organized. The CCS had a particularly strong following in Louisiana, particularly in the southern area of the state where Catholics dominated. Thought by many white conservatives to be a social reform organization, members of CCS chose to focus their attention on labor-related issues, while at the same time working to "foster a friendlier understanding between southerners "regardless of race."[2]

Perhaps the most controversial interracial organization of its day was the Southern Conference for Human Welfare (SCHW). Though labeled a communist organization by its critics since its inception in 1938, the SCHW described itself as a "southwide membership organization to promote the general welfare and to improve the economic, social, political, cultural, and spiritual conditions of the people of the South without regard to race, creed, color, or national origin." Among its members were high-profile individuals such as Dr. Mary McLeod Bethune, a black woman appointed by Franklin D. Roosevelt to head the National Youth Administration in the 1930s.[3] In 1940,

1. In the Hampton University Library, George Foster Peabody established the Peabody Collection of rare materials on African American history, now one of the largest such collections in the country.

2. "History of the Urban League," unpublished, NAACP New Orleans Papers, Earl K. Long Library, University of New Orleans, New Orleans (hereafter cited as NAACPNO Papers); Pamela Jean Turner, "Civil Rights and Anti-Communism in New Orleans, 1946–1965" (master's thesis, University of New Orleans, 1981), 7.

3. Adam Fairclough, *Race and Democracy: The Civil Rights Struggle in Louisiana, 1915–1972*

the SCHW established an office in New Orleans where a number of prominent local white women were members.[4]

As was the case during the Depression era, World War II helped to expand women's ideas about social justice opportunities. The culture of wartime America served to enlighten white women about the inequities experienced by their black counterparts. Working with the Red Cross, the League of Women Voters (LWV), and the Young Women's Christian Association (YWCA) in the war effort, a number of white women soon came to realize the hypocrisy of fighting the war against racism abroad while blacks were discriminated against at home. Prior to the civil rights movement "proper" of the late 1950s and 1960s, black and white middle-class women found common ground and were at the forefront in the struggle against Jim Crow in Louisiana. These women extended the protest tradition of the 1930s and 1940s by working on issues of social welfare through the 1950s and 1960s, when they increasingly focused on issues of race. Like their predecessors, Louisiana women of this era worked within boundaries afforded them by their gender, race, and class. They fought for equal access to public transportation and schools, and for voting rights, organizing and joining interracial organizations to further these ends. In the end, the women who participated in the movement in the 1940s and early 1950s were crucial to the achievements of the civil rights movement of the 1950s and 1960s.

The early reminiscences of Rosa Keller, a New Orleans Coca-Cola heiress, highlights the importance of white women's work and the gendered nature of their participation in non-union-affiliated organizations during the 1940s in fostering an interest in civil rights issues. Already a member of the fledgling League of Women Voters of New Orleans (LWVNO) founded in 1942, Keller worked to register people to vote and, even more, to foster interest in governmental issues and political candidates. After her mother's death in 1944, she reluctantly accepted an invitation to fill her place on the New Orleans YWCA board, a decision that propelled her into a world previously unknown to her. During the war, the integrated New Orleans YWCA worked on issues such as civil defense recruitment and providing housing for tran-

(Athens: University of Georgia Press, 1995), 56; Katherine Ann Martensen, "Region, Religion, and Social Action: The Catholic Committee of the South, 1936–1956" (master's thesis, University of New Orleans, 1981).

4. SCHW pamphlet, April 1947, Young Women's Christian Association Papers, Amistad Research Center (hereafter cited as YWCA Papers). See also Thomas A. Krueger, *And Promises to Keep: The Southern Conference for Human Welfare, 1938–1948* (Nashville: Vanderbilt University Press, 1967).

sients working in the New Orleans area. Keller recalled learning from African American members of the YWCA that their sons, brothers, and husbands were fighting and dying in segregated military units. "Our nation might have been the home of the brave," she stated, "but most surely it was not the land of the free."[5] Moreover, Keller recalled, that as "one of an interracial group who met, deliberated, and worked together, I met for the first time Negro women who were self-respecting and well-educated, women who could and should have been welcome anywhere." Indeed, organizations such as the YWCA and the Urban League, another integrated organization in which Keller was an active member, prompted many white women to reevaluate the paternalistic and discriminatory nature of the southern white community. As Keller recalled:

> I had grown up in this New Orleans community and never before had known the existence of such people. They were not acceptable in white hotels, stores, restaurants, or even public places such as parks or libraries. We never discussed these issues, but these were my friends, and I began to see things as I imagined they must surely have viewed them. It was bad enough that they were kept out of privately owned facilities, but worse was my perception that "public" meant "public for whites only." These were wrongs, inconsistent with the professed beliefs of our nation and it was high time we set about correcting them.[6]

Indeed, throughout the 1940s, while black and white teachers were forced to work separately in their own union-affiliated organizations, integrated organizations such as the YWCA, the NAACP, and the National Urban League came to function as educational clearinghouses for both their black and white members. The YWCA and the League of Women Voters helped black and white women in Louisiana find common ground not only on gender issues, but also racial issues.

"THE RIGHT KINDS OF CONTACTS"

In the South, the YWCA "generally stayed ahead of its male counterpart [the YMCA] in pressing for cooperation and equality across the barriers of race and sex," particularly in the 1930s and 1940s.[7] First organized in the

5. Rosa Freeman Keller, "Autobiography," 1977, section 37, copy in possession of the author. Rosa Keller is not the only woman who cites her involvement with the YWCA as the source of her emergent interest in racial issues. See also Sara Mitchell Parsons, *From Southern Wrongs to Civil Rights: The Memoir of a White Civil Rights Activist* (Tuscaloosa: University of Alabama Press, 2000).

6. Keller, "Autobiography," section 37.

7. John Egerton, *Speak Now Against the Day: The Generation before the Civil Rights Movement in the South* (Chapel Hill: University of North Carolina Press, 1995), 123.

United States in 1858, the YWCA was founded on the "Protestant" principles of peace, justice, and freedom. Yet in 1906, when the YWCA expanded
nationwide, no black branches in the South existed. The white reformer Grace
Dodge broached the subject at a student conference in Asheville, North Carolina, forcing the national board to address the issue. Ultimately, the board
voted to allow segregated black branches to exist as separate "subsidiaries"
of local white branches.[8] Thereafter, African American branches proliferated
throughout the South.

The history of the New Orleans branch is but one example of the history
of interracial work in Louisiana. In 1910, a white teacher at Newcomb College, a venerated southern women's college, and Louise Krause, a librarian at
Tulane University, petitioned the National Association to organize a YWCA
chapter in New Orleans. The two subsequently invited "representative women
to a parlor meeting," where they explained to the eight or nine women in attendance what a "benefit it would be to the women and girls of our city. . . .
The parlor meetings continued until a goodly number of women throughout the city volunteered to help." A New Orleans chapter was organized in
1911. The goals of the fledgling branch were to house young women and to
provide them with food and recreational facilities. Later, services expanded
into educational work, and during World War I, the YWCA provided housing and recreation centers for women—black and white—who worked in
the mills and factories.[9]

Although in its early stages the YWCA did not fully adopt a racially progressive platform, the organization continued to emphasize interracial work.[10]
As early as 1913, the national YWCA appointed its first "Colored Secretary,"
Eva Bowles, "on an experimental basis," yet it was not until 1916 that the
YWCA organized its first interracial committee. The committee, which met
in Richmond, Virginia, was formed with the "avowed purpose of laying the
foundation for more Black participation."[11] Although African American
members were disenchanted with the lack of equality within the larger organizational structure, the YWCA was more successful in breaking down ra-

8. Paula Giddings, *When and Where I Enter: The Impact of Black Women on Race and Sex in
America* (New York: Bantam Books, 1984), 155.

9. "History of the New Orleans YWCA," Young Women's Christian Association of New Orleans Papers, Special Collections, Tulane University, New Orleans (hereafter cited as YWCANO
Papers).

10. See Gerda Lerner, ed., *Black Women in White America: A Documentary History* (New York:
Vintage Books, 1992), 478.

11. Giddings, *When and Where I Enter*, 155.

cial barriers than were other women's and community organizations.[12] The
YWCA was the first predominantly white organization to offer positions of
leadership to black women.[13] Moreover, in 1936, the association dedicated
itself to building "a fellowship in which barriers of race, nationality, education, and social status are broken down in the pursuit of a common objective of a better life for all."[14]

African American women and girls were drawn to the YWCA for a variety
of reasons. Unlike the more patriarchal NAACP in which women were considered subordinate, the organization offered its female members an extensive range of social activities and leadership opportunities. For black women,
the attainment of leadership positions and the ability to function within a
women's organization as a relative equal was another advantage to their
membership.[15] By 1916, there were sixty-five "colored branches" throughout
the United States, and although they were expected to "manage themselves,"
the association made it clear that the "branches among colored women and
girls have the same status as other branches. White and colored women
within the YWCA are meeting their common task with more freedom and
are less inhibited by tradition and expediency."[16] As a Christian-based organization, the YWCA was less inhibited than its counterparts like the League
of Women Voters when it came to racial matters, although at the 1916 national convention, there was only one black representative present. Still, as
progressive as they were, the white and "colored" branches of the YWCA remained segregated until after World War II.

In New Orleans, the YWCA addressed the issue of integrating as early
as 1927, when the Girls Physical Culture Club (GPCC), a black organization
"composed of young teachers and business girls," petitioned the New Orleans chapter for admittance as a "colored" branch.[17] The YWCA noted that,
"according to population needs," the best means to reach the association's
goal of creating a cross-section of people, particularly in the South, was to
maintain "Branches" such as the "Industrial Branches, Negro Branches, and

12. Lerner, *Black Women*, 479.

13. See Susan Lynn, *Progressive Women in Conservative Time: Racial Justice, Peace, and Feminism, 1945 to the 1960s* (New Brunswick, N.J.: Rutgers University Press, 1992), 15.

14. From the 14th Biennial Convention proceedings, cited in Lynn, *Progressive Women*, 43.

15. Lynn, *Progressive Women*, 41.

16. Eva D. Bowles, "The YWCA among Colored Girls and Women," January 1924, YWCANO
Papers.

17. Miss Wilma J. Harris to Eva D. Bowles, 10 December 1927, Box 41, Folder 1, YWCANO
Papers.

International Institutes for Foreign Born."[18] In response to this request for admittance to the association, Eva Bowles, then acting administrator of "colored work" for the national YWCA, stated that the association could only go "as far as the white and colored groups in a community can agree to go together." However, she "anticipate[d] the development along interracial lines in New Orleans."[19] The general secretary of the YWCA in New Orleans (a white woman) also felt "reasonably certain that . . . action on the matter will be favorable." However, she believed it necessary to "have a group of the leading colored citizens, both men and women, [w]ho are most active in civic and religious affairs, to see if they are ready to endorse this movement."[20]

Discussion continued into the next year about forming a "colored" branch. In a letter to the director of the national YWCA, one New Orleans board member stated that it was her "opinion that a colored branch of the YWCA would contribute much to the program of social and moral uplift of the masses of colored girls in this city, a program being fostered alike by secular and religious agencies of both races."[21] Between 1928 and 1931, correspondence between the New Orleans YWCA, the GPCC, and the national YWCA continued regarding the matter of creating a "colored branch" in New Orleans. With seemingly no resolution in sight, in 1931 an interracial committee was formed to "study the needs and attitudes of colored people in New Orleans" and, among other things, "to try and convince the YWCA Board and Membership of the need of establishing a Colored Branch of this association."[22]

Between 1927 and 1934, recommendations for the formation of a black branch arose periodically at national board meetings. Finally, in October 1934, the YWCA board—with six black women and twelve white women in attendance—decided to create an Interracial Provisional Committee and al-

18. "Why New Orleans Needs a Negro Branch of the YWCA," n.d., Box 1, Folder 13, YWCANO Papers. The statement also noted that at this time, sixty-five cities in the United States had "Negro Branches"; that in 150 cities, black women had organized "club work" outside of the YWCA; and that, in total, the YWCA had 25,069 African American members.

19. Eva D. Bowles to Miss Wilma J. Harris, 20 October 1927, Box 41, Folder 1, YWCANO Papers.

20. Josephine Kelly to Miss E. D. Green, 22 December 1927, Box 41, Folder 1, YWCANO Papers.

21. Mrs. S. Nelson Boyce to the Director of the National YWCA, 28 October 1928, Box 41, Folder 1, YWCANO Papers.

22. Minutes of the YWCA New Orleans, 1931, Box 41, Folder 3, YWCANO Papers.

low for the formation of a "Negro Branch" in New Orleans. The committee raised money with the help of the local "white" YWCA for their first-year budget. Members also hired a secretary and teachers for the home economics and other education classes they sought to offer; and Straight College, a historically black college in the city, leased the girls' dormitory to the "Colored Branch" for one dollar a year.[23] As one new African American member stated: "We have in New Orleans . . . such fine outstanding Negroes and many of the white people do not get an opportunity to know them intimately. The YWCA is a medium through which the *right kind* of contacts can be made [and] interpretation [can be provided] to other groups within the community."[24]

The YWCA of New Orleans did, in fact, provide such a medium.[25] As in other areas of the country, many of the white women who worked in the New Orleans association had been reared by, and married into, well-to-do families. They were also well educated and could afford the time it took to work within volunteer associations. Although obvious social differences existed between them, white and black members joined the YWCA for similar reasons. When petitioning for admittance to the larger New Orleans association, the GPCC noted that African American "professional" women and girls in the city wanted a place to hold group meetings and educational classes, as well as to provide a place of adequate housing and food service for local and transient black women.[26] Black and white women seemed to agree that the local YWCA provided them a place for recreation and to meet friends. Little did many of the women know how important these interracial friendships would come to be.

In 1939, the national YWCA held its first Southern Regional Conference in Nashville, Tennessee. With both black and white women from New Orleans in attendance, members focused on issues of "human welfare in their region" and decided that there was "a need for more face to face relation-

23. Minutes of the YWCA New Orleans, 31 October and 27 November 1934, Box 41, Folder 3, YWCANO Papers.

24. Mrs. Cordella A. Winn to Mrs. Elizabeth S. Thompson, 20 May 1935, Box 41, Folder 4, YWCANO Papers (emphasis mine).

25. Susan Lynn suggests that the YWCA provided white and black women alike with their first interracial experiences (see Lynn, *Progressive Women*, 57).

26. "Why New Orleans Needs a Negro Branch of the YWCA," Box 1, Folder 13, YWCANO Papers. The "professional" women whom the pamphlet addresses are "businesswomen and girls" and "social workers."

ships between our different Association groups, particularly racial groups!"
Southern YWCA leaders also acknowledged the difficulty of supporting interracial organizations in the 1930s South, stating:

> We know we have to go one step at a time—that changes in custom and mores
> are not fast moving. The problems of the South, are to some extent, the prob-
> lems of the Nation and the world. The YWCA with its diverse membership can
> be an important experiment station, through which we can help build the kind
> of nation envisioned by our founders—a nation where the principles of freedom
> under God are paramount—freedom for something, a purpose, not freedom in
> a vacuum. We are challenged to create unity in diversity, to build a Christian na-
> tion, which in time, will develop into a world commonwealth.[27]

This commitment on behalf of southern associations, including the New
Orleans chapter, to racial justice and inclusiveness challenges a widely held
notion that women's activism was moribund after the success of the suffrage movement.[28] The YWCA's commitment to interracial membership contributed to its having a more progressive-minded membership than did organizations like the League of Women Voters. Such women bridged the gap
between the politically active women of the Progressive Era and the female
activists who participated in the civil rights and women's movements of the
1960s and 1970s.[29] Aside from the organization's dedication to an interracial
membership, throughout the 1930s and 1940s the YWCA protested against
discrimination in all forms, supporting the Costigan-Wagner Anti-Lynching
Bill and even establishing "Oriental" branches during World War II, when association with Japanese Americans was as scandalous as dining with an African American in public in the segregated South. Members of the New Orleans YWCA continued to attend the Southern Regional Conferences, and
some members attended the first Southern Conference for Human Welfare
Conference in 1938. It was no surprise, then, to the New Orleans association when, in 1948, it was charged with communist infiltration and promoting communist propaganda.[30]

In 1943, the YWCA decided to further its policy of interracial coopera-

27. "Findings—Southern Regional Conference, 17–20 April 1939, Box 39, Folder 3, YWCANO
Papers.

28. For instance, see Nancy Woloch, *Women and the American Experience* (New York: Knopf,
1984); and William Chafe, *The Paradox of Change: American Women in the Twentieth Century* (New
York: Oxford University Press, 1991).

29. Pamela Tyler, *Silk Stockings and Ballot Boxes: Women and Politics in New Orleans, 1920–
1963* (Athens: University of Georgia Press, 1996), 5–6.

30. "Red Infiltration into 'Y,'" *New Orleans Times-Picayune*, 18 October 1948.

tion and embarked on a study of racial practices in association branches throughout the country. The answers provided by the New Orleans association illustrate the many difficulties faced by southern branches. The New Orleans YWCA included 871 black members with full "electoral membership status" within the association. They were permitted to vote on policies that concerned their ("colored") branch as well as the New Orleans YWCA as a whole. When meetings included food, however, black women were not permitted to attend. Furthermore, African American members were barred from using the YWCA's recreational facilities, including the swimming pool, per segregation laws in the state.[31] The study secured the way for the national board to adopt its pathbreaking Interracial Charter in 1948, which admitted that "racial tensions threaten not only the well-being of our communities, but also the possibility of a peaceful world." In agreeing to integrate, the national board argued that, "women of the minority races in America form more than one-tenth of the Association constituency and have a direct claim to the organization's understanding and support. This fellowship, without barriers or race, this better life for all, is an accepted goal, which we of the National Board strive to achieve." It continued: "We shall be ever mindful of the variation in the number and range of difficulties to overcome and opportunities to progress. Where there is injustice on the basis of race, whether in the community, the nation of the world, our protest must be clear and our labor for its removal, vigorous and steady. As members of the National Board, we humbly and resolutely pledge ourselves to continue to pioneer in an interracial experience that shall be increasingly democratic and Christian."[32]

The 1940s were a risky decade for political activism of any kind, much less interracial activism. The country's patriotic support for the war effort left little room for even marginal dissent. In the 1940s, apparently "*all* forms of activism entailed high risks," whether working with the NAACP or the integrated YWCA, registering to vote, or filing a lawsuit.[33]

An awareness of inequities based on racial categories was certainly a part of the history of many southern white women. However, the drive to create interracial alliances in early organizations such as unions, the YWCA, and

31. "Questionnaire about Interracial Practices in New Orleans," 1943, Box 38, YWCANO Papers.

32. Excerpted from "The Interracial Charter of the National Board," 1944, Box 1, Folder 7, YWCANO Papers. The charter was voted on, passed, and adopted in 1946. Some associations in the South, such as Little Rock, Arkansas, and Birmingham, Alabama, voted against the charter and subsequently dropped out of national affiliation with the YWCA. The New Orleans YWCA did not.

33. Fairclough, *Race and Democracy*, 99.

the NAACP served to foster a greater awareness of racial issues while raising the consciousness of white women who were not necessarily exposed to
the extent of the disparities between blacks and whites. According to historian Jacqueline Jones, this "personal interaction between white and black
women held special significance in a society that held up the housewife-
domestic servant relationship as the only legitimate model of interracial
contact for women."[34] To be sure, interaction in biracial organizations challenged and altered this dynamic.

"WE'RE ALL WOMEN"

One organization that directly benefited from the progressive thinking held
by many YWCA members was the League of Women Voters of New Orleans.
The history of the integration of this politically bipartisan organization in
the post–World War II years highlights the many obstacles white and black
women faced when attempting to create interracial alliances. Although in
the post–World War II world women were expected to return to their roles as
wives and mothers, many looked for other ways to achieve greater meaning
in their lives. White women played important roles in the war effort, yet an
unintended consequence of their work was an increase in women's political
activism in such organizations as the American Red Cross and the League of
Women Voters.[35] Many women came away from the war years with a desire
to leave the confines created by traditional gender, race, and class roles and
enter spheres of interest previously unavailable to them such as volunteer-
ing, politics, college, the workforce, *and* civil rights activities. Female activists usually focused on priorities often marginalized, or disregarded entirely,
by men—priorities some might construe as "decidedly female" or "mother-
centered."[36] Subsequently, organizations such as the League of Women Voters

34. Jacqueline Jones, "The Political Implications of Black and White Women's Work in the
South, 1890–1965," in *Women, Politics, and Change*, ed. Louise A. Tilly and Patricia Gurin (New
York: Russell Sage Foundation, 1990), 113–14.

35. Susan Lynn, "Gender and Progressive Politics: A Bridge to Social Activism of the 1960s,"
in *Not June Cleaver: Women and Gender in Postwar American, 1945–1960*, ed. Joanne Meyerowitz
(Philadelphia: Temple University Press, 1994). See also Susan Hartmann, *The Home Front and
Beyond: American Women in the 1940s* (Boston: Twayne, 1982), esp. chaps. 2, 9, and 11.

36. See Joanne Meyerowitz, "Introduction: Women and Gender in Postwar America, 1945–
1960," in *Not June Cleaver*, ed. Meyerowitz, 106; Eugenia Kaledin, *Mothers and More: American
Women in the 1950s* (Boston: Twayne, 1984); and Rhoda Lois Blumberg, "White Mothers in the
American Civil Rights Movement," in *Research in the Interweave of Social Roles: Women and Men*,
ed. Helena Lopata, vol. 1 (Greenwich, Ct.: JAI Press, 1980), 35.

(LWV), the Parent-Teachers Association (PTA), the Young Women's Christian Association (YWCA), and even the National Association for the Advancement of Colored People (NAACP) provided women in the postwar era a place where they could effect political change without abandoning traditional social, cultural, and familial roles.[37] While middle-class African American and white women worked in the interracial organizations they created together in the 1930s and 1940s, sharing gender-oriented values, for many, the real goal was to bridge the racial divide.[38]

Unlike white women, African American women did not always have the luxury of returning to the home to "reclaim" their roles solely as wives and mothers. Historically, black women did not embody the "separate sphere" where home, family, and children took precedence. Forced to work and contribute to the family economy, whether as a sharecropper, domestic, or factory worker, black women had always embraced both work *and* family. Most black women, for instance, remained in the postwar workforce.[39] African Americans had made some economic progress during the war years. To be sure, World War II created job opportunities that led, in turn, to achievements in other areas of black life. Although absolute numbers were small, African Americans, especially women, showed a marked increase, relative to whites, in the professions and in occupations like farmers, managers, and proprietors of small businesses.[40]

In education, blacks achieved greater parity with whites between 1940 and 1960 than they had in previous decades, although differences in the quality of facilities continued. As high schools and colleges were soon to act as centers of civil rights activity, the increased numbers of blacks attending school was significant.[41]

Against the backdrop of these advances, the improved status of Loui-

37. For more information on women's political activity in the 1950s, see Susan Ware, "American Women in the 1950s: Non-Partisan Politics and Women's Politicization," in *Women, Politics, and Change*, ed. Louise A. Tilly and Patricia Gurin (New York: Russell Sage Foundation, 1990), 281–99.

38. See Meyerowitz, "Introduction," 106.

39. For more information on the work patterns of American women, see Claudia Goldin, *Understanding the Gender Gap: An Economic History of American Women* (New York: Oxford University Press, 2002); and Cohen, *A Consumers' Republic* (2003).

40. Norval D. Glenn, "Some Changes in the Relative Status of American Non-Whites, 1940–1960," *Phylon: The Atlanta University Review of Race and Culture* (Summer 1963): 111–13, 115. The author notes that although the article discusses the status of "non-whites," the percentages of Hispanics and Asians in the census were so small as to deduce that these conclusions apply mainly to the African American population.

41. Glenn, "Changes," 119–20.

siana women allowed them to further their work for civil rights. After the
Brown v. Board of Education decision in 1954, more direct challenges to Jim
Crow expanded. Still, Louisiana women joined civil rights organizations in
greater numbers, becoming members of boards and even presidents and
chairpersons. Simultaneously, a number of white women, recognizing the
need to work alongside black women to break down Jim Crow, continued to
integrate their previously all-white organizations. White women throughout
the state also worked on voter education and registration, while black women
continued to register to vote in greater numbers, all the while challenging
Jim Crow laws in the courts and in public arenas through boycotts and early
protests. Most importantly, women throughout the state began the daunting task of challenging the state legislature in integrating public schools.

The repressive political and social climate post-*Brown*, however, posed
problems for the interracial organizations and coalitions that Louisianians
had carefully groomed to that point. As historian Adam Fairclough has found,
NAACP membership dropped from 13,190 in 1951 to 1,698 in 1957, and from
sixty-five branches to seven; in 1958, the National Office of the NAACP voted
to stop organizational activity in the state altogether.[42] Virulent anticom-
munist rhetoric threatened to halt all civil rights activity, affecting white liberals who became reluctant to appear radical or extremist. Black and white
women showed their courage and dedication by insisting on integrating their
organizations.

At its inception in 1942, the League of Women Voters of New Orleans
(LWVNO) was not racially integrated. Yet, it was expected to abide by national league by-laws, which called for a membership "that would not only
be representative of the community, but that would be community-wide
in its interest in setting up programs."[43] While the LWVNO represented a
large percentage of the white community in New Orleans, it was not truly
"community-wide" because it did not represent African Americans.[44] In the

---

42. Fairclough, *Race and Democracy*, 209.

43. Emily Blanchard to Rosa Keller, 24 July 1974, in "League of Women Voters of New Orleans History, 1942–1985," typescript, copy in possession of the author, 7 (hereafter cited as
"LWVNO History").

44. In 1956, the Research Institute conducted a broad demographic profile at the University
of Michigan that revealed that the League of Women Voters was comprised of well-educated,
well-to-do community members around the country. Historian Susan Ware states that the
league was "predominantly an organization that appealed to and was made up of white, educated, middle-class women . . . living in good neighborhoods rather than 'the community.'"
Ware further notes that the league could have been more accurately called "the League of Affluent Women Voters" (Ware, "American Women in the 1950s").

1950s, the LWVNO leadership found itself uncomfortably caught between national mandates and local tradition.

The League of Women Voters for decades had regarded itself as "progressive," citing its origins in the suffrage movement of the early twentieth century and, more generally, a middle-class urban progressivism that encouraged government action on behalf of a wide range of economic, political, and humanitarian concerns. The league's primary goals were to "aid its members in how to be better citizens" and to "reflect the community and community opinion."[45] Still, while progressivism was based in democracy, in the Deep South most white southerners embraced the status quo of race relations: white over black. Like the early suffrage movement from which the organization arose, the league had never been inclusive of nonwhite or lower-class white women.[46] The social and political upheavals of the 1950s, however, led many league members around the country to seek a more active role as leaders and role models for young women, poor women, and minority women.

The League of Women Voters of New Orleans began in 1933 as an organization called the Woman Citizen's Union (WCU). Founded by Martha Gilmore Robinson, a former suffragist and women's rights advocate, the WCU's main purpose was to "educate the woman voter so that she may intelligently bring pressure to bear upon all officials in all civic and political matters." Similar to the League of Women Voters, the WCU acted as a nonpartisan organization, avoiding stands for or against an individual candidate or party, but it was politically influential nonetheless. On October 28, 1942, the WCU voted itself out of existence and became the New Orleans chapter of the League of Women Voters.[47]

45. League of Women Voters of New Orleans Charter, LWV Papers, Special Collections, Tulane University (hereafter cited as LWV Papers). Article III ("Membership"), Section 2 ("Eligibility"), states: "Any woman who subscribes to the object and policy of the League shall be eligible for membership." With "any woman" being the key phrase, nothing was ever mentioned in league by-laws, from the inception of the League of Women Voters, regarding segregation of the league because of race.

46. For more on the woman suffrage movement and its relationship with black women, see Marjorie Spruill Wheeler, *New Women of the New South: The Leaders of the Woman's Suffrage Movement in the Southern States* (New York: Oxford University Press, 1993); and Steven Buechler, *Women's Movements in the United States: Women's Suffrage, Equal Rights, and Beyond* (New Brunswick, N.J.: Rutgers University Press, 1990).

47. Minutes of the Woman Citizen's Union, 28 February 1940, LWV Papers; Martha Gilmore Robinson to the members of the WCU, 29 September 1941, and Minutes of the WCU, 28 October 1942, LWV Papers. In 1919, Carrie Chapman Catt, at the Fiftieth Anniversary Convention of the National American Woman's Suffrage Association, proposed establishing a League of Women Voters to work on achieving women's suffrage and ending other forms of political

In 1947, the past president of the Louisiana League of Women Voters and cofounder of the fledgling LWVNO, Emily Blanchard, was the first to suggest that the New Orleans league consider "opening up membership to Negro women in the community who were eligible."[48] Blanchard's appeal made no headway, however, in part because it came on the heels of her earlier request to speak to the LWVNO on behalf of the Southern Conference for Human Welfare (SCHW), a racially integrated organization. Because it was thought to be a communist front organization, the SCHW had trouble allying with more "credible" organizations; the League of Women Voters was no exception.[49]

Emily Blanchard later recalled that Martha Gilmore Robinson, cofounder of the LWVNO and much more conservative than Blanchard, refused the request on the grounds that the league should avoid any "unfortunate publicity." Robinson declared that the league did not "endorse much of the legislation which is actively being pushed by the SCHW" and that the league had no intention of "getting embroiled in the controversies which the SCHW deliberately fosters." Further, Robinson felt that that the SCHW bore "all the earmarks of a communist front group."[50] Thus, when Blanchard, a proponent of the SCHW, raised the issue of integrating the LWVNO, "there was obviously much anxiety among members concerning this suggestion," as members were fearful that the league could also be branded a "communist front group." Blanchard also recalled that "shortly thereafter . . . Mrs. Robinson brought to my home a letter from the New Orleans League which deplored my position concerning membership for Negro women and stated concretely that unless I resigned from the Southern Conference for Human Welfare, I would be stricken from the League's membership." Blanchard responded that she would "not resign from the Southern Conference for Human Welfare and would accept immediate dismissal from the League. I have had no communication with the League since."[51]

---

and legal discrimination against women. On February 14, 1920, six months before ratification of the Nineteenth Amendment, the League of Women Voters was formed nationally.

48. Blanchard to Keller, 24 July 1974, in "LWVNO History," 8.

49. Fairclough, *Race and Democracy*, 139.

50. Martha Gilmore Robinson to Ruth Preston, 2 September 1947, LWV Papers. Robinson further states that "the League of Women Voters and the Southern Conference for Human Welfare are not at all interested in the same way in influencing public opinion. There is no reason for any association between these two organizations."

51. Blanchard to Keller, 24 July 1974, in "LWVNO History," 8. Robinson commented on Emily Blanchard in the letter to Ruth Preston, stating, "Unfortunately fine liberals like Emily Blanchard . . . often let their hearts govern their hard common sense" (Robinson to Preston, 2 September 1947, LWV Papers).

Just a few years later, Rosa Keller, an elite member of the white New Orleans community and a staunch civil rights advocate, revisited the issue of integrating the LWVNO. Because of her work with the YWCA and Urban League of Greater New Orleans, and later, throughout the civil rights struggles of the 1950s and 1960s, Keller often found herself criticized by her peers. Yet, as outspoken as she was on issues of race, Keller agreed with Martha Robinson that, "obviously the forties were no time to be breaking the racial barrier." As she later explained, "'Discretion' is a delicate word to use to describe such far-reaching conditions, but if a League was to be formed in New Orleans in 1942, it had to circumvent the racial question. It was absolutely imperative that the women who formed the League must do so without incurring the wrath of the community it wished to serve."[52] This cautious stance continued to mark the LWVNO even as it began to move toward integration.

By 1953, Keller was ready to challenge established southern traditions; she held an integrated meeting in her home in the upscale "silk stocking district" of New Orleans.[53] The subject of the meeting was whether or not to consider admitting black women into the League of Women Voters of New Orleans. Keller felt it was time to raise the issue for serious consideration. As past president of the integrated New Orleans YWCA and president of the New Orleans Urban League, she believed that integration was the only path for a political group such as the LWV. While it had not been discussed since Emily Blanchard posed the idea in 1947, integration was on the minds of many league members.

The meeting included established white members of the community as well as some prospective black members. "We gathered people here one day to talk about being members of the League of Women Voters," Keller stated. "Some of the women were black. They were mostly doctors' wives. One of the white members said, 'We don't think we want niggers in our League.'"[54] Another board member in attendance frantically mailed a letter to the president of the state league, admitting: "I cannot refrain here from injecting that I loathe such evasions and compromise. . . . I have given the major portion of my time, spare or not, to the League of Women Voters, and I cannot sit

52. Keller, "LWVNO History," 8

53. The term "silk stocking district" refers to the area of New Orleans called "Uptown," where the older, more elite families in the city reside (Lindy Boggs cited in Tyler, *Silk Stockings and Ballot Boxes*, 1).

54. Rosa Keller, interview by the author, 13 March 1996, tape recording, copy in possession of the author.

idly by and see the League used and perhaps ruined by the injection of the racial question."[55]

The president of the LWVNO at the time of Keller's integrated meeting was Mathilde Dreyfous. In 1947, widowed with two children, she had married George Dreyfous, an American Civil Liberties Union (ACLU) and civil rights attorney, and relocated from the North to New Orleans. In the South, Dreyfous began her career as a dedicated civil rights activist. While her husband found himself mired in legal battles working with the Louisiana affiliate of the ACLU, Mathilde sought to encourage African Americans to get involved in civic affairs and, like Keller, often held integrated meetings in her home. She also worked on voter registration and education, and, during the school desegregation crisis in 1960, she testified before the state legislature for integration. Her friends and family remember her as a strong personality who never judged or condemned, but managed to work as "an activist without being abrasive, and listen to opposing viewpoints without offending those who felt to the contrary."[56] Dreyfous, along with Rosa Keller, pushed for integration; it was she who sought out the six African American women who would be the first to join the league in 1955.

Despite initial dissension from some members, the league's board decided to consider integrating. Keller and Dreyfous were the most fervent advocates, and Keller was appointed to head a committee to "look into the problem of Negro members." Dreyfous was further concerned that "although League by-laws stated that membership was open to all women of voting age, [the LWVNO] had no black members." She wondered if her "frail new League . . . [could] withstand what was then a bold step."[57] In a letter to the state and national Leagues, Eleanor Crawford, secretary for the LWVNO, noted that one unit group "expressed concern over the fact that 46% of [the New Orleans] population is now colored and from there went into a lengthy discussion of why we have no colored members."[58]

The LWVNO had not received any requests for admission from African American women in the New Orleans community, nor had they "gone out of their way to encourage Negro attendance . . . and do not intend to do so in the future." The board did believe, however, that "at some time in the fu-

55. Eleanor Crawford to Mrs. John G. Lee, 24 February 1953, National LWV Papers, Louisiana State Material, Library of Congress, Washington, D.C. (hereafter cited as NLWV Papers).

56. Tom Schwab, "Biography of Mathilde Schwab Dreyfous," typescript, 1992, copy in possession of the author.

57. Mathilde Dreyfous in "LWVNO History," 10.

58. Crawford to Lee, 24 February 1953, NLWV Papers.

ture there may be such a request and we want to be prepared to meet it." It was too early, Crawford explained, to "encourage such membership, that aside from any personal problems which might arise, our standing in the community and our political effectiveness would be seriously injured." Initially, "one of the chief difficulties the admission of Negro's [sic] would bring would be the operation of our unit group system," which met at individuals' homes throughout the city. The board wondered if it "would be possible for New Orleans to set up two types of classification of membership," black and white. Or perhaps black women who applied for membership might be "satisfied temporarily with general membership" and not attend meetings.[59]

In response, the national organization commended the New Orleans league for their practice of holding general, open meetings in nonsegregated places, yet it believed that there was no "magic formula" for this process. The local board was instructed to "start with the principle that all members are full members, sharing equally in the privileges and responsibilities of the organization." Per league by-laws, the LWVNO could not set up separate classifications for membership, as had the YWCA, nor discourage black women from attending unit meetings. Moreover, the national league believed that holding integrated meetings in the community was a good way to start addressing the issue as well as a way to get to know leaders of the black community, which might in turn "stimulate applications for membership."[60]

As a portent of issues to come, the national league proposed the women eliminate refreshments at unit meetings to avoid the appearance of a "social" gathering, which could possibly pose a legal problem in segregated Louisiana. The national league also suggested that local members consult with other integrated groups in the New Orleans community, such as the YWCA, to "avoid some of their pitfalls."[61] Although the New Orleans league had never encouraged members of the black community to attend league functions, for many years members held general informational meetings and workshops at nonsegregated places. One member pointed out that black women had been attending unit meetings in the Gentilly area of New Orleans, an integrated neighborhood, although without knowledge of the wider league membership. Because integrated meetings could jeopardize the league's po-

59. Crawford to Lee, 24 February 1953, NLWV Papers. She also notes that the LWVNO had for a few years held their open meetings at "places which tolerated a non-segregated audience."

60. Mrs. Robert F. Leonard to Eleanor Crawford, 3 March 1953, NLWV Papers.

61. Leonard to Crawford, 3 March 1953, NLWV Papers. Serving refreshments at unit meetings ultimately did become a legal issue that the LWVNO and other southern community organizations were forced to address after the *Brown* decision.

litical standing in the community as well as much-needed outside donations, the board decided not to push "actively" for integration. The board also decided to "plan to include Negro groups in the list which our Speakers Bureau contacts in our efforts to carry League work to the community."[62] All potentially interested groups were notified of open league meetings, including Dillard and Xavier, predominantly African American colleges. Indeed, the women concluded that while "this practice may be hastening the day when we may receive a request for membership from a Negro . . . we hope we may be educating our white members to accept colored members at some future date and the community to be accepting of the idea."[63]

Correspondence between the New Orleans league and the state and national leagues prompted the national league to send a letter to all leagues nationwide on the subject of integration. While they did not urge "membership for all races," their primary concern was that the local leagues were "promoting participation in our democratic form of government" and that each league was doing its best to ensure that it remained a "truly Democratic [sic] organization." The letter added that the "National Board realized that it would be short-sighted to grant membership to minority groups in those communities in which the very act in itself could kill the League in those communities."[64]

The New Orleans league then formed a "Membership Problems Committee" to seek information that would assist them in integration. The New Orleans board decided not to solicit or encourage black members, to continue to hold discussion meetings at nonsegregated places, and to publicize those meetings to the community regardless of race. Further, league members were asked to speak to black groups concerning issues on the league's agenda.[65] Any membership application from a black woman would be referred to President Dreyfous, who would "deal frankly with them individu-

62. Elizabeth Rack, interview by the author, 5 March 1996, tape recording, copy in possession of the author.

63. Mathilde Dreyfous to Mrs. Robert Leonard, 11 March 1953, NLWV Papers.

64. Mrs. Theo Goss to Eleanor Crawford, 2 March 1953, NLWV Papers.

65. Mrs. Theo Goss to Eleanor Crawford, 4 March 1953, Integration File, LWVNO Office Records. Only one New Orleans board member objected (privately) to the first recommendation, and another member expressed the position that if she were personally approached by a black individual for membership, she "would tactfully point out the disadvantages to both the applicant and the organization of such a step at this time, but if said applicant persisted she would have to be admitted." This member subsequently resigned for fear of "involvement in the racial question" (mentioned in the letter from State President Goss to Crawford, 4 March 1953, Integration File, LWVNO Office Records).

ally with the understanding that our membership is open to them if after our conversation they feel that they would like to join." After meeting with some of the potential black members and community leaders, Dreyfous believed that the LWVNO would "be able to meet the situation."[66]

At the national league's suggestion, the LWVNO initiated a study of integration practices throughout the country. The study took approximately three years to complete and ultimately was invaluable to their decision to integrate. Still, unlike the YWCA in the 1930s, the New Orleans league was slow to include African American women as members. League members feared that their hard work in making New Orleans a better community would be lost over the integration issue. Indeed, one benefit of league membership was its "political clout: it magnifies the voice of the individual citizen in government and politics." As league member Felicia Kahn explained, "the political climate was such that anything you did to an extreme would mean that you were less than effective in anything else." And integration in 1953 was thought by most southerners to be extreme.[67]

While many organizations had been quietly advocating integration as early as the 1930s, more overt and direct challenges to Jim Crow were not so ubiquitous as they became after May 1954. Heretofore, sporadic attacks on Jim Crow had never appeared to pose a serious threat to the racial status quo. According to law professor Michael Klarman, after the Supreme Court placed the "moral authority of the court and the Constitution behind the black demand for desegregation," southern intransigence toward federal intervention in states' rights and race issues reached a high point not seen since the Reconstruction era. Moderates all but disappeared after 1954, creating polar camps of integrationists and segregationists. Race became the focal point of southern politics, and massive resistance the dominant theme.[68] Consequently, a group such as the League of Women Voters, whose mission was to support and uphold the supreme law of the land, was pushed into the highly controversial position of siding with the pro-integration camp.

By November 1954, after attending some of the open meetings around the city, several African American women had inquired about admission. The

---

66. Mathilde Dreyfous to Mrs. Robert Leonard, 11 March 1953, NLWV Papers.

67. Nancy Neuman, *The League of Women Voters: In Perspective, 1920–1995*, League of Women Voters Publication No. 995, 1994 (Washington, D.C.: League of Women Voters, 1994), 13, 58; Felicia Kahn, interview, 5 September 1996, tape recording.

68. Michael J. Klarman, "How *Brown* Changed Race Relations: The Backlash Thesis," *Journal of American History* 81 (June 1994): 87.

women were interested in joining, but only as full participating members; they were unwilling to create a separate "Negro unit," which, in any case, violated national league by-laws. Unsure how to proceed, the board tabled the issue until December 1954, at which time they decided that President Dreyfous should attend unit meetings personally, read a statement aloud, and distribute questionnaires seeking guidance. Questions such as, "Are you satisfied with the present type of membership?" and, "Would you continue to attend meetings with a broader type of membership?" were a tacit attempt to solicit member reaction while avoiding the direct question of integration. The questionnaire accompanied a statement by Dreyfous reminding members of the national league policy, which stated that "any person who subscribes to the purpose and policy of the League shall be eligible for membership" and that "voting members shall be women citizens of voting age." Further, the league could not "refuse Negro members if they apply for membership." The statement ended by informing members that the "membership problem [had] been reopened" and asking them to "think this over quietly and unemotionally . . . bearing in mind always that the purpose of the League of Women Voters is to promote informed and active participation of citizens in government." "*Please do not discuss this problem with any non league members as publicity and inevitable misunderstanding at this time could do much damage*," the statement continued, in capital letters. "*Please cooperate to 'keep it in the family.'*"[69]

The statement's note of urgency was reflected in a letter the local league secretary wrote to the national league president: "You will notice the statement, which did not leave the president's hands, was explicit but the questionnaires, which might fall into non-League hands, was [*sic*] rather enigmatic."[70] The league admitted that they were proceeding with "some caution because there was strong feeling on the part of many Board members that any full statement should not be mailed." Some members felt that "too many copies lying about in too many homes might inevitably lead to some un-

69. LWVNO Board Minutes, 4 November 1954 and Statement—January 1955, LWV Papers, and Questionnaire . . . LWVNO, Jan. 1955, Integration File, LWVNO Office Records.

70. Eleanor Crawford to Mrs. Newton Pierce, 9 February 1955, NLWV Papers. Of the 570 members listed at the beginning of 1955, a total of 73 returned the questionnaire, with approximately 55 percent approving of integrated membership. However, as the minutes show for 16 March 1955, "The feeling of the Board is that there is enough dissatisfaction as expressed by the units, by the State Affairs Committee, and by the board members themselves to warrant the New Orleans' Board making certain recommendations to the State Board relative to the proposed State current agenda." The state current agenda was, at the time, focused on the current public school desegregation crisis in the South and the effects on the local tax structures.

desirable publicity and misunderstanding in the community."[71] Adding to the league's anxiety over the integration issue was the impact of anticommunism. As one member recalled, "anyone who was for any kind of integration was labeled a communist." Some of the league's members had already been accused of being "Reds." As Rosa Keller remembered, "so deeply was the racial barrier embedded in the social structure of the South that the terms 'Nigger lover' and 'communist red' were synonymous."[72]

Amid the turmoil of the era, and after further review of board minutes, questionnaires, correspondence from other integrated leagues in the region, and member statements, the national league concluded that the New Orleans league must comply with national LWV policy and integrate immediately. They commended New Orleans for its "trailblazing" in this area and alluded to the slow pace with which other southern leagues had been dealing with the issue. In response, the New Orleans board convened to decide how to address the next month's unit meetings. The board concluded that they should hold an orientation meeting in May 1955 for both the current white membership and prospective black members. In the meantime, board members would personally attend unit meetings to discuss the questionnaire results and to answer any questions regarding "Negro membership." The board further stated that, "if the New Orleans experience at all parallels that of other leagues with Negro members, and there is no reason to think it shouldn't, the number of new [black] members will probably be very small and should present no particular problem." In June, after a successful orientation meeting, five black women applied for membership.[73]

In the wake of the *Brown* decision, Louisiana and other southern states enacted many segregation laws designed to limit, complicate, and stall integration efforts. The New Orleans league not only faced intense criticism in the community, but was also subject to recent laws requiring "that all meetings including membership of both races shall provide for segregated seating and separate sanitary facilities." The league's only recourse was to hold meetings in the newly integrated public library system, but even those venues

71. Crawford to Pierce, 9 February 1955, NLWV Papers.

72. Rosa Keller, interview by Kim Lacy Rogers, 28 November 1978, Kim Lacy Rogers–Glenda Stevens Collection, Amistad Research Center, New Orleans (hereafter cited as Rogers-Stevens Collection); Keller, "LWVNO History," 8–9. In *Race and Democracy*, Adam Fairclough notes that in Louisiana the "Cold War had produced an ideological chilling effect that made criticism of the social order . . . unfashionable, unpatriotic, and politically dangerous" (141, 137).

73. National League to LWVNO, 16 February 1955, NLWV Papers, Statement by the Membership Problems Committee, 1955, Board Minutes 16 March 1955 and June 1955, Integration File, LWVNO Office Records.

were ultimately refused them. One librarian was "afraid to stretch his luck as he was already being harassed by those who were against it."[74] Furthermore, the league was forced to address two other Louisiana state laws that posed considerable difficulty. The first, enacted in 1924 and known as the "Ku Klux Klan Law," required all organizations to file a list of membership with the secretary of state.[75] The law in and of itself would not pose a problem, but coupled with a second law, that "teachers, who advocate or in any way contribute to integration in the public schools, or who [hold] membership in an organization which advocate[s] racial integration, are subject to dismissal and loss of tenure," it could prove harmful to some members.[76]

Considered an educational organization, the league was excluded from any laws pertaining to social organizations. However, serving refreshments put league meetings in the category of a social function, so the board did away with food or drink at meetings with both black and white members. The act pertaining to social functions, nicknamed the "Sugar Bowl Law," specified that "at any entertainment or athletic contest, where the public was invited," the persons in charge—for the league, the hosts of unit meetings—were to maintain separate "sanitary, drinking water, and any other facilities for members of the white and Negro races." They were additionally expected to "mark separate accommodations and facilities with signs printed in bold letters." This act made compliance with the law embarrassingly difficult, if not impossible; not even elite league members had the means to provide for separate black and white "facilities" in their homes.[77]

More important were the problems pertaining to the public schoolteachers' memberships. Similar to the NAACP, if the league filed its member-

74. Mrs. Thomas Crumpler to Mrs. John Lee, 14 January 1956, Integration File, LWVNO Office Records.

75. Fuqua/KKK Law, 1924, R.S. 12:401, *et. seq.* Named after Henry L. Fuqua, the law included three parts: (1) organizations must file a membership list with the secretary of state; (2) organizations were open to public inspection; and (3) it became a misdemeanor to appear in public masked, except during Mardi Gras. Ironically, the KKK later used the law against the NAACP. As in the LWVNO, the NAACP had members who feared losing their jobs in the public schools.

76. Letter to the President of the LWVUS, 14 January 1956, NLWV Papers.

77. Muriel Ferris to Mathilde Dreyfous, 7 September 1956; Mathilde Dreyfous to Mrs. Thomas Crumpler, 20 September 1956, LWV Papers. The purpose of Louisiana Act No. 579, House Bill No. 1412, regarding social functions, was "To prohibit all interracial dancing, social functions, entertainment, athletic training, games, sports, or contests and other such activities and to provide separate seating and other facilities for whites and Negroes" (cited in the afternoon edition of the conservative-leaning *New Orleans Times-Picayune*, 31 July 1956).

ship roster with the state, listing all of its members, white and black, those employed by the New Orleans public school system risked losing their jobs. The league's board finally determined that, "While advocating integration in the League and integration in the public schools are not synonymous in our minds, our action in integrating is so unusual for an organization of this type that any publicity would probably affect not only those teachers, but general League effectiveness." Moreover, the league had experienced a drop in membership from 550 to 463 during 1956; while the board did not believe that it was completely due to the matter of integration, many considered it a contributing factor.[78] By November, the league was expected to file its membership list with the state, which would inevitably "spotlight the fact of integrated membership of the New Orleans League and would put not only the Negro members, but the entire state league in the illegal position of advocating integration." The board further noted that "with the political climate reaching turbulence," retaining an integrated membership could do more harm than good: "Practically speaking, we can gain little for the Negroes but can lose much of our effectiveness in our efforts to obtain better government and fairer laws." The national league concurred, stating that "if integration were publicized it might indeed injure rather than contribute to progress" of the league and its members.[79]

It appeared that the only course for the New Orleans league was to accept the resignation of the six black members. The board concluded that, "Under optimal conditions and with broader consent and understanding, integrated membership could be tried at a later time." The difficulty and apprehension felt by the members over integration outweighed the fact that the league had only six paid black members, who, in any case, rarely attended unit meetings. As then league president Nancy Crumpler stated: "None of us are pleased with it. We have done what we feel is necessary."[80] Relaying its decision to the national league, Crumpler wrote: "As you know, the New

78. Nancy Crumpler to Mrs. John Lee, 14 January 1956, Integration File, LWVNO Office Records.

79. Board Minutes, 7 and 10 September 1956, and 11 November 1956, LWV Papers. According to the New Orleans board, "Presumed reasons for the resignations are the raise in dues, our integrated membership, and the inequality of the work load." However, one board member suggested that one reason for a drop in membership "might be the criticism that some of the unit programs were uninteresting, and that we should now concentrate on improving them" (LWVNO Board Minutes, 5 December 1956, LWV Papers). Crumpler to Lee, 14 January 1956, Integration File, LWVNO Office Records.

80. Board Minutes, 19 November 1956, LWV Papers.

Orleans League has had eight Negro members . . . six paid-up Negro members. The New Orleans League has felt the problems of working around the social situations and membership attitudes; however, they made all the necessary concessions and carried on. New Orleans membership has decreased by 100 since the legislative climate brought about passage of anti-minority legislation. . . . [We] reluctantly abandon [our] policy of integrated membership temporarily."[81]

Ultimately, three board members and the LWVNO president met with the six black members and asked them to resign. One member recalled that the situation was "very embarrassing, but the black members tendered their resignations 'graciously' as they did not want to 'imperil their jobs.'"[82] The state president recognized that the "members voluntarily agreed to resign until such time as the climate would permit their rejoining and being members without jeopardizing the league's position and strength."[83] LWVNO president Nancy Crumpler was heartbroken. In a letter to Rosa Keller, Crumpler remembered that "dreadful day" when a small committee met and decided the black members should temporarily resign for the "good of the league." Considering the state laws "oppressive," Crumpler said she did not get through the day without tears in her eyes.[84]

The League of Women Voters of New Orleans did not reintegrate until 1963, despite the efforts of women such as Rosa Keller and Mathilde Dreyfous. Some might argue that these women were solely working to integrate according to national league by-laws. Indeed, a majority of the members of the New Orleans league were intensely concerned with how integration might affect their position within the community. Of course, many others resisted any kind of integration at all, as reflected in a drop in membership during the integration years. Yet, as the history of the LWVNO illustrates, many middle-class white women willfully and deliberately ignored long-established southern ideas of class and race to initiate change. These women had been born and bred in a world that not only accepted, but also taught and lived, that white was better than black. Like the members of the

81. Mrs. Joseph Daum to Mrs. John G. Lee, 10 December 1956, NLWV Papers.

82. Mrs. Joseph Daum to Mrs. John G. Lee, 10 December 1956, NLWV Papers; Jean Boebel, interview by the author, 13 November 1996.

83. Mrs. Joseph Daum letter to Mrs. John G. Lee, 10 December 1956, NLWV Papers. It is important to note here that under national league by-laws, membership could not be terminated, thus the New Orleans league had to request that the black members resign "in the interest of the League."

84. Nancy Crumpler in Keller, "LWVNO History," 19.

YWCA, the women of the LWVNO challenged the racial status quo, and they did so within a climate of racial extremism and at great risk to themselves, to their families and friends, and to the organization they cherished.

A sustained level of commitment to racial justice is further evidenced in the numbers of women who affiliated with the Southern Regional Council (SRC). The SRC, an outgrowth of the 1920s Commission on Interracial Cooperation, worked for the "improvement of economic, civic, and racial conditions in the South." In its effort "to promote greater unity in the south in all efforts towards regional and racial development," the organization further worked toward ameliorating "race tension, racial misunderstanding, and racial distrust, to develop and integrate leadership in the South."[85] For years, the SRC was instrumental in the civil rights movement, notably sponsoring the Ashmore Project, a study to document the harmful effects of segregation. The subsequent publication of *The Negro and the Schools* in early 1954 greatly influenced the justices' decision in *Brown v. Board of Education*. Later the SRC would establish the Voter Education Project, support antisegregation protests and boycotts, and work with other civil rights organizations for the desegregation of the public schools. Its assistance during the New Orleans desegregation crisis of 1960 proved invaluable.

Since the late 1940s, the Louisiana Council on Human Relations (LCHR), an affiliate of the national SRC organization, established headquarters in seven racially troublesome areas in the state. New Orleans, Baton Rouge, Lake Charles, Alexandria, Monroe, Lafayette, and Shreveport had all experienced great social and political divisions as a result of heightening racial tensions. The LCHR planned to address these divisions with studies of racial, economic, and social conditions in Louisiana, which it would then publicize through pamphlets, newspapers, radio, television spots, and lectures. The organization also worked within communities to "find democratic solutions to local problems."[86] Its membership was made up of a majority of women, many of them high-profile female Louisianians including teacher and union activist Sarah Reed; League of Women Voters members Ruth and Mathilde Dreyfous, Rosa Keller, and Gladys Cahn (also president of the Urban League of Greater New Orleans); heiress to the Sears, Roebuck fortune Edith Stern; well-known teacher and civil rights activist Veronica Hill; civil rights activist and first female field secretary for the Congress of Ra-

85. "Constitution of the Louisiana Division of the Southern Regional Council, Inc.," n.d., Series 1, Reel 65, Southern Regional Council Papers, Library of Congress, Washington, D.C. (hereafter cited as SRC Papers, LOC).

86. *Louisiana Council on Human Relations*, pamphlet, n.d., Series I, Reel 29, SRC Papers, LOC.

cial Equality Mary Hamilton; and prominent white New Orleans socialite Elizabeth Wisner. Numerous other women served as chairs of the board, held integrated meetings in their homes, and worked to improve race relations in their cities.[87]

In the mid-twentieth century, and certainly in the postwar era, both black and white women began to test the waters by stepping outside of the socially prescribed boundaries of gender and race. They enrolled in colleges and universities, embarked on professional careers, and entered the world of politics. Their entrance into civic life allowed many of them to witness and experience, for the first time, the many disparities that existed for women and blacks. Although they pursued a female-oriented agenda, black and white middle-class women also challenged the dominant racial paradigm. In their civil rights efforts, women defiantly countered traditional assumptions of gender, class, and race, holding membership in interracial organizations, assuming positions of leadership, and pushing for legal remedies to an inherently unequal political and social structure.

Black and white women continued the tradition of dissent of the 1930s and 1940s through the 1950s, sustaining a high level of commitment toward creating a more just and democratic society. In a decade when racial extremism in Louisiana reached a high point, women did not falter. Yet in many ways, black and white women's hard work had just begun. By the 1960s, women were continuing the fight in the courts, participating in boycotts and sit-ins, working on school desegregation efforts, and forming new organizations focused on countering a southern heritage based on discrimination, disfranchisement, and segregation. The legal, social, and political challenges women endured in the 1930s, 1940s, and 1950s served to prepare them for the more trying times awaiting them in the continuing struggle for black rights in the 1960s.

87. "State Council on Human Relations, Louisiana," 1944–1972, and New Orleans Commission on Human Relations, 1947–1954, Series I, Reel 65, SRC Papers, LOC. For the years 1951–52 and 1953, in New Orleans, women made up the majority of the LCHR membership: 1951–52 membership shows 59 women of a total of 109 members, and 1953 membership shows 104 women of a total of 178 members ("Membership Lists, LCHR," 1951–1952 and 1953 respectively, Series I, Reel 65, SRC Papers, LOC).

3

HARDLY THE "SOUTHERN LADY"

Boycotts and the Vote

This is a position I did not seek or desire. I feel it is a job for a man. Since you elected me unopposed surely you see some good in me and my ability. It is my desire and determination to do all the good I can at all times for the advancement of my people.

DORETHA A. COMBRE, NAACP state president, November 1954

At the end of every school year, thousands of Orleans Parish school children participated in the historic Founder's Day ceremony. For years, the city honored John McDonogh, a white slaveholder who bequeathed most of his fortune for "the purpose of educating both sexes of all classes and castes of color." For African American children, the McDonogh Day Parade was more than simply paying respect to the individual who had helped fund their education; it paid homage to a man who was "hated and abused" by white New Orleanians for the charitable way he treated the African Americans who "worked" for him. Throughout his lifetime, McDonogh emancipated many of his slaves, and upon his death in 1850 he freed the remainder and requested that his ashes be placed in the "Negro cemetery" among his "beloved friends." For black New Orleanians, the McDonogh Day Parade was their chance to honor a rare breed of white antebellum southerner.[1]

In 1954, the New Orleans African American community challenged the way the parade had, for years, been organized. In February, four African

---

1. "McDonogh Day Bias Ironic," *Louisiana Weekly*, 8 May 1954, Amistad Research Center, Tulane University, New Orleans (hereafter cited as ARC).

American women—Ethel Young, president of the PTA council of New Orleans; Emily Davis Thomas, principal of McDonogh 24 and representative of the Orleans Parish Principals Association; Veronica B. Hill, president of the League of Classroom Teachers and national vice president of the American Federation of Teachers; and Mrs. E. Belfield Spriggins, a teacher at McDonogh 35—met with the Orleans Parish School Board. They presented a letter to the superintendent of the Orleans Parish school system, which protested the "discriminatory practices in carrying out the McDonogh Day Parade." Since the parade's inception, white school children had assembled first and marched in a processional, laying flowers beneath John McDonogh's monument in Lafayette Square. Black school children were forced to stand, sometimes in sweltering humidity and unbearable heat, waiting their turn until all of the white children paraded by the monument.

The women expressed their dismay that by the time the African American schoolchildren passed McDonogh's monument, the noted dignitaries in attendance, and most of the "interested spectators," had already left. In addition, they cited the "extra hardship on colored children . . . [due] to the lack of toilet facilities for [their] group." "For those of our children who understand the significance of this parade," the letter continued, "it is a most humiliating experience. For the rest, the parade only serves to condition them before they are old enough to think, to second class citizenship." On behalf of black Louisiana parents and their children, Young, Thomas, Hill, and Spriggins requested an end to the decades-old discrimination against black Louisiana schoolchildren so that the McDonogh Day Parade could "stand at last as a symbol of true American democracy."[2]

In response to their request that each school parade in alphabetical order according to school district, the Orleans Parish School Board cited Louisiana's segregation laws, adding that it was forced to "go along" with the admonition of the police superintendent not to alter the parade's format. Dr. Clarence Scheps, president of the school board, further noted: "[W]e live in a community in which segregation is the law and we would not be doing our duty if we did not abide by the law. We operate under the law and will continue. It cannot be done or will not be done." In early May, a number of black civic, educational, and religious associations, including the New Orleans branch of the NAACP, the Louisiana State Conference for Labor Education, and the Teamsters Local 965, called for a boycott of the McDonogh

---

2. "Three Groups Unite to Protest McDonogh Day Discrimination," *Louisiana Weekly*, 6 February 1954.

Day ceremonies. The NAACP asked all local school principals not to "impede aroused parents who refuse to permit their children to become a part of any mass demonstration fostering second class citizenship." It would, they added, be better to keep the "children home rather than see them participate in such an open display of segregation." Local civil rights leaders appeared on local radio stations and sent more than ten thousand letters to parents urging them to keep their children home that day.[3]

On Friday May 7, 1954, thousands of black schoolchildren stayed home during the McDonogh Day ceremonies. Citing only "token Negro participation," the local black newspaper called the protest the most "unified action ever undertaken by local Negroes." Among the many witnesses to the mass demonstration were a number of middle-class black women, including original petitioner Ethel Young; Fannie C. Williams, civil rights activist and the retiring principal of the all-black Valena C. Jones High School; and Mrs. Simon Marine, president of the PTA at Jones High School. Williams stated that she "had been attending these ceremonies for some time," and since this was the last year before she retired, she did not, as an American citizen, "want to miss this opportunity."[4]

School board president Clarence Scheps expressed his regret that "all Negro children did not participate in the ceremonies, because it means a great deal to them." Ethel Young countered that "the parents have spoken and gone on record as not approving of the second-class citizenship demonstration accorded their children at the biased McDonogh Day ceremonies." Marine added that she was "not discouraged. I worked hard for them not to go and I am greatly disappointed that even four children from my school had to go." The following year another mass boycott was called; not one African American child attended the ceremony.[5]

---

3. "Tell Children to Stay Away from Celebration" *Louisiana Weekly,* 8 May 1954.

4. "United Action Marred by Only Two Exceptions" *Louisiana Weekly,* 15 May 1954. The "token participation" mentioned coincided with the two exceptions wherein thirty boys from the Milne Home were forced to attend, and four eighth-grade students appeared with a ranking teacher from Valena Jones High School. The paper also noted that a few parents did allow their children to attend the ceremonies, "fearing that failure to comply with the teacher's request would mean no promotion for their children."

5. "Not to Bow to McDonogh Day 'Jim Crow'" *Louisiana Weekly,* 7 May 1955. It is important to note that the black schools, although not in attendance, did send flowers to the ceremony to pay their respects (see Arnold R. Hirsch, "Simply a Matter of Black and White: The Transformation of Race and Politics in Twentieth-Century New Orleans," in *Creole New Orleans: Race and Americanization,* ed. Hirsch and Joseph Logsdon [Baton Rouge: Louisiana State University Press, 1992], 281).

On May 17, 1954, ten days after the McDonogh Day boycott, the United States Supreme Court ruled in *Brown v. Board of Education* that separate was "inherently unequal." Following this decision, many southerners embraced "massive resistance," paralleling a reactionary anti-Communist campaign fomented by Senator Joseph McCarthy. The McDonogh Day boycott is merely one example of the ways in which Louisiana women, within a climate of potentially dangerous right-wing extremism, sought to create a more just and democratic society. By refusing to allow their children to participate in the McDonogh Day ceremonies, they taught their children and the Orleans Parish school system a lesson in how to successfully challenge white supremacy.

To be sure, the war years had dramatically altered the political, economic, and social landscape of an arguably anachronistic South. The war brought increased industrialization, mechanization, and employment to a region that had yet fully to modernize. When President Harry Truman announced his support for a civil rights agenda, to many African Americans, Jim Crow seemed destined to end. After the war, African Americans matriculated at colleges and universities in greater numbers. The efforts of the NAACP's Legal Defense Fund began to bear fruit as the Supreme Court ruled on a series of cases on behalf of African Americans in the areas of education and voting rights. In May 1950, in *Sweatt v. Painter,* the Court determined that the African American law school in Texas was inferior to the white University of Texas law school in reputation, professional connections, and the eminence of its faculty and, subsequently, ordered Herman Sweatt admitted to the white law school. The same day, in *McLaurin v. Board of Regents,* the Supreme Court ordered full integration of the graduate school of the University of Oklahoma on similar grounds. Following these two judgments, Louisiana State University (LSU), in the midst of legal action brought by the NAACP, desegregated its law school under court order; the LSU graduate school soon followed suit. By 1951, the Southern Regional Council had collected data showing that twenty colleges admitted both African Americans and whites, two of those in Louisiana.[6]

Southern University in Baton Rouge was the designated state school for higher learning for African Americans, while private Dillard and Xavier universities in New Orleans also enrolled many Louisiana blacks. Xavier Uni-

---

6. See Mark Tushnet, *The NAACP's Legal Strategy Against Segregated Education, 1925–1950* (Chapel Hill: University of North Carolina Press, 1987); and Numan Bartley, *The Rise of Massive Resistance: Race and Politics in the South during the 1950s* (Baton Rouge: Louisiana State University Press, 1969), 5–7.

versity provided the city of New Orleans with over two-thirds of its African American teachers.[7] Still, Louisiana, like other southern states, experienced only token integration of its all-white colleges and universities. In 1958, Governor Earl Long supported the construction of New Orleans branches of Louisiana State University (LSUNO) and of Southern University (SUNO). Although both schools, built within a mile of each other, were legally integrated, the intention was to have black students attend SUNO and whites attend LSUNO. However, when two hundred black students registered that fall at LSUNO, it appeared that Long had unintentionally established the "first public, state-supported university in the Deep South that admitted all students without regard to race." Integration in the public elementary and secondary schools was different, and although privately supportive of desegregation, the governor publicly signed a number of segregation bills into law.[8]

In the political arena, southern politicians had yet to progress very far on issues of race. Despite the Supreme Court's ruling in *Smith v. Allwright* (1944), which outlawed the all-white primary in Texas, African Americans still had far to go in securing voting rights. In 1956, black registration in the South was approximately 25 percent of eligible black voters compared to 60 percent of eligible white voters. In the Black Belt sections of the Deep South, the percentages were much lower.

In 1940, only 897 African Americans were registered to vote in Louisiana, due in large part to the poll tax requirement. However, with the state poll tax abolished in 1940, the numbers of registered blacks in Louisiana rose precipitously to 10,000 and, by 1947, more than 100,000 blacks were registered to vote; the numbers rose to 120,000 by 1952, and to 161,410 by 1956. Yet, due to the rise in segregationist extremism in the state throughout the 1950s, particularly post-*Brown*, the numbers declined, and by the end of the decade the state recorded only 131,000 registered blacks on its rolls.[9] In Louisiana, where African Americans made up more than one-third of the population, in 1952 only 12.6 percent of registered voters were black; by 1958, they comprised only 15.6 percent.[10]

7. Paul A. Kunkel, "Modifications in Louisiana Negro Legal Status under Louisiana Constitutions, 1812–1957," *Journal of Negro History* 44 (January 1959): 22.

8. Michael L. Kurtz and Morgan D. Peoples, *Earl K. Long: The Saga of Uncle Earl and Louisiana Politics* (Baton Rouge: Louisiana State University Press, 1992), 201, 199.

9. Kunkel, "Modifications in Louisiana Negro Legal Status," 22; Margaret Price, *The Negro and the Ballot in the South* (Atlanta: Southern Regional Council Office, 1959), 9.

10. Price, *The Negro and the Ballot in the South*, 10–11; Kurtz and Peoples, *Earl K. Long*, 198.

"IT WAS LIKE A DAILY JOB"

Even prior to the 1954 *Brown v. Board of Education* decision, Louisiana women had supported and sustained civil rights activity through organizations such as the YWCA, NAACP, and the Urban League of Greater New Orleans, and tackled discrimination and segregation through the courts, boycotts, and voter registration efforts. Registering to vote or enrolling in a formerly all-white or integrated institution was seen as an act of defiance. Women also challenged Jim Crow through spontaneous actions and confrontations in the workplace and in the more public arenas of daily life, such as on buses and streetcars. These quotidian acts of insurgency had long been, and continued to be, part and parcel of the daily lives of Louisiana's African American population.[11]

Many urban African Americans used public transportation every day. For the women who worked as domestic servants in white neighborhoods, the buses were an unavoidable necessity. With white passengers seated in the front and black passengers in the back, buses and streetcars symbolized African Americans' second-class status. If there were more white passengers than seats, the black passengers either moved farther back or were made to stand. In many instances, blacks were forced to stand over empty seats reserved for whites. Blacks paid at the front and then got off to reboard at the rear of the bus. The driver, always white, might pull away before the passenger could board or sit down, or he might purposely ignore passengers waiting at bus stops in black neighborhoods. African Americans were shortchanged, harassed, and intimidated on the buses on a daily basis.

For years, however, black passengers had shown defiance on public transportation. Examples of outright challenges and "small-scale skirmishes" on the part of black passengers are numerous, particularly by women. Outnumbering men in their use of public transportation, black women were the most vocal in their opposition to these humiliating Jim Crow practices. In one instance, a black woman threw a female streetcar conductor off the car when the conductor attempted to strike her.[12] In December 1946, Southern University of Louisiana instructor Miss Marie Davis Cochrane, with the aid of the NAACP, filed suit with the Nineteenth Judicial District Court of East Baton Rouge against the Baton Rouge Bus Company. Cochrane stated that

11. Robin Kelley, "'We Are Not What We Seem': Rethinking Black Working-Class Opposition in the Jim Crow South," *Journal of American History* 80 (June 1993): 76, 78.

12. Adam Fairclough, *Race and Democracy: The Civil Rights Struggle in Louisiana, 1915–1972* (Athens: University of Georgia Press, 1995), 83.

on October 20, 1946, she boarded a Baton Rouge bus, paid her fare, and sat with other black passengers in the back of the bus. When the bus driver demanded that she stand "and surrender [her] seat to white passengers who boarded the vehicle after them," she refused. Three police officers arrested Cochrane and held her for more than an hour. After the city court initially acquitted her of "disorderly conduct" charges, Cochrane filed a second suit in 1947, requesting twelve thousand dollars in damages "for personal injuries occasioned by [her] arrest last October on the complaint of a bus driver." A local black paper noted that the case was "of wide interest since it is common practice, not only in this city, but throughout the state for bus drivers to force Negro passengers to surrender their seats to whites." Ultimately, the case was dismissed.[13] In line with the many consumer struggles that emerged in the 1940s, buses and streetcars served as an economically viable place to contest discrimination and segregation.[14]

In 1958, the leading civil rights activists in New Orleans held a meeting and threatened to boycott. One woman recalled that black New Orleanians were asked to sit behind the [designated "colored"] screen, but often they "wouldn't do it."[15] Civil rights activists Oralean and Joyce Davis remembered blacks riding the streetcars and "sometimes taking the screens . . . and throwing them off. Sometimes you would get on the streetcars and get off because you were afraid there would be some violence or something."[16] Following the meeting, black and white civil rights activists met at midnight one Saturday and removed all the screens separating the white from the black sections on the buses and streetcars. As Rosa Keller, a longtime proponent of black rights, explained: "We were learning by that time that if you cut the opposition off before it ever formed, you had a chance of getting by with something. If you put it in the paper that the buses and streetcars were going to be desegregated tomorrow morning, you had a bunch of protesters and people carrying on and probably causing some trouble."[17] And, Keller recalled, the following Sunday "absolutely nothing happened. When it happened we said [the black riders] will be clean, and not brush up

<hr/>

13. *Louisiana Weekly*, 14 December 1946 and 1 February 1947.

14. Kelley, "We Are Not What We Seem," 105.

15. Lorraine Poindexter Ambeau, interview by the author, 17 December 2001, tape recording, copy in possession of the author.

16. Oralean Davis and Joyce Davis, interview by Kim Lacy Rogers, 19 May 1979, tape recording, Rogers-Stevens Collection.

17. Rosa Keller, interview by Kim Lacy Rogers, 7 May 1979, tape recording, Rogers-Stevens Collection.

against anyone, not to cause trouble, like the non-violent, passive resistance movement." After a week with seemingly no disturbances, Keller called her friend, "the director of public services[,] and asked if it was really going that smoothly and he said yes, [it really was] going that smoothly." Keller's insistence on "quiet integration" is significant; New Orleans's buses and streetcars desegregated without incident.[18]

While the desegregation of the buses and streetcars in New Orleans occurred without protest, five years earlier, in Baton Rouge, activists chose a different route. Even before the Montgomery (Alabama) Bus Boycott of 1955, thought by many to be the spark that began the modern civil rights movement, thousands of black women participated in a short, yet successful boycott of the Baton Rouge bus system in 1953. Baton Rouge is situated along the Mississippi River and is home to Louisiana State and Southern universities. In 1949, the city outlawed sixty independent black-owned buses that served the black community. Consequently, Baton Rouge's black community members were forced to contribute financially to a transportation system in which they were legally denied equal participation. In March 1953, in an attempt to make the monopoly Baton Rouge Bus Company system operate more efficiently, the city council passed an ordinance essentially ending segregation, allowing blacks and whites to board city buses on a first-come, first-served basis. Whites would sit from front to back and blacks from back to front, and black and white passengers were not permitted to sit in the same seat, according to state law that required the separation of passengers on inner-city routes.[19]

On Monday, June 15, 1953, after a company directive ordered compliance by all bus drivers, ninety-five white drivers staged a strike, protesting the end of segregated seating. Accusing the local NAACP of instigating the new ordinance, the striking bus drivers argued that it created a situation "in which Negroes seated in the front seats of the buses refused to move to make room for white passengers." The drivers called for return to a system in which ten or twelve seats in the back of the bus were reserved for black passengers and four in the front for whites. With all of the city's bus drivers on strike, the public transportation system ground to a halt, leaving twenty

18. Leontine Goins Luke, interview by Kim Lacy Rogers, n.d., tape recording, Rogers-Stevens Collection; Keller, interview by Rogers, 7 May 1979.

19. "City Transportation System Closed Down; Drivers Object to Ordinance over Passenger Seating," *Baton Rouge State-Times*, 15 June 1953, East Baton Rouge Parish Library.

thousand daily commuters, two-thirds of them African American, hitching rides, using taxis, or walking.[20] For four days the bus drivers met with the city council; on Wednesday, the bus drivers' wives, some with their children, marched on the parish courthouse in attempt to persuade the city council to change the ordinance. The women "stressed that they and their children were suffering because of the strike and urged the council to rescind the seating ordinance." On Friday, June 19, 1953, Louisiana attorney general Fred S. LeBlanc ruled that the ordinance was "in conflict with the state statute requiring that separate seats or compartments be provided for white and colored races," thus the ordinance did "not comply with state law."[21]

That same day, the strike, which had kept all Baton Rouge citizens off the buses, turned into a boycott by the African American community, keeping the buses nearly empty. In response to a radio plea by a member of the United Defense League (UDL), "a Negro inter-civic club organization," black citizens rallied in support of a boycott and stayed off the buses. The UDL promised free rides throughout the city, and, true to their word, the next day Baton Rouge's black citizens provided cars and taxis, "cruising the bus routes flaunting large signs reading 'Free Rides.'" In some areas of the city, black female domestics were picked up at their homes and taken to work. The few blacks who did ride the bus, apparently unaware of the boycott, were approached and told not to ride. The drivers on two empty buses noted that on any given day approximately 98 percent of their usual passengers were black. The UDL considered the boycott "virtually 100% effective as far as Negro passengers are concerned."[22]

The United Defense League served as the boycott's parent organization, with Reverend T. J. Jemison as president; Fannie Washburn, a housewife active in the local voters' league, served as the lone female on the executive board. Similar to the boycott that later occurred in Montgomery, a mass

20. "City Transportation System Closed Down," "Councilmen Air Views on Strike of Bus Drivers—Two Indicate Prompt Council Action; Bus Service Still Out," and "Prospects Dim for Settlement of Bus Strike—Council, Company, Union Hold Fruitless Conference on Issue," *Baton Rouge State-Times*, 15, 16, and 17 June 1953.

21. "Buses May Move before Nightfall—Union Attorney Expects Settlement Today, Company Stands Pat" and "Buses Roll But Boycott Is Started—Very Few Negro Patrons Seen on Buses; Private Cars Cruise City Flaunting Large 'Free Ride' Signs," *Baton Rouge State-Times*, 18 and 19 June 1953.

22. "Buses Roll but Boycott Is Started" and "Bus Boycott Continues as Parley Fails—Negro Leaders, City and Bus Company Officials Unable to Reach Agreement; Firm May Reduce Service," *Baton Rouge State-Times*, 19 and 20 June 1953.

meeting was held after the first day; all in attendance agreed to continue the boycott. After the second day, another mass rally was held in which the UDL collected over one thousand dollars to sustain the boycott. As Reverend Jemison presciently stated, "Baton Rouge will go down in the annals of history as an example of cooperation among Negroes." With "Operation Free Lift" in full swing, by the fifth day, the manager of the bus company announced that the company was losing as much as $1,600 a day. The UDL continued to hold nightly mass meetings, with an estimated four thousand in attendance. By week's end, the manager of the bus company called the boycott 100 percent effective, stating that the company's situation was worsening, and if it continued, the "no riding" policy could force the company out of business.[23]

On June 24, 1953, the bus company and the UDL agreed to a new ordinance, which the city council adopted the next day. Similar to the original one passed by the city in March, it allowed blacks to sit on a first-come, first-served basis but also reserved a limited number of seats at the front of the bus for whites and at the back for blacks. The attorney for the parish, R. Gordan Kean Jr., stated that the bus drivers had carried both black and white passengers for twenty years without any problems and that "during this time, the drivers have enjoyed pleasant relations with their passengers of both races." He expressed hope "that this relationship will continue to be pleasant." The UDL agreed to accept the new ordinance "under strong protest." At the same time, it announced financial support—having raised close to seven thousand dollars at the week-long mass rallies—for a lawsuit sponsored by the local NAACP. Aided by the New Orleans attorneys A. P. Tureaud and Louis Berry, they sought to test the validity of the attorney general's ruling and the constitutionality of Louisiana's laws governing segregation in public transportation.[24] After a mass rally that evening at a heavily guarded Memorial Stadium, with some eight thousand blacks in attendance, the seven-day bus boycott officially ended. Shouts of "stay off, stay off" and "walk, walk" were heard at the rally as the Reverend Jemison

23. "BR Negros May Petition," "To Propose New Bus Ordinance—Details Are Not Announced; Negroes Are Maintaining Boycott," and "Bus Case to Be Aired on Radio—McConnell to Cite Council Views; 'Free Rides' Continue," *Baton Rouge States-Times*, 21, 22, and 23 June 1953.

24. "Bus Ordinance Set for Action—Compromise Proposal Accepted with Protest; Test Suit Planned" and "Enact Bus Emergency Ordinance—Negroes Expected to Return to Buses Tomorrow Following Mass Meeting Tonight; Eject Student at Council Meeting," *Baton Rouge State-Times*, 24 and 25 June 1953.

urged the black community to ride the buses and offered encouragement, stating, "Justice is on our side . . . and brother, it's on the way."[25]

In Baton Rouge, as in Montgomery, black women, historically constituting the majority of riders, experienced daily harassment and intimidation at the hands of white drivers. The boycott allowed the "private misery" experienced by many black women in the community to become "a public issue and a common enemy." After Baton Rouge's black community mobilized, women were no longer alone in a daily battle for their dignity.[26] In addition, the Baton Rouge Bus Boycott provided a model for the much longer and more newsworthy Montgomery Bus Boycott, spearheaded and sustained in large part by Montgomery's black and white female citizens. The Montgomery Improvement Association modeled its transportation system, mass meetings, and ability to organize community leaders directly on the Baton Rouge boycott. The ministers of Montgomery consulted with the leaders of the Baton Rouge movement prior to mass action in that city.[27]

As in most civil rights organizations of the day, men held the majority of leadership positions in Baton Rouge, with black ministers, in particular, exerting an inordinate amount of influence within the African American community. The Reverend Jemison quickly assumed the role that Martin Luther King Jr. would in 1955 in Montgomery, negotiating a settlement with the bus company and holding nightly mass meetings encouraging the city's black residents to stay off the buses. However, the church, historically the nucleus of much protest activity, claimed a strong following among women. As was the case in Montgomery, numerous women supported the Baton Rouge boycott by working as drivers or organizers, or by simply remaining off the buses. Mrs. Almenia Freeman, a black Baton Rouge resident, drove for the free-ride system. According to Freeman: "When the bus boycott come [sic] along in 1953, I was happy with that. We met with Mr. Matthews and Reverend Jemison and others. We had meetings, and I was available to get out and drive up and down the road, take people wherever they needed to go. It was like a daily job."[28] Freeman's daughter also participated in the boycott

25. "Bus Boycott Is Lifted, Traffic Is Sub-Normal—Action in Test Case Anticipated; Car Pools Operating," *Baton Rouge State-Times*, 26 June 1953.

26. Aldon D. Morris, *The Origins of the Civil Rights Movement: Black Communities Organizing for Change* (New York: Free Press, 1984), 49.

27. Morris, *The Origins of the Civil Rights Movement*, 24–25, 56, 58, 64–65.

28. Almenia Freeman, quoted in *Baton Rouge Bus Boycott: The People*, LSU Special Exhibit Web site, www.lib.lsu.edu/special/exhibit/boycott/thepeople/html.

and was harassed by police when she refused to sit in the back of the bus. Another female free driver stated, "We got the bus people on the run and can hold out as long as they can." Another woman said, "This don't bother me . . .[but] we'll all have to go back to riding the buses before long—we have to get to our jobs."[29]

Domestics who refrained from riding the buses were also crucial to the successful boycott. As the Reverend Jemison stated, "I watched women who had cooked and cleaned the houses of white folks all day having to stand up on a long bus ride."[30] Patricia Robinson's parents participated in the bus boycott when she was a young girl. She recalled stories of her mother walking to work daily. "We started it," her mother stated. "We were in the forefront with our bus boycott." According to Robinson, her grandmother "talked about how they would stand on a different corner cause you couldn't stand on the regular bus corner . . . and somebody would pick them up and take them to work, come back and pick them up from work and take them home."[31] Without the compliance of women, the mass action would not have succeeded.

Women continued to contest discrimination on public transportation in other areas of the state. In 1958, in Shreveport, two teenage sisters, Mary and Princella Bender, sat in the only available seats, in the front of the bus. A white woman complained, but they refused to move; police arrested the sisters and charged them with disturbing the peace. Also in Shreveport, in February 1959, police arrested Dorothy Simkins, the wife of a prominent dentist, Dr. C. O. Simkins, and a well-known militant civil rights activist in her own right, "when she took a vacant trolley seat beside a white woman and allegedly refused to move when ordered to by a traffic patrolman." Challenging Shreveport's "safety" ordinance—which, following the New Orleans decision in 1957, gave trolley drivers the right to seat passengers "to ensure the safety of operations"—Dorothy Simkins was charged with "disturbing the peace" on the legally desegregated trolley.[32] In Lake Charles, Louisiana, in March 1959, following an "incident" involving Yvonne Robertson, wife of an African American physician, the NAACP filed suit to desegregate the city's

29. "Bus Boycott Continues" and "BR Negroes May Petition for Separate Bus System," *Baton Rouge State-Times*, 20 and 21 June 1953.

30. Reverend Theodore Jefferson Jemison, quoted in *Baton Rouge Bus Boycott: The People*, LSU Special Exhibit Web site, www.lib.lsu.edu/special/exhibit/boycott/thepeople/html.

31. Patricia Robinson, interview by Erin Porche, n.d., *Baton Rouge Bus Boycott: The People*, LSU Special Exhibit Web site, www.lib.lsu.edu/special/exhibit/boycott/thepeople/html.

32. "Arrested in Shreveport Trolley Seating Incident," *Louisiana Weekly*, 7 February 1959.

public transportation system. In its complaint, Robertson and Marietta Brown, the local NAACP president, argued that the city ordinance violated the Fourteenth Amendment and that they had suffered "great injury, inconvenience, and humiliation as a result of the segregation ordinance." The plaintiffs were successful when the United States Supreme Court refused to review the decision of Fifth Circuit Court, which, in a 1958 New Orleans case, ruled unconstitutional the Louisiana law requiring segregated seating on public transportation.[33]

"IT WAS A MARVELOUS EFFORT"

The successful outcomes of the Baton Rouge Bus Boycott and statewide public accommodation lawsuits energized Louisiana's black communities. United by these early successes, the state's black citizens vowed to continue to protest inequities in education and voter registration. In Baton Rouge, only 7,500 of 21,000 possible African American voters were registered. Reverend Jemison pointed out: "It is our duty and responsibility to show our enthusiasm for the privilege of voting. It is time we availed ourselves of the opportunity. This is a commencement, we are just beginning."[34] With the help of Governor Long, the numbers of registered African Americans in the state did increase sporadically through the 1950s, yet the percentages of blacks registered of voting age still did not achieve parity with whites. A number of individuals and organizations, including the NAACP, the Orleans Parish Progressive Voters' League (OPPVL) and the Louisiana Progressive Voters' League (LPVL), deemed "the NAACP in different clothes," actively pursued registering African Americans.[35] Although the state poll tax requirement had been abolished in 1940, African Americans in Louisiana continued to face a number of other challenges to their right to vote. Literacy tests, residency requirements, and the ability to be able to recite, in part or in whole, the federal and state constitutions served as ways to keep Louisiana blacks off the rolls. As one African American female voting rights activist stated: "It was a problem for us to even become registered voters. We had to go back over and over. They would say you were one day off; one of the questions was how many years, days, and months [old are you] and if you missed it by one, you were not qualified."[36] Registering to vote was an act of defiance

33. "File Suit Against Bus Bias in Lake Charles," *Louisiana Weekly*, 14 March 1959.

34. "Bus Case to Be Aired on Radio," *Baton Rouge State-Times*, 23 June 1953.

35. Fairclough, *Race and Democracy*, 131–32.

36. Lorraine Poindexter Ambeau, interview by the author, 17 December 2001, tape recording, copy in the possession of the author.

and a serious breach of the racial status quo; doing so could be dangerous, particularly during the post-*Brown* "purges" of integrated organizations actively pushed by the state's White Citizens' Councils.

Both black and white women participated in the struggle for African American voting rights in Louisiana. The NAACP, an organization with a large middle-class female constituency, led the state in voter-registration efforts. It not only encouraged its members to vote, but also worked to educate and register African Americans throughout the state. In 1954, the NAACP counted fifty branches in Louisiana, with more than 12,500 members, making it the largest civil rights organization in the state.[37]

In late 1954 and 1955, with the 1956 gubernatorial campaign approaching, the NAACP Steering Committee launched a massive voter-registration effort. Utilizing a "telephone pyramid project to increase the voting power of the Negro throughout the city," a network of middle-class women from various organizations aided the voter-registration project. Black activist Ethel Young and the PTA Council directed the program assisted by the nurses at Flint-Goodridge Hospital, one of only a few facilities in New Orleans that served the African American community. Mrs. Elizabeth Drake of Ruters Rex Clothing Company "personally accompanied a number of [her] employees to the registrar's office." One member of the NAACP's Committee on Registration commended the women working on the West Side of the city, stating, "Proportionately, I think they have encouraged more new registrants during the drive than we have even though we have a larger potential."[38]

NAACP members Oralean and Joyce Davis, sisters of A. L. Davis, a prominent New Orleans minister later affiliated with the Southern Christian Leadership Conference (SCLC) and founder of the Orleans Parish Progressive Voters' League, also worked on voter registration efforts in the city. The sisters recalled registering black New Orleanians in "leaps and bounds."[39] Leontine Goins Luke was a member of the Ninth Ward Civic League, which was created to educate and register voters. As Luke recalled: "It really was a marvelous effort. We held registration in the schools because they made it hard at the registration office. They not only give you some type of test, but then they wanted the people to recite the preamble to the Constitu-

---

37. "Annual Report, 1955," NAACPNO Papers.

38. "Committee on Registration Busy Buzzing Phones with 'Are You a Registered Voter?'" *Louisiana Weekly*, September 1954. At the time, the employees of the Ruters Rex Clothing Company were on strike for better wages and working conditions.

39. Oralean Davis and Joyce Davis, interview by Kim Lacy Rogers, 19 May 1979, tape recording, Rogers-Stevens Collection.

tion. Then they wanted them to bring a letter from the head of the household to verify that they were the person they said they were."[40] By 1954,
25,524 African Americans were registered to vote in New Orleans, approximately 25 percent of the eligible voting-age public; the Ninth Ward boasted
the second-largest numbers in the city. Considering the repressive political
climate during these years, the actions on the part of women like Oralean
and Joyce Davis and Luke are significant.[41]

The NAACP was not the only organization involved in the registration
effort. The YWCA of New Orleans also took part in the massive registration campaign. Katie Wickham, an African American member of the NAACP,
led the efforts of the YWCA in a thirty-day registration drive. With the aid
of Mrs. Venice Spraggs, a former nationally known newspaperwoman and
member of the National Democratic Committee, Wickham contacted "key
women in every town in the state" to assist in getting people to register "regardless of race, color, or religion." Out of this effort, and because the local
League of Women Voters (LWV) had yet to integrate, Wickham and other African American women founded the Metropolitan Women's Voters' League
(MWVL); Katie Wickham was its first chair and women dominated the executive committee.

Much like the LWV, the MWVL hoped to register "every eligible woman
who desires to become a voter" and especially to "stimulate voter registration among Negroes throughout the city and the state." The organization canvassed house to house and conducted a number of voter education/
registration workshops. Women learned political strategy, how to campaign,
and about the Republican and Democratic platforms. They also learned what
the city and state governments "mean to the Negro."[42]

At the end of the thirty-day campaign, the MWVL held a rally at the local YWCA building where the national chairman of the women's division of
the National Democratic Party, Katie Loucheim, addressed a crowd of local potential and newly registered voters. The editor of the *Louisiana Weekly*
wrote that, "in this new registration . . . women of the community are going
to participate like never before." He further noted "considerable speculation
that if the women get interested in politics and registration . . . there will

40. Luke, interview.

41. *Registration of Negroes in the City of New Orleans*, NAACP Report, 9 July 1954, NAACPNO
Papers. There were 14,172 black men and 11,352 black women registered.

42. "Women Vote Conscious Organize Voters League" and "MWVL to Open Vote Registration Drive in Ward 10," *Louisiana Weekly*, 8 January 1955 and 5 March 1955. Note that, of the
board, fourteen were women, while only four were men; all were African American.

be a healthy increase in registration across the board." He felt "quite opti-
mistic that when the women put their mind to it, the registration rolls will
increase to our near potential of 100,000."[43] On the eve of the 1956 gubernatorial election, 161,410 black voters were registered in Louisiana. Orleans
parish claimed the largest number of black voters on the rolls—31,289. Still,
even in New Orleans only 16.1 percent of eligible blacks were registered to
vote, and the total in the city was well below the 100,000 mark toward which
the black organizations had worked. Baton Rouge came in second with only
9,100 registered voters.[44]

In the more rural areas of the state, black voters confronted myriad obstacles when attempting to register, but many continued to move forward
in their efforts. In April 1954, Sherman Williams, Wesley Harris, Florence
Harris, Mabel Johnson, and Leola Enoch filed suit against the registrar of voters in Rapides Parish. The original petitioners, Florence Harris and Mabel
Johnson, contacted the NAACP for assistance after attempting to register
"on several occasions." They believed that they had filled out their applications correctly and "were denied registration because they could not read and
interpret the Constitution to the satisfaction" of the registrar, James McCulley. On February 2, 1953, when Wesley and Florence Harris and Florence's
mother, Mabel Johnson, again attempted to register, the registrar refused
Florence Harris and Johnson for applying "on other occasions." When Wesley
Harris asked McCulley why he would not register the two women, McCulley
"became angry and hostile and forced Wesley Harris to surrender his registration certificate, which [he] then destroyed," disqualifying Harris "on the
grounds that he was 'sassy.'" McCulley then ordered Harris out of his office.
Fellow plaintiff Leola Enoch also attempted to register to vote "on at least
four or five occasions" and believed that she also filled out her application
correctly. McCulley rejected her on the grounds that she "could not answer
the questions about the state and federal Constitution" to his satisfaction.
The petitioners argued that McCulley refused to register them "simply and
solely on account of their race and color."[45]

The female petitioners were dogged in their pursuit of voting rights.
After filling out six cards "incorrectly," Leola Enoch "finally executed a satis-
factory card," but she was subsequently asked to read "a portion of the Con-

---

43. "Women to Take Interest in Politics," *Louisiana Weekly*, 25 December 1954.

44. Price, *The Negro and the Ballot in the South*, 9, 70–71.

45. *Sherman Williams, Wesley Harris, Florence Harris, Mabel Johnson, and Leola Enoch v. James
H. McCulley, Registrar of Voters for Rapides Parish, Civil Action # 4541*, File 212, "Voting, Louisiana,
1954–55," NAACP Papers.

stitution dealing with religious freedom." Literacy tests, historically used to disfranchise blacks, worked in this case; she either "could not or did not comply and accordingly, was refused a certificate of registration." Two white witnesses testified that they, too, had filled out their registration cards incorrectly and were denied registration, thus no discrimination was involved.

Ultimately the case went before the United States District Court for the Western District of Louisiana. The justices opined that the plaintiffs had not established that McCulley "administered the registration laws of Louisiana as to discriminate against Negroes" and that "no evidence was evoked from the five plaintiffs themselves to show that the white people received better or different treatment." The judges reasoned that the plaintiffs were not allowed to register "because they could not interpret the Constitution to the satisfaction of the defendant." They pointed out that some three hundred whites as well as eight hundred blacks were denied registration for the same reasons. Judge Hunter continued:

> Human beings are subject to error and under the best system there will be a few, white and Negro, who do not receive identical treatment; but as long as these isolated cases are the extreme *exception* and there is a general policy for all, Negro and white, literate and illiterate, then there is no discrimination under the federal constitution. Unless the court goes completely beyond the record, we do not see how we could decide that the administration of the laws by the defendant penalized Negroes any more than it did other citizens. We have reached our conclusions with an acute and sustained awareness of our duty to protect the constitutional rights of all. But we are not at liberty to impose on state and local authorities our conception of what constitutes a proper administration of their offices, so long as there is no discrimination and the laws are equally administered.

The NAACP filed a notice of appeal to the Supreme Court on January 3, 1955.[46]

Women persisted in their efforts to obtain voting rights throughout the state. The experience of one woman illustrates the extreme difficulties and complications African Americans experienced. In 1959, a black woman in Caddo Parish, the farthest northwestern parish in the state, arrived at the registrar's office, and, when asked to establish her identity, she produced receipts from a doctor, a mail carrier, and a hospital. The white registrar would accept none as proof of identity. Nor would he accept, later in the day, written evidence of her identity from friends and neighbors. Informed

---

46. Opinion in *Williams et al v. McCulley.*

by the registrar the next day that she must bring in a registered voter to prove her identity, she returned with a registered African American voter, only to be told that she must produce a registered white voter. She did just that, returning with a white store owner as well as a white notary. Still, the registrar rejected both as sufficient to establish the woman's identity. After these endless complications, and only after flexing such power, did the registrar deign to allow her to register to vote.[47]

For blacks, registering to vote in the South, thought by many a white southerner to signal overt defiance of black's rightful place in southern society, could bring with it substantial economic and social risk. In Caddo Parish, blacks who attempted to register "were cut off the welfare rolls . . . [and] had difficulty selling their crops and things."[48] Despite the extreme difficulties they faced in the registration process, African American women attempted to register to vote in large numbers through the 1960s as voter registration drives, particularly in the rural parishes, intensified.[49]

As the 1950s wore on, women began to be recognized as increasingly significant players in the struggle for black equality. Even Gloster Current, director of branches for the NAACP, noted in 1959 that women had always acted as an "important part in the National Association for the Advancement of Colored People." Current cited the many women in attendance at the founding meeting who were serving in numerous capacities on the first Executive Committee of the General Committee (later to be named the NAACP) and eight who were serving on a thirty-person board of directors for the original corporation. When the NAACP began to organize in the Deep South, he noted, "much of the organizing was done by women." As membership chairs, they had "led many branches in the conduct of membership and fund raising campaigns." Current concluded that the NAACP "is deeply indebted to women for its progress, for without their aid, it could not function so effectively."[50]

Doretha Combre, a widowed single mother of six and longtime member of the NAACP branch in Lake Charles, Louisiana, illustrates the shift in the role of women in a traditionally male-led organization. In 1954, Combre, with overwhelmingly support, was named the president of the Louisiana State Conference of NAACP Branches when the previous male president re-

47. Price, *The Negro and the Ballot in the South*, 19.
48. Dr. C. D. Simkins cited in Morris, *The Origins of the Civil Rights Movement*, 111.
49. Price, *The Negro and the Ballot in the South*, 21, 70–71.
50. Gloster B. Current, "Women in the NAACP," *Crisis* (April 1959), Howard University Libraries, Washington, D.C. (hereafter cited as HUL).

tired. In accepting the appointment, Combre betrayed lingering traditional views. "This is a position I did not seek or desire," she said. "I feel it is a job for a man. Since you elected me unopposed surely you see some good in me and my ability. It is my desire and determination to do all the good I can at all times for the advancement of my people."[51] In 1959, Combre was elected to a three-year term on the NAACP National Board of Directors, one of just three female members of the board.[52]

In the 1950s, it was increasingly the case that middle-class, black and white Louisiana women were the backbone of the civil rights movement, making many of its achievements possible. As historian Kim Lacy Rogers has written, through legal challenges, boycotts, and membership in integrated organizations, black female activists of the 1950s "combined a necessary racial diplomacy with a subtle use of protest in behalf of civil rights and strategically used their few white allies to achieve modest, but visible gains in a decade of massive resistance and McCarthyism."[53] Similarly, many southern white women used their middle- and upper-class status to artfully further the cause of black rights and promote racial inclusiveness without seeming too contentious. Yet, their actions were not so unlike those of their male counterparts.

Certainly, a number of women were acutely aware of the leverage that their gender afforded them as well as the limitations that being female entailed. Whether directly challenging the gender and racial status quo by registering to vote, or in the simple act of a boycott, these women were educating their children about the proper definition of American democracy. Indeed, much like male activists of the 1950s, they went to the polls, refused to ride the buses, and joined civil rights organizations. However, what is apparent is that women were increasingly becoming highly visible actors on a traditionally limiting southern stage. In the 1960s, however, the social and political landscape of the South would continue to evolve, allowing Louisiana women to skillfully use the leeway afforded to them by their gender to address the inequality they sought to remedy.

51. "Name Mrs. Combre NAACP State Conference Prexy," *Louisiana Weekly,* 20 November 1954.

52. "Mrs. Combre Named to NAACP Nat'l Board," *Louisiana Weekly,* 17 January 1959. By 1959, the NAACP boasted 108 female branch presidents and 669 female branch secretaries of 850 throughout the country.

53. Kim Lacy Rogers, *Righteous Lives: Narratives of the New Orleans Civil Rights Movement* (New York: New York Press, 1992), 161.

4

LITTLE ROCK COMES TO NEW ORLEANS

Louisiana's School Desegregation Crisis, 1959–1962

> I can't imagine what would have happened without the women.
> BETTY WISDOM, New Orleans civil rights activist

From the end of World War II through the 1950s, challenges to Jim Crow gained momentum in Louisiana. The NAACP won a number of court cases resulting in integration of graduate programs at Louisiana State University, McNeese College in Lake Charles, and the University of Southwestern Louisiana (formerly Southwestern Louisiana Institute) among others. In addition, Governor Earl Long funneled significant funds into the creation and improvement of black educational institutions and toward programs to eliminate black illiteracy. The New Orleans League of Classroom Teachers, with Veronica Hill as acting president, had led fights for collective bargaining and equal pay for black teachers, and against segregation.[1] The president of the Orleans Parish School Board, Jacqueline Leonard, one of only two women to ever serve on the board, led the effort to alter the format of the McDonogh Day celebration. Leonard also supported the conversion of half-empty white schools for use by black children, and she was the lone board member to favor integration in 1954.[2] Despite these suc-

---

1. "Retired Teacher Praised for Work in Desegregation," *New Orleans Times-Picayune*, May 18, 1987, Amistad Research Center, Tulane University, New Orleans (hereafter cited as ARC). Veronica Hill was president of the New Orleans League of Classroom Teachers for twenty-three years.

2. "Field Notes—Louisiana," 2 August 1954, Box 4, Folder 6, Inez Adams Collection, ARC; "Mrs. Leonard Seeks Re-Election Tuesday," *Louisiana Weekly*, 30 October 1954, ARC. Although Jacqueline Leonard never openly advocated integration, she did not win reelection, possibly due to her endorsement by the *Louisiana Weekly*, the local black newspaper, and a number of other pro-integration organizations and individuals in the city.

cesses, African American children in Louisiana still attended segregated and decidedly unequal schools.

The 1954 decision by the Supreme Court in *Brown v. Board of Education* outlawing "separate, but equal" appeared to many the long-awaited end to the era of Jim Crow. After *Brown* legitimized civil rights, at least in the eyes of the courts, many white southerners reacted by maintaining Jim Crow through any means necessary. Any modicum of political moderation on issues of race that had existed up to this point ended abruptly as the majority of white southerners unified under the banner of white supremacy. White Citizens' Council (WCC) groups spread rapidly, claiming 75,000 to 100,000 members in Louisiana alone by 1957. The Citizens' Council of Greater New Orleans, headed by Orleans Parish School Board member Dr. Emmett L. Irwin, boasted a membership of more than 50,000.[3] Similarly, a reinvigorated Ku Klux Klan (KKK) responded to *Brown* by holding highly publicized rallies, demonstrations, and parades, marching through cities and towns, burning crosses, and terrorizing blacks.[4]

Louisiana women had challenged Jim Crow law long before 1954, but the real test lay in their ability to enforce implementation of the Supreme Court's decision. Their membership in interracial organizations could not have prepared black and white women for the radical anti-integration forces they would encounter in the battle to desegregate the public schools. As historian David Goldfield argues, school integration, particularly in places where blacks constituted a large percentage of the population, was a profound breach of etiquette, "akin to opening one's home to strangers—and uninvited strangers at that." In Little Rock, Arkansas, in 1957, for instance, integration "aroused deep-seated fears" of miscegenation; "that propinquity would ultimately become intimacy."[5] Confronting these fears and the white resistance to integration they engendered became the civil rights battlefront. For Louisiana activist women, seeing that *Brown* was enforced became the ultimate test of one's courage and faith.

3. "Organized Resistance Groups," n.d., Series III, Reel 121, Southern Regional Conference Papers, Library of Congress, Washington, D.C. (hereafter cited as SRC Papers); Numan Bartley, *The Rise of Massive Resistance: Race and Politics in the South during the 1950s* (Baton Rouge: Louisiana State University Press, 1969), 341–44, 90–91. Bartley notes that the actions of the citizens' councils in Louisiana were particularly effective in paralyzing black progress.

4. L. H. Foster, "Race Relations in the South, 1960," *Journal of Negro Education* (Spring 1961): 147.

5. David Goldfield, *Black, White, and Southern: Race Relations and Southern Culture, 1940 to the Present* (Baton Rouge: Louisiana State University Press, 1990), 77.

"SHOCK ABSORBERS" TO A DISTURBED SOUTH

New Orleans makes for a rich case study of the significance of women's efforts toward school desegregation. Diverse, cosmopolitan, and the second-largest port city in the country, New Orleans's "lazy, hedonistic culture seemed to discourage racism."[6] Against the backdrop of this rich cultural and social heritage, the world watched as New Orleans defied this image and erupted in mob violence in the fall of 1960. Black and white mothers bravely subjected their children, and themselves, to the ultrasegregationist and often violent crowds that gathered daily outside their homes and the integrated schools. Elite white women challenged segregationists at every level by escorting the children—white and black—to the schools, distributing information, lobbying before the state legislature, raising funds, and garnering media attention to sway public opinion. For years these women had worked within biracial organizations such as the YWCA, the NAACP, the Urban League, and the League of Women Voters. The story of a small cadre of elite white women who fought courageously during the school desegregation crises in New Orleans is a compelling example of the "politics of liberal democracy" that came to the forefront in the post-Brown years.[7]

The Brown decision in May 1954 provoked little immediate change in the southern states. In fact, barring the token integration of schools that occurred that fall in the southern Border States, the decision had relatively little impact.[8] Louisiana's response to Brown was similar to that of the other Deep South states: the state legislature in Baton Rouge immediately called an emergency session at which they censured the Supreme Court's decision. Members then adopted a series of bills in an effort to forestall any school desegregation. It prohibited the state's colleges and universities from accepting graduation certificates from students from integrated schools, cut supplies and funds to integrated schools, and gave broad powers to superintendents in pupil assignment.[9] Louisiana also had the distinction of passing the first

6. Adam Fairclough, *Race and Democracy: The Civil Rights Struggle in Louisiana, 1915–1972* (Athens: University of Georgia Press, 1995), xix (emphasis mine).

7. Bartley, *The Rise of Massive Resistance*, 345.

8. Michael Klarman, "How *Brown* Changed Race Relations: The Backlash Thesis," *Journal of American History* 81 (June 1994): 85.

9. Acts 555, and 556 respectively, in "Statistical Summary" (1961), Congress of Racial Equality Papers—Southern Regional Office, State Historical Society of Wisconsin, Madison (hereafter cited as CORE Papers, SHSW); "Letter Demanding Status of Request," Part II, General Office Files—Louisiana, NAACP Papers.

constitutional amendment mandating segregation in the public schools by placing them under state "police powers." Legislators, at least in the language of the statute, enforced segregation not *because* of race, but "for the protection and education of all children of school age in Louisiana *regardless* of race."[10] Only two legislators opposed this amendment, Mrs. Bland Cox Bruns, the only woman in the state legislature, and Bernard T. Engert. Both lost reelection for the next term.[11]

In 1955, in what is widely referred to as *Brown II*, the Supreme Court ordered the southern states to desegregate "with all deliberate speed," and a greater opposition to racial integration enveloped the region.[12] The furor over the desegregation issue was most noticeable in the state legislature, however, which immediately enacted another sweeping series of bills—"emergency legislation"—to counter the current order of the nation's highest court. First, Louisiana tried circumventing the Supreme Court order through "interposition," an interpretation of the Constitution that granted "all powers, including control over the public schools," to the state.[13] Second, the legislature passed a series of acts that, among other things, required students to be certified for "good moral character" upon entering publicly supported colleges and other educational institutions (although the law did not specifically state that this applied only to black students, that was the de facto situation). It also repealed compulsory school attendance laws, dismissed teachers and school employees who advocated integration, and banned all interracial sports and social activities.[14]

In early 1956, in spite of the legislature's actions, a New Orleans federal district court judge, J. Skelley Wright, ordered the Orleans Parish School Board to "make arrangements for admission of children . . . on a racially nondiscriminatory basis with all deliberate speed." Acting with the support of the state legislature, the Orleans Parish School Board appealed the deci-

10. Amendment 16, aka Act 753, cited in "Statistical Summary of School Segregation—Desegregation in the South and Border States—Louisiana" (Nashville: Southern Educational Reporting Service, 1961), Box 1, CORE Papers, SHSW (emphasis mine).

11. Cited in Fairclough, *Race and Democracy*, 206.

12. *Brown v. Board of Education of Topeka*, 349 U.S. 294 (1955), quoted in Morton Inger, "The New Orleans School Crisis of 1960," in *Southern Businessmen and School Desegregation*, ed. Elizabeth Jacoway and David R. Colburn (Baton Rouge: Louisiana State University Press, 1982).

13. HRC 10-Interposition in "Statistical Summary" (1961), CORE Papers, SHSW; Bartley, *The Rise of Massive Resistance*, 131–32.

14. Acts 15, 28, 249, 250, and 579 respectively, "Statistical Summary" (1961), CORE Papers, SHSW.

sion to the Fifth Circuit Court, to no avail; the Supreme Court reconfirmed its 1955 decision.[15]

Women's pursuit of racial equality in New Orleans during the school desegregation crisis highlights the differing routes they took to accomplish the same ends. For elite white women, their race, class, *and* gender, in many ways, allowed them to work from within the political and social structure. Many women found themselves successfully working within the confines of traditional "women's work." For black women, however, the politics of race loomed large and affected the routes they chose to pursue in their fight for civil rights. However, African American women similarly worked within a system that afforded them some leeway because of their gender. Ironically, their liaisons with the white community sometimes aided their efforts. For both white and black women, women's organizations provided a safe and legitimate avenue in which to voice their demands. Finally, as mothers, white and black women found that they had more in common than not; for many, this was the tie that bound them together.

After the Supreme Court rendered its second decision in *Brown v. Board of Education,* an interracial group of New Orleans women who had founded the New Orleans Committee on Race Relations (NOCRR) in 1950 established another interracial organization, the Fellowship of the Concerned (FOC). Members included Rosa Keller, Gladys Cahn, and Mathilde Dreyfous, who all had worked to integrate the League of Women Voters of New Orleans (LWVNO). Attempting to deal with the hardships the desegregation issue seemed bound to create, the women of the FOC noted that the situation was "so highly political, the women hardly know how to handle it." They believed that they should act as "God's women to be interpreters and 'shock absorbers' to a disturbed South."[16] In April 1955, the FOC organized a workshop and invited "the leadership of the various denominations of the three faiths, including both races, to study the responsibility of Christian women, in this time of social change, especially as it relates to the schools."[17] Black and white women from various progressive organizations throughout the state, including the YWCA, the League of Women Voters, the PTA, and the

15. Inger, "The New Orleans School Crisis," 85; Judge J. Skelly Wright, interview by Mary Gardiner Jones, 9 September 1968, tape recording, Civil Rights Documentation Project, New Orleans Public Library.

16. Mrs. C. J. Goldthwait to Mrs. E. M. Tilly, 22 April 1955; "Gleamings from the Workshop of the Fellowship of the Concerned," 19 May 1955, Series VIII, Reel 196, SRC Papers.

17. Mrs. M. E. Tilly to Mrs. Cottles, 25 April 1955 , Series VIII, Reel 196, SRC Papers.

National Council of Jewish Women, met to discuss the impact of the Supreme Court's decision.[18]

Between 1956 and 1960, Louisiana state legislators worked day and night to prevent desegregation in the state. The staunch segregationist William "Willie" Rainach of Claiborne Parish organized the Joint Legislative Committee to Maintain Segregation. Rainach and his counterpart, Leander Perez of Plaquemine Parish, were instrumental in introducing a number of these laws designed to obstruct desegregation efforts.[19] Judge Wright, however, ruled unconstitutional every bill the legislature passed. At the same time, the NAACP continued its legal battles against segregated schools in the state and federal courts, while African American parents petitioned the state legislature on behalf of their children.[20] In the fall of 1959, an exasperated Judge Wright, ruling in *Bush v. Orleans Parish School Board*, ordered the board to prepare a desegregation plan by the following March.[21] When a frustrated Judge Wright imposed an integration plan in May 1960 for the upcoming school year, the newly elected governor, Jimmie "You Are My Sunshine" Davis, granted himself the "sovereignty of the state to

18. "Gleamings from the Workshop," 19 May 1955, Series VIII, Reel 196, SRC Papers. Some of the tasks the women set out at the workshop follow: write the school board for reports on the school system; work to desegregate city buses, restaurants, and hotels since "if these things could be accomplished first, then the integration of the schools should follow"; find out how desegregation had been implemented in other areas of the South; encourage African American members of the community to attend previously all-white churches and synagogues; encourage black New Orleanians to register to vote; and continue to hold interracial and interfaith recreational meetings, believing it important to begin "in the homes with [their] children," to acquaint them with children of other races so that they "might be taught that we are all God's children."

19. Fairclough, *Race and Democracy*, 169–70. For example, Act 256 closed desegregated schools, Act 257 authorized the creation of private schools, Act 258 authorized grants-in-aid for private education, Act 259 provided for pupil placement by school administrators, Act 333 extended the prohibition of funds to desegregated schools, Acts 495 and 542 authorized the governor to sell schools to private interest or close them due to civil disorder, and Act 496 permitted racial classification of schools as "Black" and "White." No fewer than thirty more acts were passed and immediately annulled by Judge Wright in the "First Extraordinary Session" of 1960; eleven more were passed in the "Second Extraordinary Session"; and seven more in the "Third Extraordinary Session," of the Louisiana State Legislature. All cited in "Statistical Summary," CORE Papers, SHSW.

20. "Petition," n.d., Part II, Desegregation of Schools-Branch Action, Louisiana, 1954–55, NAACP Papers. On this particularly petition, almost three-fourths of the signers were women.

21. *Bush v. Orleans Parish School Board*, United States District Court, Eastern District, Louisiana, Civil Action No. 3630, cited in Inger, "The New Orleans School Crisis," 86.

prevent integration" and assumed command of the Orleans Parish public school system.[22]

Although the Louisiana State Legislature refused to abide by the Supreme Court's decision, many women, individually and through organizational affiliation, publicly supported desegregation. Immediately the Independent Women's Organization of New Orleans (IWO), the New Orleans Council of Social Agencies, and the Southern Conference Educational Fund opposed the actions of the legislature. The National Council of Jewish Women (NCJW), the LWVNO, the Louisiana Education Association (LEA), and the YWCA all adopted resolutions supporting the *Brown* decision. Along with United Church Women and the Louisiana Council of Human Relations (LCHR), these organizations sought ways to implement the desegregation order throughout the state. In fact, a number of progressive-minded groups such as the LWV, the NCJW, and the YWCA made the Supreme Court decision a priority on their organizational agendas.[23] Citing the fact that Louisiana was one of six states intent on defying the United States Supreme Court decision, the LCHR set up a committee and a speakers' bureau and distributed informational materials on the best way to begin to "stimulate activity designed to abolish segregated practices."[24] Similarly, the NCJW, reaffirming a 1953 resolution on public education with equal opportunity for all and its stand against discrimination and segregation, organized interfaith panel discussions on the successful implementation of the Court's ruling. The NCJW also adopted a resolution that stated that they would, "through cooperation with other groups [work] solely, and by various methods, to the best of its ability, [to] educate, and inform its members and the community to their responsibilities."[25]

"ASSAULTING THE BASTIONS OF SEGREGATION"

In June 1955, following the Supreme Court's ruling, a group of New Orleans parents, local social workers, and NAACP officials, including Lidvianna Sholes, Cornaxa Coleman, Ruth Sholes, Thelma Rose Williams, and Leah Mercier,

22. Inger, "The New Orleans School Crisis," 87. See also Earleen May McCarrick, "Louisiana's Official Resistance to Desegregation" (Ph.D. diss., Vanderbilt University, 1964).

23. "NCJW to Work toward Implementing Court Order," *Louisiana Weekly*, 13 November 1954, ARC.

24. Florence Sytz, "Program Suggestions—LCHR" (1955), Series I, Reel 29, SRC Papers; "LEA Protests Segregation Legislation," *Louisiana Weekly*, May 1954.

25. "NCJW to Work toward Implementing Court Order," *Louisiana Weekly*, 13 November 1954, ARC.

petitioned the Orleans Parish School Board to begin integrating the schools. A petition submitted to the school board on behalf of local social workers urged compliance with the 1955 desegregation order; of the ninety-five signers, seventy-four were women.[26] In July, a similar petition drawn up by local parents called upon the Orleans Parish School Board to "take immediate steps to reorganize the schools . . . on a non-discriminatory basis." Citing delay, evasion, and procrastination on the part of school board, supporters of this petition authorized the local NAACP to represent them and their children in securing "counsel for us when and where necessary and said counsel may appear before all agencies and administration boards of this State . . . [and] in all courts to represent us and protect our rights and interests in the use and enjoyment of the public schools of this community and this state." Again, the majority of the signers were women.[27]

At a function of the Urban League of Greater New Orleans in 1959, the principal guest, Miss Roberta Church, minority groups consultant for the Department of Labor, spoke eloquently and presciently on the role of women in times of crisis. Women, she said, have the power to "exert great influence both as individuals and through their organizations by taking the initiative in the community to stand for high moral principles in all areas, and by moulding [sic] public opinion to support this stand." "It is important," Church continued, "that women accept this responsibility for it is they who should see to it and insist the proper moral tone prevails in the home, the community, and the nation." In attendance at this meeting were a number of female Urban League members who took her advice to heart.[28]

In the late 1950s, a "moderate" urban, middle-class save-the-schools movement mobilized across the South in opposition to the extremist tactics of the southern state legislatures. Other respectable, progressive organizations such as the PTA and the LWV also became more vocal in their criticisms of southern ultrasegregationist factions.[29] In New Orleans, a group of elite, white "club women" began collecting information from across the South regarding public school integration.[30] Gladys Cahn and Rosa Keller had, for a number of years, worked on racial issues in the city. In 1959 the

---

26. "Ask School Board to Plan for Integrated Schools," *Louisiana Weekly,* 25 June 1955.

27. "Petition," 25 July 1955, Part II, NAACP Papers. Of the forty-seven signers, thirty-four were women.

28. "Women Should Accept Responsibility—Miss Church," *Louisiana Weekly,* 29 June 1959.

29. Bartley, *The Rise of Massive Resistance,* 320–21.

30. See Folders 17–20, Save Our Schools Papers, Amistad Research Center, Tulane University, New Orleans (hereafter cited as SOS Papers).

two organized what was the most important organization during the school desegregation crisis in New Orleans, Save Our Schools (SOS). Both women were former presidents of the Urban League of Greater New Orleans and members of the LWV and the YWCA; Gladys Cahn was also a member of the NCJW. As one member of SOS recalled, Gladys Cahn "was already ahead of her time in terms of integration."[31] Although both were dedicated to the cause of racial justice, Rosa Keller's activities rivaled those of anyone in the city, white and black.

Rosa Freeman Keller was born in 1911. Rosa's mother came from an old, southern aristocratic family, while her father, A. B. Freeman, was simply a salesman, a "nobody from nowhere." Through her father's diligence, however, the family entered the world of the New Orleans elite when his fledgling Coca-Cola business boomed in the New Orleans market. Shortly after graduating college, Rosa Freeman met Charles "Chuck" Keller, a lieutenant in the U.S. Army. The two eventually married and in 1944, after a number of itinerant years, finally settled in New Orleans. Rosa Keller immediately immersed herself in local politics. Already a member of the fledgling League of Women Voters of New Orleans (LVWNO), she worked on voter registration and community education. After her mother's death in 1945, Keller reluctantly accepted an invitation to fill her place on the New Orleans YWCA board. During the war, the YWCA worked on civil defense recruitment and provided housing for transients working in the New Orleans area. Keller credits her interest in civil rights to membership in an integrated YWCA.[32]

Soon after joining the YWCA, Keller learned of the New Orleans Urban League through Gladys Cahn, president of the board at the time. After expressing interest in the organization, she quickly became a member of the board of directors, where, she later recalled, her advanced education on issues of race began: "I did not realize it at the time, but the Urban League had never involved anyone of my type. There were Rabbis, priests, social workers, educators, and a few Jewish people whose sensitivities were much keener about discrimination than those of most of the rest of us. I was a gentile, a member of a prominent New Orleans family, and had wealth and a secure social position. We were the kind of people who usually did not develop sensitivities to the terribly underprivileged. We had no concept of

31. Jane Buchsbaum, interview by Kim Lacy Rogers, 28 November 1978, Kim Lacy Rogers–Glenda Stevens Collection, ARC (hereafter cited as Rogers-Stevens Collection).
32. Keller, "Autobiography," part 2, section 37.

how it felt to be Negro in a society not ready to accept these people except in menial capacities."[33]

Keller involved herself in racial matters in New Orleans and never looked back. In the 1940s, Keller helped found the Independent Women's Organization (IWO), a women's group created solely to aid in the mayoral campaign of deLesseps "Chep" Morrison, a moderate reform candidate. Upon his election, Morrison appointed Keller as the first woman to serve on the city board. In her role on the library board, Keller fought and successfully won desegregation of the public library system in 1954. At the same time, Keller continued to work on voter registration and education in predominantly black sections of the city. As someone "whom black people trusted and respected," she was asked to serve as chairman of the board of Flint-Goodridge Hospital, a facility serving New Orleans's black community. In this capacity, Keller worked for years on behalf of the black medical community for access to the segregated medical library and acceptance to the state's tax-supported, yet segregated medical schools.[34] In later years, she fought to get Blue Cross to extend its medical coverage to African Americans in New Orleans. Keller then worked to integrate the IWO and the LWV and, in 1958, worked behind the scenes to desegregate the city's public transportation system.

By 1959, Rosa Keller had become what historian Pamela Tyler calls an "informal liaison officer linking the black community and the white power structure."[35] The creation of Save Our Schools, with the help of her Urban League counterparts Gladys Cahn and Helen Mervis, and many others, was a logical extension of her efforts. SOS functioned as one of the most influential organizations during the school desegregation crisis in New Orleans.

Keller's involvement with school desegregation began shortly after the Supreme Court decision when she and Cahn presented a petition to the Orleans Parish School Board to "move towards desegregation." They were met with almost total resistance, but they would not give up. Emboldened by Judge Wright's 1959 order that New Orleans prepare for desegregation, Cahn and Keller again approached the school board, suggesting that they integrate two schools in the Uptown neighborhood. Both women agreed that this more elite area of the city—where Tulane and Loyola professors sent

33. Keller, "Autobiography," part 2, section 37.

34. Keller, "Autobiography," part 2, section 1.

35. Pamela Tyler, *Silk Stockings and Ballot Boxes: Women and Politics in New Orleans, 1920–1963* (Athens: University of Georgia Press, 1996), 205.

their children to school—would be the easiest place to begin. Again, the board resisted focusing instead on integrating schools in the Ninth Ward, an impoverished, working-class neighborhood already fraught with racial tension. Keller and Cahn began gathering information regarding the state legislature's special sessions, the actions of the governor, and the effects of school desegregation in other areas of the South, notably Little Rock and Virginia. In February 1960, with the backing of the Southern Regional Council (SRC), the two formed SOS to "further, by all proper and legitimate means, the continuation of a state-wide system of free public education."[36]

Though a handful of men joined, the membership of SOS was predominantly women from New Orleans's liberal elite community. As a result of continued strong anti-integrationist sentiment throughout the state, SOS strategically decided to remain all white; board members felt that they could accomplish more if they avoided integration and an extremist label. Keller's contacts in the black community agreed.[37] The Orleans Parish School Board further requested that they try not to include "too many Jews or too many known liberals."[38] Within a few months, SOS claimed more than 500 members, and, by year's end, close to 1,200 members, many of them members of the Tulane community and, much to the dismay of the school board, many of them Jewish and liberal.[39]

Cahn and Keller initially approached women they knew through their affiliations with the Urban League, the YWCA, the IWO, the NCJW, and the

36. Save Our Schools pamphlets, 1960 and 1961, SOS Papers.

37. Keller interview, 8 April 1988, Rogers-Stevens Collection. In a letter to Rosa Keller, apparently in response to a request for information regarding including black members in SOS, Paul Rilling, field director for the Southern Regional Conference, wrote that African Americans had not participated in the save-the-schools movement in the South, and that "the general thinking of Negro leadership is that they could not with integrity participate in a movement with the limited goal of keeping schools open. It has also been felt by white as well as Negro leaders that a movement aimed at bringing pressure on political figures and public opinion would be more effective strategically if it represented primarily white constituency. It is assumed that the attitude of Negro leadership is on record, that white persons will have more success with white legislators, and that it needs to be demonstrated that *white* people are interested in keeping the schools open regardless of the segregation-desegregation issue" (Paul Rilling to Rosa Keller, December 23, 1959, Series IV, Reel 144, SRC Papers). Interviews I conducted with black members of the New Orleans community corroborate this statement (Sybil Morial interview, 4 December 2001, tape recording, copy in possession of the author; Madelon Cochrane interview, 11 December 2001, tape recording, copy in possession of the author).

38. Peggy Murison, interview by Kim Lacy Rogers, 14 May 1979, tape recording, Rogers-Stevens Collection.

39. Gladys Cahn to Paul Rilling, n.d., Series IV, Reel 144, SRC Papers.

LWV. Helen Mervis, who had succeeded Keller as president of the Urban League in 1957, immediately joined the board, taking charge of organizational fund-raising. Betty Wisdom, niece of Rosa Keller and liberal Judge John Minor Wisdom, and a member of the IWO, was in charge of public relations. YWCA and league member Anne Moore Dlugos also joined the SOS board, working on membership. Rosa Keller asked Peggy Murison, a fellow league member and a recent transplant from the North, to take the SOS presidency, but she accepted only the vice presidency, believing a less visible role would be safer for her children. Murison's fears were well founded. In her stead, Mary Sand, a member of the IWO, accepted the presidency that first year. Fellow SOS members remembered Mary Sand's bravery that year: Sand's six-year-old daughter, a first-grader, was subjected daily to harassment and death threats from the ultrasegregationist mobs. As Wisdom recalled, Sand was "the most remarkable woman in SOS. She had the courage of a lion." Anne Dlugos concurred, calling Sand "the greatest unsung heroine in New Orleans."[40] Other board members included Peggy Barrett, Pat Bass, and Marjorie Stitch, also elite members of the New Orleans community. Liberal white attorney John P. Nelson Jr. and Rabbi Julian Feibelman were two of only a handful of male SOS members willing to serve on the board.[41]

SOS held its first organizational meeting at the Tulane School of Social Work, where members addressed the potential closing of the public school system.[42] Keller, Dlugos, Mervis, and Wisdom then traveled to Baton Rouge to testify for desegregation before the state legislature. As in their meetings with the Orleans Parish School Board, they were met with strong resistance. Wisdom recalled testifying in front of the state legislature as "the hardest thing I had to do at that time. I had never done anything like that before and I was terrified. I thought it would be like McCarthy and that they would reveal every discreditable thing about you." Ironically, she added, "they didn't even listen."[43]

Throughout the spring of 1960, SOS members met almost daily to discuss

40. Betty Wisdom, interview by the author, 29 November 2001, tape recording, copy in possession of the author; Anne Dlugos, interview by Kim Lacy Rogers, 30 June 1988, tape recording, Rogers-Stevens Collection.

41. List of Officers and Directors of SOS, 1960, SOS Papers.

42. Save Our Schools Board Minutes, 24 February 1960, SOS Papers.

43. Betty Wisdom, interview by Kim Lacy Rogers, 14 June 1988, tape recording, Rogers-Stevens Collection.

integration efforts in other southern communities, problems of community power structures, and methods of preventing the schools from closing.[44] The organization refused to argue the merits of segregation versus desegregation or debate states' rights issues; instead, its official stance was for keeping the public schools open. "People didn't want to give the impression that this was an extreme liberal assault on the community," recalled Peggy Murison. "They wanted it to look like we were just keeping the schools open, although in the back of our hearts a lot of us were assaulting the bastions of segregation."[45] Although most of the organizers were pro-integration, the board realized that some SOS members "differed widely as to the wisdom and timing of the court order." Consequently the organization's official stance was that "the decision was an accomplished fact and that the only realistic course was to support any reasonable plan, acceptable to the courts, which would keep the public schools open." Indeed, "the question was no longer segregation or desegregation, but open schools versus closed schools."[46]

Through the summer of 1960, the battle between the federal courts and the state continued. Governor Davis signed thirteen new bills into law, and by August, the state legislature had met in three extraordinary sessions to consider a number of bills attempting to circumvent Judge Wright's desegregation plan. The Fifth Circuit Court responded by rendering invalid every act of the governor and the legislature aimed at maintaining school segregation, including the seizure of the school board by the governor.[47] Subsequently Judge Wright authorized all first-grade children, regardless of race, to attend the school nearest their homes when school began on September 8, 1960. In response to Judge Wright's order, the state legislature enjoined Governor Davis to close the schools rather than desegregate.

Throughout the summer months, SOS carried out a massive public campaign to promote open schools. SOS members prepared several publications advocating open schools and issued daily statements to the local newspapers in response to what they deemed were "inaccuracies presented by the segregationists." SOS members also helped like-minded women form a similar "open schools" group in Baton Rouge. SOS's legal committee, led by white attorneys John Nelson and Katherine Wright, helped the board complete summaries and comprehensive analyses of the legislature's activities in the

44. Save Our Schools Board Minutes, 23 March, 6 April, 25 April, 28 April, and 9 May 1960, SOS Papers.

45. Murison, interview, 14 May 1979.

46. "Save Our Schools, Inc., 1960," SOS Papers.

47. Inger, "The New Orleans School Crisis," 87.

"extraordinary sessions." With this information in hand, SOS then sent informational pamphlets to community members. Noting the sheer breadth of bills introduced to delay integration in New Orleans, organization members wondered if the state legislature was "really concerned . . . with providing education for our children, or is it laying the foundation for the destruction of our public school system?"[48]

The League of Women Voters of New Orleans was also at the forefront of the battle. Like SOS, the league *officially* advocated "open and integrated" schools. Jean Reeves, LWVNO president from 1961 to 1964, remembered that league members were "hardworking, not afraid of controversy or politicians, and dedicated to the League of Women Voters."[49] A number of league women were also dedicated members of SOS. Under the presidency of Ruth Ann Lichtblau, the New Orleans league "adopted an emergency item for support of local public schools." Members of the league also traveled to Baton Rouge to testify on behalf of keeping schools open. Lichtblau recalled that after she testified before the state legislature, "numerous hate calls came with great frequency."[50] The National Council of Jewish Women issued a similar statement in support of the Supreme Court's 1954 decision favoring open and integrated schools. In a report on the progress of integration in

48. "Summary of Bills Introduced at Extraordinary Legislative Session, 1960," "Close Our Schools, 1960," and "To the Public School Parents of New Orleans, 1960," SOS Papers. Some of the publications of SOS that summer include, "A Stake in Our Public Schools," "Private Business and Public Education in the South," and "Constitutional Aspects of School Closings." These publications were sent to community business leaders, ministers and church members, women's and professional organizations, and every legislator in the state. SOS was not the only organization in New Orleans working to keep the schools open. Other similarly progressive organizations spoke out on behalf of open and integrated schools. The Louisiana Council on Human Relations (LCHR), founded in the early 1950s, claimed a number of female members. The LCHR supported the "elimination of the dual system of public education in the state—at all levels," and the integration of the "total student bodies" of all schools as well as "teachers and administrators at all levels." It promised to support "agencies which are attempting to accomplish [school desegregation], to publicize the inequities which continue to exist in school systems which resist such changes," and to "urge local councils to lend their efforts to initiate and follow through on desegregation programs." LCHR also offered to make its resources "available to school systems attempting to implement total desegregation and to advocate the integration of technical and vocational schools."

49. Jean Reeves to Rosa Keller, in Rosa Keller, "League of Women Voters of New Orleans History, 1942–1985," typescript, 1985, copy in possession of the author.

50. Letter from Ruth Ann Lichtblau to Rosa Keller, in Keller, "League History." Interestingly, Betty Wisdom recalls that Ruth Ann Lichtblau was not in favor of integration and that she essentially derailed efforts of the LWVNO to integrate (Betty Wisdom and Felicia Kahn, interview by the author, 10 January 2002), tape recording.

the southern states, the NCJW noted the harmful effects of the Little Rock desegregation crisis, stating: "Clearly the segregation issue posed the major moral and ethical as well as legal and political problem of this era. Despite the ugliness and the fear that has emerged from the Little Rock situation [there is] an increased recognition of the basic integrity, courage and intelligence of the majority of the community leaders of the South. The struggle of the future will be between those who will continue to delay and obstruct and those who will seek workable solutions."[51] Women such as Gladys Cahn, Marjorie Stitch, and Renna Godchaux of the NCJW took this statement to heart and brought it to their work with SOS.

In response to Governor Davis's attempt to close the public schools, another group of white New Orleanians organized the Committee for Public Education (COPE). Like SOS, members of COPE came from the elite white New Orleans community, including parents, businessmen, labor representatives, physicians, attorneys, and clergymen.[52] They were not, however, racial liberals. Most members, in fact, did not advocate integration of any sort. Rather, COPE members were, according to historian Numan Bartley, generally "more conservative . . . preferr[ing] cautious, behind-the-scenes activity to public stands." The organization was, in many ways, "more in tune with the city's mood."[53] The goals of COPE, however, were "to maintain our public schools and preserve law and order," even if it meant integration.[54] Comprised of influential, and some racially "moderate" members, the organization convinced many conservative New Orleanians to join and work toward keeping the public schools open.[55] Fearing Davis's threat to close the schools, thirty white parents, with the support of COPE, filed suit requesting a temporary injunction against integrating the public schools, while still keeping them open. Considering the extremism the state had witnessed to date, the filing of the COPE case was crucial. Affiliating with COPE, as op-

51. "School Integration—Progress and Problems," *Council Platform*, October 1957, New Orleans Branch of the National Council of Jewish Women Papers, Special Collections, Tulane University, New Orleans (hereafter cited as NCJWNO Papers).

52. "Citizens for Public Schools—News Release," June 1960, Series IV, Reel 144, SRC Papers. The organization is known as the Committee for Public Education, although the initial news release uses the title Citizens for Public Schools. It is unknown if they changed their name at a later date.

53. Bartley, *The Rise of Massive Resistance*, 336.

54. Inger, "The New Orleans School Crisis," 86–87. See also Liva Baker, *The Second Battle of New Orleans: The Hundred-Year Struggle to Integrate the Schools* (New York: Harper Collins, 1996), 338–67.

55. Fairclough, *Race and Democracy*, 237.

posed to joining SOS, which many considered a "liberal" organization, allowed racial "moderates" a third option—advocating "open schools" without advocating integration. Ironically, Judge Wright combined the COPE suit, *Williams v. Davis*, with the NAACP suit, *Bush v. Orleans Parish School Board*, arguing that they essentially sought the same result.[56]

With the public schools scheduled to open September 8, 1960, the New Orleans community braced itself. At the last minute the Orleans Parish School Board succeeded in delaying the inevitable, requesting that Judge Wright postpone integration until November 14 to allow the board "more time to devise a desegregation plan." Judge Wright agreed and the schools opened in September on a segregated basis. The New Orleans community—black and white—breathed a collective sigh of relief. For the next few months, the school board designed a complex process that included a battery of medical, psychological, and intelligence tests, as well as home visits, for potential black applicants to white schools. In the end, five girls were chosen to integrate two schools in the Ninth Ward—McDonogh 19 and William Frantz.[57] As Rosa Keller remembered, McDonogh 19 and Frantz were "the worst two schools in the city to desegregate. It was a disaster."[58] In the meantime, SOS members continued to issue press statements to the New Orleans community and held a number of mass meetings "to dramatize the cause of public education."[59]

In the months leading up to November, SOS members found themselves under increasing scrutiny by the wider state community. Although SOS made significant progress in convincing a number of local organizations to support open schools, the majority of white citizens of the state seemed intent on defending segregation and defying the directives of the Supreme Court and the state courts.[60] The organization received hundreds of letters advocating states' rights and segregation, and one poll of white parents in New Orleans showed 82 percent in favor of closing the public schools rather than integrating.[61] As one women wrote:

56. Inger, "The New Orleans School Crisis," 87.

57. Inger, "The New Orleans School Crisis," 88–89; Fairclough, *Race and Democracy*, 239. One of the girls eventually decided not to attend a white school for fear of recrimination.

58. Rosa Keller, interview by Kim Lacy Rogers, 8 April 1988, tape recording, Rogers-Stevens Collection.

59. Confidential SRC Report on the New Orleans School Project, August 30, 1960, Series IV, Reel 143, SRC Papers.

60. Gladys Cahn to Paul Rilling, 6 July 1960, Series IV, Reel 144, SRC Papers.

61. See Donald E. Devore and Joseph Logsdon, *Crescent City Schools: Public Education in New*

I have just received from your organization your pamphlet entitled, "Close Our Schools?" I am writing to say that I am not only not in sympathy with the aims and purposes of your organization, but that I most emphatically condemn it. It seems to me that you and your associates would be doing a greater service to the community and the nation if you spent your time, money and efforts maintaining our traditional way of life and in combating the steady destruction of states' rights and individual freedoms by the so-called intellectuals and liberals. Please remove my name from your mailing list.[62]

Another, comparing the work of SOS to the conquests of Hitler and Khrushchev, stated: "In my opinion, you are doing a great injustice to the cause of freedom by giving in to the social reformers, pious do-gooders, and pinks in the federal executive and judicial branches instead of fighting for our traditional way of life. I am convinced time will prove us right."[63] Other writers cited race riots in the North and quoted Bible passages or requested that SOS "quit bothering me with your integrationist tripe." One asked, "What would the NAACP do without you?"[64]

The organization also came under attack by citizens' council groups. The South Louisiana Citizens' Council published SOS members' affiliations with the Urban League and the ACLU.[65] The Citizens' Council of Greater New Orleans (CCGNO) called SOS a front group for socialism and accused board members of "working towards destroying segregation." The CCGNO asked "every sensible white and Negro person to reject any and all advice or counsel that comes from SOS" and to "stand firm against the evils of race mixing. In sum, the Council is interested in Saving Our Children and our schools, but not at the sacrifice of our children's racial purity and social well-being."[66] SOS members were labeled extremists, liberal integrationists, and "Nigger-loving communists."[67]

Orleans, 1841–1991 (Lafayette: Center for Louisiana Studies, University of Southwest Louisiana, 1991), 236–37.

62. Anonymous to Mary Sand, 25 August 1960, Folder 2, SOS Papers.

63. Anonymous to Mary Sand, 15 October 1960, Folder 2, SOS Papers.

64. Anonymous letters to Mary Sand, 1960, and 3 October 1960, Folder 2, SOS Papers. It is impossible to cite all of the letters Mary Sand received in response to the SOS mailings regarding open and integrated schools. The few letters cited are representative of the hundreds the organization received from states' rights advocates and pro-segregationists, all located in Folder 2, SOS Papers.

65. Paul Rilling to Harold Fleming, 23 August 1960, SRC Papers.

66. "Citizen Council of Greater New Orleans," n.d., Series IV, Reel 144, SRC Papers.

67. Rosa Keller, interview by the author, 13 March 1996, tape recording, copy in possession of the author.

Citing New Orleans's thriving industrial base, its tourist industry, and its importance as a world trade center, the editor of the local black newspaper had cautioned a year earlier that "'America's Most Interesting City' cannot afford the dubious luxury of becoming another Little Rock."[68] With the public school year looming just ahead, he reiterated his point in August 1960: "New Orleans and Louisiana appear ready to enjoy the dubious honor of becoming another Little Rock and the recipient of the infamous reputation that plagues that community."[69]

Apparently the lessons of Little Rock were lost on the citizens of Louisiana. As the November 14 desegregation plan deadline approached, the communitywide atmosphere bordered on hysteria. The governor called another special session on November 4. More than forty members of SOS appeared at the hearings opposing "every bill that would lead to the closing of even one school in the state of Louisiana."[70] On November 12, the superintendent of schools, Shelby Jackson, declared November 14 a school holiday, ordering all state public schools closed. The legislature sent state troopers to New Orleans to enforce the holiday, but the Orleans Parish School Board refused to comply. On the morning of November 14, three young black girls—Tessie Provost, Leona Tate, and Gail Etienne—integrated McDonogh 19, and one black girl, Ruby Bridges, integrated William Frantz.

The inevitability of a negative community response to desegregation led the school board to hide the identities of the schools being integrated. The fears of the school board were well founded. Almost immediately, New Orleans erupted in violence. Mobs formed outside the two schools, and the following day an estimated one thousand to three thousand individuals, prompted by a group of high school students, rioted downtown, destroying property and attacking black citizens. Another group of hostile parents and New Orleans citizens descended on city hall and staged a mock funeral for Judge Wright. Police used fire hoses and clubs to quell the angry mobs. At the integrated schools, hordes of screaming women cast racial epithets, threats, stones, and rotten eggs at the white and black parents who escorted their children to school. Within a few days, a majority of white parents withdrew their children from the integrated schools, "hoping that if both schools could be completely boycotted by white parents, these schools

68. "The Responsibility Must Be Shared," *Louisiana Weekly*, 1 August 1959.

69. "New Orleans Another Little Rock?" *Louisiana Weekly*, 6 August 1960; "The Integration Deadline—WDSU Editorial," 8 August 1960, Series 1, Reel 65, SRC Papers.

70. "Save Our Schools, Inc." n.d., Box 1, Folder 11, SOS Papers.

could then be closed . . . and thus the federal court would be defied by non-compliance."[71]

The situation worsened when the police chief refused to intervene. In the face of this violence, SOS took the lead and organized car pools to drive both the black and white mothers and their children to and from the schools. Betty Wisdom, Peggy Murison, Mary Sand, and Anne Dlugos all served as escorts for the girls. Anne Dlugos recalled how every morning at seven o'clock Gladys Cahn would call her with the battle plan for that day. "She was a superb organizer," stated Dlugos, "but she couldn't have done it without the others."[72] The newly created "ferry service" escorted ten white children and the four black children through the mobs the next day. All of the women were verbally abused, pushed, and spit on. Car tires were slashed and windows and side mirrors were broken. When the citizens' council published the names, telephone numbers, and license plate numbers of the female escorts, harassing phone calls and even death threats followed. "They could say things like, 'We're outside waiting for you. Don't go out of your house.' And it could get really scary," recalled Wisdom. Peggy Murison had a cross burned on her front lawn, and, at one point, members of the mob tried to force their way into her car. Betty Wisdom recalled an incident when an angry mob, brandishing tire irons, clubs, and other weapons, surrounded her and the children she was escorting. Although no one was hurt, she feared for her and the children's lives.[73] As Peggy Murison recalled, "You have heard men talk about how they were in the war; it was the same thing."[74]

Even the police harassed the female drivers. When the women tried to cover their license plates with mud to protect their identities, "The only thing the police did then to enforce the law," Wisdom recalled, "was to make us get down and brush the mud off the license [plates]." Newspapers and television stations across the country descended on New Orleans to chronicle the bedlam that engulfed the city.[75] While working on his novel *Travels with Charley*,

71. "Save Our Schools, Inc." n.d., Box 1, Folder 11, SOS Papers.

72. Dlugos, interview, 30 June 1988.

73. "Save Our Schools, Inc." n.d., Box 1, Folder 11, SOS Papers; Wisdom, interview by Kim Lacy Rogers, 14 June 1988; Wisdom, interview by the author, 29 November 2001; Murison, interview, 14 May 1979.

74. Murison, interview, 13 July 1988.

75. A number of newspapers across the country reported on the New Orleans school integration crisis: "New Orleans Disgrace," *Crisis*, December 1960, HUL; "Save Our Schools, Inc.," n.d., Box 1, Folder 11, SOS Papers; "New Orleans Police Turns Back Teen-Agers in Integration Flareups," *Atlanta Constitution*, 15 November 1960: "Officers Help Four Negroes to Integrate New Orleans Schools, New Rioting Flares in Orleans Dispute," *New York Journal American*, 30

John Steinbeck passed through the city. Describing the white women he witnessed jeering outside the integrated schools, Steinbeck wrote: "I heard the words bestial, filthy, and degenerate. But there was something far worse than dirt. These are not mothers, not even women. They were crazy actors playing to a crazy audience."[76] Within a week, the number of white children attending the integrated schools had dropped precipitously, with only two families brave enough to keep their children in the integrated schools. Because of the threats of personal violence to the children, parents, and the drivers, SOS finally relinquished responsibility to federal marshals, who escorted the children to the schools.[77]

SOS then focused its attentions on the boycott of the two integrated schools. With McDonogh 19 seemingly a lost cause, SOS members focused on keeping the few white children attending Frantz safe and educated. The black and white parents who kept their children in the schools received so much media attention that the families became the subjects of the white segregationists' wrath. For a time, the Reverend Andrew Forman kept his daughter Pamela at Frantz. The danger proved too much to bear and the Formans withdrew their daughter from the school. Two other white families—the Gabrielles and the Conners—also bravely chose to remain at Frantz. Daisy Gabrielle was determined that her daughter attend public school. The daughter of a Costa Rican immigrant, Gabrielle grew up in New Orleans. The courage she gained serving as a WAC in the Pacific during World War II must have aided her in the fall of 1960 as she bore the brunt of the mob's wrath. Each day, Daisy Gabrielle walked her daughter the three blocks to Frantz followed by "a mob of snarling, cursing women and teenaged girls." The women jeered at her, calling her a "Nigger lover," and threatened to beat her and kill her daughter, Yolanda. Over the course of three weeks, Daisy Gabrielle was harassed, threatened, pushed, spit upon, and, at one point, attacked by two women in the crowd. When asked by a reporter how she could

November 1960; "Youths Attack Negroes," *Jackson State-Times*, 16 November 1960; "Screaming Crowds March in Dixie, Fire Houses Used to Quell 2,000 Teens Spurred by Moms," *Chicago Daily News*, 15 November 1960; "Booing Crowd Greet Pupils, U.S. Marshals," *Arkansas Gazette*, 14 November 1960; "Tension Mounts with Integration," *Dallas Times Herald*, 15 November 1960; "Yelling Mobs Battle Police in Louisiana," *Arkansas Gazette*, 16 November 1960, all in Box 1, Folder 3, SOS Papers.

76. Cited in Burrell Ware, *A House Divided*, a Xavier University Drexel Center documentary, 1984, copy in possession of the author.

77. "Save Our Schools, Inc.," n.d., Box 1, Folder 11, SOS Papers; Wisdom, interview by the author, 29 November 2001; Murison, interview, 14 May 1979; Dlugos, interview.

possibly endure the daily punishment, she responded, "How can I let people outside think that everyone in New Orleans is like these women?"[78]

Peggy Murison of SOS offered to drive Mrs. Gabrielle and her daughter Yolanda to and from school. This did not stop the harassment. A mob attacked Murison's car, and more than four hundred people descended on the Gabrielle home, breaking windows and throwing rotten eggs. When James Gabrielle lost his job for keeping his daughter at Frantz, the women of SOS formed a Back-to-School Committee to raise money to "help out those families who suffered property damage" or needed help with living expenses. Although the Gabrielle's received numerous letters of support, including one from former president Eisenhower, Daisy Gabrielle could no longer take the stress. In December, the family decided to move to James's hometown in Rhode Island, where a job awaited him. As Daisy told a reporter:

> I have been boycotted, followed to my house by a mob of mothers who used obscene language with threats of beating if I did not take my child out of school. Let it be said that I feel nothing but compassion toward these women who in fear and hatred forget so easily what America stands for: freedom of thought, freedom of speech, freedom of action. It is these qualities, divine in essence, that are the core of civilization. For the sake of our beloved children, may every American mother remember in time.

In 1961, the NAACP honored Daisy Gabrielle with a "Mother of the Year" award for her "courageous and inspiring stand in the struggle for integrated schools."[79]

The majority of the ultrasegregationists' fervor, however, focused on the African American children integrating the schools. Tessie Provost, Gail Etienne, and Leona Tate were the only students, black or white, in attendance at McDonogh 19. At William Frantz, Ruby Bridges was the lone black student with four white children—the Conners' three children and Yolanda Gabrielle. One black mother involved in the school desegregation crisis believed that "some type of pressure hit them more when they were older and they could understand what they had gone through . . . a delayed reaction."[80]

The African American mothers who allowed their children to integrate

---

78. Isabella Taves, "The Mother Who Stood Alone," *Good Housekeeping*, April 1961, HUL.

79. All quoted in Taves, "The Mother Who Stood Alone"; Murison, interview, 14 May 1979; "Cite Pair Who Bucked New Orleans Race Mob," *Louisiana Weekly*, 4 March 1961; "Save Our Schools, Inc," n.d., Box 1, Folder 11, SOS Papers.

80. Leontine Goins Luke, interview with Kim Lacy Rogers, n.d., tape recording, Rogers-Stevens Collection.

the schools had a history of actively engaging in community affairs. Lorraine Poindexter Ambeau grew up in Louisiana and had always lived in integrated neighborhoods. Although her sisters attended NAACP meetings in the 1940s and 1950s "here and there," Ambeau began her activism only during the school desegregation crisis as a member of the PTA of McDonogh 19. PTA parents formed a group to work with the girls who integrated the schools. When McDonogh 19 closed the following year, Ambeau filed a lawsuit with the NAACP on behalf of her fourth-grade daughter to integrate Simms, another elementary school in the Ninth Ward.

Her children suffered at the hands of the mobs. Ambeau remembers her children involved in daily fights, and once her daughter was hit in the head with a bat. Ambeau also recalls the harassing phone calls she received, telling her "that they were going to kill all my children and set my house on fire." Still, she made light of the phone calls: "We used to set the phone on the porch so all the neighbors could answer." Ambeau pursued the lawsuits because she "wanted the best education for my children." Still, Ambeau remembers the years as "more like a nightmare. You couldn't imagine anyone could hate children and they really showed it." Because of her involvement with school desegregation, Lorraine Ambeau joined a number of civil rights organizations in the city, including the NAACP, the Urban League, and a direct-action organization, the Consumers League. She was active in picketing, boycotting, even attending training sessions at the famous Highlander Folk School in Tennessee.[81]

Another African American woman and longtime civil rights activist, Leontine Goins Luke, contributed to the desegregation efforts in New Orleans. Reared in New Orleans, Luke grew up in the Ninth Ward and was familiar with the difficulties the community faced. She helped organize the Ninth Ward Civic League in the 1930s, an organization that focused on voter education and registration. In the 1950s, Luke served on the executive board of the NAACP, where she helped the lawyers find plaintiffs to participate in the 1952 suit *Bush v. Orleans Parish School Board*. In 1954, Luke joined the many black women who organized the initial boycott of the McDonogh Day ceremonies.

Luke worked diligently on school desegregation in 1960. She visited the homes of the children who were integrating the schools "to kind of encourage the people and assure them that they would not be harmed in going to school," although unsure herself if that were true. Luke admitted that they

81. Lorraine Poindexter Ambeau, interview by the author, 17 December 2001.

"didn't expect that much trouble because New Orleans had always been a city of mixed people." Still, she acted as a contact for the children entering McDonogh 19; "should anything go amiss," the parents could call either Leontine or her husband. She also brought food and clothing to some of the black parents who were poor or who had lost their jobs due to their involvement in the integration of the schools. In fact, because of the family's involvement, Ruby Bridges's father lost his job as a service station attendant. "Ruby Bridges needed the food and clothing donated by the community because her family had many children," Luke recalled. "We also bought clothes for the girls so that they had new clothing from time to time."[82]

This community of black and white women resisted the deluge of hate that descended on the Crescent City in 1960. These women were crucial to all aspects of the integration effort, acting as escorts, counselors, fund-raisers, and publicists. Even amidst the state legislature's constant approval of the mob's actions, the families who remained in the integrated schools received an outpouring of uncompromising support from SOS. The parents and the children also received numerous letters and telegrams from all across the country, many of them from white mothers who wanted to "assure the Negro mothers that not all white people harbor ill will against the Negroes."[83] The sentiment of one SOS member expresses the feelings of many of the women involved: "I heard that it was forming and because of my children I was interested. It was people who were rallying around their own children, because they believed in the rights of all children to have equal education."[84]

Working in SOS became a full-time job for many members. The women continued to escort the children to the schools, while at the same time preparing legal analyses of the state legislature's actions and comprehensive informational packets for the city and state leaders.[85] They also worked vig-

82. Luke, interview, n.d.

83. *Crisis*, January 1961, cited in Baker, *Second Battle of New Orleans*, 383.

84. Helen Mervis, interview by Kim Lacy Rogers, 18 November 1978, Rogers-Stevens Collection.

85. The packets that SOS prepared are incredibly comprehensive and much too long and numerous to cite. Suffice it to say that the women gathered credible statistical information from the southern states regarding black and white pupil attendance through the years, complete analyses of the legal efforts to thwart integration, and information on lawsuits from other areas of the South as well as in Louisiana regarding school integration. They also meticulously gathered and researched psychological, psychiatric, and sociological studies regarding intermarriage, health issues, black/white relations, and tuition grant programs and submitted their recommendations for New Orleans. Examples of unpublished materials include: "Fact Sheet

orously to convince white parents to end the boycotts of the two schools, conducting a telephone campaign to solicit support and funds.[86] Betty Wisdom noted that by December 1960, more than a few mothers had contacted their group "frantic to get their kids back to school," but that they were afraid of reprisals. When CBS News came to New Orleans to film an episode of *Eyewitness to History,* members of SOS appeared on camera speaking eloquently about the continuous legal interference by the governor and state legislature and of the necessity of retaining a public school system. Although much of the New Orleans community now regarded SOS as liberal integrationists, the organization remained firmly committed to avoiding a debate on integration itself. In fact, when Charles Kurault asked if SOS contained both integrationists and segregationists, Mary Sand diplomatically stated that, "it contained all shades of opinion."[87]

At one point, the women of Save Our Schools, in concert with the LWV, COPE, and the IWO, turned to the New Orleans business community for support. The women believed that a strong statement in favor of open schools by local businessmen could influence community opinion. The task proved to be quite daunting. Prior to the integration of the schools, the New Orleans Young Men's Business Club and a number of other influential civic organizations refused to endorse an open-schools resolution.[88] In fact, throughout the initial desegregation fiasco, businessmen in the city had remained conspicuously silent. Even the seemingly moderate Mayor "Chep" Morrison, contemplating a run for governor that year, refused to take a stand in support of SOS or open schools. As Wisdom remembers, "Either the men felt that they had too much to lose, or they didn't have the courage of their convictions, *or* they just didn't have any convictions." Richard Freeman, Wisdom's uncle and Rosa Keller's brother, complained that every time Rosa made a speech, members of the community would call him up and say, "Get your goddamned red [Coca-Cola] machines out of my business." Even Keller's husband, an influential community leader in his own right, complained about her activities, yet Keller held firm. When her husband ordered her to end her civil rights activities and barred the subject from the house, Keller

for SOS Discussion Leaders, 1961–62," "Plans and Program for Save Our Schools, Inc, July 1, 1961–December 31, 1961," "Should We Have a Constitutional Convention," n.d., and "Tuition Grants for Louisiana, April 1961," SOS Papers.

86. Paul Rilling to SOS, 6 December 1960, Series IV, Reel 143, SRC Papers.

87. Betty Wisdom to Paul Rilling, 30 November 1960, Series IV, Reel 143, SRC Papers.

88. In fact, the Young Men's Business Club actually "commended the actions of state officials to maintain segregated schools" (cited in Foster, "Race Relations in the South," 146).

told him: "If you are serious about this, you are going to have to bar me too because I have come to this place where I cannot walk out. You fought your war and I was very helpful to you. I took care of your children and did everything like that. You were gone for two years and I took care of them. This is my war and its gotta be done. Somebody's got to do it."[89] As Betty Wisdom later reported to the SRC, "If I had to choose one characteristic of New Orleans men which, more than any other, had caused all our troubles, I think I'd choose conceited pigheadedness."[90]

Business leaders in the New Orleans community apparently feared economic retaliation by the Citizen's Councils if they supported open schools.[91] Betty Wisdom noted the apathy demonstrated by business leaders in the city, stating, "Here we have *panis and circenses* [bread and circuses] once a year at Mardi Gras and that, apparently, is the extent of the noblesse oblige and civic pride."[92] Yet, the city's business leaders could no longer ignore the economic losses in the New Orleans's tourism and trade industries. As a number of historians have noted, when the chaos began to affect the city economically, the New Orleans business elite finally rallied "in defense of order and stability."[93] To be sure, members of SOS, the IWO, the LWV, and even the conservative group COPE had already paved the way for the business community's entrance into the picture. Warlike photos and incomprehensible stories of racist New Orleans mobs circulated around the country and seemingly contributed to the softened stance of the New Orleans business community. In a letter to the *Nation,* for example, Betty Wisdom described the plight of women in SOS:

> I was there, day after day, escorting children to school past the howling harridans. The screamers shouted obscenities (Nigger-Jew bitch, dirty Jew, and others too filthy to record) and then raced home to telephone the returning families and their escorts with threats of arson, acid-throwing, kidnapping, beatings and murder. Until we began reading the stories and editorials in the outside press, we felt cut off from the world. In a crisis like ours, there are few things worse than this feeling of isolation. It induces the racists to commit ever more terrible

89. Keller, interview by Kim Lacy Rogers, 8 April 1988. At one point, Leander Perez led a boycott of the Freemans' Coca-Cola business due to Rosa Keller's actions in the school desegregation crisis.

90. Betty Wisdom to Paul Rilling, 6 April 1961, Series IV, Reel 143, SRC Papers.

91. *New York Times* article, 6 December 1960, quoted in Inger, "The New Orleans School Crisis," 94.

92. Betty Wisdom to Paul Rilling, 23 December 1960, Series IV, Reel 143, SRC Papers.

93. Fairclough, *Race and Democracy,* 253–54; Inger, "The New Orleans School Crisis," 94–95.

outrages, secure in the knowledge that no one but approving fellow citizens will ever see their actions. It induces [in] the moderates and integrationists the feeling that there is a Sisyphean task which no one approves or understands.[94]

By the end of December, the publicity and the assiduous lobbying by the women of SOS and other organizations began to pay off. More than one hundred business and professional men from the city ran a three-quarter-page advertisement in the local newspaper, and distributed to newspapers throughout the country, "appealing for an end to threats and street demonstrations and for support of the school board." SOS members jumped on the bandwagon and secured the signatures of 196 local parents in support of this statement, as well as a later statement by local clergymen who had also previously refused to take a stand.[95] Ironically, as local newspapers praised these efforts of the New Orleans men, they gave no recognition to the women who for over a year had been lobbying politicians and business leaders.[96] As one chronicler of the situation noted, "the women themselves seemed to understand that in the social climate of 1960, their signatures on a public statement would command insufficient respect to effect a significant alteration in the public mood."[97]

With the New Orleans business community behind them, SOS stepped up its effort to increase white enrollment at Frantz. Believing that McDonogh 19 "was hopeless for the time being," members compiled a list of 250 families whose children had attended Frantz and whom they regarded as "prospects for re-enrollment." While the state legislature contemplated a private-school option, the organization prepared and distributed flyers throughout the neighborhood criticizing the private school plans. They also visited the homes of approximately seventy white parents, though as one SOS statement put it, "well-founded fears of job loss" kept many parents from sending their children back to the school.[98]

Then, in early December, the state legislature froze the Orleans Parish

94. Wisdom, "Letter from a New Orleans Mother," *Nation*, 4 November 1961, HUL. Despite the title of the editorial, Betty Wisdom never had any children.

95. Inger, "The New Orleans School Crisis," 94; "Plans and Programs from SOS," 1 July 1961–December 31, 1961, Box 1, Folder 12, SOS Papers.

96. Other organizations in the city that issued statements at the behest of SOS were the Tulane Faculty Senate, the Central Trades Council, the American Association of University Women, the American Association of University Professors, the Independent Women's Organization, local PTAs and church groups ("Plans and Programs for SOS," Box 1, Folder 12, SOS Papers).

97. Tyler, *Silk Stockings and Ballot Boxes*, 228–29.

98. "Save Our Schools, Inc.," n.d., Box 1, Folder 11, SOS Papers.

School Board's funds and illegally refused to pay the teachers and staff at the integrated schools. When the Orleans Parish School Board attempted to secure loans from local banks borrowed against city property taxes, they were refused. Once again, women of the community came to the fore. Members of SOS began another fund-raising campaign, and Rosa Keller and Mathilde Dreyfous both dipped into their personal family fortunes to pay some of the teachers' salaries.[99] Another woman of the New Orleans elite community, Miss Elen Steinberg, offered a $500,000 loan to pay the teachers.[100] Finally, the mayor appealed to local businesses, the public utilities, and the newspapers to pay taxes in advance, which provided enough funds to pay the salaries of school personnel who had not been paid for almost two months.[101]

In the summer of 1961, the school board chose four more schools to integrate the following fall, and sixty-six black children applied for transfer to formerly all-white schools.[102] This time, however, the school board heeded the earlier warnings of Gladys Cahn and Rosa Keller and integrated schools in the Uptown area of the city, where some SOS members sent their children. With the New Orleans business community taking credit for the successful integration of the schools, SOS stepped up its efforts to rally support for integration. Undeterred, SOS members regrouped, and for the first few weeks of the 1961 school year they reinstated the "ferry service" until the usual harassment and mild furor over expanded integration died down. Even with McDonogh 19 closed, the 1961–62 school year ended with attendance up among both black and white students at integrated schools.[103]

The following school year, Judge Wright broadened the public school desegregation order to include integration of middle schools and high schools. In addition, the Catholic archdiocese agreed to desegregate parochial schools in the state. The state legislature again responded by enacting "emergency legislation" to hinder these efforts. Immediately, segregationists called for New Orleans schools to operate under a two-school system—one public and

99. Betty Wisdom and Felicia Kahn, interview by the author, 10 January 2002, tape recording, copy in possession of the author; Keller, interview by the author, 13 March 1996.

100. Quoted in "New Orleans Mardi Gras," *Crisis*, January 1961.

101. Inger, "The New Orleans School Crisis," 95. Eventually the state was enjoined by the federal district courts to pay the salaries of the school personnel, and three Louisiana officials were cited for contempt for having withheld the teachers' salaries ("New Orleans Mardi Gras," *Crisis*, January 1961).

102. "Plans and Programs for SOS," Box 1, Folder 12, SOS Papers.

103. Pupil attendance numbers cited in *New Orleans Times-Picayune*, 12 December 1961, and *States-Item*, 4, 7, and 8 September 1962, Box 2, Folder 17, SOS Papers.

one private.[104] Anti-integrationists called into question the effects of operating coeducational schools, particularly at the high school level, raising the specter of miscegenation. Fears of black male teenagers mingling with white females only served to heighten ultrasegregationist hysteria over desegregation. As one person wrote to the editor of a local paper, "We are all equal under God, but there are very great physical and mental differences between certain races. The desire today seems to be not so much for equal education but intermingling of the races."[105]

While most New Orleanians believed the crisis had passed, SOS continued its behind-the-scenes work, expanding its efforts outside of the city. Members sent letters to professional and civic leaders, chambers of commerce, and businessmen and clubwomen all over Louisiana, "urging them to begin forming open schools groups." SOS concentrated its energy on educating what they deemed "the four publics": city officials and politicians; business and civic leaders; parents of children in schools to be integrated; and the general community. Their educational campaign focused on the economic effects of the past year, the importance of maintaining law and order, and the negative image of New Orleans around the country and abroad. SOS pointed out the numerous problems that could arise as a result of using private schools in place of public schools. They also initiated an intensive advertising campaign, and, on a more informal level, organized "coffee parties" to allay the fears of parents who had children in schools likely to be integrated. In 1962, after two years of laboring for integration and as a result of increased enrollment by both black and white children in the public schools, Save Our Schools voted itself out of existence.[106]

"WOMEN OF COMMUNITY STANDING"

The contributions of New Orleans women during the school desegregation crisis were extraordinary. In a post–World War II climate that extolled the virtues of womanhood, home, and family, black and white women faced considerable racial and gender constraints in their political efforts. Yet, one

104. *States-Item,* 26 June 1962, Box 2, Folder 17, SOS Papers; *States-Item,* 6 April 1962, Box 2, Folders 8, SOS Papers.

105. *States-Item,* 26 June 1962, Box 2, Folder 17, SOS Papers; *States-Item,* 28 June 1962, Box 1, Folder 18, SOS Papers.

106. "Plans and Programs for SOS," Box 1, Folder 12, SOS Papers; SOS Minutes, September 1962, Box 1, Folder 6, SOS Papers.

unintended consequence of the war years was that it gave rise to women's political activism, as many believed it their civic duty to work with such groups as the Red Cross, the YWCA, and the League of Women Voters.[107] When many of the older generation of elite white women in New Orleans became concerned about issues of justice and democracy, they had to walk a fine line to avoid the appearance of repudiating the definition of women's popular role in American society.

African American women's contributions similarly had to fall in line with acceptable notions about race and gender. Membership within civil rights organizations such as the NAACP and the Urban League were construed as subversive or revolutionary. However, organizations such as the PTA and the YWCA, voluntary association "clubs," were not only considered less threatening, they were also socially acceptable avenues of female activism.[108] Moreover, members of both races accepted the maternal nature of the work that women like Lorraine Poindexter performed by providing food and clothing for black families. For these black and white women, motherhood and activism were compatible. Furthermore, middle- and upper-class women brought to their efforts what one historian calls a decidedly female ethic, "specifically to build bridges across racial lines."[109] Although forced to work within the constraints of both gender and race, their activism seems a natural progression from working for greater social welfare to working for greater justice with respect to race. Thus for both black and white women, gender and race were intimately entwined with their activism.[110]

The story of the elite white women who aided in the successful, albeit tumultuous desegregation of the Orleans Parish school system is not unique. It is, however, a story rarely told. In the many works on the civil rights movement to date, women like Rosa Keller, Gladys Cahn, Helen Mervis, and Betty Wisdom appear only at the margins.[111] More recent works have con-

107. Susan Lynn, "Gender and Progressive Politics: A Bridge to Social Activism of the 1960s," in *Not June Cleaver: Women and Gender in Postwar American, 1945–1960*, ed. Joanne Meyerowitz (Philadelphia: Temple University Press, 1994). See also Susan Hartmann, *The Home Front and Beyond: American Women in the 1940s* (Boston: Twayne, 1982), esp. chaps. 2, 9, and 11.

108. Kim Lacy Rogers, *Righteous Lives: Narratives of the New Orleans Civil Rights Movement* (New York: New York University Press, 1993), 150.

109. Joanne Meyerowitz, "Introduction: Women and Gender in Postwar America, 1945–1960," in *Not June Cleaver,* ed. Meyerowitz, 106.

110. Rogers, *Righteous Lives,* 150. See also Rhoda Lois Blumberg, "Careers of Women Civil Rights Activists," *Journal of Sociology and Social Welfare* (1980); and Rhoda Lois Blumberg, "White Mothers in the American Civil Rights Movement," in *Research in the Interweave of Social Roles: Women and Men,* ed. Helen Lopata, 33–50 (New York: JAI Press, 1980).

111. See Bartley, *The Rise of Massive Resistance,* 336; and Inger, "The New Orleans School

tributed to a reassessment of the role of SOS. Drawing on the long tradition of female activism in Louisiana since the 1930s, women in the 1960s were on the frontlines of the fight for change during the school desegregation crisis. They not only escorted the children to and from school in an extremely dangerous and hostile environment, but also subjected themselves, and their families, to death threats, harassment, and physical and verbal abuse. SOS members believed that "the whole back-to-school movement in New Orleans rested on the SOS ferry service," and, indeed, a number of parents "sent their children to Frantz because they trusted SOS."[112] Women lobbied city, state, and business leaders, politicians, and community members to accept desegregation; they prepared comprehensive analyses and informative publications; they appeared before the media to sway community opinion. Along with the LWV, the IWO, and even COPE, SOS added crucial influence in the movement to successfully integrate the schools.

Their status as elite southern white women ironically aided them in their efforts at racial conciliation. While they might have experienced some gender- and race-related barriers in other organizations, they chose to work within new organizations that afforded them opportunities *because* of their race, gender, and class. Moreover, their tactics—lobbying, education, fundraising, and publicity—fell well within the confines of traditional and acceptable forms of elite social activism; they worked within the system, not outside it. Though not exempt from harassment and violence at the hands of anti-integrationists, their elite status and female gender provided a margin of safety and brought pressure to bear on the white establishment.

Working on issues of racial justice in the early postwar era, as one historian notes, was a "watershed in women's social reform activism, one that would ultimately lead to more general challenges to discrimination based on

---

Crisis," 36, 97. One study, however, identifies SOS as "the most vocal" of the civic groups in New Orleans during the school desegregation crisis (see Foster, "Race Relations in the South," 144). For example, in his work on the rise of massive resistance in the South, historian Numan Bartley mentions Save Our Schools, but argues that it "arrived too late and failed to become an effective rallying point for middle-class white moderates." Moreover, Bartley suggests that its "disproportionate number of Tulane University faculty members, social workers, and other radicals" kept it from being of any consequence. Similarly, a study by Morton Inger and Robert Crain suggests that, because of the organization's disproportionate membership of Jews and liberal integrationists, SOS was seen as suspicious and was thus regarded as less effective by the wider community. Morton Inger went one step further in his assessment of the school crisis, arguing that, although the New Orleans business elite remained silent on the issue of desegregation, the school crisis of 1960 "ended when business leaders got involved."

112. "Save Our Schools, Inc.," n.d., Box 1, Folder 11, SOS Papers.

race and gender," particularly for women of community standing. In working for civil rights, they created within organizations such as SOS or the CRC what one historian calls a "community of subversives."[113] Ostracized from the larger New Orleans community, the women recall being labeled "reds," "scalawags," and "Nigger lovers"; they lost numerous friends of similar status, although not one of the women interviewed suggested that it hindered their activities in any way. In the end, they created for themselves a new community based on interracial cooperation, still economically privileged, but black and white together, nevertheless. This, in and of itself, was a revolutionary act for the privileged group from New Orleans. But even in their moment of success, a younger generation of female activists was emerging and exerting great influence in the student movement of the 1960s, a movement that ultimately rejected many of the genteel premises that underlay older activists' successes.

113. See Catherine Fosl, "There Was No Middle Ground: Anne Braden and the Southern Social Justice Movement" *NWSA Journal* 11 (1999): 17.

5

THE SIT-INS

If I had not been a part of the civil rights movement, I probably would have finished college, married a young man, had three or four kids, a very comfortable home, probably work- and career-oriented in some shape, form, or fashion and took part in most of the things that acceptable Americans take part in: go to church on Sunday, work Monday through Friday, picnic on Saturday, bring your kids up in the Boy Scouts. But I don't know that I would have been as valuable to myself as I feel that I am because . . . of what I did experience in the civil rights movement.

DORIS JEAN CASTLE-SCOTT, New Orleans civil rights activist

On February 1, 1960, four African American college students in Greensboro, North Carolina, entered the local Woolworth's and sat down at the "for whites only" lunch counter. Refused service, the four stayed until the store closed. The following day, twenty-seven students returned to the lunch counter and "sat in." Again the store refused to serve them. By week's end, more than three hundred college students were participating in sit-ins at downtown lunch counters as news of the student demonstrations began to spread to campuses across the South.[1] Within two weeks, sit-ins had taken place in eleven cities in four states; by April, in seventy-eight southern cities.[2] The sit-ins ushered in a new phase of the southern civil rights movement based on student-dominated, nonviolent direct action.

The sit-ins also reshaped the landscape of the civil rights movement. In the South, the National Association for the Advancement of Colored People (NAACP) had long dominated the struggle for civil rights. Throughout its history, the NAACP had adopted relatively conservative methods in their attempt to achieve legal and social parity, most notably through the courts.

1. Harvard Sitkoff, *The Struggle for Black Equality* (New York: Hill and Wang, 1981), 62–63.
2. August Meier and Elliot Rudwick, *CORE: A Study in the Civil Rights Movement, 1942–1968* (Urbana: University of Illinois Press, 1973), 101.

By 1960, the organization had achieved many noteworthy successes in education, voting rights, and employment, but in most southern states, black
citizens still fell far short of full equality. Despite the successes of the Baton
Rouge, Montgomery, and Tallahassee bus boycotts in 1953, 1955, and 1956,
respectively, and the creation of the Southern Christian Leadership Conference (SCLC) in 1957, by the end of the 1950s, civil rights activity in the South
had waned. The student sit-ins jump-started a lagging movement and brought
the black struggle for equality back to the forefront. As a new wave of younger
activists joined the fight to end Jim Crow, nonviolent direct action became
their tactic of choice, and the Congress of Racial Equality (CORE) and a newly
formed Student Non-Violent Coordinating Committee (SNCC) emerged as
formidable organizations.[3]

Although the NAACP retained its status as the chief civil rights organization in Louisiana, at the behest of the national organization the state's
local branches had ceased operations. In the late 1950s, the state legislature made membership in interracial organizations illegal, thus any movement activity had to stem from other sources. Many Louisiana citizens remained NAACP members, but sent their annual dues to the New York office.
This did not, however, end protest activity in the state. In a number of communities, white and black women challenged Jim Crow with the save-the-
schools movement in New Orleans and Baton Rouge, with boycotts and
picketing, and with court cases at the state and federal level. Prior to the
sit-ins, though, the movement lacked cohesiveness, and protest activity was,
for the most part, localized and uncoordinated. With the rise of the new
direct-action organizations, female students played crucial roles, and many
emerged as important leaders, chairing major organizations, mobilizing other
activists, and coordinating and organizing direct-action demonstrations.

The break in tone from the activities prior to the sit-ins of 1960 deserves
special attention. In the 1960s, the black struggle for equality took on a decidedly different mood. Both the tactics and goals of the movement grew
bolder. Younger activists embraced the philosophy of a utopian, "race-less"
society.[4] The ideal of a "Beloved Community" of blacks and whites living together equally and harmoniously in their protest activities, organizations,

3. For more information on the Southern University student movement in its early stages,
see Martin Oppenheimer, "Institutions of Higher Learning and the 1960 Sit-Ins: Some Clues
for Social Action," *Journal of Negro Education* (Summer 1963); and Martin Oppenheimer, "The
Southern Student Movement: Year One," *Journal of Negro Education* (Autumn 1964).

4. Howard Zinn, quoted in Clayborne Carson, *In Struggle: SNCC and the Black Awakening of
the 1960s* (Cambridge: Harvard University Press, 1981), 100.

and personal lives remained a goal.[5] But greater racial integration in the movement itself brought new tensions, ultimately resulting in internecine divisions in the increasingly radical civil rights organizations.

The female activists who joined this phase of the movement were different from their predecessors in important ways. First, many hailed from communities with long traditions of activism. Subsequently, many had been raised by strong, independent women who taught them and encouraged them to question the racial status quo. Second, younger and less encumbered by their "place" in a traditionally narrowly defined gendered framework, these women seldom accepted subservient positions in relation to their male counterparts. In fact, in Louisiana, a number of women assumed positions of leadership chairing major organizations or leading demonstrations. Finally, the women who came to the movement in the 1960s were, for the most part, not middle-class; they came from working-class and poor grassroots communities. While economic considerations had been the basis of the movement in the 1940s in particular, and the 1950s generally, the activists of the 1960s built on the successes of previous years and called for an end to Jim Crow discrimination in all areas of life. To be sure, what the struggle was ultimately about in the 1960s *was*, as Ella Baker so eloquently stated, "more than just a hamburger."

"IT WAS MOSTLY WOMEN"

By early March 1960, Southern University (SU) students in Baton Rouge prepared to join the growing sit-in movement. A predominantly black college, SU was chartered by the state in 1880, and in 1914 the university moved from New Orleans to Baton Rouge. By 1955, SU had 3,300 students and claimed to be the largest black institution for higher learning in the world.[6] In Baton Rouge, five student organizers, including junior Janette Houston, asked the Reverend T. J. Jemison, leader of the Baton Rouge Bus Boycott in 1953, to informally address SU students in hopes of getting them "excited

5. For SNCC's Statement of Purpose, which more fully outlines this philosophy, see Carson, *In Struggle*, 23–24.

6. Adam Fairclough, *Race and Democracy: The Civil Rights Struggle in Louisiana, 1915–1972* (Athens: University of Georgia Press, 1995), 265. See also Melinda Bartley, "Southern University Activism, 1960–63, Revisited" (master's thesis, Louisiana State University, 1973). Before the first sit-ins in Louisiana, Dillard University students began demonstrating in New Orleans in support of the student sit-ins elsewhere, marching on campus with signs proclaiming "Action Without Violence" and "Human Rights Are Civil Rights" ("Dillard Students Join in Nation-Wide Demonstrations," *Louisiana Weekly*, 12 March 1960).

about" participating in the sit-ins.[7] Student organizers initially gathered to discuss the Greensboro sit-ins and, according to Houston, "to decide whether we should send money to them, or whether we should go down there, or what we should do to support" them. They decided that Marvin Robinson, the president of the Student Government Association, would act as leader of their small contingent and that they should launch their own sit-ins in Baton Rouge.[8]

Janette Houston had a long history of bucking the Jim Crow system. As a child she had refused to sit in the "Negro" section of the bus. By the time Houston was in junior high and high school, the bus drivers often drove her directly to the jailhouse. "It happened so much," recalls Houston, "my dad just got tired of it. He said 'I think I would do better just buying you a damn bus.'" Houston further refused to drink from the "colored" water fountains and remembers employees at Kress and Woolworth's "putting her out" for drinking from the white fountain and for using the white restrooms. Before the sit-ins began, Houston also "led a few revolts on campus." In particular, she fought to get better cafeteria food after she discovered from her own research that Louisiana State University, the white university in Baton Rouge, had a larger budget allotment for food, libraries, and other amenities. By the time the sit-ins began in February, Houston was primed for protest. Houston emerged as one of seven leaders of the SU students, distributing flyers to the dormitories and organizing support.[9]

By early March, anticipating protest action on the campus, the Board of Trustees of Southern University warned that anyone participating in a sit-in "would be subject to stern disciplinary action." The student organizers took this as a challenge and a spur to organize. Marvin Robinson and Major Johns decided who would participate, keeping the date of the sit-in a secret. As word got out that the day was fast approaching, Janette Houston knew to "dress a certain kind of way, and look a certain kind of way. . . . We knew that we had to look good, dress decent, so in case something happened . . . we were not to have pocketbooks and a lot of stuff."[10]

On March 28, 1960, as Houston walked to class, a fellow student in-

7. "Chronology of Southern University Demonstrations, 7 March–1 April 1960," cited in Fairclough, *Race and Democracy*, 269; Janette Harris Houston, interview by Mary Hebert, 9 January 1994, Special Collections, Hill Memorial Library, Louisiana State University, Baton Rouge (hereafter cited as SC-LSU).

8. Houston, interview, 9 January 1994.

9. Houston, interview, 9 January 1994.

10. Houston, interview, 9 January 1994.

formed her that the sit-in was about to take place. The students met at the men's dormitory and headed downtown, where Houston, freshman Jo Ann Morris, and five other students sat in at the Kress lunch counter. The waitresses informed Houston that she and the others would have to stand at the black lunch counter, which, Houston recalled, was covered with crickets. She refused and sat directly between two whites who "started jumping up and running like I had the plague."[11] Police immediately arrested the group, charged them with disturbing the peace, and placed them in segregated jail cells. That evening the black community held a mass rally in support of the jailed students and called for a boycott of downtown stores over the Easter holiday. The following day, nine more students sat in, two at Sitman's drugstore and seven, including Sandra Ann Jones and Mary Briscoe, at the Greyhound bus station. Again they were arrested; however, this time the students remained in jail for almost a week while awaiting a court hearing. On March 30, 3,500 students marched downtown to the State Capitol and held an hour-long prayer vigil in support of the sit-ins. That day, seventeen students, including the speaker at the prayer meeting—Major Johns—were expelled from the university.[12]

News of the students' expulsion only increased the outrage in the black Baton Rouge community. At a mass meeting, SU students voted to boycott all classes until the school readmitted all seventeen students. After eight days of demonstrations, the SU president, Dr. Felton G. Clark, finally agreed to meet with Houston and seven other expelled students. Three thousand students sat in front of the building during the six-and-a-half-hour meeting. Houston remembers that the president of SU was basically "sympathetic," but that "his hands were tied because the white Board of Regents governed him."[13] As Major Johns described the scene, when the expelled students finally emerged at eleven thirty that evening and "announced their decision to leave the university, urg[ing] the other students to stay on and return to classes, there was an outcry. Some burst into tears, others shouted that they wanted to quit also." The next day, 250 students officially withdrew from Southern, with an additional 1,500 students unofficially leaving the univer-

11. Houston, interview, 9 January 1994.

12. Major Johns and Ronnie Moore, *It Happened in Baton Rouge: A Real Life Drama of Our Deep South Today* (New York: Congress of Racial Equality, April 1962), copy on file in SC-LSU; "Jail 16 in La. Sit-Down," *Louisiana Weekly*, 2 April 1960. It is interesting to note that H. Rap Brown's brother, Eddie Charles Brown Jr., was one of the students jailed for sitting in at the Greyhound bus station.

13. Houston, interview, 9 January 1994.

sity.[14] While NAACP attorney Johnnie Jones worked on reinstating the expelled students, the demonstrations in Baton Rouge ground to a halt. With
more than half of the SU student population either expelled or withdrawn
from classes, and support from Baton Rouge's black community waning, the
sit-ins in Baton Rouge unofficially ended.

Movement organizers throughout the state, however, continued their
support for the SU student protesters. Southern University Alumni Association chapters around the country issued statements condemning the actions
of Dr. Clark and the SU board. The New Orleans chapter of the Southern
University Alumni Association sent a telegram to Dr. Clark urging him to
"reconsider reinstating the suspended Southern University students." In
addition, the Consumers League of Greater New Orleans (CLGNO), a black
organization founded in 1959 in the wake of the Louisiana State Legislature's assault on the membership of the NAACP, had initiated "Don't Buy
Where You Can't Work Campaigns." On April 12, 1960, the CLGNO held a
march on Dryades Street denouncing the merchants' unwillingness to em-
ploy blacks and in support of the sit-ins. In what was heralded as a "double
feature night," five of the expelled student leaders, Houston among them,
joined the mass meeting at the end of the march. With the case of the expelled students now before the state supreme court, it seemed that the movement would now continue from New Orleans.[15]

It may have seemed that the Crescent City, in the midst of the school
desegregation crisis, was primed for such action. In 1957, however, the state
legislature enjoined the NAACP, New Orleans's most important civil rights
organization to date, from operating on any level. As a result, members of
the New Orleans chapter of the NAACP and local black merchants organized the CLGNO to continue civil rights activity in the city. Supported by
older members of the NAACP and the city's black ministerial leadership, the
CLGNO had for months picketed on Dryades Street, the main shopping district for the city's African American community. The groups also boycotted
white-owned businesses seeking access to jobs, lunch counters, and restaurants, and conducted "kneel-ins" at all-white churches in the city.

Women represented a significant number of the CLGNO membership.
Longtime activists Millie Charles and Madelon Cochrane, both members of
the NAACP in the 1950s, joined the CLGNO when the NAACP ceased formal

14. Johns and Moore, "It Happened in Baton Rouge"; "Fed Up Students Abandon SU in
Droves," *Louisiana Weekly*, 9 April 1960.
15. "Protest March Hits Dryades St. Stores" and "Reinstatement for 18 SU Expelled Students Sought," *Louisiana Weekly*, 16 April 1960.

operations. Millie Charles began her activism when she successfully challenged Louisiana State University to integrate its graduate school in 1956.
For a time, she was the only black student in LSU's School of Social Work.
She later worked with the NAACP on voter registration in the 1950s and
with the CLGNO during the boycotts. Madelon Cochrane, a fellow CLGNO
member, organized meetings, picketed stores, lunch counters, and restaurants, and was often arrested for her actions. Cochrane stressed the importance of women to the CLGNO: "Would you believe they listened to us then
because they knew the backbone of this organization was women. We were
there. Avery [Alexander] would call and say, 'Madelon, we need a meeting,
such and such a thing has happened.' And I would call at 3p.m. and say we
need to be at the Y[WCA] at 5 p.m., and these people were there, and it was
mostly women. Maybe eight to ten men, but all the rest were women. We
were the organizers."[16]

By May 1960, the Consumers League had achieved only limited success.
Although the number of African Americans hired by the Dryades Street
merchants had nominally increased, the lunch counters and restaurants
had yet to desegregate. By the summer of 1960, however, a group of young
black students working with the CLGNO decided on direct-action protests
in New Orleans through the sit-ins. Local black college students Rudy Lombard, Jerome Smith, and Oretha Castle, and a white student, Hugh Murray,
had joined the CLGNO protests in April during the Easter holiday. Other
local college students affiliated with the New Orleans NAACP Youth Council (NYC) also joined the demonstrations on Dryades Street. As word of the
sit-ins in Baton Rouge and across the country spread, New Orleans students
insisted on more direct action. "Of course the same systematic problem of
segregated lunch counters and other segregated facilities existed in New Orleans as in other places in the South," stated Oretha Castle. The students
believed that the lunch counters "certainly . . . needed to be dealt with in
New Orleans." Subsequently, the student members of the CLGNO and the
NYC met with the adult branch of the NAACP to discuss organizing sit-ins
in New Orleans. Yet, as they quickly discovered: "They didn't want to have
anything to do with it. We had a desire to do something in terms of the lunch

16. Millie Charles interview by the author, 12 December 2001. Madelon Cochrane, interview
by the author, 11 December 2001, tape recording, copy in possession of the author; Raphael
Cassimere, interview by the author, 2 March 2003, tape recording, copy in possession of the
author. Neither a manuscript collection nor papers exist for the Consumers League of Greater
New Orleans. Information on its activities was culled from newspaper articles and NAACP records, and through interviews.

counters and . . . we couldn't take the kind of action we wanted to within the NAACP framework." Oretha Castle further recalled: "Of course they felt that this was real kind of militant and radical action to be talking about sitting in and all that kind of stuff. So independently we decided to organize ourselves." The students organized themselves into a small cadre with the intention of beginning direct-action demonstrations in the city, but they soon decided to affiliate with the larger and more established Congress of Racial Equality.[17]

"WE WANTED TO BE ACTIVE"

The Congress of Racial Equality (CORE) originated in Chicago in 1942 as an offshoot of the pacifist organization the Fellowship of Reconciliation. From its inception, the organization adopted and applied the tactics of Gandhian philosophy: nonviolent direct action coupled with interracial cooperation.[18] The founders—who included two black men, James Farmer and Joe Guinn, and three whites, Bernice Fisher, Homer Jack and George Houser—believed that by applying the Gandhian technique of *satyagraha*, nonviolent direct action, they would eventually achieve the "resolution of racial and industrial conflict in America."[19]

CORE's first act was to establish Fellowship House, an interracial men's co-op that challenged the restrictive covenants in the neighborhood surrounding the University of Chicago. Per CORE's general philosophy, it was crucial that Fellowship House be interracial—part of the "Beloved Community" many civil rights activists struggled to create during the 1960s. CORE then committed itself to nonviolent direct-action tactics to combat other forms of racial discrimination. Charter members included an interracial group of twenty-two women and twenty-eight men. Initially, about half of the membership embraced a pacifist ideal; before becoming a member, individuals were educated in Gandhian philosophy and methods and had to "commit themselves to work as an integrated, disciplined group." Moreover, members had to agree to "democratic group discussion" when making policy decisions.[20]

---

17. Oretha Castle, interview by James Mosby, 26 May 1970, transcript, Ralph Bunche Civil Rights Documentation Project, Moorland-Spingarn Center, Howard University, Washington, D.C. (hereafter cited as RBCRDP).

18. Meier and Rudwick, *CORE*, 3.

19. Meier and Rudwick, *CORE*, 4.

20. Meier and Rudwick, *CORE*, 8–9.

Throughout the 1940s and early 1950s, CORE pursued nonviolent direct-action protests in small pockets of the country, although the organization concentrated most of these actions in the North. CORE's strength, like that of the NAACP, stemmed from its local chapters. The majority of its members were young college students who recruited new members on their college campuses. CORE immediately recognized the significance of the student demonstration movement that began in 1960, and as a result, it expanded throughout the South. At the onset of the sit-in movement and prior to the creation of the Student Non-Violent Coordinating Committee (SNCC), CORE directed its chapters to picket their local dime stores. It also pioneered the "jail, no bail" tactic employed by many civil rights activists, including those who formed the New Orleans chapter of CORE. Because the student movement embraced nonviolent, direct-action tactics, the Louisiana student sit-in movement was naturally drawn to CORE.[21]

Before 1960, CORE had failed in its attempts to organize chapters in the South. When the student sit-ins materialized in Baton Rouge, CORE's national field director, Jim McCain, spent a few weeks there establishing major "contacts that would later prove to be crucial in the organization's extensive work in Louisiana parishes." Southern University student leaders Major Johns and Marvin Robinson eventually joined CORE's field staff.[22] With the direct-action movement in Baton Rouge temporarily stopped cold, however, CORE set its sights on New Orleans, a key city that would mark CORE's presence in the Deep South.[23]

In the summer of 1960, black and white students from around the city met with Marvin Robinson from Baton Rouge and formed a CORE chapter in New Orleans. The first members came from the city's black colleges and universities—Dillard, Xavier, and Southern University of New Orleans. Within a few weeks, white students from Tulane, Loyola, Newcomb College, and Louisiana State University of New Orleans would join. A grassroots African American constituency, however, formed the body of CORE's membership; in fact, many members grew up in the city's Seventh and Ninth Wards—interracial, poor, working-class neighborhoods long steeped in traditions of dissent. Sisters Oretha and Doris Jean Castle, for example, attended school at one point or another with Raphael Cassimere, Matt Suarez, Doratha Smith, and Julia Aaron—all founding members of New Orleans CORE. Rudy Lombard, a dynamic black, male Xavier student, led the new

21. Meier and Rudwick, *CORE*, 101.
22. Meier and Rudwick, *CORE*, 107–8.
23. Gordon Carey to Rudy Lombard, 12 October 1960, quoted in Meier and Rudwick, *CORE*, 114.

chapter, which included both black and white women and men, many of whom later emerged as leaders of the civil rights movement across the state and the South. Yet, the majority of the members were strong, protest-oriented African American women including Oretha and Doris Castle, Jean, Alice, and Shirley Thompson, Julia Aaron, Doratha Smith, Katrina Jackson, Joyce Taylor, Ruthie Wells, and Sandra Nixon. In the end, many of them emerged as leaders in the southern student movement.[24]

The Castle sisters came from a long line of independent women. Oretha and Doris Jean were the older of three children. Their mother's parents were sharecroppers and their father's parents were independent farmers; and their own parents taught them the virtues of self-reliance. The Castles' mother and father both worked and, unlike many other black families in New Orleans, eventually saved enough money to purchase their Ninth Ward home. Oretha and Doris's mother, Virgie, is remembered as a "fiercely independent" woman who worked for Lea and Dookie Chase, the famous black restaurateurs and supporters of the civil rights movement.[25] "Their mother was definitely strong," recalls Julia Aaron, "you could see where they get it from." Because their father worked as a longshoreman and Virgie was gone most nights, the girls and their younger brother, John, were often left to tend to themselves. As Doris recalled, "a lot of self-awareness, a lot of independence [was] instilled in all three of us. We were left to manage by ourselves, of course with their guidance."[26]

The Castle home served as the unofficial headquarters for CORE. As Julia Aaron and others recalled: "Their house was open for meetings, anything we needed to do, we did it there. That was like our real headquarters." The Castles also housed the Freedom Riders, demonstrators organized by CORE to ride interstate buses and desegregate bus stations throughout the South.

24. Unfortunately, I have been unable to locate Ruthie Wells and Joyce Taylor, and Sandra Nixon refused to be interviewed. Consequently, the limited knowledge I have of them is from other interviewees, the CORE Papers, or newspaper articles.

25. Interviews with a number of activists suggest that the Chases often held integrated meetings for the NAACP counsel on the second floor above the restaurant. They also provided food to the jailed CORE activists and allowed Virgie to bring food home for the numerous activists who stayed at the Castle home. Katrina Jackson NaDang, interview by the author, 8 December 2001, tape recording, copy in possession of the author; Sybil Morial, interview by the author, 4 December 2001, tape recording, copy in possession of the author; Julia Aaron Humbles, interview by the author, 11 March 2003, tape recording, copy in possession of the author; Cassimere, interview, 2 March 2003.

26. Humbles, interview, 11 March 2003; Doris Jean Castle-Scott, interview by Kim Lacy Rogers, 19 January 1989, tape recording, Rogers-Stevens Collection.

"Nobody ever asked them [their parents] if it was alright for 375 people to parade through their house, would you feed them and stuff like that," recalled Doris Castle. "Somehow it was understood that they weren't going to go to jail, or march on the picket lines, but . . . [they] were going to play some part in making this all come about."[27] "We spent a lot of nights at that house," stated Doratha Smith. "That's one lady [Virgie] who should get a lot of credit. Even though she was in the background, she did a lot."[28]

Like the Castles, the Thompson sisters—Alice, Jean, and Shirley—grew up in the Ninth Ward and were the daughters of strict, hardworking parents. Their parents resented segregation, yet obeyed the informal racial laws of the Deep South. The Thompsons raised the three girls to be independent, but also defiant; they were taught never to say, "Yes Ma'am," to anyone for fear that they might unwittingly say it to a white person. Like the Castle home, the Thompson home was open to Freedom Riders who passed through New Orleans and needed a place to stay. Jean and Shirley first joined the NAACP Youth Council after meeting its president, Raphael Cassimere. Then they heard about CORE: "The youth division [of the NAACP] wasn't too active and we wanted to be active, in the midst of the movement," recalled Alice Thompson. They joined CORE immediately and there they met the Castles, Rudy Lombard, and Jerome Smith. Their parents' support for their actions cost their father his job, and eventually he was forced to leave the city to find work.[29]

Like the Castles and the Thompsons, Julia Humbles (née Aaron) was born and raised in New Orleans and attended public school in the Ninth Ward. Her father was a Baptist minister; consequently she was "raised in the church." Humbles graduated in the same high school class as Doris Castle and, along with the others, was a founding member of the New Orleans CORE. "There was a few of [us who] really got involved because [we] were so concerned about the things that were going on around the country," recalls Humbles. "[We] wanted to do something to help things, so we got together and organized."[30] Doratha Smith, also from the Ninth Ward, grew up knowing the Thompson sisters as their families were friends. Smith's family, like

27. Humbles, interview, 11 March 2003. Matt "Flukie" Suarez, interview by the author, 3 December 2001, tape recording; Castle-Scott, interview, 19 January 1989.

28. Doratha Smith Simmons, interview by Kim Lacy Rogers, 27 July 1988, tape recording, Rogers-Stevens Collection.

29. Alice Thompson, interview by Kim Lacy Rogers, 25 July 1988, tape recording, Rogers-Stevens Collection.

30. Humbles, interview, 11 March 2003.

Humbles's, was very religious; her parents taught her that, "everybody was the same, to treat everybody the same." She initially belonged to the NAACP Youth Chapter, but quickly joined CORE. At only fourteen or fifteen years old, she attended a CORE meeting and "liked what they were doing because the NAACP wasn't doing any direct action. I thought it was exciting."[31]

Katrina Jackson became involved because family members rented a duplex from the family of Ruthie Wells, another founding member of CORE. Born in rural Greensburg, Louisiana, she attended segregated elementary and high schools in St. Helena Parish. Like many female activists in the Louisiana movement, Jackson was reared in a family of tough women. Raised by her grandmother, she remembered her as "a strong-in-the-background" kind of woman. "She would get things done, but not necessarily come out and say she was doing it." Jackson does not recall when she first became interested in the movement, although she does remember a specific incident when her grandmother would not allow her to sit down and eat ice cream at a Rexel Drug store in their small town. She believes that that incident "was one of the things that pushed me to do it." With only a fourth-grade education, Jackson's grandmother instilled in her the value of education. After graduating high school, Jackson moved to the city to attend Southern University of New Orleans. At school, the students talked about the movement, and Jackson decided that she "wanted to be in that."[32]

In August 1960, six members of this fledgling CORE group attended the Miami Action Institute in Florida and returned to a chapter primed for action. The initial CORE membership had just ten or so founding members, the majority of them women.[33] The black YMCA on Dryades Street served as CORE headquarters where members gathered to hold meetings, make signs, and prepare for the sit-ins. Dorothy "Dottie" Zellner, later an important member of SNCC, also attended the workshop in Florida that August and returned with the New Orleans contingent to help them organize their first sit-in. "Nobody fooled themselves that this was such an easygoing city that a sit-in was going to be tolerated," Zellner notes. "Everything was segregated, everything. The restaurants . . . the schools, the libraries, everything. It wasn't a secret to people that this was going to happen."[34]

31. Simmons, interview, 27 July 1988.

32. NaDang, interview, 8 December 2001.

33. My research and interviews with living members suggests that the core members of CORE were Oretha and Doris Castle; Alice, Jean, and Shirley Thompson; Doratha Smith; Julia Aaron; and Sandra Nixon; along with Rudy Lombard, Jerome Smith, and Dave Dennis.

34. Dorothy "Dottie" Zellner, interview by the author, 8 February 2003, tape recording, copy in possession of the author.

On September 9, 1960, five black students—Jerome Smith, Ruth Despenza, Joyce Taylor, William Harper, and Archie Allen—and two white graduate students from Tulane University, Hugh Murray and William Harrel, entered the Woolworth's store on Canal Street at ten thirty in the morning and sat down at the lunch counter. After five hours, police finally arrested them and charged them with "criminal mischief." All chose CORE's "jail, no bail" tactic to challenge the legality of their arrests.[35] The following day, as rain soaked the Crescent City, eighteen members of the NAACP Youth Council picketed the store "in sympathy with a sit-in." Mayor deLesseps Morrison, already mired in the city's school desegregation battles, attempted to quell the city's direct-action movement by enforcing two acts passed by the state legislature that year banning all further picketing and sit-ins in the state.[36]

Undeterred by the mayor's threats, black and white New Orleanians continued to demonstrate. The following Friday, September 16, police arrested five members of the Consumers League of Greater New Orleans and Jim McCain of CORE for picketing the Claiborne shopping area in the Ninth Ward.[37] On Saturday, police arrested Oretha Castle, along with Rudy Lombard, Cecil Carter, and Sydney Goldfinch, and charged them with "criminal mischief" for sitting-in at the McCrory's lunch counter on Canal Street. Police additionally charged Goldfinch, a white student, with "criminal anarchy" for demonstrating alongside the three African American students. The six picketers arrested the day before greeted the four CORE members as they entered the jail and awaited bail. All four chose "jail, no bail" to "dramatize to the city of New Orleans how unjust [segregation] was."[38]

On Monday September 19, 1,500 people marched to the Claiborne shopping center to protest the arrests. A mass meeting at the International Longshoreman Association union hall followed, with more than three thousand

35. Gordon Carey, field director, to Local Contacts, memorandum, n.d.; "Peaceful Sit-Ins in New Orleans and Criminal Anarchy," "Seven in Sit-In Here Arrested," *New Orleans Times-Picayune*, 10 September 1960; Despenza, "Statement of Occurrence," 10 September 1960, Reel 20, 782, 765, and 766, Congress of Racial Equality Papers, microfilm copy at Amistad Research Center (hereafter cited as CORE Papers, ARC). Jerome Smith and Ruth Despenza attended the Miami Action Institute in August.

36. "N. Orleans Stores Picketed," press clipping, 11 September 1960, Reel 20, 768, CORE Papers, ARC; "Mayor Morrison Clamps Lid on 'Sit-Ins,'" *Louisiana Weekly*, 17 September 1960, ARC. Acts 70 and 80 provided that demonstrators could be arrested and charged with disturbing the peace provided their actions "disturb or alarm the public" and bans picketing by prohibiting the obstruction of public sidewalks.

37. Carey to local contacts, 4 November 1960, Reel 20, CORE Papers, ARC; Cochrane, interview.

38. Carey to local contacts, 4 November 1960, Reel 20, CORE Papers, ARC; Castle, interview.

supporters in attendance. Jim McCain and the student demonstrators out on bail spoke as CORE leaflets calling for a boycott of Woolworth's and McCrory's circulated through the crowd. McCain read a statement by Rudy Lombard, still in jail, that called for New Orleanians to "continue to fight bias not only at lunch counters, but in any area where segregation and discrimination is found." Reporters deemed the mass meeting the largest gathering of African Americans in New Orleans history. By week's end, nineteen new students, both black and white, expressed interest in joining CORE. Members distributed leaflets, conducted voter-registration campaigns, and made plans to continue the picketing and sit-ins. Ruth Despenza and Joyce Taylor spoke at various venues around the city, attempting to raise money to pay court costs for the arrested demonstrators.[39]

The female students' contribution to the Louisiana movement had only just begun. On September 24, 1960, the arrest of Oretha Castle and the other student demonstrators turned into a much more important event than even the national CORE office could have imagined. State assistant district attorney A. I. Kleinfeldt denounced CORE as one of a number of organizations on the United States attorney general's list of subversive organizations. Subsequently, city officials charged Castle, Lombard, Carter, and Goldfinch with advocating opposition to the State of Louisiana and conspiracy to commit anarchy.[40] As the case of the sixteen Baton Rouge students rose to the United States Supreme Court level, *Lombard, et al. v. Louisiana*, began to make its way through the state courts; it eventually found its way to the dockets of the United States Supreme Court.[41]

Almost immediately, however, CORE was drawn into the city's paramount issue: the school desegregation crisis. Genevieve Hughes, a New Yorker and the first woman on CORE's field staff, flew to New Orleans to assist during the crisis.[42] She initially approached Save Our Schools (SOS), the organization attempting to bring about a smooth integration of the public school system. Hughes was met with strong resistance, however, as the all-white

39. "Four More CORE Members Arrested in 'Sit-In'" and "Arrest Six," *Louisiana Weekly*, 24 September 1960; Carey to Local Contacts, n.d., "Rudy's Statement at City-Wide Meeting," 27 September 1960, "Report of James T. McCain, New Orleans, Louisiana, 8–25 September 1960," Reel 20, 782–97, CORE Papers, ARC; "Aid from Bishop F. D. Jordan and AME Ministers of the New Orleans AME Union," by Ruth Despenza, Reel 40, 860, CORE Papers, ARC.

40. "Report of McCain," 8–25 September 1960, Reel 20, 787, CORE Papers, ARC.

41. "Plan Appeal for 16 to US Supreme Court" and "High Court Weighs Louisiana Sit-In Case," *Louisiana Weekly*, Saturday, 15 October 1960 and 24 November 1962.

42. Meier and Rudwick, *CORE*, 113.

membership of SOS believed the best way to handle the school crisis was with as little dissension as possible, and that meant keeping the direct-action movement separate from the school issue. Members of SOS had, in fact, approached CORE prior to the sit-ins, urging them to reconsider beginning direct action in the city, as the climate was already ripe for trouble and they did not want to "rock the boat."[43] By November, when two schools in the Ninth Ward were scheduled for integration, members of SOS expressed their dismay over CORE's involvement in the integration crisis.[44] Although a number of CORE members individually supported the parents and children integrating the schools, the larger organization backed off. CORE did, however, show its support by circulating a petition "in appreciation and support for the courage shown by the children and parents involved in the recent integration of the New Orleans public schools."[45]

Although CORE historians August Meier and Elliot Rudwick and Louisiana civil rights movement historian Adam Fairclough assert that the school desegregation crisis in New Orleans overshadowed the sit-in movement and led to its suspension, evidence suggests that CORE continued to hold spontaneous, small, direct-action demonstrations. As news of the sit-ins and subsequent arrests spread to the seven campuses in the city, black and white students joined CORE in greater numbers. As in other areas of the South, the New Orleans sit-ins reenergized the lagging civil rights movement led by the black male ministers.[46] The Consumers League, for example, had made little headway on behalf of New Orleans black citizens, while the NAACP branch in New Orleans existed, essentially, in name only. CORE had worked alongside the CLGNO picketing and boycotting, but the students in CORE were willing to press the city further. CORE's membership surged from an influx of students, many of them from all-white Tulane University. With this larger membership base, CORE decided to continue its direct-action campaign.

Three white women were among the newly interested student constituency from Newcomb College, a small but historic women's college located on the campus of Tulane University. Margaret Leonard and Connie Bradford

43. Betty Wisdom to Paul Rilling, August 1960, Series IV, Reel 143, Save Our Schools Papers, Library of Congress, Washington, D.C. (hereafter cited as SOS Papers).

44. Wisdom to Rilling, and Rilling to Wisdom, 24 November 1960 and 30 November 1960, Series IV, Reel 143, SOS Papers.

45. Memo from Rudy Lombard, November 1960, Series 5, Reel 20, CORE Papers, ARC.

46. Fairclough, *Race and Democracy*, 275.

hailed from prestigious southern families. A third, Jill Finsten, a Jew from Canada, had moved with her family to Florida at age fourteen. Leonard's parents were well-known liberals in Macon, Georgia, who openly advocated integration; her father was the editor of the *Macon Telegraph*, and her mother, a member of the NAACP, wrote a liberal-leaning column for the *Atlanta Journal*. Bradford grew up in a socially prominent Birmingham, Alabama, family that boasted close ties to Police Commissioner Eugene "Bull" Connor. Leonard, Bradford, and Finsten openly participated in the sit-ins and picketing.[47]

Margaret Leonard was the first white Newcomb student to join CORE. After reading about the sit-ins in the newspaper, she wrote a letter to member Sidney Goldfinch expressing her support of his activities and of CORE's work in general. He subsequently called and asked her to attend a CORE meeting, and she agreed. Leonard attended a meeting one Thursday night with a few other girls from Newcomb, but she recalls that the other girls' parents eventually forced them to drop out. After the meeting, Jerome Smith approached her and asked if she would participate in a sit-in. The following Saturday, October 15, 1960, Leonard sat in for the first time at F. W. Woolworth's. She arrived at the five-and-dime with Smith and two black women, Joyce Taylor and Anna Mae Giles. "We had some kind of little trick so that Negroes could actually eat," Leonard recalls. "I would go to the white counter and order food and then a Negro would come and sit next to me and I'd give him my food. And then, when I got through with that, I would go to the Negro counter and some Negro would have ordered it because they wouldn't serve me over there." Police arrested Leonard, along with two black CORE members, Kermit Moran and Anna Mae Giles. At the station, the police asked her "why, as a southern girl, I was doing this. . . . Why did I feel this way . . . and I just said that I always had." The second time she was arrested, Leonard states, "they didn't bother."[48]

A week later, undeterred by her first arrest, Leonard and another Newcomb student, Annette Horsch, and fourteen other CORE members, sat in at

47. Margaret Leonard, interview by the author, 29 March 2003, tape recording, copy in possession of the author; Connie Bradford Harse, interview by the author, 19 March 2003.

48. Leonard, interview by the author, 29 March 2003; Leonard, interview by John H. Britton, 3 August 1967, RBCRDP; report by Anna Mae Giles, 15 October 1960, and report by Margaret "Sissie" Leonard, 15 October 1960, Reel 40, CORE Papers, ARC; Margaret Leonard, "A Southern White Girl's First Project," *CORE-LATOR*, November 1960, Reel 13, 76, CORE Papers, Addendum, Howard University Library, Washington, D.C. (hereafter cited as CORE Addendum, HU).

Woolworth's.[49] All "voluntarily" agreed to go to the police station for ques-tioning, but none were booked.[50] Immediately Leonard's activities began af-fecting her standing in school. Like Tulane, Newcomb College was not inte-grated, and Leonard was one of only a handful of women at the college brave enough to campaign for integration. Some students snubbed her, while oth-ers said "snotty things" to her. Instead of conceding, Leonard began to "ex-amine herself" and realized that "the things that they were saying about her were not true. As a matter of fact," Leonard continued, "I decided that it was my strength and security that made me able [to participate in the movement] and if the other people were [as] strong and secure as I was, they would have done it too." Dealing with hostile students was one mat-ter; dealing with school administrators and the headmother of her dormi-tory was another. Because of her involvement with CORE, the headmother instructed the house council to give Leonard "call downs," a form of punish-ment akin to being grounded. At one point, Leonard brought a black friend from CORE to the campus cafeteria and then to her dormitory. The dean of Newcomb called her that evening and threatened her with expulsion if she ever did it again.[51]

Like Leonard, Connie Bradford joined CORE in late 1960 after attending a meeting, where, ironically, she recalls, she went "to prove that segregation was the best thing" for the South. Unlike Margaret Leonard, Bradford grew up in a traditional, white southern family that embraced the Old South men-tality. She recalls that as a child, she imagined that if a black person touched her, the color would rub off. At the CORE meeting, however, Bradford had what she called an "epiphany." She met black students "just like me," and her attitudes regarding segregation changed: "I shook their hands and talked to them. My head was turned around real instantaneously." Bradford im-mediately joined the movement and never looked back, even at the cost of her relationship with her family. At one point, when home in Birmingham during the summer of 1961, her grandparents and parents, with the help of Bull Connor, attempted to institutionalize her in Tuscaloosa, taking her civil rights work as evidence of her insanity. Word of her family's plans reached

49. Margaret Leonard and Annette Horsch were two of only four whites who participated in that second sit-in in October. Although black women members of CORE sat in, they were the only two white women involved.

50. "16 Questioned in Sit-In Probe," *New Orleans Times-Picayune*, 23 October 1960.

51. Leonard, interview by the author, 29 March 2003; Leonard, interview by Britton, 3 Au-gust 1967.

her activist friends. In an incident seemingly out of an action film, the Reverend Fred Shuttlesworth, the leader of the Birmingham movement, spirited Bradford out of her family's home and took her to the safety of Louisville, Kentucky, and the home of the white civil rights activist Anne Braden. She returned to school in New Orleans in the fall, but not before she got word that her father had forbid her to return home.[52]

Bradford remained active in CORE until her junior year, when she went to Europe on a college exchange program. In addition to the regular sit-ins, picketing, and other demonstrations, Bradford acted as CORE's photographer, documenting the harassment and hostility to which the demonstrators were often subjected. Bradford, herself, was often subjected to violence while demonstrating. In one instance, while picketing on Canal Street with fellow CORE member Pat Smith, a black female student, a white woman attacked her, shoving her against a parked car, kicking and hitting her "around the shoulders and body with her purse and her hands."[53] When sitting in, Bradford was often spit on and, in one incident, had a cigarette put out on her back. Still, she stated that she felt "extremely grateful for the support of the other New Orleans CORE members," noting that the incidents only increased her faith in the philosophy of nonviolence.[54]

Unlike Leonard and Bradford, Jill Finsten did not grow up in the South. According to Finsten, "I was the quintessential outside agitator." Finsten feels that despite what Americans believe, Canada was much like America, a truly segregated and racist society. Finsten's knowledge of a segregated world stems from growing up as a Jew. "Jews were very much a separate culture," she states. "My attitude about injustice is very much shaped by being chased home by girls who called me a dirty Jew." From these experiences, Finsten believes that the line between being Jewish and being black is very fluid; that belief subsequently affected her participation in the southern civil rights movement.[55]

Finsten applied to Newcomb at the behest of her father, who had re-

52. Connie Bradford Harse, interview by the author, 19 March 2003.

53. "Nonviolence on a New Orleans Picket Line," Connie Bradford, *CORE-LATOR*, April 1961, Reel 13, 76, CORE Addendum, HU.

54. Harse, interview, 19 March 2003; Report of New Orleans CORE Action by Connie Bradford, 16 April 1961, Reel 40, 905, CORE Papers, ARC.

55. Jill Axler Finsten, interview by the author, 23 May 2004, tape recording, copy in possession of the author. For more information on the role of Jewish women in the movement, see Debra Schultz, *Going South: Jewish Women in the Civil Rights Movement* (New York: New York University Press, 2001); and Clive Webb, *Fight Against Fear: Southern Jew and the Black Civil Rights Movement* (Athens: University of Georgia Press, 2002).

searched the college's background and "found out that it . . . was a 'good girls' school." She arrived in New Orleans in the summer of 1960 to study art history. Initially, Finsten attempted to join "the sorority crowd," but soon realized that she did not fit in there. After reading an article about Margaret Leonard's involvement with the movement in a local paper, Finsten knocked on her dorm room door and expressed interest in joining CORE. She had heard of the civil rights movement, the sit-ins, picketing, and later the Freedom Rides, and "wanted to make a contribution."[56]

Finsten attended her first CORE meeting alone and, like Leonard and Bradford, immediately immersed herself in the movement structure. She recalls that the groups were rather "smallish," mostly black, and that they sat and talked for hours about how they needed to dress well, look nice, and act proper. Every Saturday, Finsten and other CORE members picketed and sat in at the local Woolworth's on Canal Street downtown and, she recalls: "I was terrified every time I went. Every Saturday morning I had diarrhea." Finsten also worked on voter registration and recalls feeling extremely frustrated at the apparent apathy of the people that either "wouldn't vote, or didn't feel that their vote made a difference." "I could feel the sense of hopelessness," she explains: "I felt that here we are busting our butts, pounding the pavement and trying to help people and the reaction was total nothing. It really took awhile to sink in that a lifetime of being treated a certain way, . . . well, you don't want a bunch of little bright-eyed, bushy-tailed kids coming in and bossing you around. They had seen an awful lot more than I had and to them, voting was certainly not going to change their lives."[57]

Like those of Margaret Leonard, Finsten's political activities, prompted reaction from Newcomb administrators. On one occasion, the dean called her to his office and said, "I know that you're involved with CORE and I want you to know that there are a lot of us who admire what you're doing, but we can't take responsibility for you." Just knowing that the dean "admired her" made her feel very brave. When the dean then called her parents, they responded by saying that they knew of her involvement and that they were very proud of her. The main problem for Finsten, however, did not involve the school itself; as a result of her activism, Finsten became a social pariah. "Being friends with me," she states, "was like social poison." When her roommate asked her to move out, a girl across the hall, Mary Bell,

56. Finsten, interview, 23 March 2004.
57. Finsten, interview, 23 March 2004.

a sorority girl, let Finsten move in with her. The two remain friends to this day. In another incident, the mother of a boy Finsten dated begged her, "on hands and knees," to end her involvement with CORE.[58] Of course, she did no such thing.

Like Leonard and Bradford, Finsten often found herself in precarious situations. While sitting in at the local Woolworth's one Saturday, nervously chatting with a young black male sitting next to her, Finsten noticed three white men nearby. She recalls that in an instant one of the white men grabbed a hot coffeepot and poured the coffee all over her black companion. "It was just so deliberate," she recalled. "It was my first real inkling, the first time I was really scared. Nobody lifted a finger to help." On another occasion, while picketing one Saturday, Finsten noticed a white woman lean down and whisper in her young son's ear. The boy promptly walked up to Finsten and called her a "Nigger lover." She recalled her "shock" and her realization that this was how people "learned racism."[59]

By December 1960, the sit-ins were occurring with less frequency, although throughout October and into November, CORE members continued to distribute leaflets and picket daily. On December 10, police arrested Margaret Leonard and eight other students for distributing leaflets that urged a boycott of two chain stores in New Orleans. As was often the case, Leonard was the only white woman involved.[60] In early 1961, a revitalized New Orleans movement, its members fresh from the holiday break, resumed their demonstrations in New Orleans. By February, CORE members began testing the December 1960 Supreme Court ruling in *Boynton v. Virginia* prohibiting segregation in terminal facilities in interstate transportation at local Greyhound and Trailways bus stations. Two white students, Dave Hamilton and Anne Higgins, entered the Greyhound bus station to observe while two black students, Nathaniel Harry and Carol Jackson, sat at the lunch counter and placed their orders. Much to their surprise, they were served.[61]

At the same time, the Consumers League of Greater New Orleans continued its demonstrations. On March 5, 1961, in an unprecedented move, the state police arrested Elizabeth Moorland, Marguerite Thomas, and Reverend Avery Alexander for picketing a white-owned supermarket in a black

58. Finsten, interview, 23 March 2004.

59. Finsten, interview, 23 March 2004.

60. Gordon Carey to Local Contacts, "Peaceful Sit-Ins in New Orleans and Criminal Anarchy, Part II," 4 November 1960, Reel 40, 838, CORE Papers, ARC.

61. *Louisiana Weekly* notes, 18 March 1961, ARC.

neighborhood. That same evening, the state police arrested five others including Madelon Cochrane and fellow CLGNO member Nora Lee Pruitt-
Daly. All were charged with criminal mischief, vagrancy, and disturbing the
peace. Although all were released, they challenged the constitutionality of an
arrest by the state and promised to return again the following Saturday to
continue to picket the A&P supermarket and Kaufmann's department store
and to support CORE's efforts at Woolworth's and McCrory's. The CLGNO
also planned a march to city hall and a mass meeting for the following week-
end.[62] The CLGNO and CORE jointly petitioned the mayor to refrain from
arresting the picketers. Over the Easter holiday, CORE organized a mass
boycott and picket of the downtown stores, including McCrory's and Woolworth's.[63]

One incident in the spring of 1961 illustrates the dedication of arguably
the most visible female student activist in New Orleans. On a Wednesday
evening in March, Oretha Castle, her sister, Doris, and other members of
CORE staged a demonstration in front of a department store on Dryades
Street. As with other demonstrations, the picketing lasted well into the
evening. CORE then held an organizational meeting, after which Oretha
and her sister retired to their family home. While Doris sat on the toilet in
the bathroom smoking a cigarette and talking on the phone, fellow CORE
member Julia Aaron sat on the floor of the sisters' bedroom. Doris and Julia
noticed that Oretha was lying down in the bedroom she had shared with
her sister growing up, and continued to share when Oretha was separated
from her husband, which, as Doris recalled, was rather frequent at the time.
Knowing that Oretha was less than domestically inclined, Doris initially believed that Oretha was just trying to keep from doing chores. As Doris later
recalled, "My sister was a glorious person for the world, but . . . there was
nothing about my sister that was domestic."[64]

Doris finished her cigarette and went in to rouse her sister, but Oretha
seemed to be in pain, holding her stomach and moaning. She stood up from
the bed, her large frame causing her to tower somewhat over her smaller
sister, and, as she walked toward the bathroom, Doris noticed a puddle of
water on the floor where Oretha stood. Doris and Julia argued with her
about calling a doctor, and finally Oretha conceded. The doctor told them

62. "League Vows to Picket Again Sat.," *Louisiana Weekly*, 11 March 1961.

63. *Louisiana Weekly* notes, 18 March and 11 April 1961.

64. Doris-Jean Castle-Scott, interview by Kim Lacy Rogers, 19 January 1989, tape recording,
Rogers-Stevens Collection; Humbles, interview, 11 March 2003.

to come immediately to the hospital, but Oretha knew she would not make it; the head of her son was already out. Oretha asked her sister to "hold her tight," and that evening, after a CORE meeting and picketing, she gave birth to her second son, Martin Luther. For nine months, no one, not the members of CORE, nor her immediate family, had known that she was pregnant as she attended school and worked daily in the movement. In fact, the previous Friday, she had gone to the dean of Southern University of New Orleans, where she attended school, and asked for a week's leave, knowing somehow that she would give birth that next week. "She had it all worked out," remarked her sister. "Her position about it was, "I'm pregnant, I'm gonna have the baby, I'm going to school, I am doing all of these other things, now what do I do to keep it all together, keep it going.'" She went back to classes the following Monday and resumed her spot on the picket lines. As Aaron recalled, Oretha "was definitely a very, very outstanding woman."[65]

That spring, CORE faced a series of legal challenges due to the arrests of Oretha Castle and three other CORE members for criminal mischief, among other charges. The judge refused to dismiss the charges of "criminal mischief," ruling that "it is not an abuse of police power to enact laws for the preservation of public peace" and that persons who "refuse to leave an establishment are subject to arrest and prosecution under the law."[66] Represented by the white attorney John P. Nelson Jr. and the young black attorneys Lolis Elie, Robert Collins, and Nils Douglas, the four entered into a history-making court case, *Lombard v. Louisiana,* which eventually ended up at the Supreme Court.[67] After the Louisiana State Supreme Court upheld the convictions of the four arrested students, CORE attorneys filed an appeal to the U.S. Supreme Court. In 1963, Supreme Court Justice Earl Warren wrote the opinion, which overturned the Louisiana conviction, stating it was a violation of the Fourteenth Amendment and an attempt, essentially, to "quash the sit-in."[68] The judgment in *Lombard v. Louisiana,* described by one reporter as "one of the most bitterly-contested civil rights cases of [the] decade," was one of the most celebrated successes in CORE's history. When asked about the judgment, Oretha Castle simply stated: "We don't feel that the decision should necessarily cause Negroes to believe that great progress

65. Castle-Scott, interview, 19 January 1989; Humbles, interview, 11 March 2003.

66. "4 Sit-Ins Lose Round in Court, Trial Set December 7," *Louisiana Weekly,* 3 December 1960.

67. "CORE To Carry Sit-In Fight to Supreme Court," *Louisiana Weekly,* 21 January 1961.

68. "LA Supreme Court Upholds Convictions of 4 Sit-Ins," "High Court Weights La. 'Sit-In' Case" and "Supreme Court Action Clears Four Students," *Louisiana Weekly,* 8 July 1961, 24 November 1962, and 25 May 1963.

has been accomplished. America is in a sad state when it is necessary for the highest court to be obliged to rule that business establishments cannot bar patrons because of race or color."[69]

The New Orleans CORE won another significant legal battle after police arrested Julia Aaron, Connie Bradford, Doris Castle, Jerome Smith, and Dave Dennis in April for "obstructing public passage" while distributing leaflets in the rear of the Woolworth's and McCrory's stores on Canal Street. Police arrested Bradford, the only white student present, for photographing the demonstration, although she was released shortly afterward. Aaron, Castle, Smith, and Dennis chose "jail, no bail."[70] Two days later, police arrested CORE members Geraldine Conrad and Alice Thompson for picketing the rear entrances to Woolworth's and McCrory's. They, too, chose to remain in jail, although the police released Doris Castle when they discovered that she was suffering from acute appendicitis. With the five transferred to the parish prison jail indefinitely, CORE continued to picket the stores, distributing leaflets urging a boycott of the two chains, and petitioning the mayor regarding the arrests.[71] In a further attempt to thwart segregation, two white female members of CORE attempted to visit the three black women in jail. According to Anne Higgins, the two women argued with the prison warden for hours, but he still refused their request, telling them to come back another day. Undeterred, the two returned the following Sunday to visit Aaron, Conrad, and Thompson, and again they confronted what Higgins called the "meanness and brutality in the faces" of the prison officials. The warden stated that he had "decided that it would not be a good idea to set this precedent of mixing the races."[72] In 1962, the Louisiana State Supreme Court overturned the convictions of the five CORE members.

Much like the southern student movement writ large, the Louisiana student movement had sparked and refueled the lagging movement of the 1950s. Beginning with the sit-ins in Baton Rouge that spread to New Orleans and other areas of the state, young women and men, both black and white, contributed to the movement's ultimate success against Jim Crow. Dur-

69. Oretha Castle quoted in *Louisiana Weekly*, 24 November 1962.

70. "CORE Pickets Say 'Jail, No Bail' after Arrest," *Louisiana Weekly*, 22 April 1961.

71. Barbara Brent to Marvin Rich, 25 April 1961, Reel 40, 914, CORE Papers, ARC; "Jail Two More CORE Pickets," and "CORE Continues Picketing," *Louisiana Weekly*, 29 April and 6 May 1961, ARC. The picture in the paper shows an unidentified black woman picketing with a "Don't Buy Where You Can't Eat" sign.

72. Report of Anne Higgins and anonymous to CORE, n.d., Reel 20, CORE Papers, ARC. There is no indication as to the identity of the other white girl who wrote the report; however, it may have been Margaret Leonard or Connie Bradford.

ing much of its existence, a core group of African American women formed and guided the New Orleans chapter of the Congress of Racial Equality. To be sure, women like the Castles, the Thompsons, Julia Aaron, Doratha Smith, Connie Bradford, Margaret Leonard, and Jill Finsten endured harassment and violence at the hands of whites on the picket lines, in sit-ins, and in jail.

This younger generation of women stared down the ugly face of racism and brought pressure to bear on their communities in their efforts to achieve racial justice. While the commitment to the goals of nonviolent passive resistance outlined by Martin Luther King Jr. and his followers in the 1950s remained steadfast, the more direct and forceful actions on the part of a younger generation of women dramatized the inherent inequalities that defined Louisiana's social and political structure. The sustained and relentless actions on the part of Louisiana women forced community leaders to acknowledge both the inequities faced by African Americans and also, at times, their humanity. The momentum wore down community officials and ultimately led many to reassess southern mores. Despite their almost daily exposure to the ugly face of white, southern racism, it was these women who fought fiercely to participate in what became CORE's feature project, the Freedom Rides.

6

THE FREEDOM RIDES AND THE END OF THE BELOVED COMMUNITY IN NEW ORLEANS

I feel that my experiences, my sacrifices, are a necessary phase in our nonviolent efforts to secure first-class citizenship. Freedom Rides must continue until all vestiges
of travel segregation are erased. Young people everywhere should join this movement.
As for me, I would not hesitate to do the same thing over again.

SANDRA NIXON, Freedom Rider

As the New Orleans group began to emerge as a one of CORE's most
prominent chapters, its members experienced a further boost when
the national CORE planned its most famous campaign—the Freedom Rides—scheduled to terminate in New Orleans on May 17, 1961. Modeled after the 1947 Journey of Reconciliation, the riders intended to test
interstate travel facilities from Washington, D. C., through the Deep South.
Arrested riders were expected to adhere to CORE's philosophy of "jail, no
bail." New Orleans CORE members prepared for the arrival of the riders,
who left Washington, D.C., on May 4, all the while continuing direct action
demonstrations in the city. However, prior to the national rides, a contingent from New Orleans conducted "test Freedom Rides" from New Orleans
to McComb, Mississippi. Five CORE members—Alice Thompson, Doratha
Smith, George Raymond, Rudy Lombard, and Jerome Smith—agreed to act
as test riders, traveling by bus to McComb, entering the bus station, and returning home on the bus. The rides, however, did not go according to plan.

When they arrived at the station in McComb, Thompson, Doratha Smith,
Jerome Smith, and Raymond entered the bus station and sat at the counter.

While Lombard bought tickets for the rest of the group, Thompson, Doratha Smith, and Jerome Smith moved into the white waiting room. Then someone poured coffee on George Raymond, and, as Doratha Smith recalled, "all hell broke loose." Alice Thompson and Doratha Smith were pulled off their seats, kicked, and slapped while Jerome Smith was beaten with brass knuckles. "Somehow," Smith recalled, "we managed to get away. I ran to the colored section. The people knew what was going on but they didn't come out, they didn't do anything. I was being chased by some of the lovely citizens of McComb." As Alice Thompson recalled, "The FBI, television people, the police and everybody stood by and watched, and if it wasn't for a few black people in the town, [we] would have been killed." Local blacks at the station eventually surrounded Doratha Smith to protect her. "My heart was pounding so hard," stated Smith. "I thought, 'God, I am never gonna live to see another day.' I thought sure I would be killed that day and when I calmed down, I just said to myself, 'You're going to walk out of this crowd and just keep walking like you've lived in McComb all of your life.' I walked and walked until I didn't see a crowd anymore [and then] I just started running [until] I heard my name." Jerome and the others had somehow found a truck, but Smith was so frightened she had managed to outrun the truck.[1]

When Smith finally joined them, the group returned to the black section of town and "got all patched up." Alice Thompson remembered it as "the only time that I really was afraid for my life. Those people had death in their eyes and hearts, they really wanted to kill us." Jerome Smith tried to contact Attorney General Robert Kennedy, while a reporter from the *New York Times* interviewed them about the experience. Although they had planned to return to the bus station, they were warned not to try to go back. Eventually the group flagged down another bus headed for New Orleans. When it broke down about an hour north of New Orleans in Hammond, Louisiana, the FBI showed up to take them back to New Orleans, but they refused. When they finally arrived in New Orleans, members of CORE were waiting for them at the bus terminal. The five test riders went to the FBI office to give statements. Doratha Smith remembered that when she told the officer that Jerome was beaten with brass knuckles, they asked her, "Are you sure you know what brass knuckles look like?" That question, Smith recalled, only served to make her want to ride again.[2]

As a result of the massive wave of sit-ins that spread across the Deep

1. Doratha Smith Simmons, interview by Kim Lacy Rogers, 27 July 1988, tape recording; Alice Thompson, interview by Kim Lacy Rogers, 25 July 1988, both in Rogers-Stevens Collection.

2. Simmons, interview, 27 July 1988; Thompson, interview, 25 July 1988.

South, CORE's plan to hold a second "Freedom Ride" took root. To be sure, the sit-ins had once again made civil rights for blacks a part of the American dialogue. Movement leaders thought that the momentum might subside if they failed to push their agenda further. Newly energized younger activists joined the movement in large numbers.

By the mid-1960s, women were increasingly becoming highly visible and important members of the major civil rights organizations that had panned out across the South, working in both rural and urban communities to rally the masses. This trend was no more evident than in Louisiana, where a brazen and defiantly committed young woman, Oretha Castle Haley, presided over what soon became CORE's most recognizable chapter. And women continued to dominate the New Orleans movement, working through a handful of organizations and institutions to achieve varying levels of equality. In the end, ideological differences would lead African American female members of CORE to question their organization's role in creating and maintaining the highly sought after "beloved community."

"WE . . . HAD ENOUGH OF THE ARMOR
OF WHAT WE WERE ALL ABOUT"

On May 4, 1961, the first contingent of Freedom Riders, including six white and seven black men and women, young and old, students, professionals, and clergy members, left Washington, D.C., to begin the trip South to New Orleans. The Rides progressed through the upper southern states with relatively little incident. But on Mother's Day, May 14, 1961, just outside of Anniston, Alabama, an unruly mob surrounded the buses. Members of the crowd threw smoke bombs into the bus and attacked the riders as they attempted to disembark. A Trailways bus arrived in Birmingham and confronted a similar scene. Although the riders had decided to continue on to Montgomery, the bus drivers refused to take the group any farther. That evening the riders left Alabama, arriving in New Orleans by plane; CORE disbanded the Freedom Rides.[3]

3. Leon Friedman, ed., *The Civil Rights Revolution: Basic Documents of the Civil Rights Movement* (New York: Walker, 1967), 51–59; John Lewis, *Walking with the Wind: A Memoir of the Movement* (New York: Simon and Schuster, 1998), 115–77; James Peck, *Freedom Ride* (New York: Simon and Schuster, 1962); Howell Raines, *My Soul Is Rested: The Story of the Civil Rights Movement in the Deep South* (New York: Penguin Books, 1983), 109–29; Harvard Sitkoff, *The Struggle for Black Equality* (New York: Hill and Wang, 1993), 88–101; "'Democracy Test' Abandoned in Breakdown of Ala. Law, Order," *Louisiana Weekly*, 20 May 1961; Genevieve Hughes to Marvin Rich and Gordon Carey, 15 May 1961, Reel 25, 116, CORE Papers, ARC.

New Orleans quickly became Freedom Ride central. Local CORE members housed and fed the physically and emotionally injured riders. Some stayed at the Castle home, some with other local activists. At the Castles' home that evening, Doris Jean Castle, Dave Dennis, and other CORE members "got drunk on Jack Daniels, all of us with the notion," recalled Doris Castle, "that we were going to pick up the Freedom Rides."

Doris, the younger sister of Oretha, had graduated from high school in May 1960 and, while visiting her younger brother in Chicago, heard that her older sister had been arrested for demonstrating with the Consumers League. When she returned home, Oretha asked Doris to accompany her to a civil rights meeting, and without hesitation Doris joined the movement. By the time the Freedom Rides had begun, Doris had already spent time in jail. In early 1961, police arrested Doris for "obstructing pedestrian traffic by way of a picket sign," and she spent five days in the New Orleans Parish Prison.[4]

"We were here in New Orleans," Doris stated, "where the ride was to terminate anyway [and we] decided that we should go to Montgomery and pick up the ride and bring it back to New Orleans."[5] CORE sponsored a Freedom Ride rally at the Mount Zion Baptist Church in downtown New Orleans with more than one thousand supporters in attendance. Riders from the first group spoke at the rally, encouraging the continuation of the rides. The city of New Orleans officially became the "checkpoint" for the resumed rides.

Despite the violence CORE members had experienced in McComb, several CORE members in New Orleans applied to participate in the national Freedom Rides; five of the seven were women: Doris Castle, Sandra Nixon, Jean and Shirley Thompson, and Julia Aaron. Margaret Leonard, a Newcomb student and CORE alumna, and Miriam Feingold, a white Swarthmore student who would return to rural Louisiana after the Freedom Rides to work on voter registration, joined the other five women for the second leg of the Freedom Rides.[6] The participants understood the dangers they could face, particularly in the Deep South. As CORE leader James Farmer stated, CORE counted on the "bigots in the South to do our work for us."[7] On the applica-

4. "Doris Jean Castle," Reel 10, 1, CORE Addendum, HU.

5. Doris Jean Castle-Scott, interview by Kim Lacy Rogers, 19 January 1989, tape recording, Rogers-Stevens Collection.

6. "Freedom Riders from the Louisiana Area," n.d., Reel 25, 458, CORE Papers, ARC; Margaret Leonard, interview by the author, 29 March 2003, tape recording, copy in possession of the author; Miriam "Mimi" Feingold, interviews by the author, 1 and 22 December 2002, tape recordings, copies in possession of the author.

7. Quoted in Sitkoff, The Struggle for Black Equality, 89.

tion, riders were told that they were "participating in a non-violent protest against racial discrimination [and] that arrest or personal injury . . . might result." Julia Aaron's application illustrates the resolve of the participants. "My first contact with the non-violent philosophy was with New Orleans CORE," she wrote.

> This philosophy inspired my heart and soul so much that I have participated in several forms of social action with an unlimited dedication. Because of my sincere dedication and profound beliefs in CORE and its aims, I hope I'm given the opportunity to participate in this project which I feel will help to remove the sins of human injustice from our society. Consequently, I hope that you will feel that I have the "material" that will help [make the] Freedom Ride a success.[8]

Within days of the first riders arriving in New Orleans, a busload of New Orleans CORE members, "mostly female rank and file members . . . came to Montgomery to confront the CORE leaders who wanted to suspend the rides." They joined Diane Nash and the Nashville Student Union, and, as fellow civil rights activist Sheila Michaels has noted, "It was the young people in both groups who very vocally forced the continuation of the Freedom Rides."[9]

This second contingent of riders was warned not to go to Montgomery, that it would be a "bloodbath."[10] Still, one group, Margaret Leonard and Miriam Feingold among them, met in Atlanta and took a bus to Montgomery. In the meantime, Doris Castle, Julia Aaron, Sandra Nixon, and the Thompson sisters, Jean and Shirley, went in two groups directly from New Orleans to Montgomery, only to be met by a mob. As Miriam Feingold remembers: "It absolutely looked like something out of Hollywood central casting. I have never seen such a huge group of rednecks in my life." But the police kept the mob at bay as CORE had made arrangements with the local authorities not to be arrested upon arriving in Montgomery that evening. All of the riders spent the night at the homes of local blacks and prepared to continue the rides to Jackson, Mississippi, the following day. "We were told to stay away from the windows where we could be seen," said Feingold. "They would get in trouble for having white guests overnight. I gained an enormous appre-

8. "Freedom Ride Application—Julia Aaron," Reel 25, 456, CORE Papers, ARC.

9. Sheila Michaels, e-mail message to SNCC list-serve, 27 October 2001.

10. Quoted in David Garrow, ed., *We Shall Overcome: The Civil Rights Movement in the United States in the 1950s and 1960s*, vol. 2 (New York: Carlson, 1989), 967.

ciation for the people living in these communities because long after we had come and gone, they had to live with the consequences."[11]

While in Montgomery, and with the assistance of the Montgomery Improvement Association, made famous during the Montgomery Bus Boycott, and other local civil rights activists, the riders prepared to head to Jackson. Members of CORE, the Nashville Student Union, SNCC, and SCLC formed the Freedom Ride Coordinating Committee with the objective of filling the jails in Jackson in order to keep media attention focused on the Rides. The riders trained that evening in the tactics of nonviolent civil disobedience. They learned how to "curl up when people start hitting you, not to hit back and not to scream." Some of the riders made out wills or gave sealed letters to organizers for their families in the event that they were killed. Others wrote their names and family information on pieces of paper and stuck them in their pockets.[12] "That night we got on the train to go [on the Rides]," Doris Castle recalled, "I remember that we were all afraid."[13]

When they arrived in Montgomery, they were greeted by "blue shirts with sticks in their hands[;] nevertheless, [we did not] waiver. You just do it. We had to be out of our minds.'"[14] James Farmer, who joined the riders in Montgomery after his father's funeral, had planned on staying off this ride. But Doris Jean Castle persuaded him to accompany them, and the following morning, on May 24, 1961, twenty-six riders left in two "heavily guarded buses" for Jackson, Mississippi. The armed escorts prevented further attacks, and the buses proceeded to Jackson, where the riders were immediately arrested for "breach of peace" for attempting to use the bus station's white facilities. All refused to pay their bail and began serving thirty- to ninety-day jail terms.[15]

Margaret Leonard, Miriam Feingold, Doris Castle, Julia Aaron, Sandra Nixon, and Jean Thompson were taken immediately to the city jail and placed in segregated cells. "It was pretty well scripted from there," recalls Feingold. The women were processed in the Jackson City Jail and all refused to post bail. Leonard never believed that she was in any real danger due to the national attention, but New Orleans CORE member Jean Thompson, a black woman who weighed all of ninety pounds, was one of five riders beaten at

11. Feingold, interview, 1 December 2003.

12. Leonard, interview, 29 March 2003; Garrow, *We Shall Overcome*, 967.

13. Castle-Scott, interview, 19 January 1989.

14. Castle-Scott interview, 19 January 1989.

15. August Meier and Elliot Rudwick, *CORE: A Study in the Civil Rights Movement, 1942–1968* (Urbana: University of Illinois Press, 1973), 139.

the jail. "Miss Thompson was slapped in the face at least three times by the [prison farm] superintendent for not saying 'sir,'" reported James Lawson.[16] The riders spent a night in the Jackson City Jail, and the next day they were transferred to Hinds County Jail, where they remained for about a week. Julia Aaron recalled going before the judge for arraignment: "I was the first person to go . . . and when I went . . . I guess something just happened to my mouth and it wouldn't stay closed. When the judge said I was sentenced I just kept talking. It was not the plan originally for me to stay in jail, but I just got angry at the lies. That's how I ended up with the 90 days."[17]

The women posed a formidable problem for Jackson city officials. As Freedom Riders poured into Jackson, the city found itself unable to accommodate the hundreds of riders who refused to post bail. Subsequently, city officials moved the male riders to Parchman Penitentiary, an infamous prison farm in rural Mississippi. In *Walking with the Wind*, John Lewis describes Parchman as a "21,000 acre twentieth-century slave plantation owned by the state and farmed by hundreds of striped-suited black convicts who were goaded by bullwhips and cursing, kicking guards to turn a daily quota of cotton or other crops."[18] With full knowledge of these conditions, the female Freedom Riders, demanding equal treatment, began a hunger strike until prison officials eventually moved them to Parchman. Once there, they were placed in maximum security, "for their own protection."[19] Still, Miriam Feingold reported to her family that "spirits remain high and no one is giving in."[20]

Conditions at Parchman were unpleasant, to say the least. Mary Hamilton, one of CORE's only female field secretaries, and later chair of the New Orleans NAACP, described the crowded conditions and soiled linens and

16. Feingold, interviews, 1 and 22 December 2002; Leonard, interview, 29 March 2003; "Freedom Rider Beaten in Mississippi Jail," James Lawson quoted in "Freedom Riders," *Louisiana Weekly*, 3, 10, and 17 June 1961.

17. Julia Aaron Humbles, interview by the author, 11 March 2003, tape recording, copy in possession of the author.

18. Lewis, *Walking with the Wind*, 168. Harvard Sitkoff describes the conditions the riders endured at Parchman as "repetitious rounds of questioning and beatings, the pain of battery-operated cattle prods, the terror of wrist breakers, the sounds of friends groaning and crying; the backbreaking work in the fields from sun-up to sundown, the execrable food, and the filthy cots in the bug-infested cells; the capricious denial of cigarettes, reading materials, and showers; and the dreaded time in the sweatbox or solitary confinement for refusing to play Uncle Tom to the guards" (Sitkoff, *The Struggle for Black Equality*, 102).

19. Meier and Rudwick, *CORE*, 141; Feingold, interview, 1 December 2002.

20. Miriam Feingold to Auntie O, 19 June 1961, Miriam Feingold Papers, State Historical Society of Wisconsin, Madison (hereafter cited as Feingold Papers).

mattresses. From three to eight women were housed in small cells meant to hold only two people. The riders felt that the food was often inedible. As Leonard recalled, "the food started coming all mixed up, with too much pepper on it." If they were lucky, they might receive their mail, although the prison guards usually read it before it reached the prisoners. Aaron had an aunt who sent her cakes, but the jailers always "confiscated" them. Although it is well documented that a number of women endured invasive and painful vaginal searches, Leonard, Feingold, Castle, Aaron, Nixon, and Thompson did not experience this particular humiliation. They did, however, hear women who came to Parchman after them shrieking in pain.[21] Julia Aaron and Doris Castle recalled that they were not allowed to bathe or brush their teeth for over a week; for them that was the worst of the jail experience. But in an unprecedented act described by one Freedom Rider as "human decency transcending prejudice and hate," a group of white women "anonymously volunteered funds to buy toilet articles and other necessities" for the jailed female Freedom Riders.[22] Sandra Nixon recalled that on one occasion a jailer in a "bad mood shut all of the windows; the heat became unbearable and it was difficult to breathe. One of our girls seemed to be suffering with hay fever. She appeared to be suffocating." They called to the jailer to come and open the windows. When he finally arrived he told her, "Take a fool's advice and get out of here."[23] "The effort was really to break the spirit of the people," stated Castle. "And the things that were done in order to accomplish this, in retrospect, [it] was really so cruel. I can't help but to say I don't know how we stood it except that we . . . had enough of the armor of what we were all about, that our cause was right, that God was on our side, that it overshadowed the fear that, in retrospect, had to have been there all along."[24]

21. In an article in the *Louisiana Weekly*, one female rider staying with Shirley Thompson, another New Orleans CORE member who served time at Parchman, described the vaginal searches: "A female prison trustee put each girl on a bare wooden table and performed the 'search'—that's what it was called, rather than an examination. The trustee wore rubber gloves, but touched the girls with her ungloved hand, and between the 'examinations' she dipped the glove in a pan of water, which soon became red with blood. This procedure was instituted for the specific purpose of trying to degrade and harass the female Freedom Riders" ("Female Freedom Riders Get Rougher Treatment Says One," *Louisiana Weekly*, 5 August 1961, ARC).

22. This information is cited in Peck, *Freedom Ride*, 152.

23. Interview with Sandra Nixon quoted in "Felt Like a Missionary Says College Soph after Ordeal," *Louisiana Weekly*, 22 July 1961, ARC.

24. Castle-Scott, interview, 19 January 1989. Regarding conditions for women, see also Sara Evans, *Personal Politics: The Roots of Women's Liberation in the Civil Rights Movement and the New Left* (New York: Vintage Books, 1979), 68.

Under the circumstances, the women made the best of their prison experiences. Although they were placed in segregated cells, they were on the same cell block so they could still communicate with each other. They even figured out a way to pass notes to each other through the ventilation system. To pass the time the women held "workshops" where they discussed the movement and nonviolence, and gave each other ballet and modern dance lessons.[25] Margaret Leonard taught the other women French, while others taught Greek and Latin. Miriam Feingold figured out that walking back and forth in the cell 660 times equaled one mile, and "we tried to walk a mile every day."[26] Julia Aaron worked at breaking the will of the jailers. "I started a campaign with the jailer," stated Aaron, "because he wouldn't even acknowledge my presence. He'd come back there three times a day and I would just speak to him and he wouldn't say anything. I did it everyday, every time he came back I spoke to him and he wouldn't stay." Aaron continued:

> I just kind of wore him down and after that he'd go, "hmph" and then eventually he began to speak, to the point that he came back and told us that we were good girls and that we needed to go home and that these people were using us, the Communists, you know this kind of craziness. And then I told him, if you are going to talk to me then you are going to allow me to talk to you. I told him what it was like being a black person in America and not being allowed just basic human rights. They didn't even understand what the Freedom Rides were about; they had no concept what it was really about. They did change quite a bit. Of course they didn't acknowledge it but we could tell just by the way they acted that there was a difference. [By the end] we were on a first-name basis.[27]

The women also sang to pass the time, much to the chagrin of the jailers. A religious Julia Aaron "sang every day, almost all day long," recalled Castle. The jailers ordered the women to quit singing. "We not only didn't quit singing," states Leonard, "we sang louder and then we started beating on the beds, being real loud. And I do remember learning something about why you get riots because you get carried away with the spirit of being in an angry crowd." The women would sing loud enough so the men could hear and sing back to them. When the women refused to stop singing, the jailers

25. For more information on the importance of "workshops" to CORE, see Martin Oppenheimer, "The Southern Student Sit-Ins: Intra-Group Relations and Community Conflict," *Phylon* (1st Quarter 1966): 22–23.

26. "Summer Resident Tells 'Why I Was a Freedom Rider,'" *Ticonderoga Sentinel*, 3 August 1961, Feingold Papers.

27. Humbles, interview, 11 March 2003.

removed everything from their cells, including their linens, towels, tooth-brushes, and mattresses, forcing them to sleep on the steel bed frames. The jailers then turned the fans on, and, as the women remembered, "although it was June . . . it was cold." What sustained them, however, were the "semi-literate" notes of appreciation from the general prison population passed through the ventilation system. "It was a game between us keeping our spirits up and the prison officials trying to beat them down," states Feingold. It be-came increasingly clear that any "involvement in direct action demonstra-tions . . . tested the women's physical courage and mental endurance."[28]

Throughout the summer of 1961, New Orleans continued to act as home base for the Freedom Riders, but the oppressive conditions had not improved in the Crescent City. As the released riders returned to New Orleans, mem-bers of CORE, including the Castles, the Thompsons, Aaron, and the young members Patricia and Carlene Smith, housed and fed hundreds of Freedom Riders who passed through New Orleans from Mississippi throughout the summer. Local CORE members also supported the riders by staging a march to the Interstate Commerce Commission offices downtown, protesting seg-regation in interstate transportation facilities. One evening in early August, three white Freedom Riders returning from Jackson were falsely arrested and brutally beaten while staying at the home of Patricia and Carlene Smith. The three men were charged with vagrancy and, later, with aggravated bat-tery against the officers while being transferred to jail. To protest these beat-ings, CORE staged a mass sit-in outside of police headquarters. Of the fif-teen students arrested at this demonstration, nine were women, including Oretha and Doris Castle, Alice Thompson, Doratha Smith, and Carlene and Patricia Smith.[29]

Although the official Freedom Rides ended by June 1961, women con-tinued to challenge Jim Crow in interstate travel accommodations. In Au-gust, nineteen women and sixteen men were arrested in LaPlace, Louisiana, for using a white's-only restroom at a service station after leaving New Or-leans and heading to Plaquemine for a picnic sponsored by the Gay Ladies Social and Pleasure Club. Rosana Johnson, one of those arrested, reported that after being told where the "Negro" restrooms were at a service station just north of New Orleans, riders "began pouring into the white restrooms."

28. Castle-Scott, interview, 19 January 1989; Humbles, interview, 11 March 2003; Leonard, interview; Feingold, interviews; Nixon interview in *Louisiana Weekly*, 22 July 1961, ARC; *Ticon-deroga Sentinel*, 3 August 1961, Feingold Papers; Evans, *Personal Politics*, 67–68.

29. "Freedom Riders Charge N.O. Cops with Brutal Beatings" and "Arrest 15 for 'Sit-ins' at Police Headquarters," *Louisiana Weekly*, 19 August and 2 September 1961.

After charging the group with disturbing the peace and simple trespassing, police released them.[30] That same month in Shreveport, Louisiana, four members of the local chapter of CORE, including Dolores McGinnie and Marie McGinnie, were arrested and charged with disturbing the peace when attempting to integrate the white's-only waiting room at a bus terminal. Again in October, police arrested sixteen members of the Shreveport CORE, eight women among them. A Molotov cocktail was thrown into a church where the group was holding a meeting to plan a statewide "freedom ride" to test segregation laws at local bus terminals, the municipal airport, and train depots.[31]

Greater danger, however, awaited three members of New Orleans CORE in Mississippi. In an act of sheer brazenness, Patricia Smith and Alice Thompson, along with a white man from New York City, sat in at a bus terminal in Poplarville, Mississippi, where a man had been lynched two years earlier; police arrested all three. CORE members from New Orleans, Freedom Riders among them, drove to Poplarville for the trial. A group of "25 to 30 hostile-looking males" met them at the courthouse. In what seemed like a scene from an old movie, one reporter described the courtroom as a "hate-laden atmosphere [that] was tense, the air clouded with cigar smoke." A man testifying for the state reported that when Thompson and Smith sat next to him at the whites-only counter, he "snatched them . . . out of the terminal and escorted them to his half-ton truck to be taken to jail." He then turned to Thompson and Smith and said, "You're lucky I didn't shoot you." The judge pronounced all three guilty and sentenced them to another night in "the jailhouse housing the ghost of the lynched Mack Parker." When Oretha Castle tried to leave the building to telephone the FBI for protection, a group of white men followed her, forcing her to return to the courthouse. In the end, the attorneys convinced the prosecutor to dismiss the charges and, escorted by local police, the "nine CORE members were whisked out into the night."[32]

"WE PUT EVERY LAST ONE OF THE WHITE PEOPLE OUT"

As the Freedom Rides subsided, protests continued throughout Louisiana, and often with women at the center. In December 1961, Louisiana CORE

30. "43 Arrested for Using White Restroom at Service Station," *Louisiana Weekly*, 12 August 1961.

31. "Louisiana Gets into Act, Arrests 4 Freedom Riders," *Louisiana Weekly*, 12 August 1961, ARC ; "Police Still Holding 8 in Fire Probe" and "CORE Members Are Charged," *Shreveport Journal*, 26 October 1961.

32. "3 Freedom Riders Found Guilty in 'Lynch Town,'" *Louisiana Weekly*, 18 November 1961, ARC.

members conducted mass marches in their respective cities. CORE organizers sent Doris Castle to Baton Rouge to assist the Southern University students organizing demonstrations. While there, Castle was subjected to tear
gas and angry police dogs. In 1962, CORE sent Castle to North Carolina to
participate in the Freedom Highways campaign to desegregate major restaurants and motels in the state.[33] In New Orleans, police arrested 304 protesters, mainly students, for "parading without a permit," while in Baton Rouge
police arrested another 73 protesters, 29 of them women, for picketing and
sitting in downtown. To protest the Baton Rouge arrests, several hundred
students staged a march to the city jail. Fifty of the estimated 1,500 marchers were arrested after police used tear gas to disperse the demonstrators. In
an attempt to "awaken the moral conscience of the community," the arrested
students conducted a twenty-four-hour fast. Among the female participants
in the Baton Rouge demonstration were Baton Rouge CORE's chairperson,
Patricia Tate, along with Julia Aaron and Doris Castle.[34] Indeed, Louisiana
women continued to play highly visible roles in their communities.

In December 1961, with Oretha Castle at the helm, the New Orleans chapter of CORE employed "Operation Freezeout," a new technique in which they
occupied all of the seats at the "Negro lunch counter," ordered a drink and
sipped it for three hours, ordered another one, and so on, until the store
closed. At one particular demonstration, Oretha reported that she and her
fellow CORE members were splashed with a burning liquid later found to
be carbolic acid, sprayed with insecticide, and threatened by the store manager with a gun. The waitresses also dumped ammonia, iodine, and choco-
late on their heads, yet ironically enough, the ammonia fumes affected the
waitresses more than the demonstrators, and they were forced to close the
store. Oretha believed that this demonstration had sparked a more violent
response than any previous sit-in. Upon returning to the CORE office later
that day, she called the police, but to no avail. Frustrated, she called the local FBI office and the CORE national office in New York, which, in turn, informed Attorney General Robert Kennedy. After this incident, Oretha reiterated her commitment to the struggle for black equality, telling a newspaper
reporter that, "We are still picketing and sitting in but our current plan is
to stage a hunger strike."[35]

33. "Doris Jean Castle," Reel 10, 1, CORE Addendum, HU.
    34. "Police Thwart 2 'Protest Marches,' 304 Are Arrested" and "State, Federal Judges Enjoin
CORE from 'Demonstrating,'" *Louisiana Weekly*, December 23, 1961; "New Orleans Summary of
Activities, 1961," Reel 20, CORE Papers, ARC.
    35. "Doused with Acid after New Technique," *Louisiana Weekly*, 30 December 1961.

Although the Louisiana movement was most prominent in New Orleans, CORE members in Shreveport and Baton Rouge also increased pressure on state and local officials. In October 1962, police arrested eight male and eight female members of the Shreveport CORE protesting the Louisiana State Fair's segregated "Negro Day."[36] In Baton Rouge, police arrested three NAACP members, Pearl Lee George, Laura Lee Harris, and Willie Lee Harris, for contempt of court after they refused to move from the white's-only section of a courtroom.[37]

Moreover, after the United States Supreme Court reversed the 1961 convictions of the Southern University students in what had been deemed the case of "the Louisiana sixteen," a rejuvenated student movement emerged in Baton Rouge.[38] In October 1961, Southern University students Ronnie Moore, Weldon Rougeau, and Patricia Ann Tate organized a CORE chapter in Baton Rouge, with Tate as acting president. By the end of 1961, CORE members in the city "launched a full-scale campaign" against the downtown merchants. On December 11, CORE sat in at two downtown variety stores. Two days later, police arrested twenty-three student members of CORE for picketing downtown. That evening approximately 3,500 students gathered for a mass meeting, and the following day CORE held a march to the courthouse to protest the jailings. Approximately 2,000 students, "walking eight abreast," marched the seven miles to the courthouse. As historians August Meier and Elliot Rudwick reported: "Upon arriving at the courthouse they pledged allegiance to the flag, prayed briefly, and sang 'We Shall Overcome.' At this point the students in the jail began singing, 'O Students, don't you weep, don't you mourn,' and the demonstrators responded with clapping and yelling. The police dispersed them using dogs and tear gas, and later . . . fifty others were arrested." As had happened with the sit-ins of 1960, the president of Southern University, Felton Clark, banned student demonstrators on campus and threatened to suspend those arrested. Clark again closed the university, forcing students to reregister for spring classes. The retaliation by the university weakened the Baton Rouge movement just as it had in 1960. The remaining CORE members, however, "resorted to a series of 'hit and run' sit-ins" that led to the desegregation of the dime-store lunch counters in August 1963.[39] In December 1962, students at Southern Univer-

36. James Farmer to CORE Group Leaders, "Harassment of Shreveport, Louisiana CORE members," 26 October 1962, Reel 40, CORE Papers, ARC.

37. "Release 3 on Bond in 'Court Sit-In,'" *Louisiana Weekly*, 29 December 1962.

38. "The Louisiana 16," *Crisis*, January 1962.

39. "Lunch Counter Bias Is Cracked in Baton Rouge," *Louisiana Weekly*, 17 August 1963; Meier

sity staged a successful boycott of the annual campus style show when they discovered that a store that had arrested CORE members for picketing the previous year would be providing the clothing.[40]

Despite a few setbacks, the Freedom Rides and the numerous local demonstrations rejuvenated Louisiana CORE chapters and their supporters, providing members with a shared purpose. Ironically, in New Orleans, a city mired in a battle over school desegregation, many female activists received kudos and support, not only from local New Orleanians, but also nationally, for their continued commitment and bravery. In a letter to the editor of the local paper, one New Orleanian applauded Shirley Thompson and Sandra Nixon, "and all other Freedom Riders," for their courage, urging them not to quit.[41] By the end of the summer, 328 riders had been arrested in Jackson, plus another 35 at bus terminals in Houston, Shreveport, and Florida.[42] By September, most of the riders had appeared at trial and prepared to serve out the remaining portion of their sentences. Julia Aaron lost her appeal and returned to Mississippi to serve the remainder of her four-month sentence. Doris Castle withdrew her appeal, opting to remain in jail rather than pay a fine. In the face of oppressive, and oftentimes horrific, conditions in jail, Aaron, Castle, and other women like them chose to stand by their convictions.[43]

By the end of 1961, Rudy Lombard left his position as chairman of the New Orleans CORE to attend graduate school, and Oretha Castle assumed his position as local president. Oretha was certainly not the first female to chair a civil rights organization. In fact, Patricia Tate presided over Baton Rouge's CORE chapter. Recent scholarship has found that a number of women served in influential leadership positions in organizations across the South. However, what is compelling about Oretha Castle's tenure as president of the New Orleans CORE is that, aside from some significant SNCC chapters in Mississippi, she reigned over the most influential and dynamic civil rights chapter in the South. The success of the Freedom Rides drew much attention to the New Orleans chapter of CORE, leading to a surge in membership. Unfortunately, the extreme visibility of the chapter, the exciting dy-

and Rudwick, *CORE*, 167; Adam Fairclough, *Race and Democracy: The Civil Rights Struggle in Louisiana, 1915–1972* (Athens: University of Georgia Press, 1995), 289–90.

  40. Patricia Ann Tate to Marvin Rich, 10 December 1962, Reel 40, CORE Papers, ARC.

  41. Ellis Williams, letter to the editor, *Louisiana Weekly*, 5 August 1961.

  42. Meier and Rudwick, *CORE*, 140.

  43. "Freedom Riders Serve Out Terms," *Louisiana Weekly*, 9 September 1961.

namics of the movement, and an attractively interracial membership almost led to its demise.

According to the organization's statement of purpose, "Gandhian nonviolence and interracial action are the twin ideological beliefs underpinning CORE's organizational structure." To CORE, racial issues in the United States were a "human problem" rather than a "Negro problem"; its commitment to interracial membership was a fundamental aspect of its organizational composition. As founder James Farmer wrote, "We cannot destroy segregation with a weapon of segregation."[44] The New Orleans chapter, however, was one of only a handful of CORE chapters that was, in reality, interracial. Yet the New Orleans group would wrestle with divergent notions about leadership, membership, and strategy. They created a "Beloved Community," but ultimately, in New Orleans, that community failed.

From CORE's inception, students from Tulane, Dillard, Xavier, and Southern and Louisiana State universities of New Orleans had comprised its membership. While the majority of members, at times, were white, the leadership always remained black. Oretha Castle remembered that, "CORE was an interracial body at that point. We thought, here are these white kids . . . to feel that they (whites) are doing us wrong." When white and black student activists sat in at a whites-only lunch counter and were not served, it was clear to Oretha Castle that, "the whites were part of the action." However, Oretha also remembered this as her "first lesson in . . . the whole role of white folks in the black people's struggle." Although Rudy Lombard directed the local CORE group, she recalled the white students "showing us what to do . . . [f]rom the very beginning."[45]

In New Orleans, black CORE members recognized the problematic nature of interracial cooperation fairly early in the organization's existence. After the Freedom Rides, and only a year into its existence, African American members of CORE began to question the reasoning behind white involvement in the movement. As Oretha Castle recalled, conflicts arose from the very beginning. In particular, two whites, Sidney "Lonnie" Goldfinch, a Tulane student, and "Skip," a photographer in charge of publicity and public relations for the group, immediately asserted their authority. "At first," stated Oretha, "that was just the way [it was] for the most part. Honestly, my reaction to it was, 'Oh, there Skip and Lonnie goes.' I guess, though, shortly, . . .

44. Meier and Rudwick, *CORE*, 126, 11.

45. Oretha Castle, interview by James Mosby, 26 May 1970, transcript, RBCRDP.

I began to develop some kind of feelings about Lonnie always wanting to tell people what to do, but I didn't really suppose it ever got too much beyond that until . . . several months later." According to Castle:

> You had all the whites coming in with their tremendous amount of education and sophistication and then you had the blacks who we really felt, "Boy, we is some dumb compared to those white kids." They would come in meetings and they'd be talking about the philosophy of this political philosopher as opposed to that and we never even heard of what they were talking about. And too, it was that kind of intimidation on our part by what we thought was their smartness . . . but underneath . . . we'd be mumbling certain things, "Boy, they sure want to run everything and tell us what we have to do."[46]

Many whites in the movement had the education and skills that blacks had been historically denied. This situation often created tension. As happened in SNCC in 1965, many blacks viewed whites as taking over organizational leadership and decision making. In fact, historical social conditioning contributed to the divisions that were probably bound to arise.[47]

The resentment obviously felt by the black CORE members against paternalistic white students was only part of the problem. Like the Mississippi Freedom Summer campaign three years later, problems of interracial sexual relationships also plagued the New Orleans CORE. Historically, the South's system of segregation had been intimately tied to the issue of interracial sex. The taboo against sex between black men and white women was central to whites' control of blacks, while white supremacy authorized white male access to black women. When white Mississippi locals accused fourteen-year-old Emmett Till from Chicago of whistling at a white woman in 1955, for instance, two white men rousted him from his uncle's home at midnight and lynched him. Thus, when hundreds of white female college students arrived in the South to work in close contact with young black men, there was bound to be tension beyond that created by the usual cultural differences. For some, interracial relationships in the movement were a way of challenging "these taboos as vestiges of a racist society"; for these white activists, "interracial sex became the ultimate expression . . . [and] conclusive proof of their right to membership in the 'Beloved Community.'"[48]

In New Orleans, conflict over interracial relationships, notably between

46. Castle, interview by James Mosby, 26 May 1970.

47. Arnold S. Kaufman, *The Radical Liberal: The New Politics, Theory and Practice* (New York: Atherton Books, 1968), 83.

48. Doug McAdam, *Freedom Summer* (New York: Oxford University Press, 1988), 93–94.

black women and white men, was the issue that ultimately splintered the local organization. The New Orleans CORE group often hosted interracial social gatherings. As Oretha Castle recalled, "after awhile it seemed as though
the CORE chapter . . . was the place if you were white and you wanted to get
some black meat, that was where you were to come, especially if you were
male and wanted to get next to a black female." At the same time, Castle
admitted that interracial sexual liaisons had been going on "ever since we
[as black people] had been here." That was not, however, what the movement meant to Castle. "I didn't appreciate none of that shit from the very
beginning . . . . I agreed to the fact that what we were fighting and what the
struggle was all about for people [was] to be able to do whatever they wanted
to do. That was not what CORE was all about . . . certainly [not what] my interests and my struggle was about." Finally, one night, CORE hosted a party,
and one of the members who joined admitted to her that that's what "sold
him on CORE. He never heard of CORE before, but he saw all them black
men with them white women and he said 'if that's what CORE is, that's what
I want.' "[49]

As the new chair of the New Orleans CORE chapter and a proud black
woman, Oretha Castle led a charge to purge white students, and a few black
members, from the organization. As Adam Fairclough, chronicler of the Louisiana movement, notes, "Considering CORE's commitment to interracialism, it was an extraordinary episode."[50] In February 1962, Castle strategically called a meeting of the all-black Membership Committee, where they
decided: "[A]s far as we were concerned, [interracial sexual liaisons] wasn't
what the struggle was all about. So what it amounted to, we put every last
one of the white people out. Every last one of them." According to Julia
Aaron, "You can't tell a person who they [are] going to fall in love with or
have a relationship with but it was becoming a real problem in that it was
affecting our effectiveness as a group." Castle admitted that white paternalistic attitudes also contributed to the decision. "There were all of the other
things that had been building ever since perhaps the first meeting we had
ever[,] where from the very beginning the white students were very clear
that they knew what was best for us to do. . . . But I think that part of that
had to do with many of us [feeling] that we just did not know or were not
capable of participating to the level that whites were at."[51] Another New Or-

49. Castle, interview, 26 May 1970, RBCRDP; Oretha Castle, interview by Kim Lacy Rogers,
27 November 1978, Rogers-Stevens Collection.
50. Fairclough, *Race and Democracy*, 295.
51. Castle, interview by James Mosby, 26 May 1970; Humbles, interview, 11 March 2003.

leans CORE member, Doratha Smith, recalled that most of the whites were from well-to-do families and that after whites were expelled from CORE, "I questioned whether they were really interested in what we were about or if it was something new to them."[52]

In a letter to Jim McCain, director of organization for the national CORE, one African American CORE member, Carlene Smith, seemingly dismayed at what she viewed as Castle's unilateral decision to purge the organization, described at length the expulsion of fifteen members, mostly white, from the local CORE. She noted that while some members believed in the idea of an integrated society as "being the ultimate goal of CORE and of the civil rights movement as a whole," others "apparently have felt that social integration is not only objectionable in itself, and not part of the groups [sic] real aims, but dangerous to those aims because of the possible disapproval which it might provoke in the outside community." Smith reported that, after the early successful protests, membership in the local CORE group increased considerably, particularly the white membership, causing a change in the "nature and attitude of the group, a change for which the existing leadership and the organizational structure of the chapter were totally unprepared." Smith then discussed the fact that members began engaging in integrated social activities, such as dances held by CORE, while simultaneously, a "small clique of favored individuals" were the only ones with any say in major organizational decisions. For these reasons, "a number of members began to feel that they were being subjected to arbitrary rule, that they were not participants in a democratic movement, but puppets manipulated by an unknown person for unknown purposes."[53]

Smith also noted the tension that "steadily built" within the local chapter due to the change in leadership and organizational structure. She reported that, "without notice and without a hearing," and without the consent of the larger CORE membership, white students were expelled. Smith further stated that one member proposed rewriting the local constitution. Similar to the organizational structure of SNCC, a new constitution for the New Orleans group "would provide for a strong decentralization of authority and for its diffusion throughout the group." Smith believed that the combination of interracial social functions, perceived by some black members as self-serving, coupled with nondemocratic, centralized (black) authority in the New Orleans chapter, ultimately led to the organization's "prestige, pur-

52. Simmons, interview, 27 July 1988.
53. Carlene Smith to Jim McCain, 22 February 1962, Reel 40, CORE Papers, ARC.

pose, and morale . . . suffer[ing]." Julia Aaron later recalled that the goal was "to maintain the integrity of the organization and [they] kind of realized that it wasn't about relationships. It was about achieving freedom for our people. I am sure that they did the best that they could, that it was the best decision they could make at the time, but I am not sure it was right."[54]

In response to the expulsions of its white members, CORE's national office sent Richard Haley to New Orleans. Although CORE, unlike SNCC, did not reject hierarchy in principle, the obvious assertion of authority by a small number of members, as well as the seemingly unilateral decision to expel the white members, proved problematic for an organization firmly committed to interracialism. Haley recalled that, because the interracial makeup of the organization was central to its philosophy, "as a group . . . black people have been caught in a kind of psychological situation, which we tend to expect leadership to come from white people. . . . [T]his traditional, habitual relationship between black and white had to be broken."[55] After further consideration and many debates among the larger membership, the suspensions were declared "invalid" and, over time, white students slowly rejoined the New Orleans chapter. However, the group never fully recovered from this early internal dissension. "I think it zapped a lot of its strength," stated Raphael Cassimere, CORE member and president of the NAACP Youth Chapter at the time. The New Orleans group went from a small group of committed young activists bound by the experience of the Freedom Rides to a larger, but less effective and less cohesive, group. White members Margaret Leonard and Connie Bradford, both studying abroad during the purges, returned to New Orleans to find themselves unwelcome in their organization. "I was kind of sad about it," recalled Bradford, "because I really enjoyed doing it . . . [although] I always felt it was probably not appropriate to have so much white input."[56]

As the history of the civil rights movement and the New Left inform us, social movements that involve both minority and majority members are often afflicted with internecine conflict. Illustrating this phenomenon is the rise of Black Power in the mid-1960s as early idealism surrounding the creation of a "Beloved Community" waned.[57] The best-known studies of

54. Smith to McCain, 22 February 1962; Humbles, interview, 11 March 2003.

55. Richard Haley, interview by Kim Lacy Rogers, 9 May 1979, Rogers-Stevens Collection.

56. Leonard, interview, 29 March 2003; Connie Bradford Harse, interview by the author, 19 March 2003, tape recording, copy in possession of the author.

57. Kaufman, *The Radical Liberal*, 82. Kaufman asserts that with the onset of Black Power, African Americans began to reexamine the traditional assumptions of the civil rights move-

the racial rift in the movement focus on the Mississippi Freedom Summer of 1964, where hundreds of white northern college students flocked to the South to participate in the voter education/registration project. The ideal of creating a "Beloved Community" was at the center of the summer project, but from the outset questions arose about the proper role of whites. Project organizers "weeded out" those they suspected might prove to be paternalistic and self-serving. The white activists who ultimately went south brought with them a "passionate commitment to the full realization of idealistic values on which they had been taught American was based."[58]

This idealism included the creation of an interracial community, which proved problematic by its very nature. According to the sociologist Doug McAdam, the naïveté and paternalism of the white college students only served to "reinforce traditional patterns of racial dominance and submission." For both the white and black participants, this idealism remained a "psychologically burdensome dilemma."[59] Moreover, in a region of the country that traditionally upheld white women as the standard by which to judge all others, African American women, certainly women like Oretha Castle, must have found themselves constantly grappling with the importance of, and dedication to, interracialism. For many black women, their race *and* their gender had historically been their albatross. Were they to repudiate centuries of racism and discrimination, sexual abuse and pain, for the larger struggle?

"WE MEAN BUSINESS"

Although CORE historians Meier and Rudwick argue that the New Orleans chapter "never regained its earlier vigor" as a result of the purging of its white members, with Oretha Castle as acting president for the next three years, the group did, in fact, rise again to be a formidable civil rights organization in the city.[60] Black and white students continued to test interstate travel facilities and demonstrate against racial discrimination in all areas of the city. In one of the organization's first acts as a reintegrated group, eleven

---

ment, most notably its interracial quality and the politics of coalition. African Americans saw white participation as somewhat superficial, if not gratuitous and ultimately unnecessary to them achieving their political goals. Black Power advocates quickly learned that the theory that "all blacks are hurt by segregation . . . [thus they] must surely be helped by integration" was defective.

58. McAdam, *Freedom Summer*, 54, 5.

59. McAdam, *Freedom Summer*, 32–33, 38.

60. Meier and Rudwick, *CORE*, 169.

members were arrested for picketing on Canal Street. Two white women, Jill Finsten and Barbara Brent, were among the group.[61]

Throughout 1963 and into 1964, members of CORE, the Consumers League of Greater New Orleans, and the NAACP Youth Council continued to demonstrate on Canal Street. They eventually expanded these demonstrations to include the city's more established hotels, the Schwegmann's supermarket chain (which eventually closed their lunch counters rather than integrate them), the city's theaters, and the all-white Ponchartrain Beach.[62] In a highly publicized media event in November 1963, members of CORE, in concert with the NAACP and Consumers League of Greater New Orleans, staged a Freedom March to city hall followed by a sit-in to protest the segregated cafeteria at a "tax-supported building." As the media stood by, police dragged Reverend Avery Alexander, a prominent New Orleans minister closely associated with Martin Luther King, Jr. and SCLC, down the steps of city hall. Police also arrested thirty-six members of the protesting group, twelve women among them, including Oretha and Doris Castle and Sandra Nixon, who were carried out of the cafeteria in their chairs after the staff refused them service and they refused to leave. In a highly publicized lawsuit, Doris Castle and Sandra Nixon, along with Alexander, successfully challenged the state's right to discriminate in a tax-supported cafeteria.[63] As Oretha Castle stated: "We mean business. The segregated barriers in public places must come down."[64]

By 1964, members of the New Orleans CORE, jailed numerous times, continued their protests unabated in New Orleans and throughout the state. In late 1963, staunch segregationist Leander Perez publicized that he had readied what he deemed the "Dungeon" for the demonstrators: a "snake and mosquito infested" jail in Plaquemine Parish. Built as a fort by the Spanish in 1746, the jail was accessible only by boat or helicopter and apparently was crawling with rattlesnakes, water moccasins, "and mosquitoes so big they kill cattle by clogging their nostrils . . . and fire ants, which swarm over humans."[65] Yet in early 1964, the undaunted CORE members demonstrated against the Loews theater, protesting the fact that the Sonny Liston–Cassius Clay fight was to be telecast at a segregated theater. Police arrested Ruthie

61. "CORE Members Queried in NO," *Louisiana Weekly*, 1962, Reel 40, CORE Papers. ARC.

62. *Louisiana Weekly*, 4 April 1963 and 29 June 1963.

63. "36 Arrested in Direct Action Movement," "Desegregation of City Hall Sought," "City Hall Cafeteria Desegregated," *Louisiana Weekly*, 9 November 1963, 8 and 22 February 1964.

64. Oretha Castle quoted in *Louisiana Weekly*, 30 November 1963.

65. "Perez Readies 'Dungeon' for CR Demonstrators," *Louisiana Weekly*, 2 November 1963.

Wells, Shirley Thompson, and Doratha Smith. The New Orleans CORE sent telegrams to both Liston and Clay informing them of the issue. The Loews theater cancelled the telecasts after Liston released a statement saying: "I feel that the color of my people's money is the same as anyone else's. They should get the same seats. If not, I don't want those places to have the fight."[66] Two months later, on Good Friday, police arrested Doris Castle, Ruthie Wells, Doratha Smith, Alice and Shirley Thompson, Linda Smith, Alice Joseph, Katrina Jackson, and one male CORE member for forming a human chain—a "Freedom Ring"—around the cashier's box at the Loews, making it difficult for patrons to purchase tickets. After they refused to leave, police took the women in a paddy wagon to jail and did not release them until the Monday after Easter.[67]

These protests proved to be some of the last staged by the New Orleans CORE group and are noteworthy for the fact that women were in the vanguard of these demonstrations, continuing to dominate CORE even as the group's effectiveness in the community waned. In 1964, Doratha Smith assumed Oretha Castle's position as acting chair; Joyce Elbrecht became vice chairman; Linda Diane Smith, secretary; and Alice Thompson, financial secretary.[68] Doris Castle served as a "community relations" assistant for the national CORE office. Shirley and Alice Thompson both served in 1964 as field secretaries for CORE's voter registration project. By 1964, it appears that gendered notions of leadership were immaterial in the New Orleans movement.

After the purges, more conservative organizations such as the NAACP, the CLGNO, and the National Urban League reclaimed their positions of authority in the city's civil rights struggles. Although Doratha Smith had filed a lawsuit to desegregate the Louisiana Wildlife and Fisheries Building, and Oretha and Doris Castle had filed to desegregate Schwegmann's lunch counters, the more militant direct-action student phase of the movement in New Orleans diminished. Women, however, continued to play a major role in protests in the city. In August 1964, for example, four women and the Reverend Alexander of the CLGNO had hot water and Coke poured on them when requesting service at an all-white establishment.[69] The NAACP Youth Council picked up where CORE left off, picketing the Canal Street merchants. By

66. "CORE Pickets Cancel Title Fight at Theaters," *Louisiana Weekly*, 29 February 1964.

67. "6 Complain Police Use Abusive Words," *Louisiana Weekly*, 4 April 1964 and "CORE on Canal Street," by Doris Castle, March 1964, Reel 40, CORE Papers, ARC.

68. List of Officers, Reel 18, 59, CORE Addendum, HU.

69. "6 Thwarted in Café Mix Attempt Here," *Louisiana Weekly*, 1 August 1964.

the summer of 1964, African American New Orleanians had been hired in nonmenial positions at a number of stores, including F. W. Woolworth's and McCrory's.[70] And in another case, Oretha and Doris's grandmother, Callie Castle, filed a suit to desegregate Charity Hospital in New Orleans.[71]

Louisiana women were leaders, not followers, spearheading the movement from 1961 to 1964. They defined and set goals, provided an ideology justifying action, organized coordinated, initiated, directed action, raised money, generated publicity, and served as an example to others.[72] While previous histories suggest that women were marginalized in other civil rights organizations across the South, Louisiana women were not. The patriarchal structure of Louisiana's earlier movement, during the 1950s and prior to the sit-ins, did not continue after the student movement took hold. Indeed, women often outnumbered men at some of the most highly visible demonstrations in the city. Even more telling is that women continued to dominate the leadership of the New Orleans chapter of CORE.

Oretha Castle certainly paved the way for those women who followed her. For most of its existence, this unstoppable young woman acted as New Orleans CORE's chairperson. In many ways, Oretha Castle's leadership is comparable to Diane Nash's leadership in the Nashville Student Union. As one CORE member recalled, the New Orleans chapter "was led by a 'backbone' of women after 1962," and the "strongest leader of the local chapter was a woman—the strong-willed and dynamic Oretha Castle, who combined leadership, motherhood, and a rich family life during her years in the movement."[73] Castle participated in a highly visible Supreme Court case while acting as president of the New Orleans CORE. She later became one of CORE's few female field secretaries, working on voter registration in Monroe, Louisiana.

The male members of CORE acknowledge the significant role that Oretha Castle and the women played. "They were all fantastic," states Matt "Flukie" Suarez. "And for me, it was an awakening because these were women who were talking about things other than what parties they wanted to go to,

70. "Youth Council Reports On Canal St. Operation," *Louisiana Weekly*, 1 August 1964.

71. Ed Hollander to Marvin Rich, August 5, 1964, Reel 40, CORE Addendum, HU.

72. Bernice McNair Barnett, "Invisible Southern Black Women Leaders in the Civil Rights Movement: The Triple Constraints of Gender, Race, and Class," *Gender and Society* 7 (June 1993): 162–63, 167. In her study of the role of black women leaders in the civil rights movement, Barnett cites these criteria for performing leadership roles most notably attributed to the male leadership.

73. Cited in Kim Lacy Rogers, *Righteous Lives: Narratives of the New Orleans Civil Rights Movement* (New York: New York University Press, 1993), 144, 175.

what dress they wanted to buy, whose hair was such and such a way. Here were women that were concerned about serious issues, were questioning the status quo and taking action."[74]

It was female members who rejected as superficial the attempt to create an integrated "Beloved Community." Unlike what happened in SNCC in 1965, where African American men took action and called for Black Power, it was women who led the fight to retain black control of their organization in New Orleans. It would take another four years before the SNCC leader Stokely Carmichael would call for a black-led, black-only organization. Coincidentally, while many of the African American members of CORE believed that their organization was "overrun" by an influx of whites, white members were seeking inclusion and "community" in a black movement. This ultimately led to disagreement over how best to create and maintain their Beloved Community. Although CORE moved its southern regional office to New Orleans in late 1963, by the time Richard Haley arrived to take charge, "the organization had begun to lose its strength and again it grew out of the Black Power problem, [although] they weren't called that then, they weren't called that at all. But it did have to do with the system that developed between black and white in New Orleans CORE."[75]

In a description of New Orleans CORE, an anonymous observer noted that it was "consistently the case that the rank and file of Negroes involved in the civil rights movement have been women, led by a few exceptional Negro men." Although movement participants were in effect, "fighting for an integrated society," many blacks in the movement allowed "themselves to be guided by their fears, which have been instilled in their hearts since childhood." Focusing on the role of white women in the movement, the author noted that white women in the South were subjected to "enormous psychological and social pressure, meant not only to prevent them from associating with Negro men, but directed at making them fear Negro men as extraordinary in sexual capacity and rapacious sexual ethics." Moreover, the anonymous writer argued, white women were expected to adhere to a rigid sexual code, more so than black women: "Therefore, a Southern white woman who is willing to attend an integrated party must be considered an exceptional individual who is striving to overcome these factors in her environment which hinder her personal freedom." In what can only be described as a portent of issues to be addressed in 1965 by Mary King and Casey Hayden in the "Kind

74. Matt "Flukie" Suarez interview, interview by the author, 3 December 2001, tape recording, copy in possession of the author.

75. Haley, interview, 9 May 1979.

of Memo" regarding the role of women in SNCC, this author recognized the value of black women to the Louisiana movement:

> The contribution of Negro women to the movement demands universal recognition. These young ladies, some of them still teenagers, have been willing to cut themselves off from social life, job opportunities, higher education, even from family life and the possibility of marriage, in order to devote themselves to the cause of setting man free and of bringing about the reign of justice and of human rights within these United States. It is these young women who filled the jails as Freedom Riders, it is these young women who man the sit-ins and accept with dignity and patience the obscene harassment of the mob, it is these young women who carry the picket signs in front of the segregationist department stores and who look on wonderingly while those whom they must call their own people enter their doors without heeding. These young women have taken upon themselves the suffering of twenty million American citizens. Repeatedly they have sacrificed their own personal security in order to demonstrate symbolically, through dramatic confrontation of their own persons with the organized forces of an unjust society, the oppression which this society visits upon a people which it once held in slavery and which it continues to hold, employing all devices of hypocrisy and bad faith, in soul-destroying serfdom. When young Negro women were kicked and beaten in a bus station in Mississippi, they forced the nation to recognize the kind of treatment, which waits for any Negro who dares assert his rights as a human being beyond the arbitrary limit, which our society chooses to set before him. The purpose of these young women was to force collective conscience to recognize without qualification the criminal behavior of which it is capable. They succeeded in this by exposing themselves to the risk of any danger including that of death. If any Negro wants to censure any of these young women for the way they act on such social occasions as those described above, let him first make such sacrifices in the cause of justice as will entitle him to speak with them on a level of equality.[76]

As Gordon Carey, field director for CORE, stated, these student activists "ha[d] been a real vitalizing influence in New Orleans."[77] Indeed, it was the actions of young female activists, black and white, that propelled the movement forward in Louisiana in the early 1960s. Even as the events of 1962 underscored the difficulties in achieving the much sought after Beloved

---

76. Anonymous letter re: women in the New Orleans movement, n.d., Reel 40, 351, CORE Papers, ARC.

77. Gordon Carey to Local Contacts, "Peaceful Sit-Ins in New Orleans and Criminal Anarchy, Part II," 4 November 1960, Reel 40, 838, CORE Addendum, HU.

Community, these young women, and African American women in particular, pushed their differences aside and continued to fight for the cause of
freedom well into the 1960s. They would continue to exert this influence by
turning their attentions to the more severe issue plaguing Louisiana's rural
communities, where black and white women were especially aware of the
significance, if not the irony, of their work together.

7

WOMEN IN THE FIELD I

The Voter Education Project in Rural Louisiana, 1962–1964

Louisiana is a truly Southern state in its attitudes towards race relations. The pattern of daytime segregation and night-time integration is characteristic to this system. Before CORE came to Louisiana, the general attitude of the white community was a paternalistic one. However, now that the Negro in Louisiana is demanding his due, the white population has become fanatically opposed to any form of integration. White authorities, rather than integrating a facility, will close it and deny themselves its use. Various groups such as the KKK, the Citizens' Councils, and Americans to Preserve the White Race have been formed to demand rigid adherence to a policy of total segregation. Louisiana, however, is not a Mississippi. Factors influencing its "liberal" veneer are its mixed (French, Spanish, etc.) population and at least partial contact with the outside world (through trade) both historically and currently. Not far beneath this façade, however, most Louisianians are true red-neck bigots like their southern neighbors.

MIRIAM FEINGOLD, "Louisiana in Brief," May 1964

As early as 1961, the Congress of Racial Equality (CORE) had begun preparations for a comprehensive voter registration project in the Deep South. Although organizations such as the National Association for the Advancement of Colored People (NAACP) and the League of Women Voters (LWV) had been conducting voter registration campaigns in Baton Rouge, Shreveport, and New Orleans for years, a program such as one planned by CORE had yet to be implemented in the Deep South. CORE organizers sought to "promote and to study and evaluate methods for teaching and encouraging exercise of the right to register to vote in areas in the South which . . . are known to be comparatively the lowest in the region." The organization's research had found extensive governmental prohibitions,

restrictions, and harassment by local registrars with respect to black registration. Subsequently, they sought to develop educational programs that
would "be most effective in providing voters with the knowledge and will to
register." The project would culminate in a published analysis of "the best
methods of education to overcome low voter registration in various geo-
graphic and cultural areas of the South."[1]

CORE's decision to expand its campaign from urban areas to rural and
small-town Louisiana forced organizational leaders to adapt and alter their
operating style. In cities like Baton Rouge and New Orleans, college students
and middle-class men and women, many of them white, had made up the
majority of CORE's membership. In rural Louisiana, CORE began to enlist
help from impoverished and working-class local blacks who had intimate experience with the harsh realities of white hostility and resistance to change.[2]
Rural blacks had, for years, employed a variety of methods to resist white
oppression in their workplaces and in their communities. As a result, challenges to Jim Crow, small and large, had cultivated a grassroots leadership
base.[3] In expanding its campaign to rural Louisiana, CORE sought to bring
these previously informal and unorganized acts of resistance into a more cohesive and disciplined civil rights campaign. At the same time, CORE realized that it would have to work with the grassroots leadership if it had any
hopes of making inroads into areas of the state loath to accept help from
"uppity outside agitators."

Veterans of the Freedom Rides and urban direct-action campaigns provided much of the initial leadership for the voter projects in Louisiana. CORE
project organizers selected James Farmer to lead the effort. According to
CORE historians August Meier and Elliot Rudwick, "except for Martin Luther King," Farmer "was the most charismatic of all the civil rights leaders."
A veteran of the civil rights movement, most notably the Freedom Rides,
Farmer had a dedication to civil disobedience and an ability to rally and in-
spire loyalty and commitment among rank-and-file members that made him
a uniquely important addition to the CORE staff.

Despite the obvious difficulties that working in the extremely rural, "back-

1. "A Statement of the Research Aims and Methods of the Voter Education Project," Reel
73, 2195, SRC Papers, LOC.

2. August Meier and Elliot Rudwick, *CORE: A Study in the Civil Rights Movement, 1942–1968*
(Urbana: University of Illinois Press, 1973), 145.

3. See Charles Payne, *I've Got the Light of Freedom: The Organizing Tradition and the Missis-
sippi Freedom Struggle* (Berkeley and Los Angeles: University of California Press, 1995); and John
Dittmer, *Local People: The Struggle for Civil Rights in Mississippi* (Urbana: University of Illinois
Press, 1994).

woods" Louisiana presented, women rallied to the cause. Local black women, as well as women from outside these small communities, participated in great numbers in the voter registration projects that occurred in the state between 1962 and 1967. As a number of historians have noted, black women were especially important in the civil rights movement in the rural South. As was the case in neighboring Mississippi, grassroots community women in Louisiana housed and fed staff members, registered to vote in greater numbers than men, held meetings and voter education clinics in their homes, and participated in mass meetings and demonstrations more often than men.[4] In addition, a number of white, female college students from the North went south, electing to work in some of the most hazardous areas of the state as field secretaries, staff members, canvassers, and organizers.

The significance of women in the field cannot be overstated. Southern gendered notions of the role of women, white women in particular, added complexities to the voter registration project in rural Louisiana. The purging of whites by the New Orleans chapter of CORE in 1962 had forced the organization to confront the problems created when interracial groups of women and men worked together in the South. And while CORE's demise in New Orleans heralded an important issue yet to be fully explored by movement activists writ large, CORE leaders, albeit with some apprehension, continued to welcome white women to the project.[5] Despite the New Orleans purges of white members, it appears that the risky and demanding nature of the voter registration project in Louisiana superseded the questions raised by interracial relationships in the field. The influx of young white women to rural Louisiana, however, altered the context of the already controversial civil rights campaign in these local communities. Black and white women alike would challenge some CORE leaders' expectations of the role of women in the field. Miriam Feingold, Oretha Castle, the Thompson sisters—Alice, Shirley, and Jean—and Mary Hamilton, among numerous other women, proved to be integral and influential members of CORE's Louisiana field staff.[6]

4. For more information on the overparticipation of women in the civil rights movement, see Charles M. Payne, "Men Led, but Women Organized: Movement Participation of Women in the Mississippi Delta," in *Women in the Civil Rights Movement: Trailblazers and Torchbearers, 1941–1965*, ed. Vicki Crawford, Jacqueline Anne Rouse, and Barbara Woods (Bloomington: Indiana University Press, 1990); and Payne, *I've Got the Light of Freedom*, esp. chap. 9, "A Woman's War."

5. For example, Mary Hamilton, a northerner, acted as one of CORE's first field secretaries.

6. Meier and Rudwick, *CORE*, 163, 152.

"SEGREGATION HERE IS COMPLETE"

It was in Louisiana's agricultural belt that CORE initially focused its attention. Although by the 1960s Louisiana, like the rest of the South, had embraced the mechanization of agriculture and industrialization, rural life still
predominated; over one-third of the state's population lived on or near a
farm. Louisiana was the nation's number-one supplier of cane sugar and
sweet potatoes, second in rice production, fourth in strawberries, and eighth
in cotton. CORE chose Louisiana's Sixth Congressional District, which included the "sugar parishes" of East and West Baton Rouge, East and West
Feliciana, Iberville, St. Helena, and Washington, to begin the voter project. CORE focused on towns such as Bogalusa, Clinton, St. Francisville, and
Franklinton, which also produced the majority of sweet potatoes, rice, and
strawberries. The project later expanded into the northeastern section of
the state, to include Ferriday, Jonesboro, Monroe, and Shreveport of the
Fourth and Fifth Congressional Districts, a region known for its cotton production.[7]

African Americans made up over 32 percent of the state's population, and
although the majority lived in cities, blacks comprised the majority of agricultural workers. In rural Louisiana, 38.3 percent of African Americans still
lived a tenant farmer's life, working on plantationlike farms. Moreover, in
a number of these project parishes, African Americans comprised the majority of the residents: 54 percent in East Feliciana, 66 percent in West Feliciana, 70 percent in Madison, 53.6 percent in Pointe Coupee, and 55.5 percent in St. Helena. In East and West Feliciana, Franklin, Iberville, Madison,
and St. Helena Parishes, African Americans lived on only half of the me-
dian family income for the state. Most of Louisiana's black farmers, however, lived well below the country's poverty line, subsisting on four dollars
a day and living in "company shacks (unbelievably dilapidated and paid for
with reductions from wages), and eat[ing] food priced high, bought at the
'company' store." At the other end of the spectrum, of course, affluent whites
made up the majority of farm owners and employers.[8]

Unequal and inadequate access to education continued to plague rural
blacks. The average number of school years completed for black Louisianians
in the 1960s stood at 3.9, well below the national average of 8.8 years total
and 5.7 years for African Americans. West Feliciana Parish, for example, did not
have a black high school until 1960, and two-thirds of adults throughout the

7. Feingold, Davis, and Messing, "Louisiana in Brief," CORE Addendum, HU.
8. Feingold, Davis, and Messing, "Louisiana in Brief," CORE Addendum, HU.

state had fewer than four years of high school. Throughout the 1960s, Louisiana continued to operate a system of segregated education in a number of its parishes, with most of the state public school system's resources allocated to white schools. According to a number of contemporary studies, education and economic viability were important factors in contributing to African Americans' attainment of voting rights. An internal CORE study concluded that, "The resulting society is one in which a few wealthy men (white) hold tight economic control over the area while a large number of people (mostly Negro) live in conditions little better than slavery—poverty, fear, ignorance."[9]

In 1960s rural Louisiana, a plantation oligarchy was alive and well. Black voter registration, particularly in the Sixth Congressional District, stood well below the level in the rest of the state. In 1956, Louisiana had the highest percentage of registered blacks in the lower South. Yet after the state legislature established the Joint Legislative Committee in the fall of 1956 to investigate "uniform enforcement of Louisiana voter qualification laws," the number of registered black voters dropped from 161,410 to 131,068 in 1958. In 1960, the Louisiana Legislature passed a series of laws known as the "Segregation Law Package" that included an amendment to the Louisiana constitution substantially changing the voting laws. It disqualified individuals for convictions for misdemeanors, common law marriage, having an illegitimate child, and other acts that constituted "bad character." Louisiana legislators accomplished what they had set out to do; in 1961, only 82 blacks were registered to vote in East Feliciana Parish, 2,484 in Iberville, 821 in Pt. Coupee, 111 in St. Helena, 1,711 in Washington, and 1,203 in Baton Rouge. In 1962, the state passed additional laws that "prevented or severely limited" further voter registration for African Americans. By the time CORE embarked on its voter education project in late 1962, the number of registered African Americans had continued to decline, and of the Sixth Congressional District's 92,216 African American's of voting age, fewer than one-third were actually registered to vote. In Madison, Tensas (Bogalusa), and West Feliciana Parishes, where the black percentage of the population stood at 67 per-

9. Feingold, Davis, and Messing, "Louisiana in Brief," CORE Addendum, HU. See also Donald R. Matthews and James W. Prothro, "Social and Economic Factors and Negro Voter Registration in the South," *American Political Science Review* 57, no. 1 (March 1963); and Donald R. Matthews and James W. Prothro, "Political Factors and Negro Voter Registration in the South," 57, no, 2 (June 1963). The authors also suggest that a greater percentage of African Americans in a population, comparable to whites, contributed to increased numbers of black registered voters, but this was obviously not the case in Louisiana.

cent, 65 percent, and 73 percent respectively, not a single black person was registered to vote.[10]

Because rural blacks depended heavily on whites for their daily survival, at the outset CORE found itself at a disadvantage. The organization initially approached the NAACP, which had conducted voter registration campaigns in the South for a number of years. The NAACP in Louisiana, however, was itself at a disadvantage as the Louisiana legislature had successfully ended its charter in the state; thus in the early 1960s its field staff was minimal. The Southern Regional Council (SRC), a much larger and more centralized interracial organization founded in 1942, had more resources. Lacking financial resources of its own, CORE applied for a grant, admitting that "registration campaigning, in the absence of dramatic causes, is hard, grubby, tiring, unspectacular, frequently discouraging . . . [is] at least as difficult as the enlistment of local groups and mobilizing manpower," and that finances would be difficult to obtain. Project organizers also acknowledged that "voting is no panacea, nor even the ultimate weapon against discrimination." They believed, however, that "free and full participation of Negroes in Southern elections, and the consequent respect which Negro citizens will be accorded, may be the surest means of ending or at least decreasing southern preoccupation with race and the racial prejudice that grows from that." In August 1962, CORE secured a grant for a "joint and large effort to increase voter registration in the South."[11]

In the fall of 1962, CORE began to solicit volunteer field staff to work in rural Louisiana. In some parishes, the NAACP had already attempted to establish registration projects. In Lake Charles, for example, a small voter registration project was led by two women, Mrs. M. T. Brown, NAACP youth director, and Mrs. Corne, the coordinating chairman for voter registration for the NAACP.[12] In the fall of 1962, CORE's National Action Committee created a "Task Force," a group of individuals who "supplemented the regular field

10. "Negro Registration in Louisiana" (1962), Reel 23, 220, CORE Addendum, HU; "The History of Negro Suffrage in Louisiana," in *Negro Voting in Louisiana* (Baton Rouge: Committee on Registration Education, 1962) and "Louisiana—The Soft Under-Belly of the Oligarchies," *New Citizen* (April 6, 1962), both located in Box 17, Folder 4, CORE Papers, SHSW; "Population and Registration Statistics for Louisiana by Congressional Districts," 30 April 1961, Series VI, Reel 175, CORE Papers, SHSW. See also Margaret Price, *The Negro and the Ballot in the South* (Atlanta: Southern Regional Office Publication, 1959), esp. "Current Negro Registration," Box 17, Folder 4, CORE Papers, SHSW.

11. "Task Force: Freedom," November 13, 1962, Reel 44, 68, CORE Papers, ARC.

12. Report by Daniel Harrell, junior field secretary of the NAACP, September 1963, Reel 183, SRC Papers.

staff" in the South and worked anywhere from four months to a year on a weekly subsistence salary of twenty-five dollars. Noting the successes of its recruitment drives for the 1961 Freedom Rides and subsequent Freedom Highways Project, CORE created a "Freedom Task Force" comprised of "long-term volunteers, many of whom [were] college students" willing to devote at least a year to working with "Negro leaders and with other civil rights organizations . . . in smaller communities." The task force committee selected volunteer "field workers from CORE chapters and from college campuses across the nation." The project would be interracial, and CORE expected that "each person accepted must have a deep commitment to the use and practice of nonviolent methods." Applicants were additionally warned of the "long periods of time under tension, often in a hostile social climate," to which they would most certainly be exposed.[13]

The application process for Louisiana, much like the one for the Mississippi Freedom Summer, was rigorous. CORE required each applicant to fill out a three-page questionnaire listing personal information such as age, most recent school attended, college activities, and jobs held. It asked for organizational affiliations, if one had participated in any civil rights activities, and any other relevant training or experience, including skills such as typing, office work, and the ability to drive. Applicants were also asked to note whether they had ever been arrested and why; to list contacts that could be helpful should they find themselves in jail or to help publicize their activities; and to list any persons to be notified in case of arrest, harassment, or worse. CORE asked applicants to list their hometown newspapers, as well as senators and congressmen. Many applicants also chose to include a brief statement about why they wanted to participate in the voter education project. One white woman wrote: "I would like to join the task force because there is a dire need for people to work on direct action projects and on voter registration projects employing non-violent techniques. I am very interested in nonviolent action and I feel that I could be used most effectively in the South, mainly because all of my experiences have been confined to the South dealing with civil rights."[14]

Despite warnings of the rigors of the project and the dangers that were bound to ensue, during the years that CORE's voter education project ran in Louisiana, women ranked high among applicants for summer fieldwork.[15]

13. "Task Force: Freedom," 13 November 1962, CORE Papers, ARC.

14. "Application for Summer Project," 1962, and Application of Bette Anne Poole, Reel 44, 63, 70, CORE Papers, ARC.

15. Although I cannot be sure that all of the applications for the 1962–66 summer projects

Early applicants included veteran Freedom Riders Miriam Feingold, Jean
and Shirley Thompson, and Ruth Wells, also of the New Orleans CORE chapter. Mary Hamilton, a light-skinned black woman from the North, a Freedom
Rider, and a longtime CORE staff member, also worked in Louisiana. All of
these women had served on the picket lines, joined the Freedom Rides after
the first buses were bombed in Anniston, Alabama, and survived months in
Mississippi's most notorious prison. Jean Thompson and her sisters, Alice
and Shirley, along with a number of other women, worked on voter registration on and off throughout the 1960s. However, Miriam "Mimi" Feingold
remained the most committed and consistent activist in Louisiana. After
her initial 1963 summer, Feingold returned to Louisiana every year through
1967, even putting graduate school on hold for a year to work on voter registration full time in what many considered the most dangerous area of the
state, the Feliciana parishes.

Born in 1942 and raised in Brooklyn, New York, Miriam Feingold epitomized the "Red Diaper baby." Her parents were active members of the Old
Left and outspoken members of the Communist Party. Believing religion to
be the "opiate of the masses," the Feingolds were not observant Jews, yet
they instilled the central tenets of Jewish culture in their children. Consequently, Mimi grew up in a family that not only embraced an ethic of idealism, but also witnessed firsthand the struggle for social justice. Feingold's
father taught high school math, and her mother worked as a librarian. During the McCarthy era, however, both lost their jobs with the public schools.
Feingold recalls that both her parents were very active in the teachers union,
"which was very left-wing and members were [Communist] party members, if not sympathizers." She remembered attending May Day parades
and meetings in her parents' home. The New York City public school system
fired Feingold's father for insubordination when he refused to testify before
the House Un-American Activities Committee about his activities. His case

---

are complete, women were well represented in the applications that were available in the CORE
Papers. Moreover, lists of CORE's field staff through the years support this fact. According to
Doug McAdam, who conducted a sociological study of participants of the Mississippi Freedom
Summer, "The number of women who applied to the Summer Project was surprising, both in
view of composition of the undergraduate population in 1964, and the strength of traditional
barriers to women's participation in projects such as Freedom Summer." McAdam found that
41 percent of the applicants were female (McAdam, *Freedom Summer* [New York: Oxford University Press, 1988], 57, 61).

ultimately reached the Supreme Court, where his dismissal was eventually overturned, though only after he had already passed away.[16]

Like many immigrants, Feingold's parents came from families that placed great value on education; both of her parents held master's degrees. It was taken for granted that she would attend college, and Feingold went to Swarthmore, a well-known liberal arts college founded by the pacifist Quakers. Feingold started her college career as a biology major, but, "guided by what was going to be socially relevant," she changed her major to history so she could better "understand the class struggle." During her freshman year, Feingold joined the Swarthmore Political Action Club (SPAC), ultimately becoming a leader of the organization. SPAC included many students from from Old Left/Marxist families; it even included a Marxist discussion group.

Although Feingold had minimally participated in civil rights activities, she became more aware of the nascent civil rights movement while involved with SPAC. Feingold was in high school when the Supreme Court ruled in *Brown v. Board of Education*. After the ruling, she helped organize a busload of kids to go to Washington, D.C., for a march on Washington. As Feingold stated: "I was a movement waiting to happen. I was ready to leap onto anything that came along. There just wasn't anything happening then." When the sit-ins began in early 1960, Feingold worked with the Chester, Pennsylvania, chapter of the NAACP to organize a boycott and picket of Woolworth's. Feingold then became aware of SNCC through her aunt. She attended one of the initial organizing meetings and was hooked. Then she heard of the Freedom Rides organized by CORE.[17]

Mimi flew to New Orleans to join the second phase of the Freedom Rides after the initial contingent of riders disbanded following the bombing in Anniston. She remembered that her parents were worried, but supportive. After her arrest in Jackson, Mississippi, and nearly four months in Parchman Penitentiary, Feingold returned to New York to spend the summer with her family. During that summer of 1961 in Ticonderoga, New York, at her family's summer home, she kept in touch with CORE. Her family also organized "little coffees" where she would "tell her story of the rides" to raise money for the organization. The following fall Feingold returned to Swarthmore, where she and other SPAC members organized the cafeteria workers into a union. SPAC also tested a segregated ice skating rink in a predominantly

16. Miriam "Mimi" Feingold, interview by the author, 1 December 2002, tape recording, copy in possession of the author.

17. Feingold, interview, 1 December 2002.

black section of town, and, following a lawsuit, the skating rink was forced to end its segregation policies. That year Feingold also worked closely with well-known activist Gloria Richardson and other activists in Cambridge, on the Eastern Shore of Maryland. On weekends she picketed and sat in, and she was arrested several times for her activities. As the voter registration project began to take shape in early 1962, Feingold applied to work with the task force. "The minute I heard about this voter registration stuff," recalled Feingold, "I was just so excited about this. School ended before we were to report to Louisiana, so I worked on the Eastern Shore . . . for a couple of weeks and then a bunch of us, as I recall, drove from there to Louisiana."[18]

Mimi Feingold arrived in Louisiana in July 1963 to begin work with CORE's first summer task force. An interracial group of forty-six volunteers met at CORE headquarters in Plaquemine, Louisiana (Iberville Parish), chosen because of its active voter registration project. Iberville Parish's economy was based on sugar plantations that employed the majority of African Americans in the parish. According to Feingold, "The people work every day (including Sunday) from sun-up to sun-down. They live in 'quarters,' a small collection of houses, all of which look alike: wooden homes, no gas, water, sagging porches. Each house is overflowing with children; it's the only recreation the people have." The remaining black residents of the parish resided outside the Plaquemine city limits in "Negro ghettos," where they, too, had no running water, no streetlights, gravel roads, and no garbage collection. Moreover, "people [had] to draw their water from a pump, and go to the bathroom in the woods, or an outhouse," according to Feingold. "Because of the dust from the roads, nothing stay[ed] clean. . . . The houses [were] typical: wooden jobs with holes in the walls and floors, stinking drainage ditches in the front. In one area, the Dow Chemical Plant used to pour its waste products into the people's ditches until one lady's house caught fire and burned up."[19]

It was in this environment, and similar other areas across the state, that task force volunteers found themselves preparing to train impoverished and illiterate blacks to register to vote. The volunteers were subjected to a "rigorous orientation period . . . including canvassing and setting up voter education clinics in eight communities in Iberville Parish," and Pointe Coupee and Ouachita Parishes, where a number of citizens had already filed complaints with the state and U.S. Department of Justice.[20] CORE initially pro-

18. Feingold, interview, 1 December 2002.
19. Feingold to parents, 15 October 1963, Reel 1, Miriam Feingold Papers.
20. Feingold, interview, 1 December 2002, and news release, "Task Force," 24 July 1963, Reel

vided leadership in helping local blacks register to vote; however, they expected local community members to assume leadership positions and take over the registration process in each town. As Mimi Feingold wrote in her journal: "we go through a very comprehensive CORE-type training session for one week, spend one week more in Plaquemine, then get assigned to the parishes. We may engage in direct action, especially if it will help build community militancy. Louisiana is another country, although it's far from being Mississippi."[21]

Almost immediately, issues between the male and female, and black and white field staff arose. As Feingold reported in a letter to her parents: "I seem to have all sorts of petty jobs to do. I'm not finding it especially easy to get along with the group leader here, so I just try to keep out of his way and do what he tells me to do. I think one of his problems is he finds it hard to relate to white females generally." Moreover, Feingold began to see "[h]ow hard it's going to be to be a white in a non-white world. There's a lot of distrust, mixed with undue awe and respect. Certainly the white folks here haven't done very much to improve the image of the white man. You know there's a lot you read about in Faulkner and Tennessee Williams, etc. that we tend to dismiss as sickness and generally as an unfortunate product of the southern system, that [is] so very much the norm around here. There's a lot of 'sundown integration' and the hypocritical veneration of white womanhood."[22]

To be sure, gender affected every aspect of the volunteer experience. Although recruiters preferred male volunteers because of the risk involved in working in rural southern communities, a number of motivated white women sought inclusion in this predominantly male movement. According

---

45, 1570, CORE Papers, ARC. A number of women filed federal complaints in 1962 with CORE or the SRC, stating that the registrar refused to register them. The CORE Papers include the following plaintiffs for 1962: Mrs. Delore Lagodvans, Mrs. Louvenia Mitchell, Albetha Anderson, Mrs. Louise Parker, Mrs. Rebecca Johnson, Mrs. Lydia Ruffin, Lillian Pilne, Mrs. Ora Lee Williams, Mrs. Lillian Lee Pitts Robertson, Edna Johnson, Mrs. Willie Ann Robinson, Mrs. Eloise Moore, Mable Sparrow, Maudria Steward, Mrs. Girlie Mae Stewart, Mrs. Geneva Wright, Mrs. Adlie Hawkins, Mrs. Elmira Swift, Mrs. Ella Lark, and Mrs. Lavinia Lapeel. A number of men also filed complaints; however, in my research on Louisiana, I found that women were more likely to register to vote than men were, possibly because they were less likely to suffer financial repercussions.

21. Miriam Feingold journal, 12 July 1963, Reel 1, notebook 6, Feingold Papers. Throughout her career in Louisiana, Feingold kept an extensive, almost daily journal chronicling her activities.

22. Feingold to parents, 19 August 1963, Reel 1, Feingold Papers.

to Dave Dennis, CORE's Southern Office director: "We had low on the list the white females, because they cause problems usually you know. That's one thing that infuriates a white male in the South especially . . . it's that whole interracial . . . sex problem, . . . white people . . . in the South, especially, can usually stomach to see a white male and a Negro male walking down the street, or a white male and a Negro female, you know, its accepted to some extent. But it infuriates people, it causes tremendous reactions, when there's a white female and a Negro male involved."[23] Because female volunteers were lowest on the totem pole, they had to work extra hard to prove their worth. Ironically, as the sociologist Mary Aikin Rothschild explains, "In the main, they were more qualified in terms of previous social-action work and tended to have more direct political experience than their male counterparts."[24] Miriam Feingold's background certainly makes a case for this argument.

Although Feingold spent most of her time working in the Feliciana parishes, her initiation to dangers of fieldwork began in Plaquemine. For almost eight months, CORE had worked alongside the biracial Iberville Voters League (IVL) toward establishing equal job opportunities, desegregating the public schools and the parish courthouse, and incorporating two black communities deemed "unimproved Negro areas" into the city limits of Plaquemine. As Feingold noted in her journal: "segregation here is complete. Negroes are half the population in this parish, but few vote. Unemployment is tough. Apathy outside the cities is high. I know now that it was good to come here."[25]

In late summer of 1963, the city of Plaquemine erupted in a clash between whites and blacks. As CORE records document, women were hardly immune to the violence inflicted on fieldworkers. On August 19, 1963, James Farmer, along with the leaders of the IVL, led five hundred people on a march to city hall to protest the failure of officials to address black grievances. Almost immediately a mob formed. Police arrested Farmer and the other leaders and forced the crowd into a local church, using tear gas, fire hoses, and electric cattle prods. A mob surrounded the church and began lobbing tear gas into the building. Still, Plaquemine's black citizens continued their protests undeterred, and within a few days, police had arrested more than two hun-

23. Dave Dennis quotation from Mary Aikin Rothschild, "White Women Volunteers in the Freedom Summers: Their Life Work in a Movement for Social Change," *Feminist Studies* (Fall 1979): 474.

24. Rothschild, "White Women Volunteers," 476.

25. Feingold journal, 12 July 1963, Feingold Papers.

dred people. At one point, over two hundred young people marched to Sheriff Griffon's home to protest the arrest of the demonstrators. The kids were "trampled by horses, kicked in the heads, on the legs and breasts, also were forced into weeds by electric cattle prods, and were molested in the usual manner with tear gas bombs." According to CORE's historians, "The black community was galvanized into unprecedented unity by this cruelty."[26]

In another mass demonstration that September, a number of female demonstrators were severely injured when the police ordered all of the women and children out of the church. As Mimi Feingold reported: "The crowd was hysterical—injured women screaming and kicking on the beds, everyone crying and screaming. They pulled down one girl's pants and prodded her between the legs. They prodded an eight month pregnant lady until she dropped from pain." Helen Jean LeJeune was "hit on the back of the head by policemen with a billet," after he approached her on horseback and pushed her into a tree. A number of other female demonstrators later reported to the Department of Justice injuries ranging from burns, eye, lung, and stomach irritation from the tear gas, and bruised and broken body parts. One twelve-year-old black girl who had been trampled by a horse later died at Charity Hospital in New Orleans after the local hospital refused to treat her.[27]

Feingold hid in a shed with two teenage black girls, where they "listened for over an hour to the mobs. For a while we heard gunfire." Eventually, the three were discovered and taken to jail. Police arrested all of the white CORE workers, and, in all, more than four hundred demonstrators were taken to jail. At the same time, police conducted a violent house-to-house search for James Farmer, whom they identified as the leader of the group. Two African American girls heard the troopers say they were going to lynch him. Local citizens, fearing for Farmer's life, took him to a local funeral home, hid him in a hearse, and eventually drove him out of town to CORE headquarters in New Orleans. In the end, more than 150 people were hospitalized, hun-

26. "The Story of Plaquemine," n.d., Reel 20, 966, CORE Papers, ARC; "Louisiana Story, 1963," Reel 49, 246, CORE Papers, ARC; Meier and Rudwick, CORE, 221–23; Feingold, interview, 1 December 2002.

27. Injury reports by Helen Jean LeJeune, Mrs. Gertrude Jones, Elizabeth Asberry, Carolyn Smith, Evelyn Dandridge, Mrs. Pearl Cole, Mrs. Nora Scott, Rosemary Wallace, Mable Williams, Mary Rogers, Mrs. Edna Mae Price, Mrs. Myrtle Jones, Nora Lee Nelson, Miss Ida Louise Calloway, Mrs. Martha Butler, Theresa Davis, Mrs. Gertrude Jones, Everline Green, Mrs. Victoria Holland, Mrs. Nathanial Battiste, Mrs. Laura Anderson, Elnora Wade, Mildred Wade, and Baziel Johnson, August 1963, Reel 20, 966–96, CORE Papers, ARC; Feingold to Danny Feingold, 5 September 1963, Feingold Papers.

dreds of others injured, and the church semi-demolished due to police van-
dalism.[28]

After her incarcerations at Parchman Penitentiary, jail time was old hat
to Mimi Feingold. The police held Feingold and the other CORE workers
at the local fairground overnight as the town jails were not large enough
to house the hundreds of arrested demonstrators. Police then transferred
her and the other women to a jail in Port Allen, Louisiana. Being the only
white, Feingold stayed in a cell by herself. She humorously reported to a
friend, "I am being temporarily detained in the finest of Port Allen hotels,
which boasts free room and board and pink cells with bathtubs. What more
could one ask for? Ironically, I integrated the women's section." Managing
to smuggle in a pencil, and because there was nothing else available to write
on, Mimi "wrote an account of the whole incident on toilet paper," later
published in a number of newspapers. Feingold recalled that she had on a
dress that her mother had hemmed: "My mother was not a domestic sort
of woman. Hemming a dress was about the extent of her sewing ability,
and her hemming was not very good. I was able to break the stitching and
create a little entrance into the hem into which I slid the toilet paper, and
that's how it got smuggled out of the Port Allen jail."[29]

Numerous reports and accounts illustrate that gender did not mitigate
the jail experience, even in the South, where women, white women in particular, held special status. While in jail, Feingold and "the girls," the black
female demonstrators in the cell next to hers, wrote daily reports in English
and French, back and forth, on toilet paper. They complained that the police
put one of the girls in a padded cell by convincing her that she could leave
her cell to call her father. The jailers also locked their windows in the dread-
fully hot Louisiana September and gave them only dry bread to eat. At one
point, a drunken female was put in the cell with them where she promptly
vomited all over the cell, leaving "stale whisky and sour food smells all over
the place." The "girls" sang to pass the time and keep everyone's spirits up,
but as one girl wrote: "Things are pretty unbearable. . . . Most of our spirits
are pretty low." Eventually CORE bailed them out. Feingold left immediately

28. "The Story of Plaquemine," n.d., Reel 20, 968–78, CORE Papers, ARC; "Negroes Live in
Fear in Plaquemine," *Louisiana Weekly*, 7 September 1963; Feingold, interview, 1 December 2002;
"The Toilet Paper Letter," Feingold to Danny Feingold, 5 September 1963, Feingold Papers. Mimi
Feingold wrote an extensive letter to her brother Danny chronicling the demonstration and subsequent violence while in jail on toilet paper, which she hid in the hem of her dress when she
was released. The story of James Farmer's escape from Plaquemine is well known in civil rights
circles and has been chronicled by a number of individuals, including Farmer himself.

29. "The Toilet Paper Letter," n.d., Feingold Papers; Feingold, interview, 1 December 2002.

for New Orleans and spent the night with a young white couple active in the movement. From there she left for New York to visit her family.[30]

As was the case with almost all of the women activists, jail did not deter them. Mimi Feingold kept her promise to stay in Louisiana for the entire year. She expected to work in the Felicianas, but Ronnie Moore, CORE field director for the district, informed her that she would be taking over the Plaquemine office since she was "so efficient." By now, the police had begun harassing the volunteer canvassers and waiting outside the voter registration clinics, yelling "nasty remarks from their cars." Feingold stayed in Plaquemine for several months. In a typical week, she contacted 150 people, trained 60, sent 18 to the registrar's office, and got 9 registered. "It is pathetic," stated Feingold, "that some of the most enthusiastic people are the ones who have common law spouses, etc. which automatically disqualifies them."[31]

Feingold was one of only three female staff members in Iberville Parish and the only female in charge of a parish voter registration office. That September, Joan Bunche, the daughter of Ralph Bunche, an esteemed professor at Howard University in Washington, D.C., joined the CORE project in Plaquemine. According to Feingold: "She had never been in the South before, and had evidently been coddled all her life, and it's quite an experience to see her adjusting to life down here. She's a wonderful person, full of life, but totally strange to the ways of most Negroes anywhere—interesting commentary on Vernon's [Jordan] remark to me early in the summer that we know more of suffering than rich Negroes. It's certainly true in this case. She isn't at all a snob, but it's obvious in the thirty years of her life she's never had to confront anything terribly physically trying."[32] Apparently northern white volunteers were not the only ones who were naïve about the inequities and hardships that defined black life in the rural South.

Female CORE workers and local citizens in other areas of the state faced similar dangers. Ruthie Wells and Shirley Thompson, both alumni of the New Orleans CORE chapter, worked in Pointe Coupee Parish supervising nonviolent training sessions, conducting sit-ins, and picketing against the registrar of voters. In one incident, a sheriff accosted and searched Wells while she canvassed. Female CORE workers in Ouachita Parish, including

---

30. Feingold to Danny Feingold, 5 September 1963, and letters to Feingold in jail, signed "The Girls," n.d., "The Toilet Paper Letter," Feingold Papers.

31. Intimidations and Harassment Against Negroes and CORE Workers, Summer 1963 to Summer 1964, Reel 40, 529, CORE Papers, ARC; Feingold to parents, 15 October 1963, Reel 1, Feingold Papers.

32. Feingold to Charlotte Phillips, 29 September 1963, Reel 1, Feingold Papers.

Oretha Castle and local activist Sarah McCoy, found themselves under constant surveillance as police tapped their phones and harassed CORE workers at voter education clinics. When CORE workers arrived in Tallulah (Madison Parish), they were arrested for "disturbing the peace" and "told never to return on penalty of death."[33] Perhaps the most trying times for women, however, were when they attempted to register to vote. Although often refused, black women returned to the registrar's office time after time. In St. Helena Parish, for example, Lillie Lee Stewart attempted to register five times and Margaret Spears Tickles twice, to no avail.[34]

With finances running low and harassment of task force workers unceasing, by November 1963 the work in Plaquemine had "literally ground to a halt." In October, the police impounded two CORE vehicles, which they did not return for over a month, costing the organization money it could ill afford. In addition, when the cars were returned, the police had obviously tampered with them, forcing CORE to sell them for junk. Lack of transportation forced the volunteers to do voter registration work on foot and end direct action for the time being. CORE was so desperate for money that Feingold wrote her parents for help. "We are ready to do anything to get the money, including selling our blood to a blood bank. Those of us who have rare blood can get a pretty penny for it. I think I have AB negative." She hoped that her parents could help them obtain a car by raising money among their friends. With the work in Plaquemine waning, Feingold finally left for the Felicianas.[35]

In Clinton, Louisiana (East Feliciana Parish), Feingold joined an already active group of female task force workers including Alice Thompson of New Orleans, and Verla Bell, a young local organizer. The workers in the Feliciana parishes had encountered problems similar to those experienced by Feingold in Plaquemine. The constant harassment by local police and the apathy of the local blacks made their voter registration work a daunting task. As in Iberville Parish, agriculture—cotton and sweet potatoes—dominated the Felicianas. Tenant farmers and sharecroppers made up more than 80 percent of workers in West Feliciana Parish, and only a handful of blacks

33. Field Report, September 1963, Reel 183, SRC Papers; Intimidations and Harassment Activity Against Negroes and CORE Workers, Summer 1963 to Summer 1964, 21 July 1964, Reel 40, 529, CORE Papers, ARC.

34. Affidavits of Lillie Lee Stewart and Margaret Spears Tickles, 1963, Reel 175, SRC Papers.

35. Feingold to parents, 16 November 1963, also published as "A Letter from a CORE Volunteer in Louisiana," *Varsity*, 13 January 1964, Reel 1, Feingold Papers

had registered to vote since 1902. The situation in East Feliciana was only slightly better; 80 blacks were on the rolls.[36]

As was often the case in local communities, CORE workers had a difficult time securing housing for fear of repercussions by local whites. In West Feliciana Parish, for instance, black sweet potato farmers depended on contracts with the Princeville Canning Company. When CORE workers attempted to register these black farmers, the cannery canceled their contracts and farm owners threw them off the land. In spite of this constant harassment, some local leaders came from the ranks of the poor farmworkers, the unemployed, and students. In West Feliciana, a number of local women risked their livelihoods, indeed their lives, to aid the movement. Grassroots female activists housed and fed CORE workers, acted as role models by registering to vote, and even held clinics in their homes. Women, in fact, often made up a majority of those registering to vote and holding membership in local organizations. In Louisiana, as in Mississippi, women were among the first community members to come forward to house the first activists and "allay the fears of others in the community who were suspicious of new arrivals." In an environment shaped by severe racism and economic dependence, where the "mere act of survival was, in itself, a life-threatening, day-to-day ordeal," women, particularly "the mamas of the movement," sustained and furthered the civil rights activism in their communities.[37]

Two local women, Charlotte Greenup and Josephine "Mama Jo" Holmes, were among the early female leaders in West Feliciana. Greenup, "one of the most gracious, articulate, vibrant, and militant Negroes" in the parish, had a long history of civil rights activism. Originally from East Feliciana Parish, Greenup lived for almost forty years in Chicago, where she taught public school and worked as a secretary for Oscar DePriest, the city's first black congressman. She returned to her native Louisiana in the 1960s to join the civil rights campaigns and to help manage her family's 191-acre farm in West Feliciana. In her eighties when CORE arrived on the scene, Greenup housed and fed four workers, including Mimi Feingold, and helped the volunteers in any way she could.[38]

36. See Adam Fairclough, *Race and Democracy: The Civil Rights Struggle in Louisiana, 1915–1972* (Athens: University of Georgia Press, 1995), 303–4.

37. Feingold, interview, 22 December 2002. See also Vicki Crawford, "We Shall Not Be Moved: Black Female Activists in the Mississippi Civil Rights Movement, 1960–1965" (Ph.D. diss., Emory University, 1987), 67, 68–110; and Sara Evans, *Personal Politics: The Roots of Women's Liberation in the Civil Rights Movement and the New Left* (New York: Vintage Books, 1979), 53.

38. "Contacts for Clinton, Louisiana," report on Charlotte Greenup, n.d., Reel 4, 488, CORE Papers, SHSW.

In East Feliciana Parish, seventy-four-year-old Mama Jo Holmes, also described as a "militant and courageous woman," housed five CORE workers, including Mimi Feingold, when Greenup took ill. As one CORE report noted, "Talking to her [Mama Jo] is a prerequisite to knowing the community." She boldly held voter registration clinics in her home. In one instance, Mama Jo "faced down a local sheriff with a loaded shotgun" in front of her home when he arrived to intimidate the CORE workers who were staying with her. For her efforts, white vigilantes burned a cross on her lawn one evening with only Feingold and Alice Thompson in the house.[39] Other important community contacts included Eunice Scott, Dora Leonard, Janie Daniels, and schoolteachers Virginia Martin and Hazel Matthews, who joined CORE "in defiance of her principal."[40]

A number of younger female student activists followed in the footsteps of the older black women including Laura Spears, Verla Bell, and Debra Brown. Bell, Brown, and Spears worked alongside family members in the West Feliciana movement. They demonstrated, boycotted, and went to jail alongside their brothers and sisters, fathers and mothers, and aunts and uncles, thus cementing the importance of CORE's call for grassroots-based community activists.

In the fall of 1963, CORE succeeded in establishing local affiliates in the Feliciana parishes. In West Feliciana, the Committee on Registration Education (WFCRE) acted as an affiliate to CORE, working to "promote voter registration and to abolish discrimination based on skin color, religion, and national origin." To become a member, individuals not only had to subscribe to CORE's program, but also had to participate in a nonviolent direct-action clinic, attempt to register to vote, and/or participate in direct-action projects. In East Feliciana Parish, a new CORE chapter included a number of young black woman—Verla Bell as secretary and Hazel Matthews on the executive committee. Verla Bell's brother, James Bell, served as vice chairman; her sister Bettie Bell, taught at the voter registration clinic until her parents forced her to stop; and sister Annie Bell Nero also taught at the Clinton and Wilson clinics. Both chapters worked throughout the fall, picketing local stores, conducting voter registration clinics and canvassing, working to abolish segregated library facilities, trying to establish a sweet potato co-op,

---

39. *Louisiana Weekly* article and Ronnie Bouma quoted in Greta de Jong, *A Different Day: The African-American Freedom Struggle and the Transformation of Rural Louisiana, 1900–1970* (Chapel Hill: University of North Carolina Press, 2002), 182–83; Fairclough, *Race and Democracy*, 304.

40. Mimi Feingold notebook, 30 November 1963, Reel 1, Feingold Papers. Among these women, only one man was listed.

and preparing to open a Freedom School. In East Feliciana Parish, the CORE chapter also conducted jail-ins when police arrested picketers for disturbing the peace and attempting to desegregate the courtroom at an appearance of CORE members.[41]

The East Feliciana Parish chapter further formed a biracial committee to investigate basic economic needs in the area. Economic considerations trumped most other issues for rural southern blacks, and since many black agricultural workers in Louisiana relied on their white neighbors for employment, economics remained a major factor among rural Louisianians' decisions to join local civil rights organizations. In many communities, civil rights participation could lead to economic or other reprisals. For many men whose position in the family as the main breadwinner mitigated all decisions, family considerations outweighed issues of equal access and voting rights.

It is not surprising, then, that rural, black women were perhaps less inhibited than their male counterparts when it came to economics, and barely hesitated when the movement came to town. In East and West Feliciana Parishes, for example, local women acted as crucial members of the civil rights campaigns.[42] Even when the local judge, John Rarick, essentially enjoined CORE from working in East Feliciana Parish, women continued to press for equal rights. At a Sunday church service, for example, when Hazel Matthews asked for volunteers to picket, only one person, Hattie Evans, stood up; for this she received "a hearty round of applause."[43] Laura Spears lost her job due to her affiliation with CORE. The local school expelled eighteen

41. Constitution of West Feliciana Chapter on the Committee on Registration Education, Box 2, File 3, 6th Congressional District, CORE Papers, SHSW; Application for Affiliation, West Feliciana Chapter—Committee on Registration, East Feliciana Chapter, CORE, n.d., Reel 18, 58, CORE Addendum, HU; Field Reports, n.d., Reel 4, 488, CORE Addendum, HU; "Recommendation for Affiliation of the West Feliciana Chapter of CORE," Ronnie Moore, November 1963, Reel 18, 58, CORE Addendum, HU.

42. For example, in Monroe, Louisiana, on 6 September 1962, ten women and twelve men attempted to register; on 10 September 1962, twelve women and eight men attempted to register; and on 13 September 1962, twelve women and six men attempted to register to vote. In a number of cases, including this example, women returned to register until they were successful. Moreover, in an early voter registration project in East Carroll Parish organized by the NAACP, all of the fieldworkers were women, barring the NAACP director (see Southern Regional Council Papers, Voter Education Project—States, Reel 175, Voter Registration Survey for Monroe, Louisiana, 1962, and Statistical Information cited in *Atlanta World*, 29 July 1962, LOC).

43. Public notice of Judge Rarick's order, from Richard Kilbourne, District Attorney, Twentieth Judicial District, 23 August 1963; Reel 18, 58, CORE Addendum, HU; Mimi Feingold notebook, 18 November 1963, Reel 1, Feingold Papers.

students, including six girls, for three days for "disrespect" when they refused to remove CORE buttons. Of this group, Maggie Perkins, Eunice Scott,
Mary Louise Davis, Catherine Archie, and two boys defiantly returned to
school that Friday wearing their CORE pins even after the principal threatened them with further suspension and a trip before the school board. Perkins, Scott, Davis, Patsy Matthews, Josephine Johnson, and Ledora Anderson agreed to picket with CORE the following Saturday. Local activists, including many female students, remained in jail for nearly four weeks after
police arrested them for picketing white merchants.[44]

By the end of the year, CORE's influence in the Felicianas began to affect local African Americans when the Princeville Canning Company refused
to renew the contracts of black sweet potato farmers who had attempted
to register to vote. Subsequently, in early 1964 CORE focused on creating a
food cooperative for black farmers, as subsistence took priority over voting
rights. Recognizing the plight of African Americans in the Felicianas, CORE
had made successful inroads into an area of Louisiana that was thought to
be impregnable. While CORE retained its base in the Sixth Congressional
District throughout 1964, the organization began to expand its presence
throughout the state. As in the Felicianas, women were again a fundamental
part of CORE's efforts. In Shreveport, the "second-most influential person"
in the chapter was Ann Brewster, a beautician who ultimately committed
suicide in November 1963 after incurring numerous financial debts due to
her activism and "saddened by the apathy she saw in the black community."[45]
Jane Duffin worked as field director in CORE's Baton Rouge project.[46] Projects in Ouachita, Plaquemine, and Pointe Coupee Parishes were staffed with
local and national women.[47]

While all of these parishes were extremely dangerous places for *all* civil
rights activists and CORE volunteers, by the mid-1960s, gender appears
to have factored less and less into decisions about how to achieve the ultimate goal of ending Jim Crow. CORE's attempt to penetrate Plaquemine
Parish aptly illustrates the dedication and perseverance of women working
in the field. Plaquemine Parish was widely known as the "most repressive in
the state." Rich in oil and sulfur deposits, the parish is located on the Gulf

44. Mimi Feingold notebook, 18, 19, and 21 November 1963, Reel 1, Feingold Papers; "CORE
Pickets to Be Arraigned," *East Feliciana Watchman*, 1 November 1963; Reel 18, 58, CORE Addendum, HU.

45. Quoted in Fairclough, *Race and Democracy*, 332.

46. CORE to Miss Jane Duffin, 11 October 1963, Reel 182, SRC Papers.

47. Meier and Rudwick, *CORE*, 258.

of Mexico at the southeastern tip of Louisiana. Leander Perez, a staunch segregationist political boss who fought diligently to keep the state's public schools segregated, ruled the parish with an iron fist, acting as unchallenged parish president for forty years. In October 1963, the Louisiana Un-American Activities Committee, with Perez at the helm, led a raid on the Southern Conference Educational Fund offices located in New Orleans. Perez's younger African American constituents still attended one of three segregated "Negro" schools in the parish. Moreover, although African Americans made up 25 percent of the parish's total population, only ninety-five blacks were registered to vote. In one instance, when "forty Negro villages were organized for voter registration," Perez arrested a group of people who went to register and spread a rumor that the organizers, "[Reverend] Griffin and [Earl] Amedee were financially benefiting from the drive." Due to Perez's history of segregationist activities and defiance of state and federal civil rights legislation, CORE leaders knew the parish would be hostile to civil rights activity.[48]

In 1963, however, Mary Hamilton, CORE's first female field secretary, began to make contacts with African American community members with an eye toward beginning a voter registration drive in Plaquemine Parish. Originally from Denver, Colorado, twenty-eight-year-old Hamilton had been employed by CORE since February 1961. She participated in the Freedom Rides, the Freedom Highway Project, and numerous other civil rights campaigns in communities throughout the South, including Baltimore, Maryland, and Nashville, Tennessee. Described by Mimi Feingold as "larger than life," Hamilton also led major CORE projects in Gadsden and Birmingham, Alabama, before working in Louisiana.[49] Hamilton is best known, however, for appealing to the United States Supreme Court a contempt-of-court conviction she received for refusing to answer a county solicitor in Alabama when he referred to her as "Mary." In an unprecedented ruling, the Court overturned her conviction, dealing "a blow at the practice in some Southern courtrooms of addressing Negroes by their first names." When she arrived in Louisiana, Hamilton worked on voter registration in West Feliciana Parish. As Feingold recalled, "[When] she came in, the breakthrough in Clinton happened with her help. In my own little way I worshiped her."[50]

In November 1963, Hamilton and Ruthie Wells, now a fieldworker in

48. Fairclough, *Race and Democracy*, 327; Field Report, Mary Hamilton to James McCain, n.d., Reel 22. 129, CORE Addendum, HU.

49. Employee Record of Mary Hamilton, n.d., Reel 22, 129, CORE Addendum, HU.

50. "Court Backs Negro's Bid to Be Addressed as 'Miss,'" *Baltimore Sun,* 31 March 1964, Box

Pointe Coupee Parish, sought out "everyone [they] could find for information on the parish." Hamilton and Wells made initial contacts with a local minister, the Reverend Percy Murphy Griffin, the only person to run against Perez in his forty years as parish president. They also talked with Earl Amedee, a local attorney affiliated with the New Orleans chapter of the NAACP, and Isaac Jones, owner and operator of a local longshoreman's bar. They discovered through these contacts that the "Negro community [was] very frightened," particularly after Kennedy's assassination and Perez's construction of a prison he named "The Dungeon," located on St. Phillip Island and accessible only by boat or helicopter. Local blacks were so afraid, Reverend Griffin reported, that CORE would find it difficult, if not impossible, to secure churches or other buildings to hold voter education clinics. In a report to the national CORE office, Hamilton further noted that the large number of mulattos in the parish presented a problem, as "hostilities are sharp between them and us. Their relationship with the whites, I have been told, is one of benevolence on the part of whites." Despite the obstacles, Hamilton had faith that "with much personal contact we may be able to build some confidence in us."[51]

By early 1964, Hamilton and Wells had made little progress in Plaquemine. Citing the holidays, problems with obtaining Louisiana car tags and driver's licenses, and the fact that most of the black residents did not have telephones, the two found that penetrating the parish was extremely slow work. Hamilton reported to CORE that even among her "scattered visits" to the parish, "most of the time I have been unable to make any contacts." In addition, Ruth Wells decided to leave CORE and return to school the following semester. Hamilton requested that CORE assign Cathy Patterson, a white CORE worker she knew from Alabama, to fill Wells's place. In the meantime, Hamilton worked to rebuild a flailing New Orleans chapter that was still reeling from the purges of its white membership.[52]

By the end of January 1964, Hamilton's persistence began "to show fruits." Hamilton secured the aid of Reverend Victor Ragas, organizer of the local NAACP and active in voter registration for over thirty years. In addition, local blacks agreed to house CORE workers and hold meetings in their homes.[53]

2, Folder 11, Southern Conference Educational Fund Papers, State Historical Society of Wisconsin, Madison (hereafter cited as SCEF Papers); Feingold, interview, 1 December 2002.

51. Hamilton to McCain, n.d., Reel 22, 129, CORE Addendum, HU.

52. Hamilton to McCain, 3 January 1964, Reel 23, 192, CORE Addendum, HU.

53. Hamilton to McCain, 12 January 1964, Reel 18, 59, CORE Addendum, HU.

Perez quickly countered any promise of success, however, after one "fatal night" when James Farmer announced to the local press that CORE was "already in Plaquemine Parish." According to Hamilton, "retribution against the Negro community was fast in occurring" and continued through March. Perez set up police barricades on the only highway leading into the parish. In an apparent search for Mary Hamilton, police, armed with her photograph, stopped and searched all cars driven by blacks and confiscated any CORE materials they found. The police further intimidated blacks by arresting, detaining, and questioning two well-respected local ministers. Then Perez "and his agents" visited black churches, "questioning the ministers and members" regarding the whereabouts of CORE workers and informing them that "no mass meetings or CORE activity would be allowed in the parish." The local ministers warned Hamilton not to return as she would be immediately arrested. Undaunted, Hamilton reported to CORE that: "Since developments have taken a turn for the worse in the parish . . . [i]t would do us a great disservice if we abandoned this area to Perez, not only statewide, but [also] nationally. It is my opinion that if we are to work there, and I definitely feel that we must, that it will have to be attacked as Jackson, Mississippi was with the Freedom Rides. Definitely a national issue must be made of the parish, otherwise we end up with people being thrown in jail and nothing being accomplished.[54] Despite Hamilton's optimism and hard work, the Plaquemine Parish project never got off the ground. In early April, she underwent emergency abdominal surgery and did not return to Louisiana as a CORE staff member until June, the beginning of the famous 1964 Freedom Summer.[55]

"I DEEM IT NECESSARY TO WORK FOR FREEDOM NOW"

While the national CORE offices planned for its second summer of voter registration work in Louisiana, volunteer workers in the Fifth and Sixth Congressional Districts continued to put pressure on white communities on behalf of blacks. In Madison, Ouachita, and St. Helena Parishes, women fieldworkers canvassed, held voter education clinics and organizational meetings, and organized new CORE chapters.[56] In Ouachita Parish, for instance, Sarah

54. Hamilton to McCain, 1 March 1964, Reel 18, 59, CORE Addendum, HU.

55. William M. Jones, M.D. to James Farmer, 21 April 1964, Box 10, File 1, CORE Papers, SHSW.

56. Field Report—St. Helena Parish, January 1964, Reel 183, CORE Papers, SHSW; Field Report—Ouachita and Madison Parishes, 14 January 1964, Reel 15, CORE Papers, SHSW.

McCoy, described in one CORE field report as "an actionist," joined CORE's task force "disgusted by past unwillingness to act," particularly on the part of the local NAACP. As student involvement expanded in the parish, she earned a reputation as one of the few activists "who can work with the youth effectively" in Monroe.[57] CORE workers in Ouachita Parish fought on behalf of black workers at the Olin Mathieson Chemical Company. With four plants in Monroe alone, the company was the largest single employer in the area. Although African Americans constituted approximately 50 percent of the parish, the company's employees were less than 10 percent black. Subsequently, in addition to voter registration and direct action, CORE worked toward equality in hiring, pay, and promotions for local blacks.[58]

Although economic concerns remained paramount for most rural Louisiana blacks, CORE opted to focus on voter registration in the Feliciana parishes. According to Feingold, CORE worked to "keep up interest in voter registration," holding weekly meetings to teach people how to fill out the forms and prepare them to go to the registrar's office. In early January, fifteen CORE workers, including Feingold, canvassed in downtown St. Francisville without issue, although secretly the workers "were all quaking in our boots before we went, but that turned out to be energy wasted." Their efforts were not in vain; for the first time since 1902, blacks in the Feliciana parishes voted in the Louisiana primaries in 1964.[59] CORE also pursued its boycott of local white merchants, which, according to Feingold, was about 90 percent effective. Like Sarah McCoy and the students of Monroe, Feingold led a group of high school students "who [were] raring to go sit-in, and who we have to hold to tamer activities, like canvassing for voter registration."[60] The local students were interested not in voter registration, but in taking a more bold approach. In March, a group of black students demonstrated against the public library system by attempting to enter libraries in three towns in the parish. The students were met by a mob of white men brandishing guns and knives. Police arrested five of the student protesters, along with Mimi Feingold as a material witness.[61]

Police continued to keep constant watch over CORE offices in Monroe by

57. Field Report—Ouachita Parish, January 1964, Reel 5, CORE Papers, SHSW.

58. Thomas Valentine, William Brown, and Michael Lesser to Mr. Hobart Taylor, Chairman of the President's Committee on Equal Employment Opportunity, 2 March 1964, Reel 21, 54, CORE Addendum, HU.

59. "Negroes Vote for First Time since 1902," *CORE-LATOR*, February 1964, Reel 13, 76, CORE Addendum, HU.

60. Mimi Feingold to parents, 5 January 1964, Reel 1, Feingold Papers.

61. Press release, 7 March 1964, Box 2, File 5, 6th Congressional District, CORE Papers,

tapping their phones and opening CORE mail. Workers often found crosses burning in front of the homes where task force workers lived. Reprisals were much the same in the Felicianas and elsewhere. Blacks affiliated with CORE in Baton Rouge lost their jobs. Vigilantes attempted to blow up a building in St. Francisville where CORE held registration meetings and shot into the homes of local blacks who had attempted to register to vote. Feingold noted that on one Saturday, fifteen crosses burned in East Feliciana Parish and a number of others in West Feliciana Parish. Local authorities consistently harassed Feingold, often arresting her in an apparent attempt to gain information regarding CORE activities. Local police paraded newly acquired police dogs through the town, attempting to scare black citizens from participating in CORE activities.[62] In the midst of this dangerous environment, Mimi Feingold remained steadfast in her commitment. In a letter to her parents, Feingold compared the civil rights movement to the American women's struggle for the right to vote:

> It is imperative, it seems to me, that precisely those people who think this country has made tremendous strides toward granting Negroes civil rights (such as President Johnson) be constantly made aware of the impatience of hundreds of thousands of people in this country. I can't help thinking, at times like these, of the woman's suffrage movement, which also employed wild, unorthodox tactics to dramatize their plea, and which prompted men in power to say that they'd never win what they were fighting for, since they were making themselves look stupid and irresponsible. While realizing we are fighting now for a good deal more than the women were, it is interesting to note that women today do vote, despite what people said at the time.[63]

By May, CORE turned its focus on the Freedom Summer projects in Mississippi and Louisiana. Although CORE and SNCC sponsored limited projects in Alabama, Georgia, and northern Florida, it was primarily in Mississippi and Louisiana that civil rights workers and local citizens faced the most severe intimidation. CORE decided to "place its heaviest emphasis" on Louisiana, hoping to make the state "a showcase of CORE's activity."[64] Be-

SHSW; press release, 16 March 1964, 6th Congressional District, CORE Papers, SHSW; Feingold to parents, 7 March 1964, Reel 1, Feingold Papers.

    62. Intimidations and Harassment, Summer 1963 to Summer 1964, Reel 40, CORE Papers, SHSW; Feingold to McCain, 21 January 1964, Reel 23, 190, CORE Addendum, HU; Feingold to parents, 7 March 1964, Reel 1, Feingold Papers.

    63. Feingold to parents, 26 April 1964, Reel 1, Feingold Papers.

    64. Meier and Rudwick, CORE, 261.

cause of CORE's work in the Felicianas, officials refused to register blacks or whites. The objective of CORE's summer project in Louisiana, then, was "to awaken the nation to the fact that Negroes want to vote" through "Freedom Candidates, Freedom Registration, Freedom Days, and Actual Registration," culminating in a "Freedom Delegation challenge at the National Democratic Party convention" that fall.[65]

The volunteers, comprised of "college students, working girls, and those interested in . . . the Peace Corps," registered people to vote, sponsored African American candidates for leadership or political office, organized community voter leagues, and challenged exclusion of blacks from voting rolls. They also worked in freedom schools and in direct-action campaigns, tackling the issue of segregation of public facilities. Perhaps most important to rural Louisianians, however, was CORE's plan to address discrimination in employment and labor unions, unemployment, and "special problems" regarding federal surplus food distribution and federal programs such as job training and farm subsidies, as well as the particular problems of West Feliciana Parish's sweet potato farmers.[66] Per CORE's general philosophy of grassroots organization and leadership, the staff hoped to energize local leaders to organize their own communities. CORE—which is to say, brave community members like Mama Jo—supplied room and board, but volunteers had to supply their own transportation and pocket money. CORE promised to supply bail money in the event of arrest. After initial training, workers were assigned to work in a specific area of the state for the duration of the summer.[67]

Women ranked high among the fifty-odd volunteers who worked in Louisiana in the summer of 1964. Some, such as Mimi Feingold, Ruth Wells, and the Thompson sisters, had worked with CORE in earlier campaigns. Others had worked in the civil rights movement in some other capacity. Doratha Smith, a three-year member of the New Orleans chapter of CORE, wanted to work on the task force "because I feel it will give me a greater opportunity to help others to gain full-class citizenship and equality by means of the vote."[68] Sarah McCoy, a resident of Louisiana, had worked on CORE's 1963

65. Press release, 27 May 1964, Reel 20, 1007, CORE Papers, SHSW.

66. "Serve in the South," *Lafayette (La.) Grail*, 1964; "Louisiana Citizenship Program," 1964, Reel 183, SRC Papers.

67. Louisiana Summer Project—1964, Reel 25, 124, CORE Papers, SHSW.

68. Application for Field Worker in CORE Task Force—Doratha Smith, 19 May 1964, Reel 45, 1272, CORE Papers, SHSW.

task force; McCoy noted on her application: "I would like to become a task force worker because I find contentment in working for the advancement of the civil rights movement and for all mankind. Previously it has puzzled me because many Negroes are unaware of this struggle for freedom and tend to disregard the value. Therefore in order to increase their concern as well as mine, I deem it necessary to work for *freedom now*."[69] Catherine Patterson, a member of the Student Committee for Human Rights in Birmingham who had worked with Mary Hamilton in the Gadsden, Alabama, movement and in Plaquemine Parish, Louisiana, initially applied to work in the CORE office for the summer. When asked by CORE's national secretary, Marcia McKenna, to consider working in the field where volunteers were needed, Patterson accepted without reservation.[70] Catherine Cortez, a white student at Hunter College, had experience with the Northwest New York chapter of CORE since its formation in 1963.[71] Similarly, Ellen Claire O'Conner, a white woman from St. Paul, Minnesota, worked with CORE as a student at the University of Miami and with Students for Integration.

A number of women who had not previously worked with CORE also applied to work in Louisiana. They included Sharon Burger, Lois Carroll Chafee, Joanne Darken, Peggy Ewan, Leola Ford, Elinor Lerner, Judith Rollins, and Janet Weiner. Some had little previous experience with civil rights. Chafee, a new advisor to the Tougaloo College chapter of the NAACP, merely believed "in CORE's program of non-violent direct action against racism" and that belief "entails the responsibility for action."[72] Similarly, Ewan, a white woman from Clinton, Iowa, was "repulsed by the attitudes of many people." She wrote: "People's hatred of the Negro is unfounded and without justification from many standpoints. It is unfair constitutionally and is against everything that America stands for both here and abroad. I do realize that as a White born and raised in the North, I can have no conception of what

69. Application for Field Worker in CORE Task Force—Sarah McCoy, 1964, Reel 45, 1433, 1438, CORE Papers, SHSW.

70. Application for Field Worker in CORE Task Force—Catherine Patterson, 4 May 1964, Reel 45, 1333–34, CORE Papers, SHSW; Marcia McKenna to Patterson, 27 April 1964, Reel 45, 1335, CORE Papers, SHSW; Patterson to McCain, 23 April 1964, Reel 45, 1336, CORE Papers, SHSW; renewed Application for Field Worker in CORE Task Force—Cathy Patterson, 1964, Reel 45, 1339, CORE Papers, SHSW.

71. Application for Field Worker in CORE Task Force—Catherine Cortez, 4 June 1964, Reel 45, 1573, CORE Papers, SHSW.

72. Application for Field Worker in CORE Task Force—Lois Carroll Chaffee, 27 May 1964, Reel 45, 1554, CORE Papers, SHSW.

it is to live in the South, as a White or a Negro. Therefore I feel a real urge and need to go to the South and live there doing what I can for a summer and then maybe I can come back to school with a better representation of what the situation really is like and with a challenge to the other young people and adults around me."[73] The initial ideological commitment to civil rights exhibited in these women's applications played out in their work as volunteers.

In May 1964, CORE officials announced their intention to launch Freedom Summer in Louisiana in early June. Citing the small number of black Louisianians who were actually registered, CORE focused its attention on voter registration in nineteen parishes in the Fifth and Sixth Congressional Districts. CORE officials hoped not only to register blacks, but also to provide evidence for a lawsuit against a number of registrars in the state and to form a "freedom delegation" as they had in Mississippi, to attend the Democratic National Convention in August in Atlantic City.[74] On June 10, thirty-five volunteers arrived in Plaquemine, Louisiana, CORE's home base. For four days the volunteers trained in the history of the voter registration project, techniques of canvassing, principles of community organization, and CORE's philosophy of nonviolence. Volunteers learned the specifics of direct-action techniques, press relations, the economics of each parish, and the importance of boycotts and selective buying campaigns. In addition, each trainee received a copy of *Louisiana in Brief*, prepared earlier that year by Mimi Feingold, and field reports on each individual parish. On June 14, all volunteers had a canvass training session in Iberville Parish before leaving the following day to their personal parish assignments.[75]

CORE concentrated its efforts for the first part of the summer project on four areas of the state—Iberville Parish, Ouachita and Jackson Parishes, St. Helena Parish, and Tangipahoa Parish. Of the thirty-five volunteers, twelve were women, and in one parish, Tangipahoa, a woman, Mimi

73. Application for Field Worker in CORE Task Force—Peggy Ewan, 19 May 1964, Reel 45, 1428, CORE Papers, SHSW.

74. Parishes in the Fifth Congressional District include Jackson, Ouachita, Richland, Franklin, Madison, Union, and Morehouse; included in the Sixth Congressional District are East and West Feliciana, Pointe Coupee, St. Helena, Tangipahoa, Washington, Ascension, East and West Baton Rouge, Livingston, and St. Tammany. CORE press release, 27 May 1964, Box 1, CORE Papers, SHSW; Meg Redden (formerly Peggy Ewan), interview by Greta de Jong, 8 December 1996, T. Harry Williams Oral History Center, Louisiana State University, Baton Rouge (hereafter cited as THWOHC).

75. Summary Report—Louisiana Freedom Summer, 10–25 June 1964, Box 2, Folder 4, CORE Papers, SHSW; Louisiana Summer Project—1964, Reel 25, 124, CORE Papers, SHSW.

Feingold, directed the project.[76] Ronnie Bouma (née Sigal), Meg Redden (née Peggy Ewan), and Joanne Darken were assigned to Iberville Parish. Claudia Edwards, Cathy Patterson, and Ruth Wells worked in Ouachita and Jackson Parishes. Sharon Burger worked with Loria Davis in St. Helena, and Judy Rollins, Cathy Cortez, and Janet Weiner worked with Mimi Feingold in Tangipahoa. Feingold also remained in contact with local community leaders in the Felicianas.[77]

The female volunteers worked on a variety of projects. Because of the risk associated with working in the field, CORE assigned women, particularly white women, to work primarily in the offices, voter education clinics, and the Freedom Schools. It appears however, that some differences existed between female volunteers' experiences in Mississippi and in Louisiana. CORE rarely allowed female task force workers in Louisiana to canvas, one of the most difficult and dangerous jobs. Louisiana summers are brutal, and in rural areas, canvassers walked miles in a day just to talk to a small number of local blacks. But some women did. Joanne Darken noted in her diary, for example, that she "Got to Hammond around 11:30, picked her [Carolyn] up, canvassed until two, ate . . . canvassed some more. We quit around four, with 25 [potential registrants] for the day. I was feeling in good form, but don't feel I've been to enough houses."[78] Sharon Burger walked "through a dry field under a blazing sun to a woman picking butter beans—trying to get past the wall of fear a white face causes." On another occasion, Burger noted: "Loria [Davis] and I are canvassing Montpelier this afternoon and holding a clinic in a chapel there tonight. I have been soaked with sweat since I've been here. I don't remember how dry clothes feel. The work is hard—a lot of walking in a lot of sun. But I wouldn't be anywhere else doing anything else for anything. I really feel—for the first time in a long time—that there's some reason for me to be living and that what I'm doing here really matters."[79]

Although studies of Mississippi have found that the Council of Federated Organizations (COFO), an umbrella organization created in 1961 that included CORE, SNCC, NAACP, and SCLC, rarely sent women to the most dangerous areas of the state, in Louisiana women often worked in such

76. Field Report for Period 15–25 June 1964, Reel 25, 124, CORE Papers, SHSW.

77. Report for Period 15–25 June 1964, Staff Assignments, Reel 25, 124, CORE Papers, SHSW.

78. Diary of Joanne Darken, 8 July 1964, Joanne Darken Papers, State Historical Society of Wisconsin, Madison (hereafter cited as Darken Papers).

79. Sharon Burger, "Canvassing in Louisiana," in "Louisiana Summer—1964," Reel 13, 92, CORE Addendum, HU.

places: Mimi Feingold in the Felicianas; Meg Redden, Sharon Burger, and Cathy Cortez in Pointe Coupee Parish; and Judith Rollins in Alexandria are just a few examples. Moreover, unlike SNCC, CORE placed female volunteers in positions of leadership, including the high-profile job of project director held by Feingold, Davis, Rollins, Oretha Castle, Joanne Darken, and Christine Wright.

Much has been written on the apparent sexism within civil rights organizations in the South and during the Freedom Summer, in particular.[80] In retrospect, it appears that female volunteers thought they were working within a movement that "saw inequality in terms of race and class and not in terms of sex."[81] As Doug McAdam notes, however, in his study of the Freedom Summer in Mississippi, "It is not that various forms of sexism did not occur, only that they went unchallenged and largely unrecognized by the female volunteers."[82] McAdam's analysis is supported by a number of interviews conducted for this study, as several women recall that sexism was not a part of their consciousness at the time.[83] For example, Mimi Feingold stated: "The issue of women and feminism was not an issue then; it was not part of the vocabulary. It was not anything anybody thought about; nobody had defined it as an issue." She did not think it strange that she should be a high-ranking CORE member.

> I didn't see myself as a woman in the South. I was a civil rights worker like everybody else. Part of that may have been that I was raised in a family that was very socially aware and I was always raised with the idea that I would go to college and that I would be a professional. My mother was not the sort of woman that raised me to be very clothes conscious. That was very bourgeois, so I was never

---

80. See Evans, *Personal Politics*; McAdam, *Freedom Summer*; Doug McAdam, "Gender as a Mediator of the Activist Experience: The Case of the Freedom Summer," *American Journal of Sociology* 97 (March 1992); Rothschild, "White Women Volunteers"; Mary Aikin Rothschild, *A Case of Black and White: Northern Volunteers and the Southern Freedom Summers, 1964–1965* (Westport, Ct.: Greenwood Press, 1982); Sally Belfrage, *Freedom Summer* (New York: Viking Press, 1965); Mary King, *Freedom Song: A Personal Story of the 1960s Civil Rights Movement* (New York: Morrow, 1987); and Constance Curry et al., *Deep in Our Hearts: Nine White Women in the Freedom Movement* (Athens: University of Georgia Press, 2000).

81. Rothschild, "White Women Volunteers," 466.

82. McAdam, *Freedom Summer*, 105.

83. See Feingold, interview, 22 December 2002; Kathy Barrett interview, by the author, 13 January 2003, tape recording, copy in possession of the author; Dorothy "Dottie" Zellner, interview by the author, 8 February 2003, tape recording, copy in possession of the author; Jill Axler Finsten, interview, by the author, 23 May 2004, tape recording, copy in possession of the author.

into fashion and makeup and dating boys and how do you get boys to like you. So, I came into the civil rights movement with a very different orientation. If I had been raised a "normal girl" I might have been more conscious of "Oh my goodness, look at me in this very influential position as a woman." But it never occurred to me to question or think otherwise.[84]

Still, in Louisiana, as in Mississippi, sexism in the movement arose both as sexual politics and as discrimination in work.[85] Women disproportionately performed gender-specific tasks such as teaching in Freedom Schools, performing clerical-type duties in the field offices, and working in community centers. Like the male task force workers, though, female volunteers experienced long days full of hard work. Whether performing clerical duties or working in the field, their daily environment was always tension-laden. As volunteers in communities that embraced the cult of white womanhood, these white women heightened the threat to civil rights workers already at risk for their activities. CORE organizers, then, believed that keeping women in field offices or teaching in community centers lessened the risks to the overall volunteer staff. Still, as Feingold stated: "There were situations that were inherently more dangerous, like accompanying people who were registering, waiting with them, and the girls were not allowed to do that, only the men did that. But even then, I was in one or two situations that were fairly dicey."[86]

To be sure, female volunteers' assignments have at times been thought of as less significant than those of men involved in fieldwork. As a consequence, many individuals, men and women alike, tended to undervalue the work performed by women. As McAdam states, "The net effect of this policy was to reproduce traditional sex and work roles on the projects"; rebellion against these roles became the launching pad for the modern feminist movement in the United States.[87] However, this point should not be overemphasized; in most of rural Louisiana, as in other rural communities of the Deep South, any type of civil rights activity brought with it great risk. As illustrated in the reports of intimidation and harassment prepared mostly by female office workers, women were at risk no matter where they were assigned. Early in the summer, for instance, the "mutilated bodies of two Negroes were found, floating in the Louisiana river" in two parishes where CORE

84. Feingold, interview, 1 December 2002.
85. McAdam, *Freedom Summer*, 105.
86. Feingold, interview, 1 December 2002.
87. McAdam, *Freedom Summer*, 108. See also, Evans, *Personal Politics*.

operated summer projects.[88] While workers were at higher risk of attack by white roughnecks while canvassing, threats against local CORE offices, churches and meeting halls, clinics, and Freedom Houses also occurred almost daily.[89]

In line with CORE's general belief in grassroots organizing, one of the most important aspects of the summer project involved inciting local communities to act on behalf of themselves. Because women predominantly worked in community centers and Freedom Schools, their awareness of the level of a community's receptiveness to CORE was particularly acute. As harassment and violence directed at local blacks escalated, motivating the community to work with CORE took on even greater significance. Nightly meetings and rallies were a common occurrence after a full day of working in registration clinics or canvassing door to door. As a field director, Mimi Feingold often acted as a motivational speaker, talking to local blacks about the need for community action.[90] "Motivation is the most important thing," noted Feingold. "Perhaps after certain gains have been made in [a] community [and] people gain confidence. . . . This is a value which *organizers* hold, which raises questions of how much pressure from outsiders must be accepted as part of the situation."[91]

Hostile whites made no concessions for gender when it came to violence against civil rights workers. Female volunteers lived in constant fear for their lives for good reason. Ronnie Sigal, a twenty-one-year-old task force worker from Minnesota and the only white CORE worker in St. Helena Parish, stated that she "learned to live each day because I never knew if I'd be alive the next day." Sigal found herself at one point staring down the barrel of a shotgun; another time, nine armed white men surrounded her car while she was investigating a murder. In spite of these and numerous other incidents, Sigal opted to stay full-time in Louisiana.[92] In a similar incident, while returning from a voter education clinic one night, Joanne Darken was shot at driving along the highway back to Tangipahoa Parish. And while living at the home of a local family, Darken reported that "whites . . . [patrolled]

88. Ronnie Moore, "Introduction, in "Louisiana Summer—1964," Reel 13, 92, CORE Addendum, HU.

89. Examples of daily threats are too numerous to list here. See "CORE's Chronological Listing of Intimidation's and Harassment's in Louisiana," December 1961 to August 1964, compiled by Judy Rollins, Reel 45, CORE Papers, SHSW.

90. Feingold notebook, 20 June 1964, Reel 2, Feingold Papers.

91. Feingold notebook, 23 July 1964, Reel 2, Feingold Papers.

92. Jackie German, "Rights Worker Lived in Fear," in "Louisiana Summer—1964," Reel 13, 92, CORE Addendum, HU.

the road trying to find out where the CORE workers were, questioned the Wickers, and told them to watch out for Communists, evidently flashed pistols, and consequently the Wickers won't have us." Although Mr. Wicker was afraid to let CORE workers live in their home after this incident, as was often the case with local women who housed CORE workers, Mrs. Wicker remained "pleasantly determined, [she was a] 'We Shall Not Be Moved,' woman."[93]

Sexism in the Louisiana movement was most noticeable in the interactions between male and female activists. Problems were particularly acute between white women and black men. As Sara Evans notes, "The presence of white women inevitably heightened the sexual tension that runs as a constant current through racist culture."[94] Mimi Feingold recalled the district attorney of the Felicianas stating that if CORE was going to send white women to the area, he could not "protect them from the horny field hands." Certainly, "horny field hands" did not pose a threat to movement workers. Yet in McAdam's words, in creating a "beloved community that would serve as a model of what a true egalitarian society was to be like . . . [i]nterracial sex became the ultimate expression of this ideology."[95]

Although interracial sexual liaisons inevitably occurred, most of the women interviewed for this study stated that they were keenly aware of the taboo against interracial sex in southern culture and therefore refrained from such relationships. Perhaps lessons learned from the New Orleans experience had filtered into the rural movement. Feingold recalled that there was "very little playing around," as CORE had specific guidelines regarding relationships between the white and black workers. When conducting orientations, Feingold "made that very clear to other white women that this is a dynamic that [they had] to be aware of" and that she expected "everyone to behave accordingly." Feingold further recalled:

> There was always an issue, from the very beginning, among the movement people, the young black men being attracted to the white women just because they were forbidden fruit. I personally was enormously aware of that tension and I made it a point in my own behavior to be absolutely like Caesar's wife, to be above reproach. I never dated anyone the entire time I was down there; I never became physical with anybody. I just felt it was inappropriate, in this context it was especially important to maintain a sense of decorum and especially because of the

93. Diary of Joanne Darken, 23 and 6 July 1964, Darken Papers.
94. Evans, *Personal Politics*, 78.
95. McAdam, *Freedom Summer*, 93.

mind-set of the black population, not to even hold any temptation that anybody could take the wrong way.[96]

Similarly, Margaret Leonard remembered that sex was an issue for white women in the movement, and like Feingold she refrained from sexual liaisons. "It was all complicated," stated Leonard. "I don't see sex as a way to make a community. It's a way to feel good, and unfortunately in addition to that it has some ugly power stuff, pretty serious, mixed up in it. I don't think it says much about the movement though. I still think the movement was wonderful." The issue of sex was "just there because it was men and women. I think black women resented black men coming after us."[97]

Sexual tension did, in fact, become a divisive force within the civil rights movement particularly between black and white women, "creating a barrier that shared womanhood could not transcend."[98] Resentment on the part of black women had already been a problem in CORE's New Orleans chapter. In the Louisiana voter registration project some two years later, organizational leaders were sensitive to those problems. Feingold noted "that the possibility existed for the black women to be very resentful of the white women because the black men would all be trailing along after the white women and . . . the black women would be left behind."[99] Regardless of whether white women acted "above reproach," as Feingold and Leonard did, "sex became the metaphor for racial tension, hostility, and aggression." As Mary Aikin Rothschild notes in her study of white women in the Freedom Summers, "Nearly every project had real problems over interracial sex, and many white women volunteers were in a painful double bind from the moment they arrived."[100] If they rejected the advances of black men they were seen as racist, and if they acquiesced, both men and women viewed them with disdain.

Yet, even though women volunteers experienced sexism in the movement, their situation was never quite as precarious as it was for local women—the "inside agitators." These women continued to be instrumental in acting as community contacts, registering to vote, housing and feeding CORE

---

96. Feingold, interviews, 1 and 22 December 2002. See also Barrett, interview, 13 January 2003; and Connie Bradford Harse, interview by the author, 19 March 2003, tape recording, copy in possession of the author.

97. Margaret Leonard, interview by the author, 29 March 2003, tape recording, copy in possession of the author.

98. Evans, *Personal Politics*, 78, 81.

99. Feingold, interview, 1 December 2002.

100. Rothschild, "White Women Volunteers," 481.

workers, and offering emotional and physical support in spite of grave repercussions. As Peggy Ewan recalled, "Many local Negroes are active in the
civil rights work, and some are real spitfires."[101] That was certainly the case
with Charlotte Greenup and Mama Jo Holmes, who continued to open their
homes to CORE volunteers in the Felicianas through the summer of 1964.
In Ouachita Parish, Mrs. Helen Jackson and Mrs. Velma Palmer also provided housing, and Mrs. Leola "Tiny" Hood housed CORE workers in Pointe
Coupee Parish. In Rapides Parish, Dorothy Jackson, Mrs. Dorothy Bell, and
Mrs. Odette Harper Hines housed workers, and Mrs. Hines, a longtime community activist, became actively involved in the local movement.[102]

These "mamas" of the movement, as they became known, acted not only
as "substitute mother figures," but also as "new models of womanhood" for
the younger female activists, black and white.[103] The older women knew
that they were placing themselves and their families in danger. Volunteers
also knew that their mere presence in these women's homes, whether for a
meal or an extended living arrangement, subjected both to great risk. Still,
women like Charlotte Greenup and Mama Jo Holmes remained steadfast
in their dedication to the movement, illustrated by a sign outside of Mama
Jo's door that read: "It is time for you to take a stand and become a first
class citizen. A voteless people is a hopeless people. Register and vote."[104]
Greenup's attitude was, "I'm going to keep fighting until hell freezes over
and then I'll walk over the ice, hold up my sword and I'll have just begun to
fight." Feingold wrote of Greenup: "She's great! She's not afraid to say anything."[105] Mama Jo displayed a similar attitude: "I spit in their face. Let them
try to do something to me."[106] Meg Redden, formerly Peggy Ewan, similarly
recalled the bravery of Mama Jo: "She was just outrageous. She was just willing to do anything to support us. And I think that's more about her own
personal courage and the kind of person she was."[107]

101. Judi Burken, "Clinton Girl Works with CORE," in "Louisiana Summer—1964," Reel 13,
92, CORE Addendum, HU.

102. Field Reports—Ouachita Parish, Pointe Coupee Parish, and Rapides Parish, 1964, Reel
4, 96, 708, and 755. Certainly local men also housed CORE workers; however, the majority of
notations are about women. I only came across one report of a man being harassed for housing CORE workers.

103. Evans, *Personal Politics*, 53.

104. James Van Metre, "Report from Plaquemine," in "Louisiana Summer—1964," Reel 13,
92, CORE Addendum, HU.

105. Cited in Feingold notebook 10, Reel 2, Feingold Papers.

106. Feingold, interview, 1 December 2002.

107. Redden, interview, 8 December 1996.

Like Mama Jo Holmes, Odette Harper Hines in Alexandria, Louisiana (Rapides Parish), served as an important local contact for CORE volunteers. Her biographer, Judith Rollins, has recounted her story as an "inside agitator" in *All Is Never Said*. When the national CORE office contacted local black leaders in Alexandria about beginning a summer project in 1964, Hines ignored the warnings of the local black conservatives and invited the workers into her home. Judith Rollins, a black college student from Boston and the project leader for Rapides Parish, arrived at her home with two male workers. Rollins worked alongside a young local woman, Betty Chenevert, "very active and very strong," testing restaurants. As Rollins later recalled, they tested so many, they often had stomach aches.[108]

Like the "mamas," younger local women like Betty Chenevert in Rapides Parish worked hard to sustain the movement in their communities. One parish report noted that Sarah McCoy, Robertine Miller, and Vera Stewart actively participated in canvassing all summer in Ouachita Parish.[109] Similarly, in Pointe Coupee Parish, Edna Draper and Thelma Caufield, only seventeen years old at the time, worked with CORE. Caufield, described as "invaluable in every aspect of our work," epitomizes the female grassroots civil rights activist in Louisiana. The oldest of six children of a mentally disabled mother, Thelma Caufield took care of her younger brothers and sisters while her father and older brothers took construction work in New Orleans, work that was denied them in their own community because of the family's prior civil rights activities. The Caufields lived in a wooden shack with no running water. "I think Thelma did most of the work." Meg Redden stated: "She hauled the wood in to start the stove to cook and she hauled the water from a pump and did the laundry in the backyard in a big wooden barrel and she had big strong hands from wringing out the laundry that way. She was an incredibly strong young woman." Caufield did not, however, adhere to CORE's belief in nonviolence; she brazenly carried a gun. As Redden recalled, there was "really scary stuff going on then. It was really a violent period of time, when black men would be lynched, hung for no reason. There was the KKK . . . there was the fear that that kind of violence was going to happen to them when there wasn't anybody there to protect them. Even though the movement was a non-violent movement, people like Thelma Caufield, who lived in a rural area like that, totally unprotected, she really did had to have a gun just to defend herself. She wasn't using the gun in an aggressive, violent way.

108. Judith Rollins, *All Is Never Said: The Narrative of Odette Harper Hines* (Philadelphia: Temple University Press, 1995), 191–95, 196–97.

109. Ouachita Parish statement, n.d., Reel 4, CORE Papers, SHSW.

She was just using it as a defense."[110] The fact that Thelma Caulfield openly carried a gun adds to the recent scholarship on armed self-resistance in the civil rights movement.[111] Additionally, Caulfield's gun-toting ways challenges traditional gendered notions regarding the role of southern women in a social movement structure. Out of necessity, not defiance, women increasingly protected themselves in an environment of southern vigilantism and outright violence.

The daily violence and harassment began to wear on the CORE volunteers and local blacks, and CORE leaders and members began to question the philosophy of nonviolence. CORE staff reiterated its policy of nonviolence, but added an exception: "CORE workers *cannot* carry guns or knives (except inside home with mob or KKKers outside)."[112] Incidents of intimidation and harassment grew precipitously as the summer of 1964 wore on, and often women were the subjects of these attacks. In late June, for example, a white man in East Feliciana Parish threw stones and pieces of wood at two women, Mrs. Sally Smith and Mrs. Helena Hamilton, and CORE workers, including Mimi Feingold and Ronnie Sigal, as Smith and Hamilton were attempting to register. As they attempted to flee the courthouse, the man fired shots at their car and chased them to the West Feliciana Parish county line. That same day, the sheriff of East Feliciana Parish harassed five canvassing CORE workers, including Peggy Ewan, Joanne Darken, and local CORE members Verla Bell and Laura Spears.[113] The sheer amount of violence that rural Louisianians faced on a daily basis ultimately led to increased use of

110. Field Report—Pointe Coupee Parish, 30 June 1964–15 July 1964, Reel 44, CORE Papers, SHSW; Redden, interview.

111. See, most recently, Lance Hill, *The Deacons for Defense: Armed Resistance and the Civil Rights Movement* (Chapel Hill: University of North Carolina Press, 2004).

112. Louisiana Summer Task Force, Staff Meeting, 15 July 1964, Reel 44, CORE Papers, SHSW.

113. Incident Harassment report, submitted by Mimi Feingold, 27 June 1964, Reel 25, CORE Papers, SHSW; Field Report—Monroe, West Monroe, 19–25 June 1964, Reel 40, CORE Papers, SHSW. Similar incidents of harassment and intimidation occurred in Ouachita Parish almost daily. In Monroe, a hotbed of racial tension, police arrested and charged CORE workers, including Ruth Wells and eight female teenagers, with disturbing the peace for testing various public accommodations, including the local five-and-dimes, the theaters, the Holiday Inn, and the public library. Police also arrested CORE workers in Monroe who were canvassing, including two young local girls who "were threatened with detention [from school] if they refused to give their parents' names." After their arrests, the police tried to "arouse fear and suspicion on the part of Negro women" by keeping them isolated. In one incident, police stopped Ruth Wells as she walked alone on a road, shining a flashlight in her face and making "a general show of power and intimidation." The officer then told her, "You're headed for trouble." Police also broke into voter education clinics and seized the canvassing lists, leading to a "sudden change from

armed self-defense, most noticeable in the creation of the Louisiana-based Deacons for Defense and Justice.

In spite of the danger, women ranked high among the task force workers accepted to work for the mock Freedom Registration campaign, and by the end of the summer, women were directing CORE projects in a number of parishes. Cathy Patterson acted as co-leader in Jackson Parish; Joanne Darken and Judy Rollins worked in Tangipahoa Parish; and only three workers, all women—Sharon Burger, Catherine Cortez, and Peggy Ewan—remained in Pointe Coupee Parish. Janet Weiner, Ruth Wells, Claudia Edwards, Verla Bell, and Ronnie Sigal also remained in Louisiana through the end of the summer.[114] Christine Wright worked as a "Freedom Registrar" as part of the mock registration campaign, and in August, CORE appointed Feingold and Sigal as delegates to "check on [the] freedom delegation to Atlantic City" and present CORE's findings for Louisiana.[115]

Most importantly, CORE's staff members, principally the women, opted to remain working in Louisiana through the winter. Of the thirteen women who worked in Louisiana that summer, nine stayed through the end of the year, including Ronnie Sigal, Cathy Cortez, Janet Weiner, Judy Rollins, Verla Bell, and Sharon Burger. In addition, CORE organizers recommended that they, along with Mimi Feingold, Claudia Edwards, and Loria Davis, be made permanent task force workers. By summer's end, women had led five of the nine projects in the state: Claudia Edwards in Ouachita Parish, Loria Davis in Jackson Parish, Sharon Burger in East Baton Rouge Parish, Verla Bell and Christine Wright in St. Francisville/Clinton (East and West Feliciana Parishes), and Judith Rollins in Alexandria (Rapides Parish).[116] Other women joined CORE's task force for the first time. Oretha Castle, for instance, left her post as chairman of the New Orleans chapter of CORE to act as field secretary for Monroe. In addition, Castle scouted for the Fourth and Fifth Congressional Districts.[117]

---

enthusiasm to more than apathy" in the parish. The constant intimidation by police "seriously damage[d]" the voter registration project in Ouachita Parish. As one fieldworker noted, "Almost implicit in this display is the threat that any cooperation with CORE workers will in all likelihood result in some kind of trouble with the police," or worse.

114. Staff Assignments, 29 June–9 August 1964, Reel 25, CORE Papers, SHSW.

115. Press release, 1 July 1964, Reel 25, CORE Papers, SHSW; Louisiana Summer Task Force, Staff Meeting, 15 July 1964, Reel 44, CORE Papers, SHSW.

116. Project Leaders, 1 October 1964, Reel 23, 210, CORE Addendum, HU; Christine Wright's Notebook, Box 2, Folder 6, Sixth Congressional District, CORE Papers, SHSW.

117. Louisiana's Citizenship Education Program, 20 July 1964, Reel 25, CORE Papers, SHSW;

After the 1964 summer project ended, CORE reports noted that the "existent interest and enthusiasm" had waned. However, task force workers continued to canvass, hold voter registration clinics, and "rekindle lagging spirits." CORE workers also created Freedom Schools in seven towns, including areas of the state where volunteers had made little previous contact, such as Jonesboro and Donaldsonville. Volunteers expanded their efforts through the winter, working in urban communities on issues of poverty and black employment as well as encouraging the creation of cooperatives and providing new agricultural research to farmers in rural Louisiana. CORE continued its direct-action tactics of testing public accommodations and facilities across the state. They also intensified recruiting and expanded voter registration efforts to other parishes.[118]

In early 1965, CORE began preparations for what would become its third Freedom Summer. In the interim, female task force workers continued their efforts in the Fifth and Sixth Congressional Districts. Their work and that of the task force workers in Mississippi and other areas of the South had helped pave the way for the successful passage of the Civil Rights Act of 1964, which outlawed racial segregation in the schools, public venues, and employment. With the weight of law behind them and a renewed sense of democratic entitlement, CORE decided to extend its voter registration project for two more years. The harassment and intimidation of the previous two summers by whites had not forced the movement in Louisiana to flounder.

The impact of women on the Louisiana project in 1963 and 1964 cannot be minimized. Although CORE leaders preferred male volunteers for Louisiana's 1964 Freedom Summer project, female volunteers were persistent and proved to be highly motivated members of CORE's field staff. Despite the limitations for women of working in the rural Deep South, female "inside" and "outside" agitators contributed greatly to the implementation of CORE's program in the state. Louisiana's female volunteers often canvassed and led local projects as well as performed more mundane clerical duties. Female task force workers and local black women remained committed to the struggle for black freedom, despite persistent harassment and violence. Women's actions in registering to vote, housing and feeding civil rights workers, and directing educational clinics, as well as the actions against women

Field Report, 13 December 1964–24 January 1965, submitted by Oretha Castle, "Castle's Projected Schedule," n.d., for February–March, 1965, Reel IV, 294–96, CORE Papers, SHSW; Field Report, 19 January 1965, Box 1, File 2, 6, Sixth Congressional District, CORE Papers, SHSW.

118. Schedule of Activities, 4 October 1964–3 November 1964, Reel 40, CORE Papers, SHSW.

in the field, would lead to significant changes in the economic, political, and social transformation of rural Louisiana, chiefly in the formation of the Deacons for Defense and Justice, a radical self-defense organization. Extra protection afforded women the opportunity to remain committed, and their dedication to the movement only increased as CORE's program continued through 1967.

8

WOMEN IN THE FIELD II

Armed Resistance and the Pursuit of Local Leadership,
1965–1967

It's a hard struggle and a long fight and I guess if we keep the faith, we will overcome one day.

GAYLE JENKINS, rural Louisiana civil rights activist

W hile female "outside agitators" continued to play significant roles
in Louisiana's struggle for black freedom, as the movement began
to bear fruit, particularly after the passage of the Civil Rights
Act of 1964, greater numbers of female "inside agitators" joined the state
movement. As the voter education project in rural Louisiana entered its
third year, local black women gained a greater sense of agency and increasingly supported the movement despite the increased risk to themselves
and their families. While the movement's still predominantly male leadership debated philosophy and organizational structure, women canvassed,
registered to vote, taught at Freedom Schools, organized their communities, housed activists, and, when necessary, adapted movement strategy to
the changing ideological tide. Despite an increasingly hazardous climate as
southern whites became more resolute in their devotion to retaining white
hegemony, the burgeoning "Mood Ebony" that defined the Black Power
movement, and early feminist stirrings, women remained steadfast in the
fight for racial equality in Louisiana.[1]

As had happened in Mississippi, the movement in Louisiana had already
experienced its share of organizational conflict. The successful implementation of CORE's program in the state between 1960 and 1964 underscored

1. The term "Mood Ebony" can be found in August Meier and Elliot Rudwick, *CORE: A Study
in the Civil Rights Movement, 1942–1968* (New York: Oxford University Press, 1973), 331.

the fact that the organization had overcome internal divisions and indeed was a force with which to reckon. Subsequently, the program in Louisiana "remained CORE's major southern project."[2] Through the fall of 1964 and winter of 1965, CORE retained a skeleton field staff in a number of parishes in the state where local and national activists continued to implement the organization's voter education program. On the heels of CORE's numerous successes, other civil rights organizations such as the National Association for the Advancement of Colored People (NAACP) and the Southern Student Organizing Committee (SSOC) began to implement programs in Louisiana.

Women were among those few staff members who chose to remain in Louisiana and subsequently gained high-profile positions. Judith Nussbaum, for instance, was named director of research and federal programs for CORE's Southern Regional Office in New Orleans; she toured all of CORE's southern projects in February 1965 "to learn what is being done in each project" and to determine "what some of the individual problems and needs" were in local areas. Nussbaum's duties included research on the political structure and economic standards of each state, extensive research on federal programs, and "negotiating with the federal government to pressure them into getting programs into the Negro community." She also planned voter education curricula that CORE staff and locals used to assist their work in a particular community.[3] Additionally, Nussbaum worked to secure funds to assist with the planned 1965 Freedom Summer.[4]

Like Nussbaum, other women increasingly secured leadership positions in the field. Judith Rollins directed the staff in Alexandria, Louisiana, working alongside local activists Dorothy Bell, Dorothy Jackson, and Betty Chenevert. The four women sought to increase the numbers of registered black voters through the fall and winter of 1964 and 1965. Similarly, Mimi Feingold retained her position as one of three field directors for the Sixth Congressional District project, working alongside Claudia Edwards in St. Helena

2. James Farmer, quoted in Meier and Rudwick, *CORE*, 344. For information on the breakdown of the movement, see Meier and Rudwick, *CORE*, chap. 12; Clayborne Carson, *In Struggle: SNCC and the Black Awakening of the 1960s* (Cambridge: Harvard University Press, 1981), esp. 133–35, 146–49; and Sara Evans, *Personal Politics: The Roots of Women's Liberation in the Civil Rights Movement and the New Left* (New York: Knopf, 1979), chap. 4 and appendix.

3. Proposed Plan of Action for CORE, Mississippi and Louisiana Staff, 1965, Student Non-Violent Coordinating Committee Papers, Reel 68, Library of Congress, Washington, D.C. (hereafter cited as SNCC Papers).

4. Judith Nussbaum to CORE Southern Staff, 18 February 1965, and Judith Nussbaum to Dr. Matthew J. Spetter [?], 19 January 1965, Reel 21, 102, CORE Addendum, HU.

Parish.[5] Christine Wright, among a cadre of women who chose to remain in Louisiana after the 1964 Freedom Summer, also worked in the Felicianas managing the Clinton field office and assisting with voter registration.[6] In November, CORE hired former New Orleans chapter chairwoman Oretha Castle as field director for all of northern Louisiana. In this capacity, Castle's main duty was to scout for the 1965 summer project. In addition, Castle supported "Don't Buy Where You Can't Work Campaigns" in Monroe, reported on incidents of violence and harassment across the state, petitioned the Department of Health, Education, and Welfare on behalf of Jonesboro residents regarding the segregation of their local health center, and investigated the Olin Mathieson Company's hiring and advancement practices in Ouachita Parish. In the later years of the civil rights movement, when violence reached an all-time high and morale began to decline, it appears that women's commitment to gaining racial equality sustained the projects in rural communities throughout Louisiana.

By 1965, separatist rhetoric and calls for "black self-help" began to affect the mood of the larger movement. Young militant leaders in CORE and SNCC not only began to question the efficacy of the movement's interracialism, but also its philosophy of nonviolence. Three factors contributed to the increasingly divisive nature of the southern movement post-1964. First, as the civil rights movement began to make inroads into the rural Deep South, backlash from intransigent whites reached a high point not seen since the early days of Jim Crow. Second, increased violence coupled with internal organizational conflict led many African Americans to question the usefulness of whites in a movement for black freedom. Third, female activists began to realize the hypocrisy of their subordination to men in a movement that challenged black subordination to whites. In the fall of 1964, SNCC held a conference in Waveland, Mississippi, where organizational leaders and activists debated the roles of whites, and women, in the movement. By the end of 1965, these three factors coalesced, leading to deep fractures in the southern movement.

Subsequently, both SNCC and CORE decided to adapt the format of their summer programs to the altered mood of the movement. In both the

5. Field Reports, Rapides Parish, 4 January, 4 February, 5 April 1965, Reel IV, 729–835, CORE Addendum, HU.

6. Field notes by Christine Wright, 10 January and 8 February 1965, Box 1, File 21, Sixth Congressional District, CORE Papers, SHSW.

Mississippi and Louisiana movement, leaders decreased emphasis on nonviolent direct action and expanded their commitment to local control and self-determination. As James Farmer stated in an address to the National Action Committee in the fall of 1964, "The old way [direct action and voter registration] won us the right to eat hamburgers at lunch counters and is winning us the right to vote, but has not basically affected the lot of the average Negro." Believing that the "means to strengthening the black poor was the achievement of political power," CORE shifted its focus from direct action to community organization.[7] Ronnie Moore, director of CORE's Louisiana field office, articulated the need to "take a backseat" while aiding in, and facilitating the creation of, community leaders. "This is the only way," Moore stated, "we can permanently build self-supporting community units strong enough to stand on their own to solve their own problems."[8]

CORE's increased dedication to helping Louisiana's poor black community, coupled with the allocation of most of its resources to the Louisiana project, allowed its staff to make inroads into areas of state that had previously been unreachable. Black leaders in Jonesboro, Bogalusa, and Ferriday began to accept CORE's help in their own local civil rights organizations, and women were crucial to this transition. Female CORE leaders Mimi Feingold in Clinton (West Feliciana Parish) and Judith Rollins in Alexandria (Rapides Parish), for example, acted as what sociologist Belinda Robnett deems "bridge leaders," women who fluidly moved between the larger CORE organization and the local community. These women were integral to CORE gaining the trust of local blacks.[9] This, in turn, helped to increase the organization's optimism regarding the future development of its program in the state.

It is clear that women were increasingly important to this aspect of CORE's project. In smaller, local communities, women often acted as a buffer between the more removed male leadership and the grassroots local organizers. As one study has indicated, "women-centered organizing," including the building of community and interpersonal relationships, utilizing local networks, and the ability to be effective conflict mediators contributed to the survival of this phase of the movement, especially in the more rural

---

7. Meier and Rudwick, *CORE*, 330.

8. Ronnie Moore, quoted in Meier and Rudwick, *CORE*, 339.

9. For more information on female "bridge leaders" in the civil rights movement, see Belinda Robnett, *How Long? How Long? African-American Women in the Struggle for Civil Rights* (New York: Oxford University Press, 1997).

areas of the state. It was in these communities that women emerged as leaders in a historically limited public sphere of political and social action.[10]

"WE WERE SICK AND TIRED OF BEING SICK AND TIRED"

With a new sense of direction for the 1965 voter education project, CORE again solicited applications for a summer task force. In spite of the violence and harassment directed at task force workers and local blacks the two previous summers, CORE optimistically expanded its project to include the Fourth and Eighth Congressional Districts, located in northwestern Louisiana. For its third summer project, CORE intended to "reach more deeply and widely into the problems that face the Negro community" and to work harder to "develop indigenous local leadership to deal with [local] problems through basic community organization." CORE leaders hoped that spontaneous community planning, rather than "pre-selected program implementation," would occur and that, with organizational assistance, communities could decide for themselves whether to focus on the desegregation of public facilities, economic issues, or voter education. Subsequently, CORE's 1965 summer project sought to foster a "multilateral program," where a smaller staff base could address the problems of a particular community and help create programs that would eventually help them achieve their long-range goals. In the end, staff members believed that "no matter how much a civil rights staff does in a community, success will ultimately rest with the people of the community."[11]

CORE dedicated its 1965 summer project to creating multifaceted community programs. Staff members developed projects similar to those of previous summers: Freedom Schools, libraries, adult education, literacy, medical programs, and community centers. Because so many of the problems that plagued Louisiana's rural black community centered around economic viability, however, CORE placed a much greater emphasis on establishing farmer's "leagues" and cooperatives to aid black farmers in achieving greater economic independence. Veteran staff members educated new volunteers in the "various aspects of the political, social, economic, and educational structures" of each parish in Louisiana. Although community development was

10. See Susan Stall and Randall Stoecker, "Community Organizing or Organizing Community? Gender and the Crafts of Empowerment," *Gender and Society* 12, no. 6 (December 1998).

11. Summer Project Direction, from CORE Louisiana Staff to CORE National Office, n.d., Reel 10, 11, CORE Addendum, HU.

now central to CORE's program, the organization continued to place great emphasis on registering black voters.[12]

In June 1965, task force volunteers arrived in Waveland, Mississippi, in June for a week of training, and then left for their respective parish assignments. Because the 1965 summer project included fifteen more parishes, the number of task force workers also increased; CORE now had more than sixty volunteers spread out over more than twenty-four parishes in the state. Of the sixty-five volunteers working in Louisiana, twenty-two were women. In almost all of the projects, at least one woman was present, and in four parishes, women dominated the project staff.[13]

Despite the violence that CORE workers had experienced the previous summer, a number of CORE's female veterans, including Mimi Feingold, Christine Wright, Sharon Burger, and Alice Thompson, returned to Louisiana. In addition, a flock of new female volunteers joined the ranks of CORE's task force. Newcomers Pam Norrin and Pat Deamer worked in Ouachita Parish; Linda Diane Smith, Joan Grieco, and Tina Vanderpool worked in Washington Parish; and Joycelyn McKissick and Alice Gay worked in Webster Parish. Gloria Stewart, vice chairwoman and director of the membership committee, led the CORE project in DeRidder, Louisiana; Mrs. Alice Matthews was acting secretary; and June E. Thomas worked as a "reporter." In Baton Rouge, veterans Sharon Burger and Judith Rollins worked alongside newcomers Irene Davis, Judith Fleiss, Nancy Gilmore, Kathy Miller, and Loraine Roy. In Jackson Parish, where a number of violent episodes had occurred earlier that spring, spurring the founding of the Deacons for Defense and Justice (DDJ), only women—Dorothy Banks, Kendra Harris, Marian Kramer, Annie Purnell Johnson, Patsy Boone, and Shirley Thompson of the New Orleans CORE chapter—staffed the project.[14]

Although CORE's presence was now felt across most of Louisiana, the Sixth Congressional District remained organizational headquarters and, thus, the most staffed. It also remained the most dangerous place for task force volunteers. Because of the risk involved, CORE assigned relatively few women to this area of the state, but local women continued to support the movement in all parishes in great numbers. Increasingly, rural black women

12. Outline of Southern Program for Summer 1965, Box 2, File 4, CORE Papers, SHSW; Dave Dennis to Mimi Feingold, 2 June 1965, Reel 2, Miriam Feingold Papers.

13. Louisiana Personnel, 1965, Reel 23, 210, CORE Addendum, HU.

14. Parish Assignments, Addresses, and Phone Numbers, 1965, Box 2, File 4, CORE Papers, SHSW; "Louisiana Personnel," 1965, Reel 23, 210, CORE Addendum, HU; Report Form, DeRidder Chapter, 1964, Reel 18, 57, CORE Addendum, HU.

aided CORE at voter registration clinics, attended demonstrations, and even raised bail money for those arrested.[15]

The events of the 1965 summer project in the Sixth Congressional District, however, only further reinforced the movement's ideological transformation. The towns of Jonesboro, Bogalusa, and Ferriday erupted in violence, permanently altering the attitudes in CORE and its volunteer staff force toward nonviolence and interracialism. Although CORE's staff remained committed to the philosophy of nonviolence, local African American men and women refused to bow anymore to the constant intimidation and violence directed at them. Indeed, the whole "turn-the-other-cheek" attitude, rooted in the religious nature of the movement, began to wear thin. The brazenness of local women in the towns of Jonesboro, Bogalusa, and Ferriday paralleled that of women such as Fannie Lou Hamer in Mississippi and Gloria Richardson in Cambridge, Maryland, both of whom became leaders of their respective local movements. As Jonesboro activist Anne Purnell Johnson stated, "[We] were sick and tired of being sick and tired."[16]

As had black and white volunteers in the Feliciana and Ouachita Parishes in 1963 and 1964, CORE volunteers and local blacks in Jackson Parish (Jonesboro), Washington Parish (Bogalusa), and Concordia Parish (Ferriday) felt the backlash from the white community. Ku Klux Klan (KKK) members launched a "campaign of terror" across the state, and in Jonesboro, Bogalusa, and Ferriday, in particular. Klan members burned crosses and intimidated local blacks by frequently parading through their towns. Additionally, white toughs intensified their campaign of harassment against CORE workers, attacking them at Freedom Houses, or during demonstrations, and bullying them as they canvassed and helped blacks register to vote. Vigilantes also torched two Jonesboro churches where CORE often held meetings and rallies.

Women were not spared white aggression; in fact, whites often specifically directed their attacks against female CORE staffers and local women working with the movement. In one incident, police stopped CORE workers

---

15. See Watts line report for Claiborne, Washington, and Jackson Parishes. In the Jackson Parish report, Dorothy Banks noted, of a Mrs. Mason, "local woman raised $50 bond" (11 July 1965, Box 2, File 4, Sixth Congressional District, CORE Papers, SHSW).

16. Greta de Jong argues that rural black Louisianians always armed themselves. I have found, however, that the increased hostility of Louisiana's rural white community toward the civil rights movement led an even greater number of black Louisianians to take up arms (de Jong, *A Different Day: African American Struggles for Justice in Rural Louisiana, 1900–1970* [Chapel Hill: University of North Carolina Press, 2002]). Annie Purnell Johnson, interview by Miriam Feingold, 1966, tape recording, Collection UC528, SHSW.

Cathy Patterson and Doris Davis as they canvassed in Jonesboro. Davis re-called one policeman saying, "Look little Nigger girl, when you get back to the mill quarters the niggers are going to kill you, or would you like for me to do it for you to save you the thoughts of it?" The sheriff then mentioned that they had been looking for Davis because, as an office staffer, she"[did] all of the writing" and reporting of police brutality. At one point, Davis thought she heard the police talking about "tying her to a tree and whipping her."[17] Yet, despite these persistent attempts to sabotage the movement in rural Louisiana, CORE continued to conduct direct-action campaigns against lo-cal businesses and to file discrimination lawsuits against local merchants, while local blacks attempted to register to vote.[18]

When CORE's staff entered the town of Jonesboro, Louisiana, in 1965, they encountered an atmosphere much different from that of the previous summer. Following CORE's initial entry in 1964, incidents of violence against Jonesboro's black residents rose precipitously. According to Annie Purnell Johnson, the KKK had "berated blacks there one time too many."[19] In re-sponse, local black army veterans organized an armed self-defense group to protect civil rights activists, and local blacks, from police violence and white vigilantes. In early 1965, the Deacons for Defense and Justice (DDJ) was offi-cially born.[20] The DDJ was the "South's first organized black vigilante" group

17. Field Report, Chronology of Jonesboro, 19 January 1965, Box 1, File 2, Sixth Congres-sional District, CORE Pa pers, SHSW; Affidavit by Doris Davis, July 1964, Reel 44, CORE Pa-pers, ARC.

18. Summary Field Report, October 1964–April 1965, Reel 23, 192, CORE Addendum, HU; Adam Fairclough, *Race and Democracy: The Struggle for Civil Rights in Louisiana, 1915–1972* (Ath-ens: University of Georgia Press, 1995), 341.

19. Johnson, interview, 1966.

20. Researchers differ over the actual date and reasoning behind origination of the Dea-cons for Defense and Justice. Reverend Dr. L. La Simba Gray states that the Deacons were or-ganized as a result of an assault by whites throwing acid on two black women as they walked home from church in the summer of 1964. Christopher Strain, on the other hand, states that the group first organized in March 1965 as a nonprofit group after Klansmen drove through Jonesboro distributing leaflets. CORE records and field reports make slight mention of the fact that the group existed in the fall of 1964, however unorganized it may have been at that point. A new book on the Deacons reveals much more history behind the organization, however, stating that it adopted the name Deacons for Defense and Justice in February 1965. See Lance Hill, *The Deacons for Defense: Armed Resistance and the Civil Rights Movement* (Chapel Hill: Uni-versity of North Carolina Press, 2004); Reverend Dr. L. La Simba Gray, *The Deacons for Defense and Justice: Defenders of the African-American Community in Bogalusa, Louisiana during the 1960s* (Winter Haven, Fla.: Four G, 2000); Christopher B. Strain, "'We Walked Like Men': The Dea-cons for Defense and Justice," *Louisiana History* (Winter 1977); and "Summary Field Reports,"

armed with guns, ammunition, and citizen's band radios.[21] Members agreed to call themselves the "Deacons" to reflect "their religious backgrounds, and their self-ascribed roles as servants of the community and defenders of the faith." Although the original chapter and headquarters remained in Jonesboro, the organization quickly branched out to Bogalusa, a small town near the Mississippi–Louisiana border. By 1965, membership estimates of the DDJ were reported to have been anywhere between five thousand and fifteen thousand across the country. The DDJ worked alongside CORE, protecting task force volunteers as they canvassed, at demonstrations, and even at the Freedom Houses.[22]

Incidents of violence against women led the Deacons to increase their presence in Louisiana. In Claiborne Parish, Deacons guarded Pamela Smith, a local activist who organized mass meetings, demonstrations, and non-violent workshops, around the clock.[23] The Deacons also made their presence known in the Felicianas, where Mimi Feingold led the project. Workers in the Felicianas had witnessed "a rash of cross burnings and attempts by night riders to burn down the Masonic hall where registration meetings are held and CORE workers shot at three times."[24] The DDJ also protected task force workers Dorothy Banks and Kendra Harris in Jackson Parish, and Joan Grieco and "Barbara" in Washington Parish. After the arrival of the Deacons, the women reported that the presence of the DDJ helped alleviate some of the tension of working in towns that were difficult to "crack"; because of the Deacons' presence, they experienced many a "quiet night" with "no major incidents."[25] In the towns of Jonesboro and Bogalusa, Deacons worked night and day to protect CORE workers. One report noted, for

October 1964–April 1965, Reel 23, 192, CORE Addendum, HU. See also Howell Raines, *My Soul Is Rested: The Story of the Civil Rights Movement in the Deep South* (New York: Penguin Books, 1983), 416–22. Historians of the civil rights movement, as historian Lance Hill has suggested, have perpetuated "the myth of nonviolence"—that is, that the movement "achieved its goals through nonviolent direct action" (see Hill, *The Deacons for Defense*, 5).

21. Raines, *My Soul Is Rested*, 416.

22. Strain, "We Walked Like Men," 44–45; "The Deacons," *Newsweek*, 2 April 1965.

23. Watts line reports for Claiborne Parish, 28 and 29 June 1965, Box 2, Folder 4, Sixth Congressional District, CORE Papers, SHSW.

24. See de Jong, *A Different Day*, 192–95; and press release, 20 December 1965, Folder 5, Sixth Congressional District, CORE Papers, SHSW.

25. Watts line reports, Claiborne and Washington Parishes, July 1965, Box 2, File 4, Sixth Congressional District, CORE Papers, SHSW.

example, that the "Deacons have been running themselves crazy escorting people in and out of Bogalusa. Tense."[26]

As a number of historians have shown, it was not unusual in the rural Black Belt South for African Americans to arm themselves and fight back against violence directed at their families and communities. As Greta de Jong's recent study of civil rights in rural Louisiana illustrates, male and female black Louisianians willingly and openly defended themselves against white vigilantes.[27] In perhaps the most telling examples of the ways in which women contested gendered notions of their "place," women as well as men took up arms to defend themselves and their families. CORE field notes report arrests and jailings of local women for carrying concealed weapons.[28] Like Thelma Caufield and Mama Jo Holmes, women were not afraid to carry guns and challenge whites who approached their homes. As historian Lance Hill notes in his work on the Deacons, however, the role of women in the DDJ was "problematic." Because "women were excluded from organized self-defense activities in the black community," the DDJ refused to formally admit female members. According to Hill, gender divisions in the Deacons reflected a long history of black fraternal orders that almost always excluded female participation. Still, several women in Louisiana, including Ruth Amos, "attended meetings" and played active roles in the organization. Local black women even organized a ladies' "auxiliary" called the Deaconesses, and, as one reporter noted, "took target practice alongside the men."[29] Furthermore, female CORE volunteers who worked in Jonesboro, Bogalusa, and Ferriday resided in the homes of Deacon members.[30]

By 1965, Jonesboro had emerged as a town with a highly active and vocal black community, due in part to the protection afforded them by the presence of the Deacons. As in other rural towns, women stand out among the

26. Watts line reports, Washington Parish, 1 July 1965, Box 2, File 4, Sixth Congressional District, CORE Papers, SHSW.

27. de Jong, *A Different Day*, 2002. See also Timothy B. Tyson, *Radio Free Dixie: Robert F. Williams and the Roots of Black Power* (Chapel Hill: University of North Carolina Press, 1999); Robert F. Williams, *Negroes with Guns* (Detroit: Wayne State University Press, 1998); and Gail Williams O'Brien, *The Color of the Law: Race, Violence, and Justice in the Post–World War II South* (Chapel Hill: University of North Carolina Press, 1999).

28. Arrest Records, Jonesboro, 1965, Folder 2, Jonesboro/Jackson Parish, CORE Papers, SHSW.

29. Hill, *The Deacons*, 45–46; "The Deacons," *Newsweek*, 2 April 1965.

30. See Annie Purnell Johnson and Gayle Jenkins, interviews by Miriam Feingold, 1966, both in Collection UC528, SHSW; Miriam Feingold, interview by the author, 22 December 2002, tape recording, copy in possession of the author; Barrett interview, 13 January 2003.

Jonesboro activists. Annie Purnell Johnson, among others, consistently advocated for better economic and social conditions, participated in direct-action campaigns against local merchants, and worked alongside CORE volunteers to register black voters.[31] Local men were often afraid to house CORE workers for fear of economic or violent reprisals. A number of Jonesboro women, however, such as Mrs. Margaret Harris, mother of CORE worker Kendra Harris, Winnifred Grace, Mrs. Vastie Gillard, Mrs. Magnolia, and Mrs. Vatrie (Ruth) Amos, acted as CORE's "local contacts." CORE volunteers participated alongside these women in numerous demonstrations against the local skating rink, a local grocery store, and in freedom marches. Police often arrived at demonstrations in great numbers brandishing billy clubs, rifles, and fire hoses. Female demonstrators were pushed, punched, kicked, and arrested. At one demonstration, police put arrested demonstrators in a "filthy garbage truck," but "inside the truck freedom songs were still being sung." And as one female demonstrator noted, "this didn't turn us freedom lovers around. We continued to demonstrate."[32]

Police arrested many local women that summer for "unlawful assembly" and "disturbing the peace." During a series of student demonstrations in early 1965, for instance, police arrested and charged Jonesboro activists Mary and Shirley Potts with contributing to the delinquency of a minor.[33] Police also arrested women for testing local merchants' compliance with the 1964 Civil Rights Act. CORE volunteers Shirley Thompson, Kendra Harris, and Marian Kramer found themselves in jail that summer alongside local activists Nora Ames, Stella Flowers, Patsy Boone, Gloria Becker, Vidia Davis, Martha Evans, Ida Mae Osborne, Bessie Boston, Mable Barnes, Bessie Bryant, and Wanda Sue Taylor. Police arrested Mrs. Queenie Ester Thompson, Miss Brenda Barrett, Stella Flowers, Bessie Dill, Mertiel Watson, Verna Gray, Betty Jo Smith, Lela Mae Walker, and Mildred Stafford for testing segregation laws at three local eateries. The women were charged with threatening an officer, using profanity, resisting arrest, and carrying a concealed weapon. With the assistance of CORE, Thompson, Walker, and Gray filed suit against the Blue Grill Café, the M & D, and the Brooks Motel and Café. As the threats increased, women only pressed harder for the rights they believed were owed them.[34]

31. Johnson, interview.

32. Field Report—Jonesboro, 18–21 July 1965, Folder 7, Jonesboro, CORE Papers, SHSW. Of those listed as local contacts, only one male is noted.

33. Ed Hollander to Marvin Rich, 5 August 1964, Reel 40, 949, CORE Papers, ARC.

34. "Summary of Events in Jonesboro, Louisiana, March 8 through March 16, 1965," Box 1,

Although CORE had achieved some nominal success in Jonesboro, its formal project in the community soon ended. As the organization had intended, a grassroots base of activists began to exert control over the local movement, and women were at the center. CORE workers had registered a few black voters and had secured postal service for nearly three hundred families who were forced to pick up their mail when the city refused to number the streets or erect street signs in their neighborhood. By summer's end, Governor McKeithan also agreed to create a "biracial mediation committee" to address the other grievances of Jonesboro's black community.

Indicative of the increasing radical nature of the movement, internecine conflict arose in the biracial committee when the Deacons accused the older black members of acting like "Uncle Toms." As a result, in August 1965 local community members organized the Action Committee for Jonesboro Community. Again women made up a large number of the members, and even dominated the executive committee: Bessie Dill served as vice president, Mrs. C. Cowens served as secretary, and Mrs. W. C. Flanagan served as assistant secretary.[35] Ultimately, however, with only minor concessions from the local white establishment, and increased conflict between local factions, CORE decided to pull its staff out of Jonesboro. Organized civil rights activity in the town all but ended.[36]

As in Jonesboro, when CORE volunteers arrived in Bogalusa, they discovered a highly active and vocal grassroots community base. In 1956, after the Louisiana legislature enjoined the NAACP from operating in the state, local black leaders had organized the Bogalusa Civic and Voters League (BCVL). The executive committee of the BCVL was made up of twenty-two members, including a number of women. Led by Andrew Moses, the league had for years fought for equal opportunity in employment, integrated schools, the desegregation of all public accommodations and facilities, and an inte-

---

CORE Papers, SHSW; press releases, "CORE Increases Pressure in Jonesboro, Louisiana," 24 March 1965, Box 1, File 1, Sixth Congressional District, CORE Papers, SHSW; Field Reports, for March–May 1965, Folder 7, Jonesboro, CORE Papers, SHSW; "3 Jonesboro Restaurants Named in Suit," *Louisiana Weekly*, 1 May 1965, ARC; "Desegregation of Public Facilities, 1964–1965," Folder 5, Jonesboro/Jackson Parish, CORE Papers, SHSW. A number of these women were arrested more than once that summer for various civil rights activities (see Arrest Records, Jonesboro—1965, Folder 2, Jonesboro/Jackson Parish, CORE Papers, SHSW).

35. Reports on Activities, 1964–1965, 3 August 1965, Folder 7, Jonesboro Papers, CORE, SHSW.

36. Meier and Rudwick, *CORE*, 345–46; "The Long Cold Winter in Louisiana," *CORE-LATOR*, March–April, 1965, Reel 13, 76, CORE Addendum, HU.

grated police force. League leaders had also met with the mayor to negotiate access to city sewage, paved roads, street lighting, and for the inclusion of African American community leaders in city and parish decision-making boards and councils.[37] In addition to the BCVL, the unionized, but segregated, Crown-Zellerbach Corporation had fostered the development of "organizational skills and . . . collective action," of its black workers. It is not surprising, then, that the black civil rights leadership in the town stemmed from these two institutions.[38]

Before 1965, CORE activity in Bogalusa had been minimal. At the behest of the BCVL, however, CORE volunteers arrived in January. Their first act was to test local banks' compliance with the 1964 Civil Rights Act. According to longtime local civil rights leader Gayle Jenkins, when CORE came to Bogalusa, "there was no trouble, but when [local blacks] went to test the next day, without [CORE] there, testing the same places, all hell broke loose."[39] As CORE's presence increased in Bogalusa, however, tensions began to mount and Klan activity increased. Despite a rash of violent incidents, CORE staff members Mimi Feingold, Howard Messing, and Loria Davis agreed that a full-time summer project in Bogalusa was warranted. The three believed that while "there is much work to be done both in the city of Bogalusa, and in the country . . . [w]e feel that Bogalusa can easily be one of the most exciting and challenging places this summer and for a long time to come." Acknowledging the difficulties that lay before them, Feingold, Messing, and Davis reported that the "white power structure, anxious to attract industry and people to Bogalusa, will do almost anything to keep CORE out."[40]

Knowing that Bogalusa already possessed a highly motivated grassroots community base, CORE approached the leaders of the BCVL in the spring of 1965 about returning. Immediately, the mayor instructed local black leaders to persuade CORE not to return to Bogalusa; as might have been expected, the meeting caused great dissension among community leaders. The BCVL and the fledgling Bogalusa chapter of the Deacons held a mass meeting, "the largest meeting I ever saw," according to Gayle Jenkins. At the meeting, "angry blacks spurred to greater militance [sic]" challenged the leader-

37. Bogalusa Voters League Papers, 1965, Folder 2, Bogalusa, CORE Papers, SHSW; Bogalusa Civic and Voters League to National CORE, et al., 6 April 1965, Reel 40, 737, CORE Papers, ARC.

38. "The Bogalusa Story," by the Bogalusa Committee for Concern, 1965, Reel 40, 730, CORE Papers, ARC; Fairclough, Race and Democracy, 347–48.

39. Press release, n.d., Reel 10, 27, CORE Addendum, HU.

40. Meier and Rudwick, CORE, 347; Feingold, Messing, and Davis, 1964 Scouting Report—Bogalusa, Reel 183, SRC Papers.

ship of the older, more conservative BCVL.[41] With the aid of the Deacons, the BCVL reorganized. The new membership elected A. Z. Young and Robert Hicks, both CORE advocates, as president and vice president, respectively, and Gayle Jenkins to serve as its secretary.

In the spring of 1965, in coordination with the BCVL, employees of the Crown-Zellerbach Company in San Francisco and Bogalusa organized the Bogalusa Committee for Concern (BCC). Among the BCC's demands were an end to segregated bathrooms, water fountains, and time clocks. In addition, the BCC sought to desegregate the unions and end the "Jim Crow line of progression relegating [the black employees] to lower-paying, unskilled jobs."[42] In March, the BCC solicited CORE for help. BCC members urged CORE staff and local individuals to write letters of complaint, which would "institute an attack [from] the top and [from] the bottom of the power structure."[43] In the spring, company executives and members of the BCC, BCVL, and CORE routinely met with the mayor outlining their demands, to no avail.[44] When the mayor insisted on excluding Gayle Jenkins, executive secretary of the BCVL, from negotiations and further insisted on a "'survey' of the town's black population to identify its *authentic* leaders," negotiations stalled.[45]

Gayle Jenkins acted as one of three local leaders of the Bogalusa movement. Like Mama Jo Holmes and Charlotte Greenup in West Feliciana Parish, Jenkins's home was the nucleus of the Bogalusa movement. Peter Jan Honigsberg, a law student who worked in rural Louisiana in the mid-1960s and provided legal representation for the movement, stayed at Jenkins's home when working in Bogalusa. As he described it: "People from eight to eighty ran in and out, planning, scheming, organizing, phoning, gossiping, and laughing. Just as Gayle's spirited energy and vivaciousness were unmatchable in the community, so too her home stood out."[46]

Raised in Bogalusa by her widowed mother, Gayle Jenkins was in her late thirties when the movement erupted in Bogalusa. Like Oretha Castle, Jenkins possessed a "magnetism" that translated into strong leadership. "All of us—the African American residents and the white civil rights workers—looked to her for leadership," said Honigsberg. Jenkins's commitment to

---

41. Press release, n.d., Reel 10, 27, CORE Addendum, HU.

42. Meier and Rudwick, *CORE*, 347.

43. P. T. Sinclair, President of Crown-Zellerbach, et al. to All CORE chapters, 1 March 1965, Box 1, Folder 21, Sixth Congressional District, CORE Papers, SHSW.

44. Press release, Reel 40, 739, CORE Papers, ARC.

45. "Tension Eased," *Louisiana Weekly*, 1 May 1965; Fairclough, *Race and Democracy*, 363.

46. Peter Jan Honigsberg, *Crossing Border Street: A Civil Rights Memoir* (Berkeley and Los Angeles: University of California Press, 2000), 34–35.

the movement, like that of many women in the state, seemingly took precedence over everything else in her life. When her boss forbade her to join
the movement, she immediately quit. In an attempt to get the "little radical
woman" out of Bogalusa, Louisiana governor John McKeithen offered her
a secretarial job at the state capital at fifty thousand dollars a year, a hefty
salary for 1965; she refused.[47]

The presence of Gayle Jenkins—an African American *and* a woman—
at the negotiating table was significant to the process. Women constituted
nineteen of the seventy-one members of the BCC, even though not one
black woman worked at any of the three Crown-Zellerbach plants. In fact,
only one black female had ever worked for the company; "a maid hired to
serve Crown-Zellerbach executives." In 1964, the company solicited applications from local women, but when African American women applied, "they
were told Crown-Zellerbach [was] no longer hiring," even though the company continued to hire white women. Subsequently, when company officials
and the mayor finally consented to meet with the BCVL, Jenkins's presence
proved to be more than necessary. As Adam Fairclough has described the
scene: "During a four-hour session on July 15, A. Z. Young, Robert Hicks,
and Gayle Jenkins pressed for the hiring of black women and fairer promotion procedures. The trio proved articulate and determined, appealing in
turn to the company's self-interest and its sense of fair play. Gayle Jenkins
made plant manager Ferguson squirm by repeatedly challenging him to defend the existing transfer procedures. Ferguson could not, admitting 'this
is a problem.'" Initially, the meeting produced only minor concessions on
the part of Crown-Zellerbach, but eventually, constant pressure forced the
company to accede to all BCVL demands.[48]

The persistence of women like Gayle Jenkins in Bogalusa is noteworthy.
Considering her status as the only female member of the executive committee of the local civil rights organization, Gayle Jenkins never felt "biggity"
about her involvement in the Bogalusa movement. In 1965, thirty-eight-
year-old Jenkins had three children, including a daughter attending Dillard
University in New Orleans and a nine-year-old son who, in 1966, integrated
a formerly all-white school. Along with her duties as secretary of the BCVL,
Jenkins worked on voter registration, picketed, tested local eating establishments, and sought compliance with the Civil Rights Act by applying to work
at Sears. "I took the test," she recalled, "[but] nothing happened." When test-

47. Honigsberg, *Crossing Border Street*, 35–36.
48. Fairclough, *Race and Democracy*, 376–77.

ing accommodations at the local Ackman Café, the waitress brought the water, slammed the glass on the table, brought the food and said, "Would you Niggers care for anything else?" An incensed Jenkins asked to see the manager. When picketing, Jenkins recalled, police not only arrested the demonstrators, "but hosed, beat them, etc." Like many other African American women, Gayle Jenkins had had enough: "Whites think black women are slovenly. All the Negro women go to work for fifteen dollars a week, cook, wash and iron and take care of the white ladies children and you just don't feel like it when you get back home so I wouldn't say that we're lazy, [we're] just tired and that's the way it [is] with everything."[49]

Like her older counterpart, seventeen-year-old Hattie Mae Hill fought the Bogalusa power structure in demanding equal rights. Hill joined the Bogalusa movement in January 1965 after attending her first civil rights meeting. Believing that "the older people can't do it all by themselves," Hill took the initiative and cofounded a civil rights youth group in Bogalusa, working as its secretary. Instead of shying away from the movement during Bogalusa's violent period, Hill marched, picketed, and tested facilities "at noon and at three" during the 1965 school year. Throughout the summer of 1965, Hill participated alongside CORE members in marches and demonstrations. In one instance, Hill was struck in the back of the head by a solid object (she thinks a billy club) as she marched. When members of the DDJ tried to assist her, a fight ensued between the marchers and local whites. In the melee, a Deacon accidentally shot a white man. Police arrested Hill and brought her in for questioning. After many hours, Hill told the police she wanted to go home. According to Hill, the policeman told her that "the man in the hospital wanted to go home too." Illustrating Hill's courageous streak, she responded, "'Well hell, he should have been home, then he wouldn't have gotten shot.'"[50]

In October, Bogalusa's youth organization called a boycott of a local fair, which allowed blacks to attend only on certain days. The students decided to boycott not only the fair, but also the schools affiliated with it. Every day for two weeks students marched to the school board office, petitioning the superintendent for a better heating system, better books, and general access to the fair. In what is locally known as "Bloody Wednesday," police beat the black protesters, arresting fifty-nine juveniles and charging them with "failure to

49. Jenkins, interview, 1966.

50. Hattie Mae Hill, interview by Miriam Feingold, 1966, Collection UC528, SHSW; Fairclough, *Race and Democracy*, 368.

move on." Hill recalled police beating women and handcuffing them to telephone poles and trees. "If you were in a car, they would snatch you out and start beating you. They beat just about everyone." Lynn Teidman, a nurse, tried to help Hill to a local minister's car; a white man grabbed her and held her down until the police came and arrested her. When police called parents to retrieve their children from jail, the students, including Hill, held a spontaneous jail-in. Friends of the jailed protesters tried to throw food through the windows, but police moved the students to solitary confinement. When the case finally went to court, Hill remembered that "the 'Uncle Toms' got up and lied . . . no one could get their stories straight."[51]

The reports of attacks on women in Bogalusa occurred on a regular basis. At a demonstration in April 1965, a white woman hit BCVL member Patricia Smith in the stomach while she picketed.[52] Police often harassed Hattie Mae Hill for her participation in the protests. While she was picketing in front of a department store one afternoon, police referred to her as "Nigger," "bitch," and "trash."[53] When ten-year-old Anne Ruth Hutchinson and her twelve-year-old sister, Brenda, entered a local diner with their "Freedom Hats" on, the white waiter called them "Nigger" and pushed their food at them. When they left, a white man followed them.[54] Mrs. Ora Lee Robinson reported to CORE that police arrested her for disturbing the peace when she intervened to stop a white man from beating Barbara Hicks, a local black female activist. Robinson reported to CORE that police pushed her and grabbed her "around her neck and began to squeeze." When her son attempted to intervene, the policeman told her "All you Niggers are going to jail."[55] In another case, a group of white men severely beat two local women, Mrs. Lilly Sampson and Daisy Sheppard, when they attempted to test a bar and restaurant in Sun, Louisiana, approximately three miles from Bogalusa. After the two were refused service, eight or nine men brandishing guns followed them. At one point, the deputy sheriff of Washington Parish threw Sampson to the ground and "pistol beat her in the face while another man pistol whipped and kicked Sheppard." Only after the Deacons arrived did the beatings end. Police arrested Sampson and Sheppard for disturbing the peace and resisting arrest. Refusing to stand down, Mrs. Sampson ultimately filed charges

51. Hill, interview, 1966.
52. Incident report, 16 April 1965, Folder 6, Bogalusa, CORE Papers, SHSW.
53. Incident report, 15 May 1965, Folder 6, Bogalusa, CORE Papers, SHSW.
54. Incident report, 28 May 1965, Folder 6, Bogalusa, CORE Papers, SHSW.
55. Incident report, n.d., Folder 6, Bogalusa, CORE Papers, SHSW.

against the sheriff, Vertress Adams, for attempted murder and aggravated assault.[56]

Like the local black women, CORE's white female field staff also continued to suffer. As one reporter wrote after a trip to the South, "Racists hate Northern Negroes worse than southern ones, white civil rights workers worse than black ones, white Yankee females worst of all." The story of "Donna," a twenty-two-year-old CORE volunteer from California, illustrates the dilemma of the white female "outside agitator" working in the rural South. After dismissing the warnings of CORE organizers of the dangers faced by white females, Donna committed to CORE's 1965 summer project in Bogalusa. When she first arrived, Donna recalled that, "she jumped at every loud noise, couldn't sleep at night, and broke out in a nervous rash." She remembered that the volunteers, women in particular, were kept under twenty-four-hour guard by the Deacons and warned "never to stand close to a lighted window at night; at one tense moment when the volunteers were isolated in an empty house, she was even issued a small pistol." According to Donna, "You never stop being afraid there, but you stop being scared."[57]

The fear that women like Donna experienced was, according to one reporter, "both a healthy and realistic state of mind for a white female Yankee civil rights worker billeted with a Negro family in the Deep South."[58] Although CORE directed its members to adhere to the philosophy of nonviolence, in towns like Bogalusa they had no choice but to accept armed protection from the Deacons, particularly as white aggression expanded and violence against women escalated. According to Gayle Jenkins, without the Deacons, "Bogalusa probably would have been destroyed. We felt that it was important that Negroes took a stand for the betterment of our people and for the betterment of our children."[59]

Certainly, the presence of the DDJ allowed the women a modicum of safety. Local activists note, in fact, that the reason the men organized a chapter of the Deacons for Defense and Justice in Bogalusa was due, in part, to the numerous, and seemingly endless, assaults against black women and children. The straw that apparently broke the camel's back came when someone in a truck with Mississippi plates poured acid on a group of women

56. Incident report and statement by Daisy Sheppard, 20 February 1966, Folder 6, Bogalusa, CORE Papers, SHSW.

57. Shana Alexander, "Visit Bogalusa and You Will Look for Me," *Life*, 2 July 1965. "Donna's" last name was not provided.

58. Alexander, "Visit Bogalusa and You Will Look for Me."

59. Jenkins, interview.

as they left church one morning.[60] Obviously whites made no concessions for race, gender, or age when it came to dishing out violence; according to Charles Sims, the leader of the DDJ in Bogalusa, "those most in danger are the women."[61]

The idea of white females and black males interacting on any level provoked the greatest hostility toward CORE's female staff. Beverly Lee, a white female veteran of the Mississippi movement was initially assigned to the Baton Rouge office, but within a few weeks transferred to Bogalusa. Lee noted that after only a few days, she preferred "to accompany a Negro girl when canvassing or at any time when in close company with the local people who don't know me." Aware of the white southern mentality regarding any kind of close physical contact between white women and black men, Lee refrained from close contact with local black males, including black male CORE coworkers. However, Lee expressed her optimism, stating that, "the community will sooner or later accept integration with only the normal amount of questioning as they would give a Negro girl and boy. I'm truly convinced this will happen far sooner when they see friendships arise between Negro and white girls."[62]

Even with the protection afforded by the Deacons, CORE's female volunteers increasingly found themselves subjected to severe harassment and intimidation. Police arrested local activist Jacqueline Butler, CORE's Southern Regional Office researcher Judi Nussbaum, and CORE volunteer Beverly Lee as they picketed a shopping center in July 1965. Sheriff Vertress Adams threw Butler into the back of his patrol car, which, as Butler reported, contained a K-9 police dog. Butler hit her head, causing her to be dazed from the blow. She recalled the four officers in the car talking "segregationist talk" among themselves as they took her to jail. When they arrived at the station, Adams "slung [Butler] into the wall of the building . . . grabbed the back of [her] dress collar and twisted it tight." When she told him he was choking her, he twisted the dress tighter and threw her through the door of the station. Frightened because she could not see if the police had also arrested the other picketers, she was "booked, mugged, fingerprinted and put into a cell." After the assault, Butler did not recall much more of the incident, except that her head hurt so much she felt sick. Her real nightmare, however, had not yet begun. Within a few hours, an officer came and told her

60. See Raines, *My Soul Is Rested*, 418; Gray, *The Deacons*, 4–8, 11; and Jenkins, interview.

61. Alexander, "Visit Bogalusa and You Will Look for Me."

62. Field Fellowship Report by Beverly D. Lee, 27 June 1965, Folder 10, Bogalusa, CORE Papers, SHSW.

that she had been released on bond. As she went to fill out the papers, she realized that the police were releasing her into the hands of a mob of thirty whites that had gathered outside, shouting threats that they were going to rape and kill her. After pleading with the officer to let her stay, he finally relinquished and allowed her a phone call. Police eventually allowed Butler to wait until another CORE volunteer, "Gail," arrived to pick her up.[63]

Gayle Jenkins, Hattie Mae Hill, and the many other local women who actively participated in Bogalusa's black struggle for freedom illustrate the determination of black women to sustaining the movement in such an extremely hostile area as Bogalusa. Similarly, white CORE field staff members like Judi Nussbaum and Beverly Lee also represent a dedicated group of women willing to risk their lives for their principles. It was often women who sustained injury during arrest, found themselves beaten by whites on the picket lines, were denied service at local eating establishments, and stared down the barrel of a gun. It is not surprising, then, that many began to carry weapons.

When CORE initiated a project in Ferriday, Louisiana, women were among the first to seek inclusion. According to local activist Robert Lewis, when CORE first arrived in Ferriday, "amazingly, only women would join."[64] Alberta Whatley and her granddaughter Mary were among the numerous women who worked with CORE task force volunteers hoping to change the racial status quo in Ferriday. Like Mama Jo Holmes and Charlotte Greenup in the Felicianas, Alberta Whatley opened her home to CORE volunteers. Essie Mae Lewis, Robert Lewis's wife, also openly advocated greater equality in her community. In 1966, the Lewises established the first NAACP chapter in the area, with Robert Lewis serving as its president from 1966 to 1972. Aside from the Lewises and the Whatleys, a number of other local young women pressed for integration of the schools, public facilities, and equal employment opportunities. Like their sisters in the struggle in Bogalusa and Jonesboro, women in the Ferriday movement refused to adopt the nonviolent philosophy of CORE, arming when necessary and standing their ground against intransigent whites.[65]

When CORE arrived in July 1965, in "response to attempts by the white

63. Incident report by Jacqueline Butler, 17 July 1965, Folder 6, Bogalusa, CORE Papers, SHSW.

64. Robert Lewis and Essie Mae Lewis, interview by Greta de Jong, 25 November 1996, THWOHC.

65. de Jong, *A Different Day*, 182–83, Robert Lewis and Essie Mae Lewis, interview; Ferriday Freedom Movement Papers, Collection 376, SHSW (hereafter cited as FFM Papers).

community, and especially the KKK, to interfere with a voter registration drive among the black population," local blacks and CORE task force workers organized the Ferriday Freedom Movement (FFM). Under the guidance of CORE's Southern Regional Office, the FFM soon branched out from voter registration and began demonstrating against local merchants who refused to hire blacks, testing restaurants, lunch counters, the local movie theater, and the town library. FFM members also held "a march to city hall to protest police brutality." Integration of the local trade school, swimming pool, and bowling alley, as well as the hiring of "a substantial number of Negro policeman chosen from some respected members of the community," were among their demands. In addition, the FFM asked for the integration of Concordia Parish Hospital and for the hiring of black nurses.[66]

Although the male members of Ferriday's African American community were slow to embrace the movement in their town, women rose to the challenge, and female leadership there was essential. According to Robert Lewis, when members of the FFM met after a Klan bombing, "amazingly only women and children were there." Women dominated the movement in Ferriday and were primed to assume the leadership positions. Men, however, held fast to hardened gender roles. When twenty-two-year-old Mary Whatley offered to serve as president of the FFM, according to Robert Lewis, "The folks didn't want to follow her." Subsequently, Lewis led the Ferriday Freedom Movement. Women served in all other capacities though, including Mary Whatley as vice president, Dorothy Caston as secretary, and Jessie Dixon as treasurer.[67]

Initially, high school students made up the majority of the members of the FFM, but as the civil rights movement got off the ground, older members of the community joined, demonstrated, and marched. Established female members of the community like Essie Mae Lewis and Alberta Whatley sustained the Ferriday movement. According to Lewis, "the local people who became involved were mainly women and children . . . young adults." Alberta Whatley acted as "the mother of freedom movement in Ferriday because . . . when no one else would allow the CORE person to come to the gates, she would allow them in her home."[68]

Essie Mae Lewis served as a role model for younger local women. Born

66. "History," and FFM List of Demands, 1965, Box 1, Folder 1, FFM Papers. See also Meier and Rudwick, *CORE*, 350–51.

67. Minute Book, 27 July 1965, Box 1, File 2, FFM Papers; Robert Lewis and Essie Mae Lewis, interview, 25 November 1996.

68. Robert Lewis and Essie Mae Lewis, interview, 25 November 1996.

in 1927, Lewis grew up in a sharecropping family, attended school through the seventh grade, and, at age seventeen, married Robert. Robert and Essie Mae lived in Ferriday quite aware of their subordinate lot in life. Robert Lewis acknowledged two methods used to control blacks: violence and economic pressure. According to Lewis, economic pressure brought the worst repercussions "because . . . we had to rely on jobs . . . from the white community." When white men lynched Emmett Till in Mississippi, Lewis recalled that his boss made sure he saw the newspaper report, "as a kind of warning of what might happen if [I] stepped out of line." Essie Mae's grandmother, however, did not accept this treatment. At one point, she had had enough of whites referring to her as "Ma" and "Auntie," brazenly telling one man, "I ain't your damn ma, and I ain't your auntie."

Black women in Ferriday were apparently subjected to some of the worst forms of racial abuse in the state. The Lewises recalled stories of whites accosting black women, including a young prostitute who was kidnapped, then repeatedly raped and beaten for two weeks. Moreover, a tradition existed in Ferriday's white community that "young white males were not 'men' until they had slept with a black woman. So white men were often seen downtown trying to pick up black women." Not surprisingly, these women had no recourse; if they saw fit to complain to the police, "it wasn't going to do any good because they would get you uptown, they would beat you instead."[69]

Although by 1965 the movement had yet to reach Ferriday, the Lewises were aware of civil rights activity in other areas of the South, particularly the actions of the NAACP. "We yearned for some of the same rights," stated Robert Lewis. As the movement gained momentum through the 1960s, particularly after the murders of the three civil rights workers in Mississippi in June 1964, a desire among Ferriday's black community "to fight back against oppression really began to increase." Like many members of the Ferriday community, the Lewises were initially afraid to get involved. When CORE arrived in the summer of 1965, however, staff members "helped them to see that they were American, just like everybody else." In addition, the incidents of violence directed at the black community, particularly the bombings of two local homes, served to strengthen the resolve of locals. In the summer of 1965, Essie Mae participated in Ferriday's first march alongside other local women such as Ernestine Brown, Katie Brown, and Geraldine Johnson.[70] Essie Mae also participated in picketing and boycotts where she, like others,

69. Robert Lewis and Essie Mae Lewis, interview, 25 November 1996.

70. Greta de Jong's interview with Ernestine Brown is in her possession, but she identifies Ernestine Brown as a "local leader" from Tallulah (de Jong, *A Different Day*, 198).

found herself subjected to violence at the hands of whites. At one demonstration, female activists had hot water poured on them, and a local activist, "Mrs. Melancon," was hit with a bicycle chain and badly cut. According to the Lewises, the demonstrators refused to leave as they "knew [we] had the right to assemble peacefully. None of [us] tried to fight back, and none ran away." The Lewises also had their house bombed, and Mr. Lewis spent time in jail. Women like Essie Mae, the Whatleys, and local youths "played key roles" in the Ferriday movement; they "were the heart of the movement in Ferriday."[71]

In August, Robert Lewis and Samuel Morgan, accompanied by five female FFM committee members—Dorothy Caston, Geraldine Henderson, Rosie Tennessee, Beverly Long, and Mary Whatley—presented a list of grievances to the mayor. When the mayor refused to meet their demands, FFM members staged a march to city hall. In addition, only women—Dorothy Caston, Jessie Dixon, Rosie Elaine, Geraldine Henderson, Beverly Long, Lillie Mae Savage, Rosie Tennessee, Gertrude Walker, and Ruby Lee Witherspoon—worked on the voter registration campaign. The women also organized a letter-writing campaign to the local editor, arranged protests, and volunteered to integrate the local theater.[72] Through the fall of 1965, members of the FFM and CORE engaged in battle with local whites resigned to maintaining the racial status quo. Through the fall, women kept up the pressure by boycotting local merchants; testing cafés, hotels, and snack bars; raising money; and organizing community marches. When the FFM again approached the mayor with a list of demands in the spring of 1966, Mary Whatley, "Mrs. Smith," and "Miss Walker" were chosen to represent the organization.[73]

In addition to the numerous demonstrations, boycotts, and meetings attended, Ferriday's female activists were among the first to fight on behalf of their children for integrated schools. In November 1965, FFM members Irma J. Smith, Dorothy Caston, and Pinky Mae Carter filed suit against the Concordia Parish School Board. Represented by CORE attorneys Lolis Elie, Robert Collins, and Nils Douglas, the women cited discrimination in school construction, budget allotments, and disbursement of funds to the local black schools, and requested the desegregation of four grades by January 1966.[74] In December, the Concordia Parish District Court ordered the integration of

71. Robert Lewis and Essie Mae Lewis, interview; de Jong, A Different Day, 258.
72. Minute Book, 25 July–25 October 1965, Box 1, Folder 2, FFM Papers.
73. Minute Book, 28 October 1965–12 May 1966, Box 1, Folder 3, FFM Papers.
74. Press release, 30 November 1965, Box 1, Folder 5, FFM Papers.

grades one and two and eleven and twelve; in February, Marie Jones, Ethel Lewis, and David Whatley, grandson of Alberta, integrated Concordia Parish High School. In April, Donna Lewis integrated the first grade.

Integrating the schools, however, did not happen as smoothly as the parents had hoped. The black students suffered abuse at the hands of white students. In addition, teachers segregated them in the classrooms and forced them to use separate toilets and sit at separate tables in the lunchrooms. When eighteen mothers and seven fathers filed a petition with the Commission of Education listing a series of complaints and requesting integration of the local Headstart program, local whites turned their attention on the black parents, harassing them at their homes and on the streets. Despite the constant barrage, the parents filed a petition with the Department of Health, Education, and Welfare for assistance.[75]

As Ferriday's school integration struggles continued, CORE workers canvassed and worked on voter registration while local blacks demonstrated the segregation of public accommodations. As a result, incidents of violence in Ferriday increased, forcing the DDJ to increase its visibility in town. In December 1965, Klan members firebombed the Lewis home and fired shots into the homes of Mrs. Willie Lee Calhoun and Alberta Whatley. When "bullets were fired into the Freedom House where CORE volunteers lived," the DDJ came out in full force. According to one volunteer, "the Freedom House [was] armed like a 'small Alamo.'"[76]

In March 1966, police arrested Carrie Washington and David and Mary Whatley as they posted protest signs around town. Police and white men slapped Washington and pushed her to the ground, and dragged her by her feet as her head hit the ground. Another man slapped Mary Whatley, knocking her glasses off her face. When she hit him back, another man came up behind her and hit her on the back of the head with a soda bottle. Reeling from the assault, Whatley, bleeding badly, staggered toward the car, but the police grabbed both her and Washington and put them in the police car. When Whatley requested to see a doctor, the police told her that he was "sorry [that he] didn't kill them all."[77] CORE lawyers eventually took the

75. Mrs. Rosetta Miller to Mrs. Ester W. Smith, 4 May 1966, Box 1, Folder 2, FFM Papers; Field Reports, 16 February 1966, 2–7 April 1966, Folder 5, FFM Papers; Alberta Whatley to CORE, 21 January 1966, Series of complaints, n.d., 7 January 1966, 7 and 11 February 1966, Folder 17, FFM Papers.

76. "Night Riders Intimidate Freedom Fighters with Shootings, Burnings," *Louisiana Weekly*, 25 December 1965; press release, 26 December 1965, Reel 21, 104, CORE Addendum, HU.

77. Statements of Carrie Washington and Mary Whatley, 19 March 1966, Box 1, Folder 12, FFM Papers.

case to federal court.[78] When members of the FFM continued to test facilities, in May 1966, the KKK burned crosses all across the town. As Richard
Haley, director of the Southern Regional Office, reported, "We feel the Ferriday Freedom Movement deserves the highest praise for its direct challenge
to this lawlessness." Indeed, FFM members continued to test local restaurants and resumed testing of the local theater.[79]

By the summer of 1966, internecine conflict began to overshadow the
Ferriday movement, paralleling issues that began to arise in other organizations across the South. Earlier that year, the NAACP appointed Mary Jamieson, a white woman from Long Island, New York, and the first white student to attend Grambling College, as field director for Louisiana. Jamieson's
tenure as field director epitomized the "women-centered organizing" model
that became a fundamental component of the latter stage of the civil rights
movement "proper." For instance, although she worked for the NAACP, Jamieson "recognized CORE's dominance in certain areas (of the state) and tried
to work closely with the organizations that CORE sponsored," like the FFM.
However, a power struggle ensued when members of the FFM and other local activists insisted on organizing a NAACP chapter in Ferriday, believing
that the NAACP was more "recognizable among [the] black community,"
and because the NAACP simply had more economic resources. Even Robert
Lewis left the FFM and became president of the newly organized NAACP,
believing that the NAACP had "a better chance of gaining [local black] support." Jamieson's ideological commitment to bridging the divide between
FFM and NAACP members and her ability to cultivate friendly relations
among divergent interests resulted in success. Throughout the remainder
of the summer, Jamieson worked with the members of the NAACP, FFM,
and CORE, testing the local swimming pool, theater, and other public facilities.[80] However, Jamieson's role as one of few female leaders in the NAACP
was short-lived. Because she resisted NAACP directives to let the local organizations fend for themselves, in early 1966 NAACP leaders fired Jamieson for insubordination. Nevertheless, it was only through her diligence
that the three organizations finally agreed to work together to achieve the
same ends.[81]

78. Richard Haley to David Whatley, 23 March 1966, Box 1, Folder 12, FFM Papers.

79. "Negroes Served at Two Ferriday Restaurants, Crosses Burn Later," *Louisiana Weekly*, 7
May 1966.

80. Fairclough, *Race and Democracy*, 402–3.

81. Robert Lewis and Essie Mae Lewis, interview; correspondence between FFM and Mary
Jamieson, Box 1, Folder 1, FFM Papers; Fairclough, *Race and Democracy*, 401–3.

"NOBLESSE OBLIGE WAS NOT WHERE IT WAS AT"

As CORE's 1965–66 project wound down, notions of Black Power began to take hold in Louisiana's rural communities. According to Mimi Feingold, "There began to be some small expressions of resentment. . . . I don't want to belittle it, but it would come from young people who had reasons to resent the civil rights workers quite apart from anything radical." CORE members debated whether whites should remain in the organization. Even Feingold recalled:

> There was a big discussion about whether we should stay or not, and we ourselves were arguing that we should not stay. Also within the SDS circles, the white movement circles so to speak, there was a very strong growing feeling, which, in a way, was a reaction to the black power stuff, that whites should be dealing with their own stuff. That noblesse oblige was not where it was at, that people should be dealing with their own particular issues, so that we didn't belong there anyway. What interested me was the overwhelming sentiment of the people at that meeting was "Please stay. We love you, we want you here, we want you to continue to help us."

Although some locals "genuinely wanted [their] help," Feingold recalled that "there were a couple of young people, one young woman in particular, who spoke out very strongly, that we didn't belong there anymore."[82] It seemed that CORE had met its goal of having local communities become self-sustaining entities.

Despite the movement's ultimate embrace of Black Power by 1966, white women remained committed to the Louisiana movement through the summer of 1967. Mimi Feingold, now a fixture in the Louisiana rural movement, worked in the Felicianas full time until the fall of 1965, when she returned to Wisconsin to attend graduate school. Feingold remembers the increased militancy of the movement in the Felicianas, relating to her parents how she was "constantly struck by how the movement combines country-style Negro religion and black power rhetoric." As Feingold reported to a friend in August 1965, "Meetings here start with several long prayers and a long-meter hymn or two, and even 'We Shall Overcome' sounds like a Negro hymn! Then the president of the League gives a rousing speech, sprinkled with anti-white sentiment, but those statements really refer to the bad white folk

82. Feingold, interview, 22 December 2002.

around here, and don't extend to the white folk in general."[83] Illustrating her profound dedication to her friends in Louisiana, Feingold returned in the summers of 1966 and 1967, continuing her work organizing the local communities in and around the Feliciana parishes, which had become her second home.[84]

These divisions in the movement over black self-determination led many whites, inside and outside the southern civil rights movement, to question rising black militancy and separatist rhetoric. Aside from CORE and SNCC, organizations like the NAACP also grappled with the direction of their programs. Amid the growing disenchantment within the southern movement, a group of predominantly southern white student activists from SNCC regrouped and acknowledged the almost inevitable end to interracialism in the movement. Already feeling isolated because of their involvement in a movement that challenged the central tenets of their upbringing, white southern activists began to question their own dedication to the struggle for black equality. In response to what many considered an "urgent and growing need for communication and education in the South," in April 1964, forty-five student leaders and representatives from seventeen predominantly white southern campuses across the South gathered in Nashville. The interracial group of young men and women addressed what they considered the problem of the "moderate" southerner: those supportive of the civil rights movement, yet increasingly marginalized by their race and southern heritage. The students agreed to look into "the extent of involvement in civil rights by students at Southern campuses . . . to ascertain the amount of interest in action along other political, social, and economic lines, and to assess their student needs and set up a structure through which felt needs in those areas could be met." As longtime SNCC member Sue Thrasher stated, "[We] needed to find other people like [ourselves]."[85]

From this initial meeting, the Southern Student Organizing Committee (SSOC) was born. As Ella Baker had done during the organization of SNCC

83. Feingold, interview, December 22, 2002; Feingold to Russell, August 12, 1965, Reel 2, Feingold Papers.

84. See Feingold notebooks nos. 11 and 12 for summers 1966 and 1967, Reel 2, Feingold Papers.

85. Southern Student Organizing Committee History, 1964, Reel 44, SNCC Papers (hereafter cited as SSOC History, 1964); Sue Thrasher quoted in Evans, *Personal Politics*, 44; Sue Thrasher, "Circle of Trust," in Constance Curry et al., *Deep in Our Hearts: Nine White Women in the Freedom Movement* (Athens: University of Georgia Press, 2000). See also Catherine Fosl, *Subversive Southerner: Anne Braden and the Struggle for Racial Justice in the Cold War South* (New York: Palgrave Macmillan, 2002), 280, 300–301.

in 1960, Anne Braden, a longtime white female activist and cofounder of the Southern Conference Educational Fund (SCEF), acted as a mentor working closely with the student leadership to develop the new organization. Although SSOC basically operated as an affiliate of SNCC, Braden warned against the creation of a separate "white student organization." Thus, while members agreed that the organization would be interracial, they also acknowledged that, as a predominantly white organization, their main focus was to challenge "white southerners to shed racial prejudice."[86] SSOC also aligned itself with other similarly progressive organizations such as Students for a Democratic Society, the United States National Student Association, and the American Friends Service Committee.

SNCC member and SSOC leader Robb Burlage penned the organization's manifesto "We'll Take Our Stand," modeled after that of the Agrarians, a group of early twentieth-century writers and intellectuals who promoted an agrarian vision of the South's future as an antidote to the dehumanizing effects of modern life. In this new version, SSOC members declared that "as Southern students from most of the Southern states, representing different economic, ethnic, and religious backgrounds . . . we will here take our stand in determination to build together a New South which brings democracy and justice for all its people." The statement further declared: "We hereby take our stand to start with our college communities and to confront them and their surrounding communities and to move from here out through all the states of the South—and to tell the Truth that must ultimately make us free. The Freedom movement for an end to segregation inspires us all to make our voices heard for a beginning of true democracy in the South for all people. We pledge together to work in all communities across the South to create nonviolent political and direct action movements dedicated to the sort of social change throughout the South and nation which is necessary to achieve our stated goals."[87] SSOC members vowed to end poverty, segregation, and racism, to work toward "full and equal opportunity for all," to create a democratic society "where politics pose a meaningful dialogue . . . an end to man's inhumanity to man," and " a world working toward the easing of tensions of the Cold War with positive emphasis on peace, disarmament, and world-wide understanding."[88]

86. SSOC History, 1964.

87. See Dorothy Dawson Burlage, "Truths of the Heart," in Curry et al., *Deep in Our Hearts*, 119–20.

88. SSOC History, 1964; text of "We'll Take Our Stand" quoted in SSOC History; Thrasher, "Circle of Trust," 230; Carson, *In Struggle*, 102–3.

As in other civil rights organizations, notably the Southern Christian Leadership Conference (SCLC) and the NAACP, SSOC was, for the most part, male-dominated and male-led. More so than southern white male activists, white female activists had reason to feel alienated in the southern civil rights movement. It was on their backs that much of the burden of southern segregationist ideology was laid. Thus, the women who joined SSOC, particularly after the Waveland Conference in 1965, did so with an enhanced sense of what their role in the southern movement meant. Although females represented less than one-third of the officers, one-seventh of the executive committee, and one-fourth of the Continuations Committee, the women who did participate were essential to the organization's success. Sue Thrasher, the only female elected to serve on the executive committee and one of only a handful of women in leadership positions, acted as SSOC's executive secretary.[89]

In SSOC, as in the larger movement, women performed much of the more mundane organizational work, such as clerical duties, visiting white campuses and talking to students, and setting up local affiliates. As one female member of SSOC noted, traditional female characteristics such as "self-assertion . . . interpersonal, organizational, and administrative" skills, "abilities that are commonly encouraged in women," were essential to SSOC. Founding member Dorothy Dawson (later Burlage) recalled that "the movement grew because of such personal connections and relationships, often encouraged and developed by women."[90] Again, "women-centered organizing" constituted an essential element of SSOC's agenda. SSOC organizers encouraged women to create intimate, interpersonal relationships, reifying traditional notions of skills considered uniquely female. According to Anne Braden, "SSOC just wouldn't have happened without the women."[91]

Kathy Barrett, a young white woman from Baton Rouge, chose to work in rural Louisiana amid the heightened tensions in the movement over the place of whites and women. Barrett, a young Loyola University student, served as a campus traveler and on the executive committee of SSOC for the state of Louisiana. A substantial portion of SSOC's program focused on traveling to campuses across the South. SSOC members visited campuses in twelve southern states to assess students' opinions of, and the extent of their involvement in, the civil rights movement. In addition, campus travelers helped students to "communicate with other active [civil rights] groups

89. SSOC History, 1964.
90. Burlage, "Truths of the Heart," 120.
91. Cited in Evans, *Personal Politics*, 46.

in their area or region." To be sure, women contributed greatly to this aspect of SSOC's agenda.[92]

Born in 1944, Barrett grew up in Baton Rouge, attending segregated schools and witnessing the beginnings of the civil rights movement in Louisiana firsthand. Barrett daily walked through black neighborhoods and rode segregated public transportation to school. During the Baton Rouge Bus Boycott of 1953, and other periods of activity in that city, such as the Southern University sit-ins and boycotts, Barrett's parents forbade her to go downtown. According to Barrett: "I lived a really insulated life. I was a naïve girl. The best thing I can say about my awareness of the civil rights movement in high school was that I was vaguely aware and I just had this feeling that it made sense." Barrett recalls that, by the age of eighteen, she felt strongly that one had a responsibility" to support or defy the Jim Crow status quo. The momentum of the civil rights movement demanded a response. You had to take a position on civil rights, when I was doing it. You had to make a choice and you had to live your life accordingly. There was no in between in Louisiana."[93]

Barrett graduated from high school in 1962, and after a short period of study in early 1963 at the Sisters of St. Joseph, a New Orleans convent, she began attending Loyola University, majoring in history. Almost immediately upon arriving in New Orleans, Barrett joined both CORE and the Tulane Liberals Club, an integrated "democratic organization" that supported the civil rights movement in the city. During summer and winter breaks, Barrett worked with CORE in Hattiesburg, Mississippi, and rural Louisiana, teaching at Freedom Schools and canvassing for the voter registration project. When the Klan bombed two churches in Jonesboro, Barrett helped CORE's staff rebuild them. Although she participated in picketing and testing restaurants in downtown New Orleans with CORE, Barrett still recalls only having "a vague idea of what was occurring in the South."[94]

Barrett's involvement with SSOC began after a meeting with Constance "Connie" Curry, a longtime civil rights activist and founding member of SNCC. Curry had delivered a speech to an interracial "Democratic Party group" at Loyola to which Barrett belonged. Curry personally recruited Barrett for the National Student Association (NSA) conference in Minneapolis so that Barrett could learn more about the southern student movement. Shortly after

92. Barrett, interview, 13 January 2003.
93. Barrett, interviews, 13 January 2003 and 3 February 2003; Kathy Barrett, e-mail message to the author, 20 January 2003.
94. Barrett, interview, 13 January 2003.

this conference, Barrett decided to drop out of school to work with SSOC full-time. Working with SSOC "made a whole lot of sense to me," states Barrett. "It seemed to me at that point, even though I wasn't fully appreciative initially when I went to work for SSOC, [that] the move towards Black Power . . . was present very much. It seemed to me that as a white southerner, where the work I needed to do was with other white southerners. They had to be convinced that change was here, that it was going to come and I took the position that this had to be dealt with. That civil rights was a part of human rights and that we had to acknowledge this, we had to do it and convince people that it was the right thing to do."[95]

Like a number of other female SSOC members, Kathy Barrett worked as a campus traveler. In this capacity, Barrett assisted "people who struggled for integration on their campus." The main purpose of campus travelers was to get local student groups to affiliate with SSOC, a daunting challenge for a white female southerner working in a Deep South state that had witnessed extreme resistance to school integration. Louisiana was certainly "a land where a girl, according to Old South gentile traditions, does not travel freely or alone." As she traveled the state, Barrett was fully aware of the fact that "one of the worst things that you could be in the white community was a Nigger lover." According to Barrett, "As a white southerner, I envisioned the elimination of racism through a joint effort in all communities. This mission led me to work with the southern students to organize activities in support of civil rights." She met with students at predominantly white campuses— "not black campuses because they were doing their own thing"—discussing issues ranging from integration and civil liberties to the threat of nuclear war and the draft. Barrett remained with SSOC until late 1965, when she decided to return to school full-time. She continued to affiliate with CORE and work in the movement in small ways. In 1966, Barrett worked alongside fellow SSOC staffer and CORE activist Cathy Cade at an "adult open school [in New Orleans] . . . akin to a settlement house," teaching classes to local women on everything from sewing to reading, to the burgeoning women's movement.[96]

White women like Kathy Barrett, who joined the movement in late 1964 and 1965, found themselves working in a quite different movement from the one whites had joined in 1960 and 1961. Years of violence and constant struggle had given the movement, and its members, an edge. According to

95. Barrett, interview, 13 January 2003.
96. Barrett, interview, 13 January 2003; Barrett, e-mail; *The Road from New Orleans,* documentary by Robert Rowen (copy provided by Kathy Barrett, ca. 1964).

Barrett: "One of my struggles as a campus traveler [was] to realize the needs of students like myself. I know that lots of times when myself or my friends [were] meeting Negroes in the movement for the first time they'll hear the southern accent and come up and ask 'Where are you from?' and when you tell them they don't really believe you." At the same time, women began to question their role in a movement led by men. Like many other white women who joined the movement in later years, Barrett felt increasingly isolated. "I felt connected to the students I made contact with," states Barrett, "but because of what was going on in the movement, and what was happening to CORE and what was happening to SNCC, being a woman, working alone . . . I did feel very, very isolated. I was out there wandering around in the white community trying to figure out how to make things connect with something that wasn't going so well." And, Barrett continued, "In rejecting the dominant culture, where does your experience leave you to connect with other people?"[97]

Paralleling racial divisions in the movement, as early as 1965, a number of young white women began to question their marginalized status not only because of their race, but also because of their gender. As the call for black self-determination increased, and black men sought to assert their dominance in a society that they believed had emasculated them since slavery, the movement became more "masculinized."[98] Still, white women continued to join civil rights organizations, believing that their participation in a movement for the liberation of blacks was important to its success. As historian Sara Evans notes, "From the beginning, a cluster of young white women committed themselves to the revolt of black youth."[99] This was certainly the case in rural Louisiana. Even amid heightened dissension, white women like Kathy Barrett chose to remain in the movement.

While in SSOC, Barrett traveled alone to campuses in Louisiana and Arkansas. Yet like many female activists, Barrett downplays her role in the Louisiana movement, believing that, "at best, my participation in the Louisiana Civil Rights movement may deserve a footnote. My uniqueness only deserves mention as a white, born and raised, Louisianian." However, as her father indicated in a 1964 interview, since Kathy was young, she was a "born idealist . . . ideally suited" for the type of work she performed in

97. Barrett, interviews, 13 January 2003 and 3 February 2003; Rowen, *The Road from New Orleans;* SSOC Program Update, 1965, Reel 44, SNCC Papers.

98. For more information on the masculinization of the movement, see M. Bahati Kuumba, *Gender and Social Movements* (Walnut Creek, Calif.: Altimira Press, 2001).

99. Evans, *Personal Politics,* 42.

SSOC and later, with SDS; the Pageant Players, an activist New York street theater group; and the women's movement. He believed that the work she and other white women performed was an "extension of [southerners'] conscious[ness]." Besides working with CORE and SSOC, Barrett also attended an activism workshop at Highlander Folk School with the Bradens in 1965 and was present at the Waveland Conference in Mississippi, where the role of women in the civil rights movement was first openly debated. Yet, Barrett remained committed to working within the white community to affect change. "When people were saying 'Black people belong in the black community, if you want to support us go work in the white community,' I was getting an affirmation of what I was deciding to do." In 1966, Barrett left Louisiana for New York to work in the peace and nuclear disarmament movement.[100]

By 1966, CORE's focus on targeting local problems and working within local community structures had won them some "clear victories . . . in other instances groundwork was laid for future successes." Across Louisiana, local blacks began to vote for the first time; more ran for office and organized community groups to work toward equal treatment in public services. In Monroe (Ouachita Parish), for instance, community members created "Project Uplift," a program "to have surplus food distributed to the poor." Although voter registration continued to be an uphill battle in most places, in East Feliciana Parish, with the aid of a federal registrar, over two thousand blacks registered to vote in only eighteen days, "an increase of one thousand percent." In addition, in towns across the state, blacks increasingly demonstrated for greater access to public accommodations and schools, and against job discrimination. That summer, Bogalusa boasted of being "the most marched city in the country."[101]

In 1966, with congressional elections approaching, CORE, with the assistance of the Southern Regional Council, initiated yet another voter education/registration project, concentrating on areas of Florida, Louisiana, Mississippi, and North and South Carolina. In Louisiana, CORE's project had been greatly pared down to only six parishes—Caddo, Baton Rouge, Claiborne, Madison, Ouachita, and Orleans.[102] With the passage of the Voting Rights Act in 1965 and the placement of federal registrars in a number of

---

100. Barrett, interview, 13 January 2003; Barrett e-mail.

101. Draft Louisiana Summer 65 Brief Summary, Box 2, File 5, CORE Papers, SHSW.

102. "Introduction," 25 February 1966, Series VI, Reel 185, SRC Papers, "Biracial Group Plans Big Voter Drive in Seven Southern States," *National Observer*, 10 January 1966; Financial Report, 15 July 1966, SRC Papers.

parishes, the drive to increase black registration finally began to bear fruit. By the end of 1966, the number of black Louisianians registered to vote had increased from 30 percent of the blacks of voting age to 47 percent.[103] In some areas of the state, the percentage of blacks registered to vote reached as high as 80 and 90 percent. Perhaps the greatest achievement of 1966, however, was a twenty-two-mile march from Bogalusa to Franklinton, organized by members of the BCVL. When the 242 marchers arrived at the courthouse in Franklinton on July 11, 1966, and were met by 300 supporters, six marchers entered the courthouse and successfully registered to vote.[104]

By the end of 1966, however, the movement in the South in general began to splinter as a result of "weak and fragmented leadership" and a louder call for a black separatist movement. CORE's successes in 1964 and 1965 were overshadowed by an escalation in militancy in the Louisiana movement. CORE increasingly found itself under attack for its adherence to nonviolence and interracialism. With some local CORE affiliates already members of the Deacons for Defense and Justice, organization delegates voted at the 1966 national convention to "eliminate the requirement of chapter affiliates to adhere to the technique of nonviolence in direct action."[105] At the same time, fearing that their organization might appear militant and thus, not trustworthy, NAACP leaders refused to associate on any level with SNCC and CORE, an old argument reconstituted. With the civil rights movement in rural Louisiana basically moribund, the Southern Regional Council (SRC) took over sponsorship of the voter education projects.[106]

By the end of 1966, the civil rights movement in Louisiana had entered a new phase. Most of Louisiana's male leadership left CORE and went north to work in other aspects of the movement. It is significant, however, that those who chose to remain were women like Mimi Feingold and Kathy Barrett, dedicated to seeing their vision of an egalitarian society achieved. Through 1968, under the rubric of the SRC, a much smaller contingent of CORE members continued to work in communities in certain areas of rural Louisiana. Local women, such as Charlotte Greenup and Odette Harper Hines, also continued to support the movement in their communities.

103. Negro-White Voter Registration in the South, Summer 1966, press release, 5 August 1966, Series 1, Reel 73, SRC Papers.

104. "Negroes Finish Louisiana March," *New York Times*, 12 July 1966; Voter Education Project, memos and reports for 1966, Reel 73, 2194, SRC Papers.

105. Akinyele O. Umoja, "The Ballot and the Bullet: A Comparative Analysis of Armed Resistance in the Civil Rights Movement, *Journal of Black Studies* (March 1999): 563; Meier and Rudwick, *CORE*, 397.

106. Fairclough, *Race and Democracy*, 401–3.

While a number of historians chronicling the movement in Mississippi have argued that the 1964 Freedom Summer project heralded the effective end of the rural southern movement, the Louisiana movement illustrates the commitment of CORE's female members and local women activists alike to sustaining the momentum of the previous two summers.[107] CORE female staff members continued to work toward changing the racial status quo in rural Louisiana well into the late 1960s. Mimi Feingold, for example, returned to Louisiana in both the summer of 1966 and the summer of 1967, working in the Felicianas and in Weyanoke, Louisiana. According to Mimi Feingold, when she finally bid farewell to Louisiana in 1967, "It was very much with my own feeling that we did not belong in the South anymore, that whites needed to deal with issues that were more immediate to ourselves."[108]

Between 1965 and 1967, female activists, both black and white, proved that gendered notions of a woman's role in society were misplaced. Despite the enormous risk of remaining in the movement post-1964, female inside and outside agitators played integral roles in sustaining the movement in rural communities while adapting to the changing nature of the movement.[109] As the male leadership bickered over organizational structure, ideological commitment, and personal gain, in communities like Jonesboro, Bogalusa and, especially, Ferriday, women led by example. They continued to register to vote, ran Freedom Schools, organized community groups, and taught, fed, housed, and supported movement activists in other ways. As Bernice McNair Barnett argues, local black women "provided valuable leadership roles in their homes, churches, social clubs, organizations, and communi-

107. Barring Meier and Rudwick's study of CORE, the majority of the literature on the movement that discusses the demise of the movement and its relation to Freedom Summer focuses on SNCC and Mississippi. See Sally Belfrage, *Freedom Summer* (New York: Viking Books, 1965); Carson, *In Struggle;* John Dittmer, *Local People: The Struggle for Civil Rights in Mississippi* (Chicago: University of Illinois Press, 1994); Cheryl Lynn Greenburg, ed., *A Circle of Trust: Remembering SNCC* (New Brunswick, N.J.: Rutgers University Press, 1998); Mary King, *Freedom Song: A Personal Story of the 1960s Civil Rights Movement* (New York: Morrow, 1987); John Lewis, *Walking with the Wind: A Memoir of the Movement* (New York: Harcourt Brace, 1998); McAdam, *Freedom Summer;* Alphonso Pinckney, *The Committed: White Activists in the Civil Rights Movement* (New Haven: New College and University Press, 1968); Carol Polsgrove, *Divided Minds: Intellectuals and the Civil Rights Movement* (New York: Norton, 2000); Emily Stoper, *The Student Non-Violent Coordinating Committee: The Growth of Radicalism in a Civil Rights Organization* (New York: Carlson, 1989); Howard Zinn, *SNCC: The New Abolitionists* (New York: Beacon Press, 1965).

108. Feingold, interview, 22 December 2002.

109. See Miriam Feingold, "Chronicling the 'Movement,'" *Reviews in American History* (March 1974): 152.

ties," even when the "triple constraints of race, gender, and class" did not allow for them to be thought of as leaders in a largely male-led movement.[110]
In a similar vein, white women like Miriam Feingold are what white activist
Joan Browning deems "invisible revolutionaries. . . . [Y]oung white women
[who] committed their lives to the revolt of black youth and shared most
of that revolt's complexities"; the constraints put on them due to their race
and gender.[111] Although the civil rights movement in general continued to
lose momentum, black and white women alike continued to adapt to what
they believed was a fight not yet wholly won.

110. See Bernice McNair Barnett, "Invisible Southern Black Women Leaders in the Movement: The Triple Constraints of Gender, Race, and Class," *Gender and Society* (June 1993): 177.

111. Joan C. Browning, "Invisible Revolutionaries: White Women in Civil Rights Histori-
ography," *Journal of Women's History* (Fall 1996): 198. See also Curry et al, *Deep in Our Hearts;*
Evans, *Personal Politics;* and Mary Aiken Rothschild, "White Women Volunteers in The Freedom
Summers: Their Life in a Movement for Social Change," *Feminist Studies* 5 (Fall 1979).

EPILOGUE

I really think I can tell you that I was color blind and just when I found out that I was color blind, I was forced to relearn about color.

JANE BUCHSBAUM, New Orleans community organizer

By the mid-1960s, the struggle for black equality had begun to enter a new phase. Stokely Carmichael's call for "Black Power" in 1966 heralded the demise of the movement; Martin Luther King Jr.'s assassination in 1968 essentially ended it. Black Power shook the movement to its foundations. Across the South, African Americans began to embrace black separatism; the Louisiana movement did not escape this trend. As early as 1964, blacks had questioned the usefulness of including whites in rural projects. Even white CORE members wondered whether they could be effective in the new climate of black nationalism. Miriam Feingold, as one of a handful of CORE'S white female field directors, acknowledged the problems white leaders faced in rural communities. Although she noted that the "black-white emphasis" hid the fact that few local blacks were good organizers, Feingold felt that the white organizer's role was to provide information, conduct research, and simply "participate in things." Feingold still believed, however, that she and her fellow white field staffers could "overcome their whiteness," that there would "always be a place for whites in the community."[1]

The determined optimism felt by white activists like Feingold could not quell the rise of black radicalism. Although CORE supported voter education projects in Louisiana through 1967, the problems that had plagued the organization were only compounded. Local blacks increasingly questioned white

1. Miriam Feingold notebook, 1964, 23 and 24 July 1964, Reel 2, Miriam Feingold Papers.

female staff members' behavior around black men as well as the necessity of continued white presence in leadership positions in towns like Bogalusa and Jonesboro, where, they argued, local black leaders already existed. Longtime CORE member Oretha Castle openly criticized the national organization's bureaucratic structure and called for more localized community organizing. Additionally, the younger CORE members' alliances with the Deacons for Defense and Justice marginalized a number of older black activists and white liberals whose allegiance to the movement lay with Martin Luther King Jr. and the philosophy of nonviolent civil disobedience. CORE's effectiveness was further hindered in the summer of 1966 when it openly repealed its philosophy of nonviolence and adopted the Black Power slogan, an action that led to the resignation of some of CORE's most influential white supporters, including the liberal white author Lillian Smith, a twenty-year member of the national advisory committee. By year's end, only five task force workers remained in the state, and CORE's presence as a force in the Louisiana movement had all but ended.[2]

As the civil rights movement "proper" came to an end, the movement segued into the era of the Great Society. War on Poverty programs replaced integration initiatives. Civil rights activists joined neighborhood improvement associations, and civic groups aimed at reforming public facilities, utility services, and public school systems. Local activists placed greater emphasis on equal opportunity, community development, and political representation than on integration. As one historian has noted, the civic leaders and policymakers implementing President Lyndon B Johnson's Great Society, in essence, "professionalized the civil rights movement."[3]

Female activists were part of this transformation. Black and white women who had struggled together during the civil rights era now served on biracial committees and in government bureaucracies working to ameliorate societal ills and furthering efforts begun in the classical civil rights movement era. In many areas of the state, elite white women continued to use their personal connections and resources seeking successful implementation of Johnson's initiatives in Louisiana. African American women in rural and urban communities founded, led, and supported neighborhood improvement leagues in large numbers. As they had in the civil rights era, Louisiana's female ac-

2. August Meier and Elliot Rudwick, *CORE: A Study in the Civil Rights Movement, 1942–1968* (New York: Oxford University Press, 1973), 391–417; Adam Fairclough, *Race and Democracy: The Civil Rights Struggle in Louisiana, 1915–1972* (Athens: University of Georgia Press, 1995), 381.

3. See Kent B. Germany, "Making a New Louisiana: American Liberalism and the Search for the Great Society in New Orleans, 1964–1974" (Ph.D. diss., Tulane University, 2001), 2.

tivists adapted their skills to the changing nature of the movement and persisted in their efforts toward a more just and equitable society.[4]

By the end of 1966, all but a handful of resolute whites had resigned
from major civil rights organizations such as SNCC and CORE. The purging of whites from the movement had a profound effect on women in particular. For many, their work in the movement was a career; for many more,
it was a calling. As Dorothy Zellner, one of the first white staff members of
SNCC and an early supporter of CORE in Louisiana, stated, the purge was
"extremely painful. I think it was probably the most painful thing that happened to me, including my divorce. I felt that I had found my vocation; this
was what I was going to do with the rest of my life. In my mind, I had made
a lifetime commitment. And my first reaction was these people were telling
me I can't stay, and I got here before they did."[5]

On the heels of a waning Louisiana movement, the National Association for the Advancement of Colored People (NAACP), viewed by many as
moderate in the climate of Black Power extremism, resumed its position
as the leading organization in the state. NAACP members embraced their
newfound role as a conduit between blacks and white liberals seeking to
maintain biracial working affiliations. Although the NAACP continued to
advocate for voter registration across the state, it also openly protested police brutality, employment discrimination, segregated education, as well as
working with local whites toward the successful implementation of Great
Society programs.[6]

As a logical extension of their work in the civil rights movement, women
advocated for greater equality and access to public resources for blacks in
communities across the state. Working with a variety of civil rights and
War on Poverty organizations, the large female presence that had character-
ized the Louisiana struggle for equality remained in force through the early
1970s, as women easily extended their civil rights activism to their work with
such programs as the Volunteers in Service to America program (VISTA),
the Women in Career Services (WICS), the Model Cities Program, and Head
Start. In New Orleans, in particular, women often dominated neighborhood

4. Information provided throughout Kent B. Germany, "Making a New Louisiana: American Liberalism and the Search for the Great Society in New Orleans, 1964–1974."

5. Dorothy "Dottie" Zellner, interview by the author, 8 February 2003, tape recording, copy in
possession of the author; Ruby Doris Smith Robinson quoted in Clayborne Carson, *In Struggle:
SNCC and the Black Awakening of the 1960s* (Cambridge: Harvard University Press, 1981), 229,
336–42; Meier and Rudwick, *CORE*, 390–91.

6. Fairclough, *Race and Democracy*, 384–85.

community organizations. Female activists in the newly organized "alphabet soup" of civic groups like SOUL, BOLD, and COUP utilized civil rights movement tactics such as picketing and sitting in in New Orleans. All of these organizations included women with experience in the civil rights movement. Oretha Castle Haley, for example, became a highly articulate spokeswoman in New Orleans during the 1970s working with BOLD.[7] A group of six women led the New Orleans Welfare Rights Organization, while women comprised a majority of the members of the Desire Area Community Council.[8]

Similarly, white women continued to work with progressive organizations such as the League of Women Voters, the Community Relations Council, the Urban League, the Louisiana Council for Human Relations, and the NAACP. Women also created new organizations in an effort to tackle issues of poverty, unemployment, and illiteracy. Betty Wisdom and Felicia Kahn, for example, organized Carrollton Central, a unique housing/community/employment/day-care/health-care facility located in a poor black neighborhood in New Orleans.[9] Rosa Keller continued her work in the city with the League of Women Voters, in the Urban League, and in various other biracial and political organizations until her death in 1997.

Throughout the twentieth century, black and white women, in myriad ways, challenged the racial status quo in Louisiana. As early as 1924, black women insisted on equality when purchasing property, in employment, and in education. Through the 1930s and 1940s, black women organized boycotts and fought for voting rights, the integration of institutions of higher learning, and equalization of teacher salaries. In the 1950s, white women fought to integrate previously all-white organizations and challenged the racist state legislature in the aftermath of the *Brown* decision, while black women boycotted public transportation systems, registered to vote, and challenged discrimination and segregation in schools. By the 1960s, black and white women were working together all over the state by sitting in, marching, picketing, and conducting voter registration campaigns. This diverse group of women worked within, and outside of, an economic, political, and social system dominated by men, ultimately gaining the ability to cultivate the leadership skills they used through the "long civil rights movement" of the 1970s and 1980s.

The civil rights movement in Louisiana could not have endured or suc-

7. See Germany, "Making a New Louisiana," 559–61, 577.

8. See Germany, "Making a New Louisiana," 175, 418.

9. Betty Wisdom and Felicia Kahn, interview by the author, 10 January 2002, tape recording, copy in possession of the author.

ceeded without the women who participated. Their work has been, at times, overshadowed by the larger-than-life histories of the men. Yet, the strength, perseverance, dedication, and persistence of the women who worked at the forefront of the Louisiana's struggle for black equality is not unusual in the history of the modern civil rights movement. Regardless of economic standing, religious affiliation, southern traditions, gender, thousands of women in Louisiana stridently fought in the struggle for human dignity. Through the years, women adapted to the changing tide of the movement; they took a backseat when asked to, and assumed the mantle of leadership when called. And when the civil rights movement "proper" abated, these women continued to educate their communities on the meaning of democracy in America.

This study furthers our understanding of leadership in the civil rights movement by highlighting the significance of women to this particular social and political movement structure, its goals, and ultimate successes; it expands our concept of what constitutes a leader. The modern civil rights movement was, for all intents and purposes, "gendered" terrain. Gender-based assumptions affected recruitment, placement of actors, their participation and actions, and, ultimately, movement outcomes. "Women-centered organizing" was key in the rural areas of the state and in smaller community structures where building relationships was central to building an activist base. In many ways, female civil rights activists were more community-oriented; they utilized interpersonal skills in planning and coordinating, in conflict mediation, and in creating indigenous leadership. Women were often more pragmatic and diplomatic and thus able to bring the larger movement to the grassroots level.[10]

Women also experienced unprecedented levels of power and leadership in the Louisiana civil rights movement. As the sociologist Bernice McNair Barnett has observed, "Leadership is multidimensional and embedded within a structural context."[11] Consequently, when accounting for social, political, and cultural conditions, it is necessary to look at the roles of women and the actions they performed in a gendered context. In rethinking the traditional notions of leadership, it is apparent that women, particularly at the grass-

10. See Bernice McNair Barnett, "Invisible Southern Black Women Leaders in the Civil Rights Movement: The Triple Constraints of Gender, Race, and Class," *Gender and Society* 7, no. 2 (June 1993); and Susan Stall and Randy Stoecker, "Community Organizing or Organizing Community? Gender and the Crafts of Empowerment," *Gender and Society* 12, no. 6 (December 1998).

11. Barnett, "Invisible Southern Black Women," 177.

roots level, acted in extraordinary ways. Historical circumstance shaped the definition of leadership and, subsequently, the evaluation of leadership qualities and the roles women performed. The movement itself, however, provided a unique structure within which women were able to perform certain duties that, in effect, constitute the traditional definition of a leader. Indeed, women emerged as leaders and, ultimately, heroines in a historically limiting political and social public sphere.

BIBLIOGRAPHY

MANUSCRIPT COLLECTIONS

Inez Adams Collection. Amistad Research Center, New Orleans.
Congress of Racial Equality (CORE). Southern Regional Office. Papers. State Historical Society of Wisconsin, Madison.
———. Papers. Copy of microfilm collection on file. Amistad Research Center, New Orleans.
———. Papers. Addendum. Copy of microfilm on file. Howard University, Washington, D.C.
Feingold, Miriam. Papers. State Historical Society of Wisconsin, Madison.
Ferriday Freedom Movement. Papers. State Historical Society of Wisconsin, Madison.
Independent Women's Organization Papers. Special Collections, Howard Tilton Memorial Library, Tulane University, New Orleans.
Keller, Rosa Freeman. Papers. Amistad Research Center, New Orleans.
League of Women Voters of New Orleans. Office Records. League of Women Voters of New Orleans Office Files, New Orleans.
———. Papers. Special Collections, Howard Tilton Memorial Library, Tulane University, New Orleans.
National Association for the Advancement of Colored People. Papers. Library of Congress, Washington, D.C.
———. Papers. New Orleans Papers. Special Collections, Earl K. Long Library, New Orleans.
National Council of Jewish Women, New Orleans Branch. Papers. Special Collections, Tulane University, New Orleans.
National League of Women Voters. Papers. Library of Congress, Washington, D.C.
National Young Women's Christian Association. Papers. Library of Congress, Washington, D.C.
Save Our Schools. Papers. Amistad Research Center, New Orleans.
Southern Regional Council. Papers. Library of Congress, Washington, D.C.
Southern Student Organizing Committee. Papers. Library of Congress, Washington, D.C.

Student Non-Violent Coordinating Committee. Papers. Library of Congress, Washington, D.C.

Tureaud, P., Papers. Amistad Research Center, New Orleans.

Young Women's Christian Association of New Orleans. Papers. Special Collections, Howard Tilton Memorial Library, Tulane University, New Orleans.

INTERVIEWS

Barrett, Kathy. By the author. 13 January 2003. Tape recording. Copy in possession of the author.

Boebel, Jean. By the author. 13 November 1996. Tape recording. Copy in possession of the author.

Buchsbaum, Jane. By Kim Lacy Rogers. 28 November 1978. Tape recording. Kim Lacy Rogers–Glenda Stevens Collection. Amistad Research Center, New Orleans.

Cassimere, Raphael. By the author. 2 March 2003. Tape recording. Copy in possession of the author.

Castle, Oretha. By James Mosby. 26 May 1970. Transcript. Ralph Bunche Civil Rights Documentation Project. Moorland-Spingarn Research Center, Howard University, Washington, D.C.

———. By Kim Lacy Rogers. 28 November 1978. Tape recording. Kim Lacy Rogers– Glenda Stevens Collection. Amistad Research Center, New Orleans.

Castle-Scott, Doris Jean. By Kim Lacy Rogers. 19 January 1989. Tape recording. Kim Lacy Rogers–Glenda Stevens Collection. Amistad Research Center, New Orleans.

Charles, Millie. By the author. 12 December 2001. Tape recording. Copy in possession of the author.

Cochrane, Madelon. By the author. 11 December 2001. Tape recording. Copy in possession of the author.

Davis, Oralean, and Joyce Davis. By Kim Lacy Rogers. 19 May 1979. Tape recording. Kim Lacy Rogers–Glenda Stevens Collection. Amistad Research Center, New Orleans.

Dlugos, Anne. By Kim Lacy Rogers. 30 June 1988. Tape recording. Kim Lacy Rogers– Glenda Stevens Collection. Amistad Research Center, New Orleans.

Feingold, Miriam "Mimi." By the author. 1 December 2002, and 22 December 2002. Tape recordings. Copies in possession of the author.

Finsten, Jill Axler. By the author. 23 May 2004. Tape recording. Copy in possession of the author.

Freeman, Almenia. Interview for *Baton Rouge Bus Boycott: The People.* N.d. LSU Special Exhibit Web site. www.lib.lsu.edu/special/exhibit/boycott/thepeople/html.

Haley, Richard. By Kim Lacy Rogers. 9 May 1979. Kim Lacy Rogers–Glenda Stevens Collection. Amistad Research Center, New Orleans.

Harse, Connie Bradford. By the author. 19 March 2003. Tape recording. Copy in possession of the author.

Houston, Janette Harris. By Mary Hebert. 9 January 1994. Transcript. Special Collections, Louisiana State University, Baton Rouge.

Hill, Hattie Mae. By Miriam Feingold.1966. Transcript. Collection UC528, State Historical Society of Wisconsin, Madison.

Humbles, Julia Aaron. By the author. 11 March 2003. Tape recording. Copy in possession of the author.

Jemison, Reverend Theodore Jefferson. Interview for *Baton Rouge Bus Boycott:
The People* N.d. LSU Special Exhibit Web site. www.lib.lsu.edu/special/exhibit/
boycott/thepeople/html.

Jenkins, Gayle. By Miriam Feingold. 1966. Tape recording. Collection UC528. State
Historical Society of Wisconsin, Madison.

Johnson, Annie Purnell. By Miriam Feingold, 1966. Tape recording. Collection UC528.
State Historical Society of Wisconsin, Madison.

Kahn, Felicia. By the author. 5 September 1996. Tape recording. Copy in the possession of the author.

Keller, Rosa. By the author. 13 March 1996. Tape recording. Copy in possession of
the author.

———. By Kim Lacy Rogers. 28 November 1978, 7 May 1979, and 8 April 1988. Tape recordings. Kim Lacy Rogers–Glenda Stevens Collection. Amistad Research Center,
New Orleans.

Leonard, Margaret. By the author. 29 March 2003. Tape recording. Copy in possession of the author.

———. By John H. Britton. 3 August 1967. Tape recording. Ralphe Bunch Civil Rights
Documentation Project.

Lewis, Robert, and Essie Mae Lewis. By Greta de Jong. 25 November 1996. Transcript. T. Harry Williams Oral History Collection. Louisiana State University,
Baton Rouge.

Luke, Leontine Goins. By Kim Lacy Rogers. N.d. Tape recording. Kim Lacy Rogers–
Glenda Stevens Collection. Amistad Research Center, New Orleans.

Mervis, Helen. By Kim Lacy Rogers.18 November 1978. Tape recording. Kim Lacy
Rogers–Glenda Stevens Collection. Amistad Research Center, New Orleans.

Morial, Sybil. By the author. 4 December 2001. Tape recording. Copy in possession
of the author.

Murison, Peggy. By Kim Lacy Rogers. 14 May 1979, 14 June 1988, and 13 July 1988.
Tape recording. Kim Lacy Rogers–Glenda Stevens Collection. Amistad Research
Center, New Orleans.

NaDang, Katrina Jackson. By the author. 8 December 2001. Tape recording. Copy in
possession of the author.

Poindexter Ambeau, Lorraine. By the author. 17 December 2001. Tape recording. Copy
in possession of the author.

Rack, Elizabeth. By the author. 5 March 1996. Tape recording. Copy in possession
of the author.

Redden, Meg (formerly Peggy Ewan). By Greta de Jong. 8 December 1996. Transcript.
T. Harry Williams Oral History Center, Louisiana State University, Baton Rouge.

Reynolds, Isaac. By James Mosby. 27 May 1970. Transcript. Ralph Bunche Civil Rights

Documentation Project. Box 298. Moorland-Spingarn Research Center, Howard University, Washington, D.C.

Robinson, Patricia. By Erin Porche. For *Baton Rouge Bus Boycott: The People.* N.d. LSU Special Exhibit Web site. www.lib.lsu.edu/special/exhibit/boycott/thepeople/html.

Simmons, Doratha Smith. By Kim Lacy Rogers. 27 July 1988. Tape recording. Kim Lacy Rogers–Glenda Stevens Collection. Amistad Research Center, New Orleans.

Suarez, Matt "Flukie." By the author. 3 December 2001. Tape recording. Copy in possession of the author.

Thompson, Alice. By Kim Lacy Rogers. 25 July 1988. Tape recording. Kim Lacy Rogers–Glenda Stevens Collection. Amistad Research Center, New Orleans.

Wisdom, Betty. By the author. 29 November 2001. Tape recording. Copy in possession of the author.

———. By Kim Lacy Rogers. 14 June 1988. Tape recording. Kim Lacy Rogers–Glenda Stevens Collection. Amistad Research Center, New Orleans.

Wisdom, Betty, and Felicia Kahn. By the author. 10 January 2002. Tape recording. Copy in possession of the author.

Wright, Judge J. Skelly. By Mary Gardiner Jones. 9 September 1968. Tape recording. Civil Rights Documentation Project. New Orleans Public Library.

Zellner, Dorothy "Dottie." By the author. 8 February 2003. Tape recording. Copy in possession of the author.

NEWSPAPERS AND MAGAZINES

Baltimore Sun
Baton Rouge States-Times
CORE-LATOR
Crisis
East Feliciana Watchman
Good Housekeeping
Lafayette Grail
Life
Louisiana Weekly
Mother Jones
Nation
National Observer
Newsweek
New Orleans States-Item
New Orleans Times-Courier
New Orleans Times-Picayune
New York Times
Shreveport Journal
Southern Exposure

WEB SITES AND DOCUMENTARIES

Baton Rouge Bus Boycott: The People. www.lib.lsu.edu/special/exhibit/boycott/thepeople/html.

Rowen, Robert. *The Road from New Orleans.* Documentary. Copy provided by Kathy Barrett. Ca. 1964.

Ware, Burrell. *A House Divided.* Documentary by Xavier University Drexel Center. 1984.

DISSERTATIONS AND THESES

Bartley, Melinda. "Southern University Activism, 1960–1963, Revisited." Master's thesis, Louisiana State University, 1973.

Crawford, Vicki. "We Shall Not Be Moved: Black Female Activists in the Mississippi Civil Rights Movement, 1960–1965." Ph.D. diss., Emory University, 1987.

de Jong, Greta. "A Different Day: The African-American Freedom Struggle and the Transformation of Rural Louisiana, 1900–1970." Ph.D. diss., University of Pennsylvania, 1999.

Germany, Kent B. "Making a New Louisiana: American Liberalism and the Search for the Great Society in New Orleans, 1964–1974." Ph.D. diss., Tulane University, 2001.

Martensen, Katherine Ann. "Region, Religion, and Social Action: The Catholic Committee of the South, 1936–1956." Master's thesis, University of New Orleans, 1981.

McCarrick, Earleen May. "Louisiana's Official Resistance to Desegregation." Ph.D. diss., Vanderbilt University, 1964.

Turner, Pamela Jean. "Civil Rights and Anti-Communism in New Orleans, 1946–1965." Master's thesis, University of New Orleans, 1981.

BOOKS

Ayers, Edward. *Promise of the New South: Life after Reconstruction.* New York: Oxford University Press, 1992.

Baker, Liva. *The Second Battle of New Orleans: The Hundred-Year Struggle to Integrate the Schools.* New York: Harper Collins, 1996.

Bartley, Numan. *The Rise of Massive Resistance: Race and Politics in the South during the 1950s.* Baton Rouge: Louisiana State University Press, 1969.

Belfrage, Sally. *Freedom Summer.* New York: Viking Press, 1965.

Braden, Anne. *The Wall Between.* New York: Monthly Review Press, 1958.

Buechler, Steven. *Women's Movements in the United States: Women's Suffrage, Equal Rights and Beyond.* New Brunswick, N.J.: Rutgers University Press, 1990.

Cantarow, Ellen, ed. *Moving the Mountain: Women Working for Social Change.* New York: Feminist Press, 1980.

Carson, Clayborne. *In Struggle: SNCC and the Black Awakening of the 1960s*. Cambridge: Harvard University Press, 1981.

Chafe, William. *The Paradox of Change: American Women in the Twentieth Century*. New York: Oxford University Press, 1991.

Charron, Katherine Mellen. *Freedom's Teacher: The Life of Septima Clark*. Chapel Hill: University of North Carolina Press, 2009.

Coles, Robert. *Children of Crisis: A Study of Courage and Fear*. Boston: Little, Brown, 1967.

Collier-Thomas, Bettye, and V. P. Franklin, eds. *Sisters in the Struggle: African-American Women in the Civil Rights-Black Power Movement*. New York: New York University Press, 2001.

Congress of Racial Equality Publications. *Negro Voting in Louisiana*. Baton Rouge: Committee on Registration Education, 1962.

Crawford, Vicki L., Jacqueline Anne Rouse, and Barbara Woods, eds. *Women in the Civil Rights Movement: Trailblazers and Torchbearers, 1941–1965*. Bloomington: Indiana University Press, 1990.

Curry, Constance, Joan C. Browning, Dorothy Dawson Burlage, Penny Patch, Theresa Del Pozzo, Sue Thrasher, Elaine DeLott Baker, Emmie Schrader Adams, and Casey Hayden. *Deep in Our Hearts: Nine White Women in the Freedom Movement*. Athens: University Press of Georgia, 2000.

Davis, Angela. *Women, Race, and Class*. New York: Random House, 1981.

de Jong, Greta. *A Different Day: The African-American Freedom Struggle and the Transformation of Rural Louisiana, 1900–1970*. Chapel Hill: University of North Carolina Press, 2002.

Devore, Donald E., and Joseph Logsdon. *Crescent City Schools: Public Education in New Orleans, 1841–1991*. Lafayette: Center for Louisiana Studies, University of Southwest Louisiana, 1991.

Dittmer, John. *Local People: The Struggle for Civil Rights in Mississippi*. Urbana: University of Illinois Press, 1994.

Durr, Virginia. *Outside the Magic Circle: The Autobiography of Virginia Foster Durr*. Tuscaloosa: University of Alabama Press, 1985.

Egerton, John. *Speak Now Against the Day: The Generation before the Civil Rights Movement in the South*. Chapel Hill: University of North Carolina Press, 1995.

Evans, Sara. *Personal Politics: The Roots of Women's Liberation in the Civil Rights Movement and the New Left*. New York: Vintage Books, 1979.

Fairclough, Adam. *Better Day Coming: Blacks and Equality, 1890–2000*. New York: Penguin, 2001.

———. *Race and Democracy: The Civil Rights Struggle in Louisiana, 1915–1972*. Athens: University of Georgia Press, 1995.

Fosl, Catherine. *Subversive Southerner: Anne Braden and the Struggle for Racial Justice in the Cold War South*. New York: Palgrave Macmillan, 2002.

Friedman, Leon, ed. *The Civil Rights Revolution: Basic Documents of the Civil Rights Movement*. New York: Walker, 1967.

———, ed. *Southern Justice*. New York: Pantheon Books, 1966.

Garrow, David, ed. *We Shall Overcome: The Civil Rights Movement in the United States in the 1950s and 1960s*. Vol. 2. New York: Carlson, 1989.

Giddings, Paula. *When and Where I Enter: The Impact of Black Women on Race and Sex in America*. New York: Bantam Books, 1984.

Gilmore, Glenda Elizabeth. *Defying Dixie: The Radical Roots of Civil Rights, 1919–1950*. New York: Norton, 2008

Goldfield, David. *Black, White, and Southern: Race Relations and Southern Culture, 1940 to the Present*. Baton Rouge: Louisiana State University Press, 1990.

Goodwyn, Lawrence. *The Democratic Promise: The Populist Moment in America*. New York: Oxford University Press, 1976.

Gray, Reverend Dr. L. La Simba. *The Deacons for Defense and Justice: Defenders of the African-American Community in Bogalusa, Louisiana during the 1960s*. Winter Haven, Fla.: Four G., 2000.

Greenburg, Cheryl Lynn, ed. *A Circle of Trust: Remembering SNCC*. New Brunswick, N.J.: Rutgers University Press, 1998.

Hartmann, Susan. *The Home Front and Beyond: American Women in the 1940s*. Boston: Twayne, 1982.

Height, Dorothy. *Open Wide the Freedom Gates: A Memoir*. New York: Public Affairs, 2003.

Higgenbotham, Elizabeth. *Too Much to Ask: Black Women in the Era of Integration*. Chapel Hill: University of North Carolina Press, 2001.

Hill, Lance. *The Deacons for Defense: Armed Resistance and the Civil Rights Movement*. Chapel Hill: University of North Carolina Press, 2004.

Honigsberg, Peter Jan. *Crossing Border Street: A Civil Rights Memoir*. Berkeley and Los Angeles: University of California Press, 2000.

Jones, Jacqueline. *Labor of Love, Labor of Sorrow: Black Women and the Family from Slavery to Freedom*. New York: Basic Books, 1985.

Kaledin, Eugenia. *Mothers and More: American Women in the 1950s*. Boston: Twayne, 1984.

Kaufman, Arnold. *The Radical Liberal: The New Politics, Theory and Practice*. New York: Atherton Books, 1968.

Keller, Rosa Freeman. "Autobiography." Unpublished. 1977. New Orleans Public Library.

———. "League of Women Voters of New Orleans History, 1942–1985." Unpublished. 1985. Copy in possession of the author.

Kelley, Robin D. G. *Hammer and Hoe: Alabama Communists during the Great Depression*. Chapel Hill: University of North Carolina Press, 1990.

Key, V. O. *Southern Politics in State and Nation*. New York: Vintage Books, 1949.

King, Mary. *Freedom Song: A Personal Story of the 1960s Civil Rights Movement*. New York: Morrow, 1987.

Krueger, Thomas A. *And Promises to Keep: The Southern Conference for Human Welfare, 1938–1948*. Nashville: Vanderbilt University Press, 1967.

Kurtz, Michael L., and Morgan D. Peoples. *Earl K. Long: The Saga of Uncle Earl and Louisiana Politics*. Baton Rouge: Louisiana State University Press, 1990.

Kuumba, M. Bahati. *Gender and Social Movements*. New York: AltaMira Press, 2001.

Lee, Chana Kai. *For Freedom's Sake: The Life of Fannie Lou Hamer*. Urbana: University of Illinois Press, 1999.

Lerner, Gerda, ed. *Black Women in White America: A Documentary History*. New York: Vintage Books, 1992.

Lewis, John. *Walking with the Wind: A Memoir of the Movement*. New York: Simon and Schuster, 1998.

Liebling, A. J. *The Earl of Louisiana*. Baton Rouge: Louisiana State University Press, 1961.

Litwack, Leon. *Trouble in Mind: Black Southerners in the Age of Jim Crow*. New York: Knopf, 1998.

Lynn, Susan. *Progressive Women in Conservative Times: Racial Justice, Peace and Feminism, 1945 to the 1960s*. New Brunswick, N.J.: Rutgers University Press, 1992.

McAdam, Doug. *Freedom Summer*. New York: Oxford University Press, 1988.

McGrath, Robert C. Jr. *American Populism: A Social History, 1877–1898*. New York: Hill and Wang, 1993.

Meier, August, and Elliot Rudwick. *CORE: A Study in the Civil Rights Movement, 1942–1968*. Urbana: University of Illinois Press, 1973.

Morris, Aldon D. *The Origins of the Civil Rights Movement: Black Communities Organizing for Change*. New York: Free Press, 1984.

Murray, Gail S., ed. *Throwing Off the Cloak of Privilege: White Southern Women Activists in the Civil Rights Era*. Gainesville: University Press of Florida, 2004.

Neuman, Nancy. *The League of Women Voters: In Perspective, 1920–1995*. Publication No. 995. Washington, D.C.: League of Women Voters, 1994.

O'Brien, Gail Williams. *The Color of the Law: Race, Violence, and Justice in the Post–World War II South*. Chapel Hill: University of North Carolina Press, 1999.

Olson, Lynne. *Freedom's Daughters: The Unsung Heroines of the Civil Rights Movement from 1830 to 1970*. New York: Scribner, 2001.

Parsons, Sarah Mitchell. *From Southern Wrongs to Civil Rights: The Memoir of a White Civil Rights Activist*. Tuscaloosa: University of Alabama Press, 2000.

Payne, Charles M. *I've Got the Light of Freedom: The Organizing Tradition and the Mississippi Freedom Struggle*. Berkeley and Los Angeles: University of California Press, 1995.

Peck, James. *Freedom Ride*. New York: Simon and Schuster, 1962.

Pinckney, Alphonso. *The Committed: White Activists in the Civil Rights Movement*. New Haven: New College and University Press, 1968.

Polsgrove, Carol. *Divided Minds: Intellectuals and the Civil Rights Movement*. New York: Norton, 2000.

Price, Margaret. *The Negro and the Ballot in the South*. Atlanta: Southern Regional Council Office, 1959.

Raines, Howell. *My Soul Is Rested: The Story of the Civil Rights Movement in the Deep South*. New York: Penguin Books, 1983.

Ransby, Barbara. *Ella Baker and the Black Freedom Movement: A Radical Democratic Vision*. Chapel Hill: University of North Carolina Press, 2003.

Robinson, Jo Ann. *The Montgomery Bus Boycott and the Women Who Started It*. Knoxville: University of Tennessee Press, 1987.

Robnett, Belinda. *How Long? How Long? African-American Women in the Struggle for Civil Rights*. New York: Oxford University Press, 1997.

Rogers, Kim Lacy. *Righteous Lives: Narratives of the New Orleans Civil Rights Movement*. New York: New York University Press, 1993.

Rollins, Judith. *All Is Never Said: The Narrative of Odette Harper Hines*. Philadelphia: Temple University Press, 1995.

Rothschild, Mary Aikin. *A Case of Black and White: Northern Volunteers and the Southern Freedom Summers, 1964–1965*. Westport, Ct.: Greenwood Press, 1982.

Schultz, Debra. *Going South: Jewish Women in the Civil Rights Movement*. New York: New York University Press, 2001.

Sindler, Allen. *Huey Long's Louisiana: State Politics, 1920–1952*. Baltimore: John Hopkins University Press, 1956.

Sitkoff, Harvard. *King: Pilgrimage to the Mountaintop*. New York: Hill and Wang, 2008.

———. *A New Deal for Blacks: The Emergence of Civil Rights as a National Issue*. New York: Oxford University Press, 1978.

———. *The Struggle for Black Equality*. New York: Hill and Wang, 1981.

Stoper, Emily. *The Student Non-Violent Coordinating Committee: The Growth of Radicalism in a Civil Rights Organization*. New York: Carlson, 1989.

Sullivan, Patricia. *Days of Hope: Race and Democracy in the New Deal Era*. Chapel Hill: University of North Carolina Press, 1996.

Theorharis, Jeanne, and Komozi Woodward, eds. *Groundwork: Local Black Freedom Movements in America*. New York: New York University Press, 2005.

Tushnet, Mark V. *The NAACP's Legal Strategy Against Segregated Education, 1925–1950*. Chapel Hill: University of North Carolina Press, 1987.

Tyler, Pamela. *Silk Stockings and Ballot Boxes: Women and Politics in New Orleans, 1920–1963*. Athens: University of Georgia Press, 1996.

Tyson, Timothy B. *Radio Free Dixie: Robert F. Williams and the Roots of Black Power*. Chapel Hill: University of North Carolina Press, 1999.

Webb, Clive. *Fight Against Fear: Southern Jews and the Black Civil Rights Movement*. Athens: University of Georgia Press, 2002.

Wheeler, Marjorie Spruill. *New Women of the New South: The Leaders of the Women's Suffrage Movement in the Southern States*. New York: Oxford University Press, 1993.

Williams, T. Harry. *Huey Long*. New York: Bantam Books, 1970.

Woloch, Nancy. *Women and the American Experience*. New York: Knopf, 1984.

Woodward, C. Vann. *Origins of the New South*. Baton Rouge: Louisiana State University Press, 1951.

———. *The Strange Career of Jim Crow.* New York: Oxford University Press, 1974.

Zinn, Howard. *SNCC: The New Abolitionists.* New York: Beacon Press, 1965.

ARTICLES

Abrahams, Naomi. "Negotiating Power, Identity, Family, and Community: Women's Community Participation." *Gender and Society* 10 (December 1996): 768–96.

Acquaro, Kimberlee, and Peter Landesman. "Out of Madness, A Matriarchy." *Mother Jones,* January/February 2003, 56–63.

Alexander, Shana. "Visit Bogalusa and You Will Look for Me." *Life,* 2 July 1965.

Ambrose, Edith Rosepha. "Sarah Towles Reed: Teacher and Activist." *Louisiana History* 37 (Winter 1996): 31–60.

Badger, Anthony. "Huey Long and the New Deal." In *Nothing Else to Fear: New Perspectives on American in the Thirties,* edited by Stephen W. Baskerville and Ralph Willett, 65–103. Manchester; and Dover, N.H.: Manchester University Press, 1985.

Barnett, Bernice McNair. "Invisible Southern Black Women Leaders in the Civil Rights Movement: The Triple Constraints of Gender, Race, and Class." *Gender and Society* 7 (June 1993): 162–82.

Blumberg, Rhoda Lois. "Careers of Women Civil Rights Activists." *Journal of Sociology and Social Welfare* (1980): 708–29.

———. "Rediscovering Women Leaders of the Civil Rights Movement." In *Dream and Reality: The Modern Black Struggle for Freedom,* ed. Jeanne Swift, 19–28. New York: Greenwood Press, 1991.

———. "White Mothers in the American Civil Rights Movement." In *Research in the Interweave of Social Roles: Women and Men,* edited by Helen Lopata, 33–50. New York: JAI Press, 1980.

———. "Women in the Civil Rights Movement: Reform or Revolution?" *Dialectical Anthropology* 15 (1990): 133–39.

Braden, Anne. "A Letter to White Southern Women from Anne Braden." Southern Conference Educational Funds Publications, 1972.

———. "A Second Open Letter to Southern White Women." *Southern Exposure* 4 (Winter 1977): 50–53.

Browning, Joan C. "Invisible Revolutionaries: White Women in Civil Rights Historiography." *Journal of Women's History* 8 (Fall 1996): 186–202.

Cable, Sherry. "Women's Social Movement Involvement: The Role of Structural Availability in Recruitment and Participation Processes." *Sociological Quarterly* 33 (1992): 35–50.

Collins, Robert F., Nils R. Douglas, and Lolis E. Elie. "Clinton, LA." In *Southern Justice,* edited by Leon Friedman, 120–21. New York: Pantheon Books, 1966.

Congress of Racial Equality Publications. "The History of Negro Suffrage in Louisiana." In *Negro Voting in Louisiana.* Baton Rouge: Committee on Registration Education, 1962.

———. "Negro Registration in Louisiana." In *Negro Voting in Louisiana.* Baton Rouge: Committee on Registration Education, 1962.

Current, Gloster. "Women in the NAACP." *Crisis* (April 1959): 205–11.

Evans, Sara. "Women's Consciousness and the Southern Black Movement." *Southern Exposure* 4 (Winter 1977): 10–14.

Feingold, Miriam. "Chronicling the 'Movement.'" *Reviews in American History* (March 1974): 152–60.

Feingold, Miriam, Loria Davis, and Howard Messing. "Louisiana in Brief." Unpublished Congress of Racial Equality document. May 1964. Copy in possession of the author.

Fosl, Catherine. "There Was No Middle Ground: Anne Braden and the Southern Social Justice Movement." *National Women's Studies Association Journal* 11 (1999): 24–48.

Foster, L. H. "Race Relations in the South, 1960." *Journal of Negro Education* 30 (Spring 1961): 138–49.

Gerson, Judith M., and Kathy Peiss. "Boundaries, Negotiation, Consciousness: Reconceptualizing Gender Relations." *Social Problems* 32 (April 1985): 315–31.

Glenn, Norval D. "Some Changes in the Relative Status of American Non-Whites, 1940–1960." *Phylon: The Atlanta University Review of Race and Culture* 44 (Summer 1963): 1–25.

Hall, Jacquelyn Dowd. "The Long Civil Rights Movement and the Political Uses of the Past." *Journal of American History* 91, no. 4 (March 2005).

Hirsch, Arnold R. "Simply a Matter of Black and White: The Transformation of Race and Politics in Twentieth-Century New Orleans." In *Creole New Orleans: Race and Americanization,* edited by Hirsch and Joseph Logsdon, 262–319. Baton Rouge: Louisiana State University Press, 1992.

Inger, Morton. "The New Orleans School Crisis of 1960." In *Southern Businessmen and School Desegregation,* edited by Elizabeth Jacoway and David R. Colburn, 82–97. Baton Rouge: Louisiana State University Press, 1982.

Irons, Jenny. "The Shaping of Activist Recruitment and Participation: A Study of Women in the Mississippi Civil Rights Movement." *Gender and Society* 12 (December 1998): 692–709.

James, Joy. "Resting in Gardens, Battling in Deserts: Black Women's Activism." *Black Scholar* 29 (1999): 2–7.

Johns, Major, and Ronnie Moore. "It Happened in Baton Rouge: A Real Life Drama of Our Deep South Today." Congress of Racial Equality Publications, April 1962.

Jones, Jacqueline. "The Political Implications of Black and White Women's Work in the South, 1890–1965." In *Women, Politics, and Change,* edited by Louise A. Tilly and Patricia Gurin, 108–29. New York: Russell Sage Foundation, 1990.

Kelley, Robin. "We Are Not What We Seem: Rethinking Black Working-Class Opposition in the Jim Crow South." *Journal of American History* 80 (June 1993): 75–112.

Klarman, Michael J. "How *Brown* Changed Race Relations: The Backlash Thesis." *Journal of American History* 81 (June 1994): 81–118.

Korstad, Robert, and Nelson Lichtenstein. "Opportunities Found and Lost: Labor, Radicals, and the Early Civil Rights Movement." *Journal of American History* 75, no. 3 (December 1988): 786–811.

Kunkel, Paul A. "Modifications in Louisiana Negro Legal Status under Louisiana Constitutions, 1812–1957." *Journal of Negro History* 44 (January 1959): 1–25.

Lynn, Susan. "Gender and Progressive Politics: A Bridge to Social Activism of the 1960s." In *Not June Cleaver: Women and Gender in Postwar America, 1945–1960*, edited by Joanne Meyerowitz, 103–27. Philadelphia: Temple University Press, 1994.

Marx, Gary T., and Michael Useem. "Majority Involvement in Minority Movements: Civil Rights, Abolition, and Untouchability." *Journal of Social Issues* 27 (1971): 81–105.

Matthews, Donald R., and James W. Prothro. "Political Factors and Negro Voter Registration in the South. *American Political Science Review* 57, no. 2 (June 1963): 355–67.

———. "Social and Economic Factors and Negro Voter Registration in the South. *American Political Science Review* 57, no. 1 (March 1963): 497–508.

McAdam, Doug. "Gender as a Mediator of the Activist Experience: The Case of the Freedom Summer." *American Journal of Sociology* 97 (March 1992): 1211–40.

Meyerowitz, Joanne. "Introduction: Women and Gender in Postwar American, 1945–1960." In *Not June Cleaver: Women and Gender in Postwar American, 1945–1960*, edited by Meyerowitz, 1–16. Philadelphia: Temple University Press, 1994.

Nasstrom, Kathryn L. "Down to Now: Memory, Narrative, and Women's Leadership in the Civil Rights Movement in Atlanta, Georgia." *Gender and History* 11 (April 1999): 113–44.

Oppenheimer, Martin. "Institutions of Higher Learning and the 1960 Sit-Ins: Some Clues for Social Action." *Journal of Negro Education* 32 (Summer 1963): 286–88.

———. "The Southern Student Movement: Year One." *Journal of Negro Education* 33 (Autumn 1964): 396–403.

———. "The Southern Student Sit-Ins: Intra-Group Relations and Community Conflict." *Phylon* 27 (First Quarter 1966): 20–26.

Parr, Leslie. "Sarah Towles Reed, Class of 1904." In *Lives of Learning in a Southern Setting: The Education of Women at Newcomb College*, edited by Beth Willinger and Susan Tucker. Baton Rouge: Louisiana State University Press, forthcoming.

Payne, Charles, M. "Men Led, but Women Organized: Movement Participation of Women in the Mississippi Delta." In *Women in the Civil Rights Movement: Trailblazers and Torchbearers, 1941–1965*, edited by Vicki Crawford, Jacqueline Anne Rouse, and Barbara Woods, 1–11. Bloomington: Indiana University Press, 1990.

Poussaint, Alvin F. "The Stresses of the White Female Worker in the Civil Rights Movement in the South." Paper presented at 122nd Annual Meeting of the American Psychiatric Association, 13 May 1966, Atlantic City, N.J.

Reagon, Bernice Johnson. "My Black Mothers and Sisters or On Beginning a Cultural Autobiography." *Feminist Studies* 8 (Spring 1982): 81–96.

Robnett, Belinda. "African American Women in the Civil Rights Movement, 1954–1965:

Gender, Leadership, and Micromobilization." *American Journal of Sociology* 101 (May 1996): 1661–93.

———. "African-American Women in the Civil Rights Movement: Spontaneity and Emotion in Social Movement Theory." In *No Middle Ground: Women and Radical Protest,* edited by Kathleen Blee, 65–95. New York: New York University Press, 1998.

Rothschild, Mary Aikin. "White Women Volunteers in the Freedom Summers: Their Life Work in a Movement for Social Change." *Feminist Studies* 5 (Fall 1979): 466–95.

Schornstein, Felicia. "A Southern Negro's Attitude on the Race Problem." Typescript. Copy in possession of the author. 1947.

Schwab, Tom. "Biography of Mathilde Schwab Dreyfous." Typescript. Copy in possession of the author. 1992.

Stall, Susan, and Randy Stoecker. "Community Organizing or Organizing Community? Gender and the Crafts of Empowerment." *Gender and Society* 12, no. 6 (December 1998): 729–56.

Strain, Christopher B. "'We Walked Like Men': The Deacons for Defense and Justice." *Louisiana History* 38 (Winter 1977): 43–62.

Taylor, Joseph T. "Desegregation in Louisiana—One Year Later." *Journal of Negro Education* 24 (Summer 1955): 258–74.

Taylor, Verla. "Gender and Social Movements: Gender Processes in Women's Self-Help Movements." *Gender and Society* 13 (February 1999): 8–33.

Taves, Isabella. "The Mother Who Stood Alone." *Good Housekeeping,* April 1961.

Umoja, Akinyele O. "The Ballot and the Bullet: A Comparative Analysis of Armed Resistance in the Civil Rights Movement." *Journal of Black Studies* (March 1999): 201–26.

Vanauken. "Freedom for Movement Girls—Now." Southern Student Organizing Committee, 1969.

Ware, Susan. "American Women in the 1950s: Non-Partisan Politics and Women's Politicization." In *Women, Politics, and Change,* edited by Louise A. Tilly and Patricia Gurin, 281–99. New York: Russell Sage Foundation, 1990.

Washington, Cynthia. "We Started from Different Ends of the Spectrum." *Southern Exposure* 4 (Winter 1977): 14–18.

Wieder, Alan. "One Who Stayed: Margaret Conner and the New Orleans School Crisis." *Louisiana History* (Spring 1985): 194–201.

INDEX